T0291423

THE MANUAL OF
MUSEUM
MANAGEMENT
for Museums in Dynamic Change

GAIL DEXTER LORD

Third Edition

ROWMAN & LITTLEFIELD
Lanham • Boulder • New York • London

Acquisitions Editor: Charles Harmon
Acquisitions Assistant: Lauren Moynihan
Sales and Marketing Inquiries: textbooks@rowman.com

Credits and acknowledgments for material borrowed from other sources, and reproduced with permission, appear on the appropriate pages within the text.

Published by Rowman & Littlefield
An imprint of The Rowman & Littlefield Publishing Group, Inc.
4501 Forbes Boulevard, Suite 200, Lanham, Maryland 20706
www.rowman.com

86-90 Paul Street, London EC2A 4NE

British Library Cataloguing in Publication Information available

Library of Congress Cataloging-in-Publication Data

Names: Lord, Gail Dexter, author.
Title: The manual of museum management : for museums in dynamic change / Gail Dexter Lord.
Description: Third edition. | Lanham : Rowman & Littlefield, [2024] | Series: A Lord cultural resources book | Includes bibliographical references and index.
Identifiers: LCCN 2023048763 (print) | LCCN 2023048764 (ebook) | ISBN 9781538162118 (cloth) | ISBN 9781538162125 (paperback) | ISBN 9781538162132 (epub)
Subjects: LCSH: Museums—Management—Handbooks, manuals, etc. | Museums—Planning—Handbooks, manuals, etc.
Classification: LCC AM121 .L66 2024 (print) | LCC AM121 (ebook) | DDC 069/.068—dc23/eng/20231026
LC record available at https://lccn.loc.gov/2023048763
LC ebook record available at https://lccn.loc.gov/2023048764

♾™ The paper used in this publication meets the minimum requirements of American National Standard for Information Sciences—Permanence of Paper for Printed Library Materials, ANSI/NISO Z39.48-1992.

For Barry, who is on every page.

CONTENTS

CASE STUDIES

Chapter 7

Chapter 1

WHEN

Museum Management in Dynamic Change

Welcome to the third edition of *The Manual of Museum Management*!

The enthusiastic reception of the first two editions in 1997 and 2009 and their many translations around the world demonstrate a continuing need for a concise and practical book on museum management.

This edition, like its predecessors, is for everyone involved in or curious about how museums large and small are managed, including people already working inside museums—managers, staff, trustees, and volunteers; those thinking of starting a museum; those joining the profession; and people who are part of the museum ecosystem—participants, neighbors, descendant communities, students, governments, foundations, donors, and museum service providers. As museums become more and more popular, the circle widens.

The subtitle *"For* Museums in Dynamic Change" reflects a decade of social and political upheaval that directly impacted museums in ways often unexpected. The global pandemic, for example, resulted in as yet untold tragedy and also shuttered museums and led to fundamental shifts in working life that are ongoing. The climate crisis required museums to change practices related to infrastructure and operations that had been unquestioned for decades. Growing demands for social and racial justice challenged museums in their very systems of organization, human resource policies, and governance. New research foregrounded the colonial roots of museology leading to questioning by staff and public of almost every museum function.

However, museums and the people who work in them are incredibly resilient and retain significant public trust. The intent of the subtitle is to highlight that museum leadership, management, and staff are not victims of, but participants in dynamic change. Museum staff and management are formulating values that inspire new ways to create and communicate meaning from the evidence and stories that museums collect, research, and display. More museums are implementing the repatriation and restitution of artifacts, works of art, and specimens that were looted, stolen, or purchased under duress. At a time when museums are being held to account for issues like climate justice, equity, and inclusion, many museums are changing their human resources priorities and sharing authority with communities with regard to the stories they tell, the content they collect, and the research they conduct.

To explore the museum management challenges and the emerging new management ideas and initiatives, I have enlisted the help of thirty museum leaders to share their experiences by contributing case studies. I am most grateful for their wisdom and creativity.

WHEN: A New Museum Definition

The challenges and changes taking place are so profound that the main debate at museum forums, including the International Council of Museums (ICOM),[1] has been focused on the very definition of what museums are. Created in 1946 as part of UNESCO, the cultural wing of the United Nations, today ICOM is the world's largest museum organization with 45,000 members representing 138 countries and territories around the globe. In 2022, after five years of passionate debate, ICOM adopted the following newly revised definition of the term "museum":

> A museum is a not-for-profit, permanent institution in the service of society that researches, collects, conserves, interprets and exhibits tangible and intangible heritage. Open to the public, accessible and inclusive, museums foster diversity and

sustainability. They operate and communicate ethically, professionally and with the participation of communities, offering varied experiences for education, enjoyment, reflection and knowledge-sharing.[2]

This new museum definition is more than aspirational but less than prescriptive as it sets out the basis for international acceptance in a respected and often trusted institution of culture in different ways, in various places and times. This means that the application of the definition varies from country to country, and from jurisdiction to jurisdiction, sometimes forming the basis for legislation, funding, and association memberships, more often forming a framework for professional practice and training.

The key points of difference from previous definitions are the proactive, community-based approach: museums are characterized as "accessible and inclusive," they foster "diversity and sustainability," and they "operate and communicate ethically, professionally and with the participation of communities." This *Manual* explores how and what is involved in managing museums in dynamic change and why it matters.

We humans have collected, valued, and revered objects of nature and our own creation for millennia, but the history of museums as we know them can be counted in mere hundreds of years that equate to the modern colonial era. That's why the greatest concentrations of museums on a per capita basis are located in the industrialized countries of what is often referred to metaphorically as "the global north." These two charts illustrate the disparity between the distribution of museums and population worldwide. The implications are profound because those who live in the "global south" have less access to museums than those in the "global north." Equally

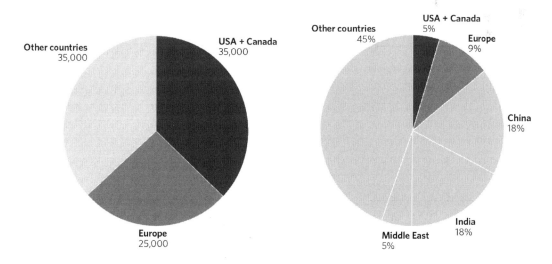

MUSEUMS IN 2020

Other countries 35,000

USA + Canada 35,000

Europe 25,000

POPULATION IN 2020

Other countries 45%

USA + Canada 5%

Europe 9%

China 18%

India 18%

Middle East 5%

95,000 Museums worldwide
More than two-thirds of
the world's museums are located
in the "global north".

50,000 residents per museum
in the "global north".
Other regions count 100,000-250,000
residents per museum.

Figure 1.1.   Distribution of Museums and Population Worldwide.   *Lord Cultural Resources.*

significant are the implications for collections because former colonies suffer from loss of their material and spiritual culture due to external domination only to be informed when they demand repatriation that they lack the museums in which to protect them.

The idea of museums—particularly the ways in which they represent beauty, nature, and science; tell stories; and display power—are equally compelling in the global south. Indeed, museums continue to be created in countries that were former colonies. Many of these countries practice museum management in innovative ways, often working within the limitation that numerous specimens, works of art, and artifacts of great value to their people and communities that were plundered and acquired by conquest or through unequal treaties can now only be experienced in the countries and places of the colonizers. Where museums and collections are located leads to different perspectives on equity, restitution, and repatriation. Nonetheless, as Cara Krmpotich explains in her case study "Repatriation Is Not Loss," repatriation can and should benefit knowledge sharing at the very core of museum management worldwide.

In the mid-1990s, when the first edition of this *Manual* was being written, the museum sector was surprised when Sir Nicholas Serota, who contributed the preface to that first edition, then director of the Tate Gallery, innovated a process of reinterpreting and reinstalling the Tate art collection in February of every year. While many museum goers were delighted and attendance boomed in what had been a low visitor month, there were many who told our audience research team that they were disturbed that the interpretation of works was changing. They longed for a return to the "good old days" of the museum's authoritative voice.

Flash forward
thirty-five years,
and museums
today are actually
sharing authority
with communities.

Flash forward thirty-five years, and museums today are actually sharing authority with communities. This new edition of the *Manual* features case studies by Marc Mayer, Daniel Hammer, and Yvonne Tang with Muna Faisal Al Gurg and Terry Simioti Nyambe who explore the many ways in which community voices contribute important information as well as perspective to museum research, interpretation, and exhibitions. Joy Bailey-Bryant explains in her contribution how community consultation leads to museum relevance.

Cultural change takes time, sometimes leading and sometimes following social and economic change.

In the cultural sector, museum management has been slower to adapt than, say, the performing arts, possibly because of their different funding models and possibly because of the museum focus on preservation, but museums are in dynamic change.

The discipline of history itself has been transformed by historians, led by Holger Prize–winning professor Natalie Davis, shifting from the stories of "great men" to the experiences of the people, including women, the enslaved, and the marginalized. These narrative shifts have slowly made their way into museums. The impact on museum management, though, has been slower: women and persons of color remain a distinct minority in positions of management, particularly in larger institutions,[3] a challenge addressed by Karen Carter, Lisa R. Biagas, and Sandra Jackson-Dumont in their case studies.

It has been the emergence of culturally specific museums like the Smithsonian National African American Museum of Culture and History (2016) and "big idea" museums like the Canadian

Museum for Human Rights (2014) that began to transform management thinking. I have been honored to collaborate on both of those groundbreaking projects, learning a great deal about how new museum types impact management models. One cogent example was provided by Lonnie Bunch III, founding director of the Smithsonian National African American Museum of Culture and History in his 2021 International Museum Day address when he said, "Museums cannot be community centers, but they can be centers of community." This book explores the new attitudes, training, and skills required to make that happen.

"Where and When" are vital points of difference when considering the approaches museum management takes to massive global issues such as poverty, social justice, climate change, and the lasting effects of the pandemic. In his case study, John G. Hampton describes a noncolonial philosophy of museum management—creating a human museum culture of caring, empathy, and equity.

While the extent of the tragic human loss and the long-term impacts of the COVID-19 pandemic will not be fully known for some time, the impact on museums has been to reinforce the reality that museology is an international discipline in which knowledge, science, and aspiration are interconnected. Case studies by Dov Goldstein and Anjani Kumar Singh, while continents apart, demonstrate how heritage can inspire teamwork to complete great projects even during a pandemic.

Although in some ways competition for collections and talent is baked into museum culture, the pandemic encouraged collaboration at every level within museums, between and among them. The pandemic also replaced a prevalent 1980s aspiration for a corporate management style with an aspiration for a more caring approach encompassing social justice, inclusion, and transparency.

The racial and social reckoning unleashed worldwide by the murder of George Floyd in 2020 accelerated demands by artists, scientists, funding bodies, communities, and the public for museums to be more responsive to issues of antiblack racism and equity. Cheryl Blackman and Umbereen Inayet have contributed a powerful case study on "awakening" the City of Toronto's historic house museums through multidisciplinary expressions of their untold stories.

These new approaches have been fueled by the growing awareness that museums are institutions that arose from modern colonialism: a political and economic system that is in decline, but has not disappeared.

Many basic museum functions—including collecting, research, visitor experience, and management—were formed by the culture of colonialism including hierarchy, authoritarianism, and ethnocentrism. Museum staff and community stakeholders are challenging management and boards to change that model by, for example, initiating diverse representation in hiring practices and collection development and greater transparency to ensure ethical funding sources. Contributors Tim Johnson and Gwendolyn Perry Davis reflect on these issues in their case studies.

Digital Technologies

We could not have anticipated the societal changes that digital technologies have wrought! The social media frenzy was boosted by the forced isolation experienced by hundreds of millions of people during COVID-19, and museums were swept along by the tsunami of demands to which they responded with unprecedented access and connection.

As Ali Hossaini explains in chapter 4, digital connection both within organizations and the ways they interact with their communities will only become a higher priority as time goes on—to the great benefit of museums. These influences are not confined to visitor experience alone (although much attention has focused on that dimension) but extend into and connect to different aspects of the museum's operation. In her case study, Natalie MacLean explains how museum management can assess their institution's digital readiness and prepare staff for the present and future.

While digital technologies—including artificial intelligence and augmented and virtual reality—present opportunities and challenges for museum management, the digital divide between rich and poor, urban and rural, and global south and global north create even greater museum management challenges.

One of the most influential trends impacting museums—and one that managers need to respond to continuously—is digital communications technology. New tools and platforms, data storage, and knowledge management have transformed and will continue to change the way museum management is practiced.

Hybrid Platforms and Multiple Locations

In her case study "Learning Is Everywhere" Judith Koke helps us understand how to best use a blend of online, onsite, and offsite opportunities to connect people to the museum, while Frederic Bertley shares how the Center of Science and Industry he directs has "scaled the museum walls" by adapting effective and potent forms of content delivery to reach prospective audiences where they are.

Balancing more than one modality at a time—and how to integrate and amplify multiple content channels or to differentiate them for specific audience segments—will be key to engagement success with users of all kinds. Annemies Broekgaarden describes how the famed Rijksmuseum is experimenting with new methods of engaging families and children with art history.

"Hub and spoke" models—where a main site for interaction connects with and supports experiences remotely—are becoming more common because they reach museum users "where they are," much as library branches do.

These strategies for connection and impact require extreme flexibility and intentionality with a holistic understanding of and commitment to meeting people's needs. Partnerships with community organizations and other entities are key to leveraging strengths and embracing collaboration in new and unprecedented ways. Rosalia Vargas offers a strategy for networking based on her experience as CEO of an expanding network of science centers called Ciencia Viva in Portugal.

Changing Modes of Governance

Museums are also moving (or being moved) from the governmental sector to the independent not-for-profit sector and to innovative mixed models of governance that encompass elements of both. This transformation, which is highly challenging for museum management, has been motivated in large measure by the increasing concentration of wealth in private hands and the consequent reduction in government support of museums, the arts, and many other services. At the same time, there is a significant growth of private museums. These trends are welcomed by some because not-for-profit governance adds vitality to public sector–owned institutions. These trends are also deplored by others, who see a future of growing financial insecurity ahead.

Whether dependent mainly on government or on philanthropic and corporate support or a combination of all three, museum management is often under real or imagined pressure to reflect major funder policies and values in their work, which may be inconsistent with museum ethics, scientific research, the philosophy of Indigenous people, the lived and historic experience of communities, and the well-being of museum staff.

Perhaps museums belong in "the plural sector," a term suggested by management scholar Henry Mintzberg,[4] meaning a third sector of society composed of social forces and associations including public and private organizations but not dominated by either. Are museums already becoming pluralist institutions by acknowledging multiple perspectives and promoting critical thinking? This pluralist approach may be one factor in why museums are often cited as among the most trusted institutions in society—more trusted than media, journalism, and even universities.[5] The following charts on museum trust developed by Wilkening Consulting for the American Alliance of Museums in 2021 demonstrate the level of trust the American public has for museums of *all* types and that the top three factors in their trust are the factual basis of museums, the authentic objects they present, and their research focus. It is significant that the next four factors are the new directions that museums are taking in this time of dynamic change.

> Are museums already becoming pluralist institutions by acknowledging multiple perspectives and promoting critical thinking?

Does public trust support the role of museums in "soft power,"[6] an influence that is based neither on military power nor economic hegemony but on cultural understanding? Is soft power a useful way for museums to apply their knowledge, research, and convening capacity to influence policy in many fields?

These themes thread through this *Manual* as does the creativity and resilience of museum management and staff.

No Going Back

The global north experienced rapid growth both in the number and the size of museum buildings from the 1980s to now. This led to an expansionist museum management style.

The proliferation of museums in the global south, however, is also stimulating museum management innovation and sensitivity to place making and meeting economic needs for economic growth and tourism. Museums have benefitted from a tremendous expansion totaling an estimated 95,000 museums worldwide.

Will the museum sector continue to expand?

The climate crisis suggests that expansion may be "clicks not bricks." Will museums in the global south develop more as experiences and activities rather than brick-and-mortar

> The climate crisis suggests that expansion may be "clicks not bricks."

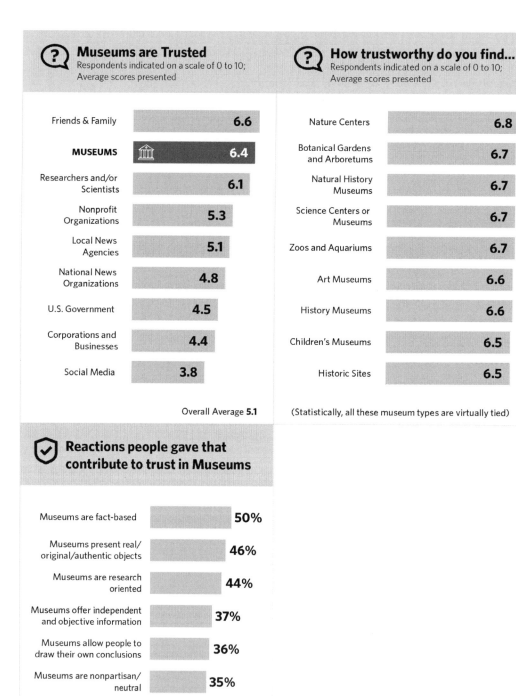

Museums are Trusted
Respondents indicated on a scale of 0 to 10;
Average scores presented

Friends & Family	6.6
MUSEUMS	6.4
Researchers and/or Scientists	6.1
Nonprofit Organizations	5.3
Local News Agencies	5.1
National News Organizations	4.8
U.S. Government	4.5
Corporations and Businesses	4.4
Social Media	3.8

Overall Average **5.1**

How trustworthy do you find...
Respondents indicated on a scale of 0 to 10;
Average scores presented

Nature Centers	6.8
Botanical Gardens and Arboretums	6.7
Natural History Museums	6.7
Science Centers or Museums	6.7
Zoos and Aquariums	6.7
Art Museums	6.6
History Museums	6.6
Children's Museums	6.5
Historic Sites	6.5

(Statistically, all these museum types are virtually tied)

Reactions people gave that contribute to trust in Museums

Museums are fact-based	50%
Museums present real/original/authentic objects	46%
Museums are research oriented	44%
Museums offer independent and objective information	37%
Museums allow people to draw their own conclusions	36%
Museums are nonpartisan/neutral	35%
Museums employ/consult experts	31%
Museums share multiple viewpoints	29%
None of these/I don't trust museums	6%

Museums and Trust. Research by
Wilkening Consulting on behalf of the
American Alliance of Museums, 2021.

Figure 1.2.   Public Trust in Museums.   *Research by Wilkening Consulting on behalf of the American Alliance of Museums.*

buildings? Sarah Sutton and Elizabeth Wylie provide cogent insights on "Journey to the Green Museum" in their case study. Sean Stanwick, Robert LaMarre, and Javier Jimenez Fernandez-Figares detail the challenges of managing museum infrastructure in their contributions to chapter 7.

In some circumstances, change of museum governance from being a government department to an arm's length agency or pluralist civil society organization will be a priority. In other situations, forging closer relationships with communities is the institutional focus. Many museums must grapple with surviving conflict, disease, and corruption. All museums, in one way or another, are being confronted with the urgency of climate change, which requires museum managers to be incredibly resourceful in how they use their tools both for disaster preparedness and to meaningfully take part in the green economy. Compelling challenges persist in terms of repatriation of collections and reinterpreting them through multiple perspectives.

All this change requires clarity of mission and vision. Kathleen Brown and Mary Kershaw treat us to their conversation on how words can help staff and the board achieve clarity and unity of purpose and help develop the best course for the museum's future direction.

Multiple Perspectives and Creative Thinking

In brief, there is no "one size fits all" approach to museum management and there are no immutable management fundamentals.

This third edition of *The Manual of Museum Management* therefore applies the knowledge and experience of the international museum sector through the lens of how museum management can facilitate the creation of meaning through the preservation of authentic experience in collaboration with communities in a spirit of respect for science and multiple perspectives.

Achieving these aspirations requires diverse skill sets! So how do managers and directors of museums large and small deal with this ever-increasing complexity and advance their organizations in this climate of change and risk?

Being a museum director is like being CEO of at least six different enterprises—education, research institute, facility management, hospitality, community organization, and entertainment. Today we might add more areas of responsibility: social justice, economic revitalization, innovation, and cultural diplomacy. These responsibilities exceed the abilities of any one individual, and that is why new professional practice areas, inclusivity and team work, are the very essence of museum management.

And there's no going back!

Decolonizing Museum Management: Toward a Human Institution

By John G. Hampton

We are operating in an era of significant change. Museums are facing multiple existential issues and questions: we are confronting the generational impacts of our colonial roots, misconceptions of neutrality, leadership structures, and poor staff diversity.

There is also greater scrutiny of funding models, donors, and supporters, and an expanded role that museums are being called on to play in the community. All of this is happening under growing movements for improved labor practices, reduced workload, and better support for the mental health not only of our staff but also our audiences. In the face of these potentially overwhelming changes, our role as museum leaders is to be attentive to where these needs intersect and how we can weave multiple priorities together to create a cohesive fabric that can support the cultural future we need.

The MacKenzie Art Gallery's work with our Equity Task Force could serve as an example of this type of weaving of multiple challenges and solutions. The impetus and the urgent matter at that time was to look at racial justice and systemic barriers within our own institution, to try to identify and address those; but when we start untangling that, you can't just look at racial barriers independently. They ended up connecting to our accessibility initiatives, which connected to the issues artists and staff were exploring in our exhibitions, which developed some standards that influenced our respectful workplace policy. All of these systems are interconnected. When you try to orchestrate them in a calculated manner, then that may seem like a daunting task, but if you open yourself organically to where all of these elements come together, then they are mutually informative. Opportunities emerge from these intersections where work in one direction can help support multiple goals.

This attentiveness to mutually supportive aims helps find far-reaching impacts with relatively simple gestures. I am not advocating for complexity but for a human-oriented approach, one that must be coupled with respect for our own limitations. We can't expect ourselves to be able to address every need all at once but focus on what we can accomplish in a thoughtful, healthy way.

At a recent Canadian Arts Summit Executive Director's Peer-to-Peer session, there was a beautiful moment where one of the participants reminded us of our need to take care of ourselves. For those of us who take a servant leadership approach, we can sometimes overlook how our own mental, physical, and spiritual health is critical to how we are able to support others. It is difficult to guide an institution or community down a healthy path if you are not in a good place yourself, and in relation to this community. The challenges facing museums that I articulated earlier are fundamentally human problems that require our best selves to address.

While none of the language I have used so far has explicitly addressed decolonization, I think these crises stem from a colonial rupture—a distinction between types and parts of our humanity. I would generally describe the moment we are in as an ethical turn for museums, and I see decolonization as one framework for guiding us through this turn, toward an alternative form of organizing in a way that honors interdependence and interconnection.

Most museum professionals have a broad understanding of the connection between museums and colonialism. We know about the history of the museum as an imperial trophy case, of the "parade of spoils," and of the systemic exclusion of nonwhite, nonmale, nonnormative artists and voices from cultural institutions. However, we often fail to acknowledge the influence that Indigenous philosophies have had on European ideals that helped establish the contemporary museum. Concepts like equality and freedom were heavily influenced by Indigenous critiques of European nations,[7] which helped inspire epochal turns like the French Revolution and the subsequent shift of the Louvre from a palace to a public museum. While I believe in the museum's proposition that culture belongs to the people, the modern museum is built on a narrow definition of humanity, one that suggests the cultures of others are "ours" to consume, preserve, and present as "we" see fit. This ideology is felt not only in our collections and exhibitions but also in the spirit in which we work and our efforts to rectify these wrongs.

As my father, Eber Hampton, wrote, there have historically been two goals of "Indian education": assimilation and self-determination.[8] As we write new policy and procedures, as we hire Indigenous staff into predominantly white institutions and provide mentorship on how to integrate and succeed, we need to ask if our decolonization efforts are acts of self-determination or assimilation. I consider myself quite adept at walking in two worlds, conducting myself in a respectable manner, and translating from Indigenous concepts into Western ways of speaking and working. However, as I work with emerging Indigenous leaders, I have to ask whether this is a skill that should be imparted on new generations or rebelled against. "Here I am," wrote my father, "a Chickasaw, an educated Chickasaw. It means I survived the brainwashing to some extent; I survived the genocide, physically. Now I am a qualified brainwasher. I can do to my students what was done to me."[9]

To avoid inadvertent assimilationist tendencies, we must look within ourselves and question our motives. When seeking to impart a lesson about professionalism to a young Indigenous cultural worker or model methods for succeeding in the cultural sector as it is currently configured, I suggest taking a moment to reflect on what system this advice upholds (I also suggest the same beyond Indigenous relations).

As a museum embarks on a journey of decolonization, it is easy to get lost in the enormity of the task, trying to identify an end goal. Is the intention to dismantle all colonial institutions? Is it to build new institutions? Is it to completely restructure? Anyone who has revamped just one policy in their institution knows that it is a process. You look at *The Manual of Museum Management* or other resources that provide best practices and standards, evaluate the needs of your own team, and ensure compatibility with other policies. It takes time and effort. If you are trying to Indigenize your whole institution, you have to look at every policy, every corner, every individual, and you don't have a manual of best practices to follow. How do you adopt a worldview that has not yet existed within the museum world? Establishing a new philosophy and structure in this way from the ground up can sound like an impossible task, but thankfully we don't have to tackle it like that, and you are not alone.

Embedded within the museum is a memory of ideals that have not yet been fully realized. It is a dream that requires an opening up to an expanded view of humanity and collectivity. This is not just a project for one institution or sector but a collective cultural shift. Whether you know it or not, you are surrounded by community members who are doing work that you can amplify and build from. As you seek to weave threads together for multiple solutions, look outside the walls of your institution and consider how you can connect with what is already happening in the broader community. Identify calls for action that can work as solutions to your problems and areas where you can offer solutions to others' problems.

To decolonize museum management, we must prioritize being whole humans in relation. Being human is not a state. *Being* is a verb; it is a shared action, and we are continuously doing it. To solve our existential problems, museums must engage us as humans, including our communities, staff, and ourselves (yes, managers are people too).

If we can be true to ourselves as humans, prioritizing the human aspects of our institution (as well as our impacts on nonhuman relatives), then we don't need to have a complete image of our final destination. Instead we can look for the next step. You likely have a sense of the general direction you are going, what you are walking away from, and who is walking alongside you, so focus on ensuring you have solid footing for that journey so you can be a support when you're needed.

Figure 1.3.   Exterior of MacKenzie Art Gallery, featuring Duane Linklater's 2018 LED text work *Kâkikê/ Forever*. These words offer an Indigenous interpretation of the spirit of the treaties between Indigenous and non-Indigenous nations, signaling a shared relationship with a land that precedes—and will outlast— us all.   *Photo by Don Hall. Image courtesy of the MacKenzie Art Gallery.*

Museum Relevance through Community Conversation

By Joy Bailey-Bryant

All cultural institutions seek to share stories with their communities. Performing arts centers through dance, music, and theater. Libraries through collection, preservation, and documentation. As hybrid institutions that exhibit, collect, document, preserve, research, and educate, museums bear the responsibility of communicating vast and complex stories to broad audiences who may not be well acquainted with museums. How then to determine what stories will be meaningful and relevant?

Market analysis can be useful because it *identifies* the actual and potential audiences and communities your museum serves through analysis of such demographic and psychographic categories as residents, tourists, and student, age, and employment status. However, museums that aspire to be relevant need to build on that data to *understand* needs and motivations.

Figure 1.4 depicts the process of gaining information to understand your audiences and community motivations leading to relevance and collaboration to achieve shared outcomes. The largest circle represents the large body of knowledge that can be learned about your audience. As information is refined the circles become smaller and the information becomes more useful until it is distilled to focus knowledge on both community needs and the museum's mission.

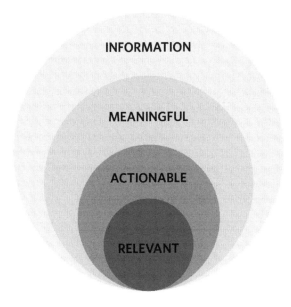

INFORMATION refers to the mass of data on people, places and communities that is available.

MEANINGFUL represents understanding what is most important to your audience.

ACTIONABLE addresses how the museum and community work together to move this knowledge of each other forward in a tangible way.

RELEVANT is the smallest circle because it focuses on how the museum and community can work together to achieve common goals that have impact.

Figure 1.4.   From Information to Relevance.   *Lord Cultural Resources.*

Meaningful for Your Community

Figure 1.4 is not only a process of refining information but also a progression from one-way information gathering to engaging directly with communities in a two-way conversations that provides the museum with opportunities for the museum to communicate and to learn from each other.

The museum should be able to

- communicate your mission and vision;

- raise its visibility;

- manage public expectations;

- create relationships with individuals and groups; and

- better understand community needs, motivations, and interests.

The community should be able to

- express their needs (such as, for example, health, jobs, and education);

- learn the strengths and limitations of what museums do;

- make suggestions regarding stories they would like the museum to tell and content and artifacts the museum could study and collect;

- identify opportunities for partnerships, collaborations, activities, and programs; and

- inform the museum's planning processes with their experience and opinions.

This process goes by many names—community consultation, public engagement, audience input—but the meaning is the same: dedicated efforts to listen to, understand, and respond to the communities that your museum seeks to serve. Establishing a goal of gaining information that is most actionable by your institution will help the museum to be relevant.

Actionable for the Museum

In the mid-2000s, O'Reilly Media popularized the term "2.0" to refer to shifts in the World Wide Web from being a primarily flat resource to a two-way communication tool between Web programmers and users.[10] The term has been coopted in many sectors including culture and now refers to any participatory information sharing platform to gain input and share output.

In this time of hyper information gathering, there are many tools that can assist you in understanding the needs, wants, and motivations of your communities. Civic or public engagement is one of the most effective because it allows the public to speak for themselves. Community engagement has been a popular communication technique since it was used in many fields for years and gained international validity in the United States in 2009 when one of the first actions of newly elected president Barack Obama was to establish a national Office of Public Engagement.

This method is not without hazard. Public consultation processes that do not properly consider their participants can endanger an institution's current standing with their established supporters *and* fail to meet their objectives with any new communities because they tend to confuse or frustrate the very public they are intent on reaching. Any engagement process must consider the diversity of communities, the forum to optimize feedback, and a schedule in line with a project's lifespan that gains strength in tandem with community input.

The following are guidelines for successful community engagement:

- **Open.** Anyone who is interested should be aware of and understand how they can contribute and participate. They should feel welcomed. Meeting locations, formats, and times should be adapted to suit the people or groups that you are seeking to engage.

- **Accessible.** Improve access by using a variety of communication tools from in-person to digital and hybrid. Prepare for translation and providing for special needs including child care. Think carefully about locations where people will feel comfortable.

- **In-depth.** "Deepen the dialogue" by facilitating smaller focus groups that are targeted and specific to particular needs.

- **Expansive.** The more feedback you gain, the larger your circle of contacts will grow. Develop options to engage your broadening public incrementally through the process.

Although gaining public input can take many forms, two of the most common information-gathering techniques are *observation*, a powerful tool because it allows for the use and investigation of information that you or staff may have noticed about your communities, and *conversation*, the simplest format to seek feedback from people that you seek to serve.

Observation. An observational bias occurs when researchers only look where they think they will find positive results or where it is easy to record observations.

Conversation. Getting people talking about themselves is the easiest and at times one of the most enjoyable parts of this process: ask participants how they enjoy culture, what motivates and deters them from attending an event or visiting a cultural venue, and what opportunities they perceive. Here are a few suggestions of the most common ways to engage in productive conversations with communities:

- **Digital engagement.** Approximately 15 percent of adults in the United States participate in the arts via electronic media only.[11] There are currently any number of platforms that can assist you in set up (Facebook and WordPress immediately spring to mind), and as technology evolves, more will certainly emerge. The only requirements for participation should be registration, giving participants access to view and comment on conversations and key topics, as well as topics of their own.

- **Individual interviews.** One-on-one, intimate conversations between the museum and individual relevant community members are valuable in understanding the community and soliciting guidance about future action. Individual interviews should address people that represent the community or "recognized leaders"; these may be, for example, political leaders, neighborhood advocates, business owners, active private citizens, and youth.

- **Surveys.** The most common form of gaining feedback, surveys are useful for expanding the numbers and types of participants wherever they are located. This format of communication is amenable to flexible schedules and alternative methods of feedback, particularly among teenagers and working professionals, two groups who are not regularly represented in public forums.

- **Workshops.** These small, informal gatherings are great for exploring levels of access and barriers to participation at your institution. Workshops seek open and frank dialogue with diverse groups of people, in a welcoming setting, frequented by the audiences you are trying to reach. You can also do "focused group workshops," which allow for engagement of small conversation groups of a particular type to share information and gather feedback.

- **Focus groups.** These group discussions are closely monitored and controlled by key factors such as age range, occupation, and usage patterns depending on the goal of the research. Moreover, conducting focus groups presents an opportunity to gather information from members who may not attend or would feel uncomfortable at large public forums.

- **Town hall–style meetings.** Community-wide convenings in the form of facilitated town hall meetings. This is a labor-intensive endeavor most suited for positioning your institution on a large stage. Meetings should be arranged to best meet the scheduling needs of community members, from families to youth to commuting professionals.

Relevance

Having developed meaningful communication with communities on a regular basis, museum management will be able to incorporate their needs, aspirations, and motivations into its plans and activities—within the realistic context of the museum's mission and vision. Museum management will have a better understanding of the stories, content, and ideas that matter to people and can incorporate this knowledge into exhibitions, content, and collections plans and staffing priorities.

Being relevant is a process (not a special event).

All this is in constant change, so it's an ongoing conversation. And don't forget to thank everyone in the community and museum staff for their participation and hard work. Share the results of the work, and keep staff and community updated on the results. Being relevant is a process (not a special event).

Chapter 2

WHY

Purposes of Museum
Management and
Leadership

There's a memorable aphorism used to distinguish management and leadership: Management is about "doing the *thing* right," while leadership is about "doing the *right* thing."

This chapter sets management in the context of leadership with particular emphasis on the museum's foundational principles, starting with values.

2.1 Values

Values are essentially about principles and standards of behavior. Values motivate us; values are formed early in life and evolve through experience with our communities and surroundings.

The term "values" was not much discussed a decade ago and was not listed in the index of our previous *Manuals*. There was instead a tendency to attach some value-like adjectives to the museum's mission statement—and that limited approach missed a great opportunity for the museum staff and leadership to think deeply about the values that they want to instill and implement in the museum: in the ways they work (for example collaboratively versus compartmentalization), how they see each other (in a spirit of equality or as part of a hierarchy based on qualifications), and how they approach the public (with respect or as problems—like noise and security—to be controlled).

Until recently, systems of compartmentalization, hierarchy, and control were the default values of museums—convenient for senior management and leadership and less than comfortable for most everyone else. This resulted in workplaces that were often experienced as oppressive, exclusionary, or even toxic.

Here are some of the key points to consider when developing your museum's values:

- Values matter because they guide work behavior, are the foundation of human resources policies, and create a social atmosphere that makes the museum a great place to work and visit.

- The values of a museum team should be developed by all staff through a process facilitated by a committee representing the diversity of people and departments and assisted by the museum's human resources team.

- The starting question is this: "How do we want to work together?"

- The committee should reach out to museums and other organizations it admires to learn from their values, as well as what does and doesn't work.

- The process of developing a values statement may include a confidential staff survey, workshops, and breakout groups. It might also be helpful to involve an external facilitator.

> Think of museum values as a big tent—big enough for one and all: staff, management, and leadership.

Think of museum values as a big tent—big enough for one and all: staff, management, and leadership.

While management plays a key role in *facilitating* these processes, every team member should have the opportunity to *lead* in the creation and implementation of a values statement. Here are two examples of museum values statements from the Museum of Science in Boston and the MacKenzie Art Gallery in Regina.

- **Museum of Science—Boston, Massachusetts (2020)**

Everyone: We are everyone's Museum. We pursue equity and celebrate every person for who they are. We foster an inclusive environment in which we value and respect diversity.

Service: We serve our colleagues and community. We hold ourselves accountable to be a trustworthy public resource, and to support a sustainable, just, and evidence-based future.

Learning: We love learning. We are curious about the world and want to share our joy and wonder with others. We value open minds and recognize that everyone has more to explore, discover, and create.

Connection: We find strength in connections. We collaborate across communities, organizations, and disciplines to make science relevant and accessible to all.

Boldness: We dream big. We boldly push ourselves forward, pursuing new ideas and challenges. We experiment and learn from our failures as we seek to inspire purpose, spark imagination, and encourage hope.

- **MacKenzie Art Gallery—Regina, Canada (Values Statement 2013)**

As the board, staff, and volunteers of the MacKenzie, we:

Represent the MacKenzie to the best of our ability at all times.

Celebrate one another's successes, work toward shared goals, and recognize the unique value of each member of the team.

Are stewards of an enduring and ever-deepening public trust rooted in our permanent collection, in the legacy of our predecessors, and in the achievements of the present.

Welcome the community to the Gallery with the highest standards of hospitality and share our passion for the arts with creativity and innovation.

Work with the highest professional standards, accountable for our decisions and actions, and responding with creativity and innovation to opportunities that will benefit the Gallery.

Believe passionately that art transforms us and advances knowledge and our understanding of the world around us.

Believe that artists and their engagement with our visitors are indispensable to the success of the MacKenzie.

Research, exhibit, and celebrate the past, present, and future of the Indigenous peoples in collaboration with contemporary Indigenous creators, knowledge keepers, and publics.

Are proud to take the work of Saskatchewan artists to the national and international stage and to bring the art of Canada and the world to Saskatchewan.

2.2 Vision, Mission, and Mandate

Contrary to popular belief, the purpose of management is not to exercise power but to make it *easier* for the staff of the organization to do their jobs by *facilitating decisions*.

Contrary to popular belief, the purpose of management is not to exercise power but to make it easier for the staff of the organization to do their jobs by facilitating decisions.

To "facilitate" means to make things easier than they would otherwise be. The purpose of management in museums is to facilitate decision making and implementation of strategies, goals, objectives, and, in some cases, tasks throughout the organization that lead to the achievement of the museum's vision, mission, and mandate.

Tough job? You bet.

In 2020, the need for greater institutional accountability became apparent with respect to: diversity, social and environmental justice, the duty of care for staff and visitors, working from home, trade unions, and the increased public scrutiny of funding sources and board member affiliations.

By 2021 there were almost two dozen unfilled director positions at museums in the United States. This surprising number of vacancies was commonly attributed to the "unrealistic" expectations for leadership in such diverse areas as collection and audience growth, community accountability, and fund-raising, which made it "almost impossible" to find one leader who could do it all. But, of course, that's why a management team guided by strong foundational statements is so essential. Few tears should be shed for the "glory days" of the "all-knowing" museum director whose every word (right or wrong) was automatically obeyed.

Museums are complex cultural institutions uniquely concerned both with collecting and preserving the material cultural heritage while simultaneously *communicating its meaning*—whether that meaning arises from works of art, archaeological and historical artifacts, or scientific specimens.

The social, political, and scientific dimensions of the communication of meaning results in an institution that fuses research, interpretation, education, and community connection with the "hardware" functions of housing and caring for tangible and intangible collections as well as welcoming the public.

To align these sometimes conflicting directions, museums are defined by three foundational statements: the vision, the mission, and the mandate.

These three statements are usually incorporated into the museum's legal framework, whether it is a legislative act, if the museum is a government agency, or with a constitution and bylaws, as is likely the case for museums in the charitable or not-for-profit sectors. Each type of statement is described shortly. Appendix A presents examples of foundation statements currently in use by a number of museums, which graciously gave permission to reprint them in this *Manual*.

Vision

The *vision* expresses the impact the museum wants to have on its community and the world. It answers the questions, "Why does this museum matter? What difference does it make?" Vision statements respond to changing conditions of "the now." They are often changed through strategic planning processes or a communication audit. Today, museum management places a great emphasis on developing the institution's vision with staff, board, and community stakeholders. Often a director brings a vision to that position. A visionary director has to have the ability to inspire all the stakeholders with that vision and to have the humility to modify that vision when support is not forthcoming.

The vision statement inspires!

The vision statement inspires!

Mission

The *mission* states the purpose and intent of the museum. The original mission or purpose of the museum is usually embedded in its founding charter or legislation. It answers the questions, "What is this museum? What does it do?" Mission statements change infrequently and usually in response to a new or changed function. Because change is constant, it is important that museum management and the board regularly review the mission statement to ensure that it reflects both the actual functions and intent of the museum. The mission statement directs our sights toward the long-range reason for the museum's existence.

The mission is the foundation of all museum policy.

The mission is the foundation of all museum policy.

Mandate

The *mandate* articulates the range of material and immaterial culture for which the museum assumes responsibility in terms of academic discipline, geographical range, chronology, and specialization. The mandate is often buried in the museum's enabling legislation. It locates the museum in the context of its external responsibilities and lays the foundation for the museum's relations with other museums as well as government and educational institutions and the private sector. The mandate answers the questions, "What is the scope of this museum? Are you avoiding duplication of efforts with other museums and related organizations?"

The mandate makes good neighbors.

The mandate makes good neighbors.

The following case study describes the process that the Museum of Northern Arizona employed to develop new foundation statements.

Foundation Statements: Making Change

**By Kathleen Brown in conversation
with Mary Kershaw**

Sometimes museums get so caught up in the delivery of their programs and exhibitions that we forget why we are doing them in the first place! We have all seen or experienced "mission creep" in the context of trying to be "all things to all people" in how we serve the needs of our communities—and sometimes this can come across as being unfocused, disjointed, or "flabby." Impact is hard to achieve or assess when the museum's resources are spread so thin and operational focus is so diffuse.

The hard work of defining or recapturing what a museum's essential "why" is—its reason for being—can be daunting. But essential to high impact and sustainability is a laser focus on what you are trying to achieve and why it is important. Even when your institution is almost one hundred years old and deeply rooted in an ethos of service and community, your purpose can become clouded by competing interests, dated thinking, and ossified structures.

Kathleen Brown sat down with Mary Kershaw, executive director of the Museum of Northern Arizona (MNA) in Flagstaff, to talk about the institution's journey toward clarity and focus.

Kathleen: When we first started talking about strategic planning at MNA, you knew from the very beginning that you needed to address the vision and mission statements. Why did you think that this was how you were going to move the organization forward?

Mary: When I joined MNA in 2019, one of the first things I did was talk to people about the institution. I talked to staff, board members, volunteers, stakeholders, funders, donors, the whole range—as many as I could—to get an idea of what they thought about MNA and what they valued.

What was really interesting to me—and something I'd never experienced anywhere else—was that everyone had a different view of MNA. There was no single vision of what MNA is. Instead, there were a variety of very strongly held visions that were in many ways mutually exclusive—we were a museum of native American art and culture. Or we were a learning institution for scientific research. We were a specialist geology museum. We were a visitor attraction on the Colorado Plateau. You get the idea. There are a whole range of different identities, and that led to a number of difficulties.

Kathleen: What kind of difficulties?

Mary: Conceptually and structurally, the organization really was very atomized, and there was not a lot of synergy—between people or working departments. But more than anything it made it difficult to move forward with any impact. Because of multiple identities—and then the variety of activities and priorities that would fall under each of those identities—it meant that there were unrealistic expectations about what MNA should be or could be doing, and that was a recipe for real frustration. To the staff and the board, as soon as you made a progress in one area there was somebody from another area saying, "Yeah, but what about this?" So that lack of focus and lack of clear identity was very apparent from the outset. Our mission and vision statements reflected this—becoming laundry lists—so that there was "something for everyone" rather than focus and clarity as to what MNA is truly about.

It occurred to me that the easiest way to identify and to establish a clear identity and build consensus around it was a robust, strategic planning exercise.

Kathleen: What was the board's role in your process? How did you get them engaged and committed?

Mary: It was relatively easy to get the board on side! What I identified as this disparate range of expectations was not new—there was whole-hearted agreement that yes, this existed. They were very enthusiastic about strategic planning, so that was relatively simple. And they also believed that the foundation statements had lost their power to organize and focus MNA's activities. What we did then was organize a working group, and we brought Lord Cultural Resources in to help us through the planning process. Moving the process forward with the strategic advisory group was a way to engage the board. For me, that was really important, because it gave essential background and context, which meant that everyone was working on the plan from the same starting point rather than coming from this spread. This provided us a level playing field, and then we could look at priorities. It was critical that the board was engaged, and they really were—they embraced it!

To address the foundation statements, we worked through a series of plenary and small group discussions with the board, senior staff, and the Lord team to recapture key ideas and words that resonated. Then drafted and redrafted several rounds of iterations (five in total), arriving finally at the core of what we are, do, and aspire to do.

Kathleen: How was the board thinking about MNA's legacy?

The MNA is almost one hundred years old and we're looking at our centennial—that was also a strong motivation for looking at where we've been and where we're going. MNA is an organization that really cherishes its history and legacy. The identity and role of our founders as far back as 1928 is something that is very present in all of MNA, so it was essential that we just didn't say everything that's gone before is gone, and we're just looking at new. So, we did take a good look at the existing mission and vision and the history of MNA and what the priorities of MNA have been over time. And the drafting process allowed us to strip away all of the distracting language and focus on intent and outcomes: being *a gateway to understanding the Colorado Plateau, engaging local, regional, and global audiences with life-enriching knowledge and experiences.* MNA has always been about appreciating and understanding this unique place in the world. *We illuminate the connections between people, place, and time through science, art, and culture* is a vision that everyone could embrace!

Kathleen: How would you describe what is different about the "before" and "after" versions of your statements?

Mary: The key differences are that the new ones are much shorter, much more focused, and, to my mind, more actionable. We didn't just throw everything out. We distilled what we thought essential, affirming that we are a place-based institution, and using that fact to weave together the variety of activities that we engage in and looking at the connections between people, place, and time

Kathleen: How have board and staff responded to this change?

Mary: The board especially is very excited. They enjoyed the process and they felt elevated and educated by it. I think they now feel they have a better sense of the potential of MNA. Not just what we have been—which has been remarkable history—but even more so by what we can be. And they feel energized by having been a part of that.

The staff at first had a healthy dose of skepticism: "Yeah, another strategic plan, we'll do it, and it'll sit on the shelf, and we'll just move ahead and keep doing what we do." But what we're doing now is using the mission, vision, goals, and objectives in every aspect of what we do organiza-tionally. So, my report to the board—and the reports I get from senior staff—are now structured around our goals and objectives: at staff meetings, people are connecting their presentations to our goals and objectives; setting our budget is linked to our goals and objectives; our board discussions about what the priorities will be for next year are drawn directly from our goals and objectives. Everyone now understands that this is a real, living, working document, and that's really helpful in identifying new opportunities as they arise.

We now have a sort of touchstone to say, "Okay, this is what we're doing this year. How does this new opportunity fit in, change, or be scheduled for some other time." It gives us a framework to make those decisions rather than just running pillar to post: "Oh, there's something over there—let's run toward that. Wait a second—here's something else—let's run toward that." Not that any of the things were banned, but it just meant you never reached your target, right? Because something else always came up. Sharpening that focus meant we can have real impact.

Kathleen: How has your community responded?

Mary: I did a presentation to our members at our Member Appreciation Day on a beautiful Saturday afternoon and over sixty people attended and participated in a really good Q and A. We've also sent it out to our donors, supporters, and stakeholders, and we're following up with meetings. We've had a number of people close to MNA who wanted to be with us and talk about it, and a number of people who had drifted a little bit away from MNA. It's been a really good tool for us—a conversation starter—about where we're going. It gives us a way to talk about MNA.

Overwhelmingly the response has been a real delight that there is a focus and also a recognition that there was a lack of focus. I would say everyone we've spoken to has really welcomed that clarity and the transparency. To a prospective donor or legacy donor who asks you: "What's new at the museum?" Well, there's a lot that's new, and that gives you some freshness and currency that might not have been present before. Foundations and individuals that support us have been very pleased to see this, and I think will only tie them closer to us. A number of high-level members have increased their membership to a giving society that we've just started in support of the museum. So I would say, yes—it has been a very, very good tool.

I think the other thing that is a critical success factor is that, although there's a huge amount of background, documentation, and data that informed it, the final plan is really short, sharp, focused, and very attractive.

The work that went into building it was valuable because it gathered us together and pointed us in the same direction, and it gave a context for making difficult choices and for people to understand and see how those choices were made. The process was difficult, but now that we have the final results, we make sure that we use it, and we use it in a way that is transparent and widely communicated, which is what unleashes the power of the statements and the plan.

Figure 2.1.   Dawn at the Grand Canyon, one of the most iconic geological features of the Colorado Plateau. The Museum of Northern Arizona, founded in Flagstaff, Arizona, in 1928, was conceived of and continues as a "gateway" to understanding the Plateau's magnificent landscapes, natural history, and Indigenous people and cultures. *Photo by Murray Foubister, CC BY-SA 2.0, via Wikimedia Commons.*

2.3 Museum Functions, Goals, and Objectives

All foundation statements refer to museum functions. While there are hundreds of activities that take place in museums, these activities can actually best be understood and organized in six functional areas distributed among two massive categories: assets and programs.

The museum's asset functions are collections (both tangible and intangible), documentation (which includes myriad activities involving research and consultation with descendant communities), and preservation (which encompasses both the active aspects of preserving objects, stories, art, archives, and specimens as well as the maintenance of the museum building—the container).

The museum's programming functions include research and the creation of new knowledge; interpretation, which is the ever-changing explanation of meaning through learning processes; and display, which is most often thought of as exhibitions but also includes digital presence, publications, tours, events, and so much more.

Seen in this way we can understand the inherent tension within museums between the introvert asset functions of the museum and the extrovert programming functions.

As many have observed, the best way to achieve "perfection" for the asset functions—collecting, documenting, and preserving—would be to keep the museum's collections in a dark, locked room, whereas "perfection" for the program functions of research, display, and interpretation would be to make them as publicly accessible as possible.

It is the daily job of leadership to pull together the assets and the programming personalities of museums. Innovative, sustainable, and relevant museums (as distinct from "community attics") require not only the administrative tools of management but an inspiring vision, mission, and mandate, with strong leadership and united staff who share meaningful values.

The greater the integration of museum functions, the more relevant and meaningful museums become, and the more their communities will value and use them.

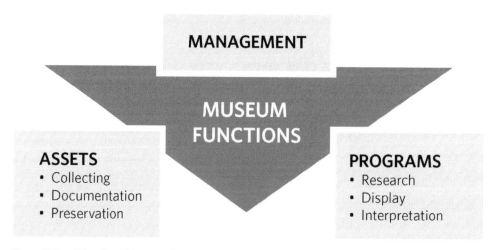

Figure 2.2.   Triangle of Museum Functions. *Lord Cultural Resources.*

The terms *goals* and *objectives* are often used interchangeably—some see objectives as broader and goals as more specific, whereas others see goals as broader, while objectives are more particular to a given time period or budget. Here are two distinct definitions to avoid any confusion for these terms.

The goals of a museum may be defined as: The long-range qualitative levels of achievement relative to the museum's vision and mission. Goals will likely address levels of excellence and fundamental change to be achieved in core museum functions such as collection development, community engagement, visitor services, and financial sustainability toward which the institution is striving. They may be articulated for a given period of the museum's development in a strategic plan or in a master plan. Achieving them may take years.

The objectives of a museum may be defined as: The short-range, quantified expressions of particular steps on the way to the longer-range goals. Such objectives are placed on a timetable or schedule for fulfillment, and they are usually specific to a one-year or two-year planning period. They may be articulated as part of a one-year plan of action or as part of a budget exercise. Again, if the opposite usage is preferred, with objectives as the longer-range qualitative levels and goals as the shorter-range quantified targets, the effect is the same—both apply the mission and mandate to specific museum functions.

2.4 The Roles of Management

In order for museum management to facilitate the achievement of vision, mission, values, mandate, goals, objectives, and functions, it must be adept at playing not one but five roles:

- to *inspire* with a sense of the museum's *vision, mission,* and *values*;

- to *communicate* the museum's *mandate*;

- to *lead* toward the museum's *goals*;

- to *control* the attainment of *objectives*; and

- to *evaluate* the fulfillment and impact of museum *functions.*

We can all relate to the idea that most managers cannot perform all five roles equally well. Yet understanding each of these roles in museum terms can help museum managers build on their strengths and identify and improve in those roles in which they may be weak. The diagram developed for this chapter illustrates how these roles are integrated and mutually supportive.

Inspiring with Vision, Values, and a Sense of Mission

A good museum manager has a clear sense of the museum's mission and inspires others to join in its fulfillment. This sense of mission is a stable well of creativity from which the manager derives original solutions to problems, redirects struggling staff toward the essential objectives, or sets challenges that lead the museum to greater accomplishments.

The manager's comprehension of the mission must be so infectious that people who meet them (from staff and volunteers to donors, visitors, and the general public) want to get involved. The manager must believe in the mission: for them it must resonate emotionally and intellectually.

If inspiration is not forthcoming, it may be a weakness of management, or it may be that the mission is out of date, has become irrelevant, or is less significant in the now.

If this is the case, management should set about working with the museum's governing body and staff to review and revise the mission statement. It is surprising how frequently trustees meet to discuss the museum's mission only to discover divergent views despite their prior confidence that everyone shares a common sense of purpose. Generally, major revisions to the mission statement are undertaken only as part of a strategic planning process (as described in this chapter's case study). Getting the mission right may take time, but it is essential to the long-range direction of the institution because the mission is the core around which *policies* should be formed. Without a fully understood and relevant mission, policies remain an empty form. However, when they are supportive of an agreed-upon mission, policies can more effectively be directed toward common goals.

> Without a fully understood and relevant mission, policies remain an empty form.

Figure 2.3.   The Roles of Management: Inspiring with the Mission. *Lord Cultural Resources.*

Communicating the Mandate

A museum manager must understand the mandate of the institution and be able to communicate it to others clearly and concisely, both within the museum and beyond its walls.

As such, the museum's director must be aware of the extent and limitations of that mandate and also of its relationship with the mandates of other institutions. By exercising the mandate consciously, the manager (or director) and the museum may be said to be "communicating" the mandate clearly to visitors, funders, the museum's governing body, and staff.

"Use It or Lose It" applies to mandate.

If a museum is not fulfilling its mandate, and if that mandate is of real interest and concern to others, then another institution—a new museum or an existing museum or related institution—may compete for, or fulfill, that mandate.

> "Use It or Lose It" applies to mandate.

Usually it's not a question of a complete replacement but of a gradual encroachment from other institutions expanding their field of activity. If, for example, a museum of Asian art is not very active in exhibiting or collecting contemporary Asian art, then a museum of contemporary art in the same city may expand into that field and effectively usurp the Asian art museum's mandate, leading to competition for collections and exhibitions.

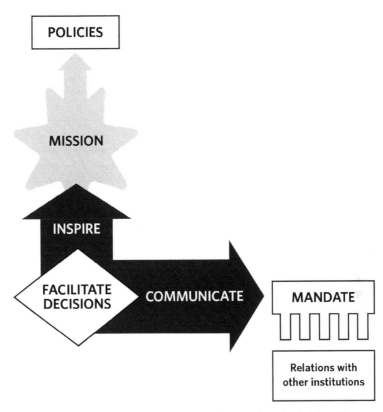

Figure 2.4. The Roles of Management: Communicating the Mandate. *Lord Cultural Resources.*

On the other hand, a lack of clarity about the museum's mandate can also lead the institution to distractions that interfere with the accomplishment of the museum's purposes. It may, for example, be tempting for the County History Museum to offer an exhibition on dinosaurs because of their popularity, even though there were never any such creatures in what is now that county. This exhibition might be admissible as part of a temporary program of "Opening a Window on the World," but if such exhibitions become a major activity, absorbing the energies of staff while the permanent collection of archaeological and historical artifacts is neglected, then the museum is losing sight of its mandate.

Leading toward Goals

Management and leadership are related but are not identical: management is about "doing it right," while leadership is about "doing the right thing." A leader is constantly aware of the institution's goals and, therefore, is able to guide others toward their achievement. Also, leaders have a vision that helps prioritize goals and objectives.

For example, once it has been decided that one of the goals of the museum's documentation program is the conversion of all of its records to an electronic format with an image of every object, it will require leadership as well as good management to steer toward that goal and to dedicate the necessary staff and resources to its achievement despite the many other demands on time, funds, and facilities.

This goal may be very important for the particular director because it will lead to an expansion of the museum's audiences through its website and digital media. It will also require leadership to balance the dedication to that goal with the requirements of a temporary exhibition program that also needs attention from the same registrar who is responsible for the documentation conversion project.

Or consider the leadership needed to achieve the management goal of diversifying the museum's staff. Long-range institutional goals should be identified in plans such as strategic plans or master plans that link those goals to the museum's mission (and therefore to its policies) and mandate. The director needs to report to the staff and the governing body on the progress toward achieving goals. Without a regular reporting process by management, goals can be forgotten and the museum becomes confused and demoralized by "goal confusion."

The importance of strong leadership has become increasingly apparent in the museum field in recent years. This is partly because of the popular success of museums, and partly for the opposite reason, related to the decrease in public funding for museums in many jurisdictions.

Leadership, therefore, is needed more than ever to balance the myriad demands on these institutions, and to keep them on the path to fulfilling their missions, mandates, goals, and objectives. Inspired leadership is an indispensable factor in the successful management of museums.

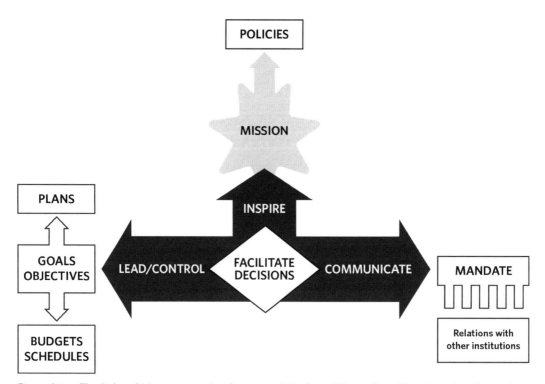

Figure 2.5. The Roles of Management: Leading toward Goals and Controlling Objectives. *Lord Cultural Resources.*

Controlling Attainment of Objectives

To achieve the broad institutional goals articulated in the museum's plans, management must break those goals down into short-range, measurable objectives that, taken together, will lead to the qualitative change that is expressed in the goals.

Many museums, for example, are endeavoring to "decolonize" their collections and their interpretation of those collections. "Decolonization of the collection" could be a goal, but it will mean completely different things in different contexts. And while the goal is stated on the asset side of museum functions, many of the objectives will be programmatic, involving research and education, as well as communication. To complete the objectives managers use a variety of tools discussed in chapter 6.

Evaluating the Fulfillment and Impact of Museum Functions

Are we there yet? And is "there" where we wanted to be? It's important for the funders to know in terms of future funding and for staff to know in terms of morale and for the museum's many publics and stakeholders too!

The achievement of a museum's mission, the accomplishment of its mandate, and even the attainment of short-term objectives on the way to long-range goals can be understood in the big picture when these are related to the museum's goals for its core functions. The evaluation of the six core functions of collecting, documentation, preservation, research, display, and interpretation should be made in terms of both *effectiveness* and *efficiency*:

- *Effectiveness* measures the extent to which the museum's efforts achieve the intended result, which should have been quantified as far as possible in the work plan for that function. Effectiveness evaluates impact. For example, until recently few art museums collected art by Indigenous people, considering it to be "ethnographic specimens" and not "art." In the past, most art museums had goals to expand their collections by filling gaps in "style" or "school" or "geography." Now is different and curators increasingly see that there have been bigger gaps based on racism and ethnocentrism. Evaluating this type of collection growth may require inputs from external sources, including descendant communities.

- *Efficiency* measures results in relation to the effort required—in person hours, in money, in space (which is often at a premium in museums), or in the use of facilities or equipment. The term "cost-effectiveness" is sometimes used to describe efficiency measured in financial terms; "person-effectiveness" and "space-effectiveness" would be equally useful concepts, but all three are really measures of efficiency.

In recent years, as museums have become more aligned as pluralist institutions with diverse funding sources, it is its funders and donors, both public and private, who are challenging the idea that museums should be evaluated only in terms of their own museological functions. Stephen Weil pioneered this approach in his important book *Making Museums Matter* in which he asserts that museums "matter" when they fulfill social needs.[1] It's worth mentioning again that Lonnie Bunch III, secretary of the Smithsonian Institutions, famously said, "Museums are not community centers but they can be centers of community."[2]

Museums, in fact, are increasingly being evaluated in terms of the impacts they achieve for society. There is a strong trend to evaluate museums in terms of the *outcomes and benefits* they achieve for society as a whole—such as economic impacts, job creation, and skills training.

In Canada and elsewhere there is a new emphasis on truth and reconciliation with Indigenous peoples. In the United States and elsewhere there has been a move to evaluate museum performance in terms of diversity, equity, inclusion, and belonging. These initiatives have lasting impacts only when they are implemented in all museum functions and in museum governance.

This is where figure 2.6 can be very helpful. Figure 2.6 has been built from all the figures discussed in this chapter. It illustrates the five roles of management in relation to museum functions and policies. And at the very heart of the diagram is the reminder that the purpose of management is to make it easier (for it will never be easy!) for people who work and volunteer in museums to do their jobs well.

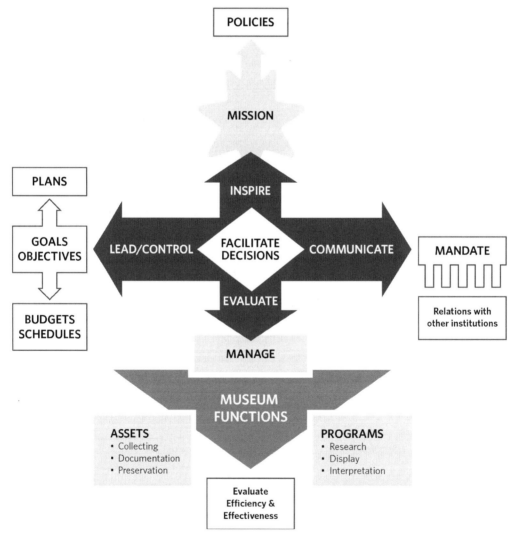

Figure 2.6.   Summary of Museum Management. *Lord Cultural Resources.*

Repatriation Is Not Loss

By Cara Krmpotich

As a repatriation scholar, I am often asked to weigh in on questions of repatriation when they appear in the headlines. Public and professional concerns about repatriation are often framed by ideas of "loss": museums will lose their collections, science will lose opportunities for knowledge, the public will lose access to important human heritage.

Concerns that repatriation results in loss are surprisingly short sighted and run contrary to the available evidence. I believe museums are better served by an understanding of repatriation as a creative practice: repatriation contributes to the creation of belonging, cultural expressions, knowledge, and understanding. All of these attributes are at the core of contemporary museum practice. From a museum perspective, then, we should be leaning into—not shying away from—repatriation.

In English, repatriation is the return of someone or something to their homelands. It applies to cultural heritage but also to refugees and the war dead. At its heart then, the word reflects an understanding that belonging is connected to place, and that displacement creates hardship and ruptures. In the cultural sector, we have expanded our use of "repatriation" to include the return of knowledge, images, seeds, sound, and archives. The term "rematriation" has also been offered by Indigenous leaders to invoke the return of traditional governance models that center women's knowledges and leadership in cultural continuity and community well-being; rematriation is an Indigenized form of return with a lineage outside Western legal practices and statehood. In African-European contexts, "restitution" is commonly used. It is a term that evokes the dual needs of restoration and justice and speaks to the material violence of displacement. There are important antecedents for "restitution" in the return of Nazi spoliated artworks and family belongings to Jewish Holocaust survivors (on the overlaps between the contexts of Nazi spoliation and Indigenous repatriation, see Glass 2004 in further reading).

When people speak of repatriation as a loss to museums, they are ignoring the fact that the loss has already happened: someone or something is already lost from their homelands. The remains, belongings, artifacts, or knowledge have been displaced from their home and taken into the museum. Repatriation requests seek to reunite that which is lost; they seek a return home. I am not being naïve about the reality of human displacement, malleable political borders, and the remaking of cultural identities: *where* home is and *who* identifies with that home can be complex and multifaceted. But in the case of museums in colonial metropoles, the museum, its staff, and activities rarely resemble *home*. Items may have been in a museum for decades, even hundreds of years, but as public historian Robert Archibald offers, our childhood home comes to be the basis for future comparisons and sense making. Our homelands act as a barometer, a suite of expectations, against which subsequent experiences are understood and assessed. For ancestral remains, cultural patrimony, and even mundane or everyday cultural belongings, the museum experience of being accessioned, cataloged, numbered, stored with limited interactions, curated, researched, interpreted, and exhibited deviates significantly from their premuseum lives. The possible relations an artifact or ancestral remain can have shift substantially when those remains or artifacts enter a museum (Matthews 2016 in further reading).

There are, of course, instances when museums and staffs more closely resemble home; where the geographic and cultural distance between artifact, collection, institution, and staff is not so great. With this fact, it is useful to remember that museums' roles in repatriation are not limited to that of the returner. Museums are also very frequently the recipient of repatriated materials (Collison and Krmpotich 2020 in further reading). Equally, we need to acknowledge that repatriation has led to the creation of museums, including the Haida Gwaii Museum, U'mista Cultural Centre, and the National Museum of the American Indian. Whereas the Haida Gwaii Museum's earliest collections included items repatriated from private citizens as well as museums, and the National Museum of the American Indian was created through repatriation legislation, the U'Mista Cultural Centre was created as a condition for the return of a confiscated potlach collection. However, increasingly, and even to some degree with U'Mista, we see communities and nations desiring caring and collective spaces for their belongings and patrimony. What they create are often museums and museum-like spaces where they can enact local practices of care, knowledge sharing, and history making. Items with spiritual roles to play may be restored not (only) to a museum but to a temple or place of worship.

The MacKenzie Art Gallery, led by John G. Hampton, proactively repatriated a statue learned to be stolen to Varanasi, India, where it has rejoined the Kashi Vishwanath temple and is once again part of an active community of faith (Warwick 2021 in further reading). Furthermore, repatriation can become a powerful event in a community's or nation's sense of self and sense of history. Sara Baartman's story of repatriation, for example, is embroidered into the tapestries telling San History at the Origins Centre, University of Witwatersrand, South Africa.[3] Back with their communities, repatriated items contribute to precisely the kinds of cultural expressions and human meanings museums so ardently seek to convey. Repatriation has not been a detriment to any of these museums; on the contrary, these examples speak to the ways repatriation is a generative force for museums, cultural spaces, and history making.

It is worth addressing earlier museum expectations that repatriated materials should only be returned if they could be received into a local museum. This goes against the spirit of repatriation, which is about the return of control or agency over a person or object, as much as it is their physical return. The United Nations Declaration on the Rights of Indigenous Peoples identifies repatriation as a right for Indigenous nations and a duty of states. In repatriating, museums forego the right to stipulate conditions of care, preservation, interpretation, and circulation. It is useful to say it plainly: when museums repatriate, they are not owed anything in "return." And indeed, when we start from the perspective that repatriation is not a loss for museums, our sense that museums should benefit in some way from participating in repatriation becomes unnecessary.

And yet, museums with colonial origins or in colonial centers report myriad ways in which they have gained by engaging with repatriation (Conaty 2015; Curtis 2006; Peers 2004; Shannon 2017 in further reading). The paradox of repatriation is that the work entailed in returning ancestors or cultural belongings home almost always leads to a deeper understanding by the museum of the items no longer in their care and the cultures, communities, and nations related to them. The building of relationships, trust, and understanding through the work of repatriation can carry over into future conservation, curatorial, and educational collaborations. A museum's expanded understanding usually begins with the requirement to investigate provenance in meaningful ways, which brings historical specificity and current knowledge to bear on a museum's collections and histories (Bruchac 2010; Digital Benin n.d. in further reading).

I am currently part of a team supporting efforts by the Anatomy Museum, University of Edinburgh, to conduct provenance research, identify descendant communities in Canada, and contact communities' governing bodies about potential ancestral remains held in Edinburgh.[4] The museum's proactive approach to repatriation sees our team confronting the racism of phrenology as a scientific pursuit and seeking approaches to repatriation that do not perpetuate the harm of past museum practices. Rather than descendants having to locate and search an online database that uses museological and osteological terminology, our team is taking responsibility for researching, assessing, and correcting errors in documentation and returning some semblance of humanity to the ways ancestors are identified in museum documentation.

Through introductory letters and virtual sessions, we share what we know, what we don't know, learn what communities desire to know, and what next steps are appropriate. There is no law compelling the Anatomy Museum to undertake this work or the other ongoing repatriation commitments they have in Africa and Asia. This instance of the Anatomy Museum is an important illustration of how "loss" as a framing for repatriation is misplaced.

Curator Malcolm MacCallum reports the return of hundreds of skulls over time, beginning with an early repatriation in the 1940s, to a more intensive period of returns in the 1990s and 2000s, and now again in the 2020s. Unlike collections of material culture, where people continue to create material anew and acquisitions can be commissioned or otherwise pursued, the repatriation of ancestral remains does not lead to a growth in collections. MacCallum, like his colleagues, has identified gains for his museum from participating in repatriation, including conducting research at the behest and with prior and informed consent of communities seeking greater information about their relatives and expanding disciplinary understandings of collections to include culturally specific knowledge, values, ethical beliefs, and histories.

MacCallum summarizes it well: "We have a duty of care to the individuals in our collection and we also have a growing awareness of being global citizens."[5] In this instance, the creative aspect of repatriation can be understood as an evolution in the way museums enact duties of care and engage in the very processes of repatriation itself.

Beyond provenance research, engaging in repatriation work requires us to develop our understandings of cross-cultural diplomacy, governance, and law; spirituality, animacy, and agency; cultural expressions of kinship, grief, mourning, responsibility, and care; and interrelationships between tangible and intangible culture. Arguably, when museum staff and boards grow their understandings in these areas, their capacity to care for, curate, interpret, and activate collections for a diverse public improves.

Figure 2.7.   The goddess Annapurna, once part of the Norman MacKenzie Collection of the University of Regina, was repatriated in 2020 and now sits in a newly constructed Annapurna temple inside the Kashi Vishwanath temple corridor, a short distance from the shore of the Ganges River in Varanasi where she was stolen from in 1913. *Photo by Don Hall. Image courtesy of the MacKenzie Art Gallery.*

Figure 2.8.   Divya Mehra, *There Is Nothing You Can Possess Which I Cannot Take Away (Not Vishnu: New Ways of Darsána)*, 2020. Purchased by the artist from a Hollywood memorabilia store and artificially aged, this bag was filled with sand to match the weight of the Annapurna sculpture and now sits in the void left from the repatriated sculpture. Collection of the MacKenzie Art Gallery. *Photo by John G. Hampton. Courtesy of John Hampton.*

2.5 Governance

Museum governing bodies do not manage museums—yet a chapter on museum management and leadership needs to discuss governance to clarify its important roles.

Museums are managed by designated staff hired by the director. Even in an entirely volunteer-operated museum, some participants are designated as board volunteers who are responsible for maintaining its charitable or other legal status, while others are designated as unpaid staff. They may be the same people who metaphorically change hats, but the distinction is nonetheless significant if this fledgling museum is to grow.

The roles and responsibilities of museum boards vary with the type of board as outlined shortly, its location and history, and are the subject of many excellent books and publications.[6] To clarify the distinction between the roles of management and governing boards, here are six of the basic roles of *governing* boards.

- Recruit and negotiate a contract with the museum's director, to evaluate their performance, and to terminate their employment if necessary.

- Maintain the legal requirements of the museum legislation or charter.

- Provide for the continuity of the museum's mission, mandate, and policies.

- Participate in the museum's strategic and long-range planning.

- Ensure that the museum has adequate operating and capital funds to fulfill its mission, mandate, policies, and plans, including the responsibility to make and solicit donations.

- Collegiality and ethical management of the board itself.

Despite the wide variety of circumstances in which museums around the world have been established, there are four principal modes of governance that may then be combined in so many different ways that all too often staff, the general public, and board members themselves do not really understand where in the museum the power and accountability is located and how this impacts management.

That's why it is useful to briefly describe the four basic types of governance:

- line departments

- arm's length institutions

- independent nonprofit or charitable organizations

- private ownership

Those involved in establishing a new museum should carefully consider which mode of governance will best meet the long-term needs of the institution. And those

> Those involved in establishing a new museum should carefully consider which mode of governance will best meet the long-term needs of the institution.

responsible for existing museums should also review governance issues, because what may have been a suitable form of governance fifty years ago may no longer be appropriate.

Current societal trends toward decentralization and privatization are sometimes reflected in the tendency to change the governance of museums that were once part of government agencies or public authorities to the independent nonprofit or charitable sector model.

More broadly, museums are now very often conceived as "civil society" institutions with mixed public and private funding, but with accountability both fiscal and moral to the public at large. The process of reviewing and possibly changing a museum's governance is called *institutional planning*, which generally follows a *strategic plan* or a *governance review*.

This section outlines the main characteristics of each of the four basic modes of governance and the different roles of their boards. It concludes with figure 2.9, which summarizes all four modes: line departments, arm's length institutions, independent nonprofit or charitable organizations, and private ownership.

Line Departments

National, state, provincial, county, and city museums and galleries are often part of the cultural departments of the relevant level of government. Line department museums form part of a government, university, religious/social organization, or corporation. This is equally true of specialized museums in their respective departments: a postal museum, for example, may be part of a national postal or telecommunications service; a geology museum may be part of a university's geology department; and an automotive museum may be established within the public relations department of a car manufacturer. These are all examples of *line department museums*.

Their employees are civil servants if the museum is a government line department, or employees of the university, other entity or corporation that owns the museum.

The director of a government line department museum may be appointed by the departmental administration or may be recruited through the civil service process; directors of university or corporate line department museums, and of some government museums, may be engaged in the same way as other departmental administrators. In any case, the governance of the line department museum is integrated within that of the larger body.

Line department museums are funded primarily through allocations from the budget of the owning organization. This is usually not grant aid but a line item in the department budget. Some line department museums are therefore free of charge, while others charge admission and raise additional revenue in other ways, but all have a central allocation from their governing body to sustain them. The collection and the buildings of line department museums are usually owned by the parent body.

Many government line department museums around the world share a common problem in the disposition of their earned revenues, which typically go to a central government finance department and do not benefit the institution directly. As a result, many of these museums have little incentive to provide retail or food services of good quality, and their shops and cafés sometimes reflect this. Amending this accounting principle so that line department museums can keep their earnings has resulted in vast improvements in food services, retailing, rentals, and special events in many national museums.

Because they are part of a larger departmental body, most line department museums do not have a membership organization. Some have recruited "friends" groups both as a means of retaining earned income and of obtaining financial support. Volunteers are also often more difficult to recruit in a line department museum because of the perception that everything is being done by paid staff.

If a line department museum has a board, it will likely be an *advisory board* without decision-making authority on any of the six board responsibilities listed earlier. Instead it will advise the owner or governing authority on those and other matters listed in its terms of reference. That is why it is especially important to reinforce the point that boards do not manage museums. Prospective directors and senior staff should closely examine the terms of reference for the advisory board to ensure that this is clear.

In some instances the advisory board may advise the department administration or the president of the university or corporation on the selection of the director. But in any case the trustees are advisory only, having neither decision-making authority nor that responsibility. This type of board is often passive, seeing itself as a "watch dog" for the owner rather than a partner in the museum's progress, goals, and plans.

Many governments—national, state, provincial, county, or municipal—operate museum systems in which several museums are grouped together to form a *museum service*. These associations of multiple museums are cost-effective for their administrations due to the centralization of at least some functions. The constituent museums may share their governing authority's accounting, personnel, maintenance, security, or other services, adding only the curatorial and programming staff that are unique to each museum.

Many museum services have found it cost-effective to centralize conservation and documentation functions for all participating institutions, and in some cases to erect or renovate nonpublic collection storage and laboratories in one central location. The disadvantages of such services for the participating museums can be loss of independence and difficulty in maintaining a distinct identity and public image, which may affect fund-raising, but if well managed they can be both efficient and effective in providing a wide range of museum experiences for residents and visitors throughout the jurisdiction of the presiding government.

Arm's Length Institutions

Although many levels of government, universities, and corporations operate their museums as line departments, some have discovered advantages to establishing them as *arm's length institutions*.

Arm's length refers to the distance between head and hand, which appears to allow the hand a certain degree of autonomy, although it is ultimately controlled by the head. The arm's length approach is intended to ensure that the museum is independent of partisan politics or corporate self-interest and to encourage the institution to find additional means of support besides government, university, or corporate funds. Arm's length museums in the governmental sector are sometimes referred to as agencies.

To continue the metaphor, the "arm's length" may be the distance from wrist to shoulder, or merely from elbow to shoulder, and institutional planning may consider whether the "distance" is sufficient or excessive. A governance review might recommend greater autonomy for the museum so that it can earn, raise, and retain more revenues and build closer ties to communities. There are, though, many situations when such a review might recommend that the government or institutional or corporate owner take a more active role in order to ensure adequate financial support for the museum.

Arm's length museums differ from line department museums in that they normally have a *governing board* appointed by the senior political authority within that jurisdiction or by the president of the university or the institutional or corporate owner.

The government department or owner is usually represented on this board, along with representatives of stakeholders and/or the general public. This governing board is not merely advisory but actually determines policy and long-range plans and engages the museum's director. Because these boards exercise real power and influence, the method of appointing board members or trustees and their qualifications are matters of utmost importance. Regulations for board appointment and roles are usually part of the legislation establishing the museum, so this is not a board function as in an independent museum. The museum director/CEO is usually consulted for their recommendations as to who should be appointed because the director/CEO will have the best understanding of what skills and representation are needed on the board to support the vision and mission. However, when the arm's length relationship is very tight (from shoulder to head as it were), the director/CEO may be excluded from the board selection process.

The benefit of arm's length governance is that it places the main funding responsibility on the owning organization whether government, institutional, or corporate. The disadvantage is that due to the large presence of the owner, board members continue to see themselves as "watch dogs" rather than dynamic partners in achieving the museum's vision, mission, and plans.

In arm's length scenarios, museum staff may either be considered civil servants or employees of the government department, university, or corporation, or they may be employed directly by the museum.

The collection and/or the land and buildings of a museum at arm's length are usually but not always owned by the government or the owning organization. Owing to a heightened perception of their autonomy, arm's length museums are sometimes more successful in attracting donations of both funds and objects for the collection than line department museums. Volunteers may also be more likely to support an arm's length museum than a line department institution. However, to avoid confusion, many arm's length museums establish separate, independent friends organizations to raise money and support in order to ensure donors that their gifts provide tax and other benefits.

Government funding for museums at arm's length may be an annual allocation (as in line department museums), but it often takes the form of an annual dedicated grant rather than a departmental allocation. The amount of this annual grant is typically determined from year to year, thus making the arm's length institution less certain of its annual budget levels than the line department museum.

On the other hand, the arm's length museum is usually free to raise additional nongovernmental funds from philanthropists, foundations, or corporations or even to attract grants from other levels or departments of government. Museums at arm's length typically do not have the line department museum's problem of their earned revenues going to a general government finance department but are able to access both government and earned revenues for their own purposes—an advantage that is usually made evident in a more visitor-centric approach to amenities like café, retail, parking, rentals, events, and activities.

Independent Nonprofit Museums

The terms *nonprofit and not-for-profit* refer to a legal status that figures prominently in the official definitions of what is a museum.[7] Indeed all four of the museum types referenced here are likely *not-for-profit*. Very few government, university, or social enterprise line department museums or their agencies at arm's length are operated for profit. Likewise, many privately owned museums are non-

> From a management perspective, the key word is "independent" because it fundamentally changes the board role from advisory to governing.

profits. This category is significantly different because these museums are *independent* nonprofit organizations formed under legislation that specifies that their purposes must be *in the public interest* and *not for private benefit*. In many countries this type of museum is eligible to receive tax exemptions and may confer tax benefits to its donors. It must be pointed out that line department and arm's length museums may be able to receive and confer similar benefits when the owner is a nonprofit. From a management perspective, the key word is "independent" because it fundamentally changes the board role from advisory to governing.

The boards of museums incorporated as *nonprofit or charitable organizations* are governing, not merely advisory bodies. The board may be self-perpetuating or elected from the membership of the organization, or it may consist of both appointed and elected members. Whatever its specific form or size, the board collectively assumes legal and financial responsibility for the museum, subject to the laws governing this type of organization in the country or jurisdiction in which it is incorporated.

In the past, it was common for such museums to have constituent memberships, with the board as an executive body of the members, elected at an annual general meeting. Today, however, membership is usually just a program operated by the museum, with a separate set of bylaws governing the board's methods of recruitment and replacement of trustees. Membership programs are maintained as means of ensuring public support and achieving the museum's societal mission, as well as a minor revenue source.

To achieve charitable or nonprofit status, the museum organization will usually have applied for and obtained registration, letters patent, or a charitable tax number allowing it to provide tax-deductible receipts for donations and to receive other benefits allowed by government policy in each jurisdiction. Consequently, the museum organization must comply with a broad range of government regulations in order to maintain that status. For example, it may be necessary to establish a separate corporation to operate retail or catering because the nonprofit museum itself may not be allowed to operate these directly. There may also be regulations to prevent unfair competition with the for-profit sector.

The nonprofit or charitable organization typically owns the museum collection, land, and buildings and employs the museum staff. However, there are many independent nonprofit or charitable trusts that operate museums in government- or city-owned buildings and some that care for city-owned collections.

The museum director is appointed by the trustees. Funding is likely to be a mixture of public and private funds, including income from endowments, donations, and visitor spending in the museum. Volunteers, generally, play a prominent role in these museums.

The board of the independent not-for-profit museum is a governing board that takes on responsibility for all six roles listed at the beginning of this section, and often more. The governing board is a full partner with the museum in its progress, goals, and plans. Nonetheless, the board does not manage the museum, nor does it hire (or fire) any staff other than the director/CEO. Because the board has ultimate legal and financial responsibility for the museum, the relationship between the board chair and the director/CEO is key because together they constitute a powerful leadership team. However, the director/CEO and the museum management team require exceptional leadership and management skills and tools for success in this complex governance situation.

Private Ownership

One or another of the three previous modes of governance is found in virtually all public museums around the world. In addition, there are a number of museums that are owned and operated by private individuals, foundations, or companies.

These museums may be operated as private charities or may be intended to earn a profit for their owners. However, it should be noted that profit-making museums would not be classified as museums under the ICOM definition of *museum*, nor the definitions of the British Museums Association and the American Alliance of Museums, all of which define museums as non-profit-making institutions.

The individuals or the incorporated companies that operate private museums normally own the collections and own or lease the building. The funding for private museums comes directly from their owners and from earned revenues.

The director is usually employed by the owner, who may also appoint an advisory board or committee. Staff are employees of the individual or the private company. Volunteers are rare.

Mixed Model of Ownership and Governance

Mixed models of museum ownership are emerging in part to encourage private investment in public museums (which some see as creeping privatization) and in part to change the passive watch dog style of governance that tends to accompany line department and arm's length museums to a more activist, energized private-public model. Such as:

* museums owned by government but operated by nonprofit associations;

* museums owned by for-profit entities like developers but operated by nonprofit organizations, such as universities, schools or social agencies, that receive regular government funding, grants, and philanthropic support; and

- museums owned by government but operated by self-perpetuating boards with governing authority.

- In the United Kingdom, the national museums (now all free admission) are operated by separate boards that negotiate multiyear funding agreements with government based on strategic plans. While government funding remains extremely important, additional and alternative sources of funding such as fund-raising, events, commercial activities, and philanthropy are almost equally so.

- In 2003, Spain's national museum, the Prado, became an independent institution, still strongly linked to government but as a special status institution with its own board and the long-range goal of reducing its level of state support from 80 to 50 percent.

- In Canada the national museums were made into "Crown Corporations" in 1990—which means that they have boards that operate at arm's length from government and control their own budgets. In 2006, the government established a new process for board appointments that invites volunteers from the public. However, board appointments are made by the responsible government department and the director is appointed by the government. Two new national museums were founded: in 2014 the Canadian Museum for Human Rights[8] in Winnipeg and in 1997 the Canadian Immigration Museum[9] in Halifax.

- The Louvre and other French national museums operate under special contracts with government, control their own budgets, and have managing boards.

- The Barbados Museum and Historical Society functions as a national museum but is a private-public partnership with government as a generous supporter.

While city museums, or museums in the local authority sector, still tend to be line department government institutions, many of the new museums being initiated by cities and regional governments—often with the goal of urban regeneration or economic development—are being established as charitable institutions with independent boards. For example:

- In establishing the Lowry art center in Salford Quay, Salford City Council transferred their collection of L. S. Lowry's paintings and drawings to the fully independent Lowry Trust that manages the art center and its museum. This is an exceptionally dynamic art center, which with the Imperial War Museum of the North across the canal has stimulated economic development in a region of England that was formerly classified as one of the most deprived in Europe.[10]

- New York City has one of the most extensive systems of urban museums—thirty-three in total, so far—which are all independent nonprofit museums that receive a total of $200 million from New York's Cultural Affairs Department in return for agreeing to shared policies of public service and diversity, equity, and inclusion. Additionally, part of this cultural exchange funding included a capital budget of more than $1 billion over the next four years, which extends their support through capital spending construction and renovation.[11]

- In 2023, the State of Bihar in India opened the Bihar Museum, a new type of storytelling museum for India that focuses on the region's cultural heritage—displaying relevant artifacts, artworks, and collected stories as well as operating a dedicated children's

Factor	Line Departments	Arm's Length	Nonprofit	Private
Ownership	Government, University, or Corporation	Government, University, or Corporation	Association or Public Company	Individual or Private Company
Role	Advisory	Governing or Advisory	Governing	Advisory
Funds	Annual Allocation	Granted and Earned	Earned, with Grants and Endowment	Private and Earned
Donations	Less likely	More likely	Most likely	Not likely
Staff	Civil service, University or Corporation staff	May be civil service or museum staff	Association employees	Company employees
Volunteers	Difficult	Possible	Important	Rare

Figure 2.9.   Modes of Museum Governance. *Lord Cultural Resources.*

museum—showcasing the history of the region, state, and its people. This is a state museum with a wider range of management autonomy than has been the norm.

Figure 2.9 summarizes the four basic modes of governance of museums and galleries. The fifth, mixed mode presents various combinations of these factors, depending on local circumstances.

Any change in the museum's institutional status must be carefully considered: a government line department museum may envy the freedom of an arm's length institution, but is it prepared for uncertainty in its annual funding? On the other hand, a nonprofit or charitable organization struggling to finance the local public art gallery may be advantaged to move to arm's length status by appointing civic representatives to its board. Any decision to change status should be taken only as the result of a careful *institutional planning* process that examines all possible impacts of the change.

What these disparate examples have in common is greater reliance on mixed sources of funding and new models of governance resulting in museums that are more accountable to a wider range of stakeholders, more dependent on earned revenues from the general public (even when admission is free)—and are even more complex to manage!

Reclaiming a Region's History at Bihar Museum

By Anjani Kumar Singh

The Bihar Museum was conceived in 2010, then planned and executed at a phenomenal speed, with the first phase opening in August 2015. Subsequent galleries were inaugurated in 2017 for a fully operational museum.

The uniqueness of the museum is not only due to the process and master planning—developed in collaboration with Lord Cultural Resources—but also because of its specific location: Patna, India.

The Bihar Museum lays claim to the roots of Indian history and spirituality, which in the last half century have survived many challenges, with its glorious history and legacy obscured due to colonial and postcolonial policies and management. The museum was created as an antidote to these challenges, and the chief minister, Nitish Kumar, had a vision that the Bihar Museum could help reclaim some of this lost pride and valued history.

The museum has been operational now for over seven years, including the era of the COVID pandemic. The historical, artifact-based galleries showcase the rich history of Bihar, and additional attractions like the Children's Gallery, Diaspora Gallery, and the Regional Art Gallery also bring into focus the contemporary, living heritage of Bihar, which engages a variety of audience demographics.

Since 2010 the chief minister's leadership and vision, combined with the continuity of the museum management including Anjani Kumar Singh—who was appointed director general of the museum in 2003—have aided in implementing the vision and mission of the museum.

In India, as in many other countries, the museum culture is undergoing a paradigm shift as it moves away from colonial structures to embrace its own identity, reflecting local and regional narratives, as well as amplifying the voices of all its stakeholders, not just the decision makers.

The Bihar Museum is helping to lead this transition through its various exhibitions, programming, and events. In doing so, the museum has successfully placed itself on the international map, through its Museum Biennale, an innovative asset that invites museum staff from cultures around the globe to participate in an exchange of ideas—bringing the world to Bihar.

The first edition of the Bihar Museum Biennale was held in 2021. As the pandemic forced all of us to pivot and adapt to the new normal, so did the Biennale, by moving many of its panel discussions, museum walks, and master classes online.

The Bihar Museum is also one of the first museums in India to be planned in an integrated manner, anticipating the needs of its various audiences and collections, while connecting the museum with international visitors and its primary stakeholders—local communities.

For example, along with international programs like the Biennale, the museum also displays exhibitions of contemporary Indian artists like Himmat Shah, Jatin Das, Dheeraj Chaudhary, K. G. Subramaniyan, Jyoti Bhatt, and Jai Jharotia, along with programming and workshops created around these artists.

As a growing institution, the Bihar Museum has also partnered strategically with other museums, including entering into an MoU with the National Museum Institute in New Delhi, creating infrastructure for the conservation lab of the museum. The museum's ambition is to create a world-class lab for the conservation of art works from Bihar and neighboring regions. The museum is also partnering with the India Foundation for the Arts to conduct research into various local folk arts, with an emphasis on encouraging female artisans to explore contemporary design and modern techniques.

Bihar has a sizable diaspora, and its peoples have migrated to various countries like Mauritius, Fiji, Surinam, Trinidad, and South Africa, often as indentured labor. Therefore, the museum has dedicated a gallery on the Bihari diaspora which tells the story of their sociocultural and political history. The museum has also engaged a team of experts to further enrich these stories through research.

There are many challenges ahead, of course. For example, even as Indian museums are coming into their own, staff resources are often scarce, and staff are required to be transplanted laterally from other institutions or trained for specific roles in the museum.

In response, the Bihar Museum has been collaborating with local institutions like Upendra Maharathi Institute, Kilkari (a children's hobby center), and Pratham (a learning organization) to ensure that its offerings are rooted in the cultural context of its unique identity.

The approach has worked and is attracting large audiences. In fact, the museum was created to accommodate about two thousand visitors per day, but during some weekends, summer vacations, and the New Year break, visitor numbers have crossed the five thousand threshold. These visitor numbers are not only due to increased tourism but are also due to locals from Patna and neighboring towns.

Fifty percent of the Bihar population is under twenty-five years of age, so the children's section of the museum is an important aspect to the overall museum and is designed as an interactive space. Here children are allowed to fully experience and examine the artifacts and to explore and learn in fun ways. The Bihar Museum is also developing a section designed specifically for the visually impaired, so they can experience major artifacts from the museum in a tactile format.

To keep pace with the high volume of families and children visiting over summer holidays, the museum undertook a visitor evaluation in 2022, gathering qualitative feedback from children. Our team is now responding to these findings and incorporating experiential learning from the educational sector. This will not only increase the engagement among children but also aims to redistribute those high visitor numbers among the other galleries, through planned activities and tours. This ability to respond with agility to audience needs has also led to longer opening hours than most other museums in India.

Meanwhile, regional tourism has increased because of the museum. Patna, for example, wasn't on the tourist map and was a pass-through for the religious tourists visiting Bodhgaya, Nalanda, Pawapuri, and other religious sites. This has changed because of the Bihar Museum opening, leading to many new hotels and F&B businesses opening in and around Patna. The museum eventually became a one-stop attraction for experiencing Bihari culture, not just through its galleries but also because of its restaurant—which offers authentic Bihari cuisine at an affordable price—and the Bihari crafts available at its gift shop. In fact, the museum remains the only place in Bihar with both authentic cuisine and artisan-created artifacts, offering a wholistic cultural experience to visitors.

During the Museum Biennale of 2023, Bihar Museum continued its leadership role by publishing catalogs of its collections, special exhibitions, mentoring visitor services staff, and building local capacity for museum resources. It is pursuing its goal of striving for the highest international standards while being locally rooted—celebrating our proud history, the work of contemporary artists, and telling our stories.

Figure 2.10.   Visitors explore their families' roots as they navigate through the world map using a touch table in the Bihar Museum's Bihari Diaspora Gallery. *Image courtesy of Lord Cultural Resources.*

2.6 Board Roles and Responsibilities

Trusts and boards around the world hold their museums' collections and other assets in *public trust* not only for the public of today but also for their descendants. They are *fiduciary* in character—a word describing trusteeship of property for others, meaning in the case of museums that trustees have an obligation to manage the property of others (in this case, the public) with the same diligence, honesty, and discretion that prudent people would exercise in managing their own property.

As a consequence, although there may be many specific differences in the constitutions of museum boards around the world, governing boards have the following six main responsibilities in common. Advisory boards are generally expected to make *recommendations* on these same issues to a higher body, whereas governing boards make *decisions* on them:

- recruit and negotiate a contract with the museum's director (who may have the titles CEO or president as well), to evaluate their performance, and to terminate their employment if necessary;

- maintain the legal requirements of the museum legislation or charter;

- provide for the continuity of the museum's mission, mandate, and policies;

- participate in the museum's strategic and long-range planning;

- ensure that the museum has adequate operating and capital funds to fulfill its mission, mandate, policies, and plans, including the responsibility to make and solicit donations; and

- collegiality and ethical management of the board itself.

Thus, the board appoints the director and delegates to that director the responsibility to recruit, evaluate, and if necessary dismiss all other museum staff. The director is not generally a board member but attends all board meetings ex officio and recommends policies and plans to the board consistent with the museum's mission and mandate. The board is responsible for raising money so that the museum can achieve the plans it has approved. This fund-raising role may encompass:

- supporting staff fund-raising and revenue generation activities;

- acting as an advocate on behalf of the museum to public and private funders including government, corporations, and foundations; and

- making donations and inviting others to make donations.

Trustees are both formal and informal advocates for the museum in the community, which includes the political arena as well as the private sector.

The board's role, as indicated earlier, is that of guiding and monitoring policies rather than policy formulation, which is a management function. However, there can be a fine line between the board in its monitoring role and being a "rubber stamp" for management. When a board is a rubber stamp, it will not likely be effective in fund-raising or museum advocacy. Conversely, there is a very serious problem when boards interfere with management functions by trying to write policies, frame budgets, or decide on procedures.

Balancing the role of the board and the responsibilities of management so that both are able to perform their jobs well is one of the main challenges facing museum leadership. Another major challenge centers on the board's advocacy functions and the degree to which trustees should reflect the diversity of the community in order to be more effective in advocating for the museum. Museums are increasingly adopting operational policies on diversity, equity, access, and inclusion (DEAI). There is a growing public demand that these policies be reflected in the membership and operations of the museum's governing body as well. The case study by Tim Johnson reveals the benefits of board diversity.

The Value of Indigenous Representation on Cultural Boards

By Tim Johnson

Since I left the Smithsonian Institution's National Museum of the American Indian in 2015, I transitioned into my current career phase, where I am working to establish Indigenous legacy spaces within my home region and community, which means getting involved with various organizations from the Niagara region of Southern Ontario through Toronto and beyond.

Most of the organizations with which I am involved as a board member or trustee are connected to my primary objective of advancing broad public knowledge of the Indigenous experience that involves culture, history, and the visual and performing arts. As a result, I was recruited to several boards that are strategically aligned to my own life and work.

Throughout the Niagara region my ancestors' footprints are found, going back to my seventh great grandfather, Joseph Brant, my sixth great uncle John Brant, and others throughout time. I have a deep personal interest in the history that took place along the Niagara River corridor, and, of course, my Indigenous community of Six Nations of the Grand River is only an hour and fifteen minute drive from Niagara.

The Shaw Festival Theater, for example, based in Niagara-on-the-Lake, is one of the most distinguished repertory theater companies in North America. I have been attending the Shaw Festival for more than thirty years because of its intellectually entertaining content that is presented through its plays every year. I've found the curation of material to be compelling and generally universal in terms of themes. What was missing, of course, was any content associated with Indigenous peoples and Indigenous actors within the ensemble. But that began to change over the past few years. Several Indigenous actors have since joined the ensemble and the play *This Is How We Got Here*, written and directed by Métis playwright Keith Barker, launched the 2022 season. I hope it has been useful having me on the Shaw board in terms of energizing and sustaining those conversations.

I am also on the board of the Niagara-on-the-Lake Museum, and this an important role to me for a couple of different reasons. First, I spent a number of years volunteering to help establish what is known as the Landscape of Nations, Six Nations and Native Allies Commemorative Memorial. It's a wonderful work created by artists Tom Ridout and Raymond Skye, located on the Queenston Heights battlefield, which is a Niagara Parks venue. This meaningful memorial recognizes the participation and involvement of Indigenous Allies—their forces and warriors—in assisting the Crown during the war of 1812. There's a very deep and complex history to those relations.

I also serve on the board of trustees of the McMichael Canadian Art Collection, which is one of the most extraordinary fine art centers in Canada and places a significant emphasis on Indigenous artists as being part of what is considered to be "Canadian Art."

When one considers Canadian art, one has to take into consideration Indigenous art in the thinking and the visualization of what that means—whether it resides in the form of Inuit art, the compelling aesthetics from the West Coast, or the work of Anishinabek artists and the Woodland School that was advanced by Norval Morrisseau. You cannot think about Canadian art without fully considering and incorporating Indigenous arts.

The idea of showcasing and emphasizing Indigenous influences on Canadian society and culture is ongoing, propelled by the Truth and Reconciliation Commission (TRC) with its 94 Calls to Action, which has brought heightened attention to the Indigenous experience within Canada.

What I've found in my work with cultural organizations is that the result of national initiatives such as the TRC's 94 Calls to Action, or international instruments such as the United Nations Declaration on the Rights of Indigenous Peoples (UNDRIP), is that leaders in many different sectors within Canada are paying closer attention and actually doing what they can to help facilitate, or to at least to play a part, in the reconciliation process.

This is occurring on many fronts simultaneously: in education systems, municipal governance, provincial agencies, and cultural organizations. It seems that there is a great deal of sincere interest in these initiatives, and I will stand behind the term "sincere" because while it is sometimes hard to discern true sincerity in a person, I have had enough longstanding relations with people from these different sectors to know that most participants are fully supportive of what they are doing in the context of reconciliation.

For all of the reasons I've outlined, it seems essential that Indigenous professionals serve on the boards of major arts and cultural institutions, because Indigenous people can bring to a given board table a sense of justice and community.

These Indigenous perspectives are vital, particularly in the nonprofit sector, where organizations strive to develop a community culture that ensures everyone is treated fairly and equally and help people understand that they're a valued part of a community.

Governance usually requires a hierarchy, but the extent and scope of that hierarchy is something that needs to be transparent so that everyone understands what goals an organization's board is working toward. This is important not just for morale but for the actual capacity building of the organization.

Indigenous peoples can share unique community values and offer leadership experience to contribute. We come out of our own cultures with skills that are directly applicable to the not-for-profit sector, and with an emphasis on equity, diversity, and inclusion (EDI).

I've done a lot of work with the Shaw Festival in this area—which generally curates its plays based on the works of George Bernard Shaw or his contemporaries, but as described earlier, is now branching out—and I have been a member on their EDI committee.

Within that framework, how does EDI apply to theater ensembles, to the organization, or to the board? Policies and changes certainly need to be delivered with precision and direct action in order to arrive at outcomes that are inclusive.

Shaw has done a tremendous job over the past several years in diversifying its ensemble. The skill set of the company's multitalented theater professionals is extraordinary, and the audience has proved to be open to new approaches. Although there's been a couple of complaints about people of color playing particular characters, for the most part it has strengthened the organization and the audience experience.

In terms of the numbers, the Shaw has performed better than ever as it changes and adapts. So you have a quantitative and a qualitative result that is significant. The organization, having had the courage to move in this direction, is performing phenomenally well.

Having also sat on the Governance and the Nomination Committee of Shaw, I witnessed that the board has diversified, along with other layers within the organization, including senior management. Indigenous Peoples and BIPOC representation on boards, even by the very fact of their presence and advocacy, can have a positive effect on an organization.

At the McMichael Canadian Art collection, we have an institution that essentially started as a platform for the Group of Seven—artists whose work captured the Canadian landscape in a particular aesthetic. That organization could have simply stayed with its Group of Seven programming mandate and probably would have been okay.

However, for an organization that takes seriously being one of the leading visual arts organizations in the country, the collection's vision and curatorial and program offerings have become quite inclusive and now represent the broader scope of what Canadian society and culture actually is.

Much credit should be given to the executive team, the curators, and its board for placing a particular emphasis on Indigenous art. The result is this wonderful mix of art, exhibitions, and programing that has come to represent all different sectors of Canadian culture.

In terms of the bigger picture, if an organization is going to seek to diversify the members of its board, then it must pay attention and listen carefully to what those members have to say. Those perspectives are critically important in developing and offering the right balance of representation.

When an organization's culture is positive, productive, and functional—as opposed to dysfunctional and resistant to any change—then the product is generally better. That's certainly been my experience through the various organizations with which I've worked, including the Smithsonian.

After all, the best project teams produce the best outcomes, and that's always what you're striving for—both on the micro-level and on the institutional level, trying to achieve the outcome of a truly forward-thinking work culture that respects all the people involved.

Figure 2.11.   Rick McGraw, director and chair of Muskoka Discovery Centre Revitalization, and Gary Getson, chair of the board of the Muskoka Discovery Centre, present Tim Johnson with a beautiful custom-painted oar to mark the occasion of the opening of the permanent exhibit *Misko-Aki: Confluence of Cultures*. Tim spent three years working closely with Muskoka Discovery Centre leadership to integrate Indigenous principles and practices within the organization. *Photo by author.*

Board Procedures

At a time when members of the museum staff and the public are increasingly concerned with the ethical consumption of culture, board membership and procedures are being questioned. How are values such as equity, social justice, climate activism, and antiracism addressed by the museum board?

> The dynamic change museums are experiencing requires transparency, discussion, and dialogue.

The dynamic change museums are experiencing requires transparency, discussion, and dialogue within the museum, among trustees and museum leadership, and between the museum and the many communities it serves. This is very challenging for museums, which until recently were relatively closed, even secretive.

Museum directors need to work with their trustees to fully inform them of the issues behind the policies so that the board may make informed decisions. In this regard, the culture of the board is also important—as the case studies in this *Manual* demonstrate. Diverse boards need to be welcoming and ensure that new board members have a sense of belonging, empowerment, and agency.

All board members need to be scrupulous in separating their museum role from their personal, professional, and business interests. They also need to distinguish governance from management functions. An effective nominating committee that continuously evaluates board performance and that involves the director in the recruitment and training of new board members can be enormously helpful in clarifying governance and management roles and in addressing issues of board diversity. The board chair and the museum director have key and mutually supportive roles to play in maintaining an atmosphere of open discussion, access to information, and collegiality. It is generally found that museum directors spend about 50 percent of their time working with the board when it is a fiduciary board and somewhat less when it is an advisory board.

The roles and responsibilities of the board are usually regulated by a *constitution, bylaws,* or equivalent document that establishes, for example:

- the number of trustees and their means of appointment or election;

- qualifications of board members;

- roles and responsibilities;

- public trust commitment and degree or limitation of personal liability;

- length of trustees' terms of office and rotation off the board;

- frequency, location, quorum, and minuting of meetings;

- policy on public access to board meetings or minutes;

- financial accounting practices and spending and borrowing rules;

- responsibilities and means of selection of officers of the board;

- board committees;

- remuneration of board members and provision for expenses; and

- procedures in the event of dissolution of the board.

Board Committees

There are many sizes of museum boards. A large board of sixty to seventy people is sometimes considered desirable for fund-raising and community representation. Smaller boards of twenty to thirty people are sometimes considered to be more active and engaged. Smaller museums in smaller communities may find even fewer members—seven to fifteen people—more efficient.

Most boards find it advisable to appoint their members (usually called *trustees*) to *board committees*, in order that the board can work on a wide range of issues simultaneously. In doing so, boards should set *terms of reference* to establish the mandate of the committee and its limitations. It is an important principle that while boards work through committees, it is the board as a whole that makes policy decisions.

Committees may recommend but should not approve policies and should report to the board regularly on the implementation of policies or plans. The following are among the committees most commonly appointed:

- *Executive Committee*: It may be advisable to appoint an executive committee to facilitate decisions between board meetings. This committee should normally include the board president or chair and the other senior officers and the museum director ex officio.

- *Nominating Committee*: This is a critically important committee that has two main responsibilities: first, the ongoing evaluation of board performance and making recommendations for changes in governance or board procedures; second, identifying strengths and weaknesses of the board and recruiting trustees who will strengthen the board.

- *Finance Committee*: It is often useful to strike a committee to focus exclusively on finances. This committee may have responsibility for capital fund-raising as well, but it is usually concerned only with ongoing operating funds. It normally works with staff to recommend the annual budget to the board, monitors financial reports, and ensures that the museum's accounts are audited.

- *Development Committee*: While the finance committee may be concerned with the operating budget, a development committee addresses the board's fund-raising role, including annual giving, corporate sponsorship, planned giving, and the many programs and activities the board undertakes to raise money. Specific subcommittees may be formed to spearhead special campaigns, such as acquisition funds, endowment development, or capital funds for renovation, expansion, or new construction projects.

- *Long-Range Planning Committee*: Long-range planning is a board function that is frequently delegated by the board to a committee that will work with museum management and planners to develop the strategic plan or the master plan as needed. The committee takes responsibility for the planning process, reports regularly to the board, and recommends the resultant plan to the board for approval. When a planning process or a capital project is underway, this group may become or may appoint a more specialized *steering committee* for that process or project.

- *Acquisition Committee*: Curators have the professional responsibility for collection development, but because additions to the collection affect the long-range future of the institution, many museum boards have established acquisition committees to which curators present proposed acquisitions for approval—sometimes only those above a certain monetary value. Such a committee can be instrumental in encouraging donations to the collection or finding sponsors for acquisitions that are beyond the museum's budget. The acquisitions committee is usually also responsible for approval of deaccessioning recommended by the curators through the director.

Of course, boards may appoint additional committees as needed. However, some committees are problematic—exhibition committees, for example, can be appropriate if they focus on exhibition policy and on sponsorship for proposed exhibitions, but too often they go beyond the limits of a board's concern to make decisions on exhibition selection or priorities that should be delegated to staff. Such a committee can also present conflict-of-interest problems if its members include collectors whose acquisitions may be affected by the "insider knowledge" that their participation in an exhibition committee gives them.

The museum director is an ex officio member of all board committees and should give priority to participating in the executive committee and the acquisition committee. The director may share or delegate this responsibility to other staff members for committees that concern them: the chief financial officer may work with the finance committee, the head of development with the development and membership committees, the chief curator with the acquisitions committee, and so on.

> Boards malfunction when they attempt to direct the day-to-day activities of the museum instead of delegating those decisions to staff.

Boards malfunction when they attempt to direct the day-to-day activities of the museum instead of delegating those decisions to staff.

Board members need training and development, just like staff and volunteers. Most museums find it useful to provide each incoming member with a *trustees' manual* that includes all the relevant vision mission, mandate, and policy statements and the board constitution or bylaws, as well as a history of the institution, current plans, staff organization charts, budgets and financial reports, a list of board roles and responsibilities, and an outline of the committee structure. The new trustee should attend at least one *board orientation session*, which should include a tour of the building and introduction to the division or department heads.

Board members need to be assured about the extent of their personal and collective liability for the museum's actions. This varies according to the legal provisions of each jurisdiction, but in general the incorporation of a nonprofit society or similar association should have the legal effect of placing liability on the institution collectively. As part of their fiduciary responsibility, trustees also need to be assured that the museum's insurance is adequate for its risks and resources and that they are personally protected from any allegations of liability for actions that the museum undertakes.

Ethics

Museum boards should adopt a *code of ethics*, both for themselves and for the museum. A code of ethics protects the trustee as well as the museum's interests and is written in the spirit of "Justice must not only be done, but must be seen to be done."

The code should subscribe to relevant international conventions and national, state, provincial, or local laws affecting artifacts, specimens, or works of art, as well as to the Code of Professional Ethics of the International Council of Museums (ICOM) and parallel guidelines promulgated by the museum profession in each country, such as the British Museums Association's Code of Practice or comparable documents of the American Alliance of Museums.

These codes of professional practice and ethics affect staff as well as trustees and should be developed for the museum in its entirely and included in the staff manuals and employment contracts. The implementation of codes of professional practice and ethics is key to maintaining the public's trust.[12]

The board's code of ethics should also aim to eliminate conflicts of interest for trustees with collecting activities related to those of the museum. Obviously, it is an advantage for the museum to have trustees who are also collectors in its field, especially as it may result in future donations; however, because the museum itself is involved in the collecting field, it is important that the trustee should declare to the board his or her collecting activity, and of course any related business interests. A record should be kept of any advice given to the trustee by staff members affecting his or her collecting activity, and the trustee should normally be expected to give the museum first refusal on collecting opportunities that arise. The code should require a trustee to withdraw from any deliberations affecting his or her business interests or from which he or she might benefit, directly or indirectly. The code should also require confidentiality of the trustee, and collegiality with fellow trustees in pursuing the interests of the museum, as well as minimal requirements for attendance at meetings and museum functions.

There is a growing demand for greater transparency about the composition of museum boards and potential conflicts board members might have with the museum's values due to their business interests and activities. It is a significant challenge for museum leaders of the future to develop policies in this area of museum ethics.

It is important for the board to maintain appropriate relations with the museum director. The director recommends policies and plans to the board, implements approved policies and plans, and is responsible for the day-to-day management of the museum. The board should give the director unwavering support as long as museum policies and plans are being implemented in a professional manner and should not be involved in day-to-day administration. The board should expect from its director timely reports and recommendations, full disclosure of relevant information, and a commitment to the museum's mission that goes beyond personal enthusiasms or career goals.

Board relations with staff should be regulated by a board policy statement that may be included in the board's code of ethics. Normally, staff should report to the director, and the director should report to the board, except for staff delegated by the director to report to board committees. In a unionized museum there will be provisions for grievances in a collective bargaining agreement. The human resources department generally addresses staff problems and concerns including harassment and racism. However, the code of ethics should also provide for extraordinary occasions of disagreement or conflict, whether these are professional concerns or grievances over employment conditions, so that the board may serve as an ultimate level of appeal within the institution. In such cases the policy should provide procedures so that the board can help to resolve the dispute in a constructive way that does not undermine the director but responds judiciously to staff concerns in light of the museum's mission and policies.

Chapter 3

WHAT

The Museum Ecosystem

A temple-like structure with pillars and ascending stairs is still the most common symbolic representation for "museum"—a temple of the muses.

In practice, this image is being deconstructed and museums are being reimagined and reconstructed as institutions that are interconnected with communities in many ways. This interconnectedness is often referred to as the museum ecosystem.

This is an important opportunity for museums to consider because their sustainability, and perhaps their very survival, depends on community support. How museums support communities is less clear and much debated. In *Cities, Museums and Soft Power*[1] museums are characterized as "sleeping giants" because despite their size they ignore many community concerns around them.

Management, though, has the potential to awaken the sleeping giant.

Museums are not isolated institutions, and in almost all cases they exist within a thriving ecosystem of people, communities, public and private agencies, learning and health organizations, workplaces, retail shops, food services, communications networks, and other economic drivers—in a phrase, everything and everyone all at once.

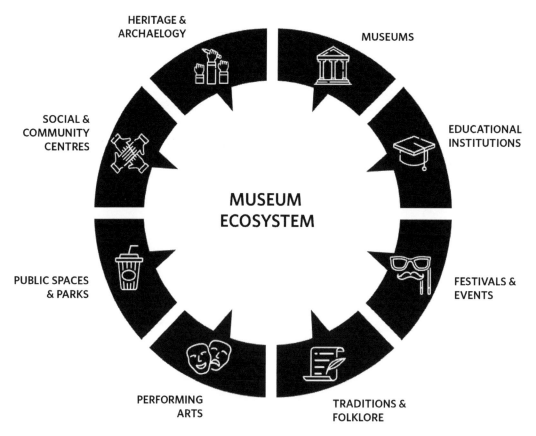

Figure 3.1.   Museum Ecosystem. *Lord Cultural Resources.*

This chapter focuses on eight dimensions of the museum ecosystem, local, regional, and national—and in our globalized and environmentally challenged world, the ecosystem always has international links.

> Museums are not isolated institutions, and in almost all cases they exist within a thriving ecosystem of people, communities, public and private agencies, learning and health organizations, workplaces, retail shops, food services, communications networks, and other economic drivers.

- People

- Creative economy

- Learning places

- Other museums and associations

- Governments and foundations

- Tourism

- Service organizations

- Public realm

3.1 People

In an increasingly financialized world, there is a tendency for museums to think of people as consumers, both onsite and online.

Certainly maintaining accurate participation data is very important, but it is equally important to look at the many people who pass by the museum every day without even glancing at the front door: they are part of the human ecosystem weaving around the building at all hours.

The museum means something to them too: for some it could be a friendly landmark, because museums generally improve property values; while for others it may be threatening, because its continual expansions encroach on green space and foreshadows gentrification. Negative experiences—as well as positive ones—are passed down through the generations, so a history of exclusion, poor labor practices, or ethnocentrism and racism ensure that some people will just hurry past the property line, barely noticing the signage.

Parents may remember when their kids were not welcomed into museums except in controlled school visits—so they don't visit as a family. Indigenous and racialized people whose art and collections might comprise a significant proportion of what is on view or in storage may feel excluded because their "stuff" was stolen or because the meaning of those objects has been misinterpreted or ignored.

Then there are the never-collected materials of working people and immigrants who will not see themselves represented in the museum until collection and exhibition policies change.

> Museum management needs to be critically aware of what attendance numbers actually mean.

Museum management needs to be critically aware of what attendance numbers actually mean: sure, those numbers may be growing, but are they keeping pace with increases in population or are they amplified through tourism but not by residents? There are numerous strategies to overcome these challenges, but the first step is for museums to understand how people fit into their ecosystem. "Awakening Spadina House" is a truly remarkable case study of how the sleeping giant of a city museum system was awakened by activating people in its ecosystem.

"Awakening Spadina House"

**By Cheryl Blackman and Umbereen Inayet
in conversation with Gail Dexter Lord**

Gail: How did the idea of "Awakenings" happen?

Cheryl: The journey began in 2018 when I joined the City of Toronto as the director of Museums and Heritage Services. I was given a clear mandate for change. A decision had been made to create one unit for the ten historic museums. Located in ten wards throughout the city, two of the museums—including Spadina House—are designated National Historic Sites. A city which has grown up around each of them.

I viewed all these sites as opportunities to create community hubs. So, I began working with my colleagues to shape a new vision, mission, and program narrative—not only for the entirety of our sites, but for each of the ten sites.

We launched our strategic plan at the beginning of the pandemic, in 2020, with the aim to be antiracist and to decolonize the experience of these "sites" by telling their stories, not through our voices, but through the voices of the communities. We also wanted to tell the untold stories; that is, to tell the full story. We wanted to make sure that we were creating space for voices that had not been heard.

Umbereen: Cheryl asked me to think about a creative strategy that encompassed the strategic plan. I started to meditate on it and realized that because of the pandemic we were all seemingly connected by circumstance almost overnight. And so "Awakenings" came to me, and I started to write—and I created a ninety-six-page PowerPoint for Cheryl in one day.

We knew we had the ten sites. What could we do with them? How would we use them for education, using different artistic modalities? I think that as people of color we know how to deal with limitations. We weren't waiting for the pandemic to end and the doors to open. We needed to respond in that time of extreme fear, panic, grief, and anger.

During the pandemic everybody was consuming culture over their phones and computers. It was an ideal way to collect the untold stories and truths within each of the museums. These are mainly the stories of Black, Indigenous, and People of Color and new Canadians who were historically there—and are here today in even greater numbers—but were not represented in the narratives of these sites.

Creativity, it turns out, is a perfect tool to help address intergenerational trauma and healing. The historic houses showed what erasure looks like, and how they could be transformed to illustrate what a new present and future could be.

Gail: Thinking about how you transformed Spadina House, please describe the big themes of "Dismantle" and "Rebuild." What did you dismantle? And why rebuild?

Cheryl: The poet Audre Lorde, in 1978, said: "The master's tools will never dismantle the master's house. They may allow us to temporarily beat him at his own game. But they will never enable us to bring about genuine change."

We were working within systems never designed to accommodate the kinds of voices that we were now bringing to these spaces. Museums are not neutral and never have been. Being a member of a racialized community and bringing racialized and Indigenous artists into spaces also means that we have to confront the realities that the community hasn't felt welcomed, and as a result, there may be concerns of tokenism.

Umbereen: "Dis/Mantle" is a concept that we created with the black Toronto-based visual artist Gordon Shadrach, who is a great portrait painter. Spadina House is full of Austen family[2] portraits, one of which is a portrait of the laundress Mrs. Pipkin—a formerly enslaved woman who had escaped enslavement in Baltimore in 1852 and made her way to Toronto where she worked. We dismantled the colonial narrative of Spadina house by reimagining the house as belonging to Mrs. Pipkin, turning the house into an Afro futuristic narrative where Mrs. Pipkin was now the homeowner. This was an active, defiant act of an artistic intervention. It was an anticolonial move.

Gail: The house displays portraits that Mrs. Pipkin might have had—for example, one of Frederick Douglass,[3] and a magnificent portrait[4] by Gordon Shadrach of Mrs. Pipkin herself as the owner of the house. What does it mean to rebuild? And why did you think it was important to rebuild as well as dismantle?

Umbereen: The *Dis/Mantle* exhibition was an incredible success. When we thought about the closing of the show, and what type of legacy we wanted to leave for the future, we started to think about the younger generations, which will be the ones to rebuild. That is also why we had youth-friendly programs and focused on self-care and building a safe space for our youth through connection with poetry and art.

Gail: This is a big change for staff and the community. What processes did you use to make this work?

Cheryl: I don't want to romanticize this change journey, because change management is a lot of work, and it is hard work. I think what we did was to create this new vision to be leading centers of experiences and critical dialogue about Toronto's past, present, and future. Through many meetings with staff and stakeholders, we focused on trying to understand what community wanted and needed from these.

Umbereen: We knew we needed a community to help support us, to teach us, and guide us along the way, and to also help cultivate support and cultural capital. For example, Professor Mark Campbell from the University of Toronto and Professor Natasha Henry from the Ontario Black History Society brought a scholarly approach to the work, encompassing music, history, and culture. Natasha taught us a lot about our connections to the Underground Railroad and about streets that have connections to former slave owners.

Weyni Mengesha, artistic director of Soul Pepper Theater, helped us bring these stories to life using a theatrical lens. She also partnered with Myseum[5] and asked them to re-create a conference that took place at Toronto's St. Lawrence Hall in 1851. Julien Christian Lutz, professionally known as Director X, was the first mentor on an annual program we launched through the initiative. He mentored our film program and emerging filmmakers. Ashley Mackenzie Barnes, a black, queer curator in Toronto, is our mentor for our very first exhibition during Pride, to create our first 2SLGBTQ+ exhibition, and Roger Mooking is a biracial multidisciplinary artist who has contributed to a number of our creative projects dedicated to mental health and healing. This task force and many other artists have been with us through the journey.

Countless people have supported us, including the NBA team the Toronto Raptors. We also have a small but mighty internal team at the City of Toronto and support from their marketing and sponsorship team, and they have been tremendous partners to us in this work— Awakenings.

Umbereen: From our perspective our philosophy is inspired by Ghandi, *Be the Change You Want to See in the World.*

Figure 3.2. Detail of *Refashion* (Mrs. Pipkin), oil on wood panel by Gordon Shadrach, 2022. This work of art was commissioned by the City of Toronto, Heritage Division, for "Awakening Spadina House." It has been accessioned into the City of Toronto collection. *Photo by Gordon Shadrach. Image courtesy of City of Toronto.*

3.2 The Creative Economy

The past forty years have seen the growth of what is now called "the creative economy,"[6] which includes, for example: arts, music, design, and knowledge-based professions such as health care, finance, law, engineering, research, technology, and communications. One hundred years ago during the industrial era, when many of our museums were founded, fewer than 10 percent of the population was employed in this way; today it is between 40 percent and 50 percent of larger cities around the world[7] where there is also a great concentration of museums.

In the past, museums relegated this type of creativity to specialist museums such as design and science, and they marginalized the creative contributions of Indigenous and racialized people to ethnographic museums. The ecosystem approach challenges museums to see the full spectrum of the creative community as part of their mandate in terms of collections, displays, staff, and interpretation.

Because few museums have expertise in all aspects of the creative economy, they need to reach out and consult the practitioners to more deeply explore and be energized by this creative ecosystem, working together for mutual benefit.

3.3 Learning Places

Educational services are usually an important part of a museum's institutional role in the view of funders—and almost always in fulfilling its own sense of mission.

> The museum's relationship to universities, colleges, and schools at all levels is therefore another important dimension of its institutional context that requires adroit management.

The museum's relationship to universities, colleges, and schools at all levels is therefore another important dimension of its institutional context that requires adroit management. The possibilities may range from cross-appointments of professors for museum research or curatorial duties, to signing a contract with the local school board agreeing to provide a certain number of tours and educational activities to school parties for a fixed level of reimbursement throughout the school year.

Some museums have found it advantageous to propose a "time share" agreement with schools, whereby the museum is open every morning, for instance, only to school groups for their educational use. Others have gone further to form "museum schools," where the students attend school at the museum.

The American Museum of Natural History in New York has established its own university and the World War II Museum in New Orleans has created an MA program in World War II history, in partnership with Arizona State University among many other innovative partnerships.

In establishing relationships with educational institutions, the museum director or education officer should remember that the museum can be an excellent venue for *informal* learning, while the schools and universities usually provide the preferred setting for *formal* education. Retaining this distinction of roles usually helps to ensure that each institution does what it can do best, without attempting to supplant the other. After all, as Judith Koke explains in her case study, learning experiences are everywhere in the museum ecosystem.

Learning Is Everywhere

By Judith Koke

Many people consider the words "education" and "school" as practically synonymous, and yet most people spend less than 5 percent of their life in classrooms.

In fact, most of what we all learn across our lifetimes happens in informal or free-choice learning environments, at work, at home, and in the community. As part of that learning ecosystem, museums have yet to truly maximize this opportunity, remaining deeply focused on attracting audiences to cross their physical thresholds.

Yet museums can derive tremendous benefit from working in and with a diversity of organizations to achieve projects they simply cannot do as well on their own. Community organizations bring their audiences, and the trust they have established with those groups, into new relationships with the museum. Effective community partnerships build cultural competency among museum staff and leverage new connections on behalf of the museum. With shifting concepts on how education can center the learner and the recognition of the importance and longevity of free-choice learning, museums are recognizing the opportunity to support learning across geography, different learning needs, and stages of life.

Currently, the majority of museum programs located in communities serve youth and family audiences. An early example is Project Butterfly Wings,[8] a partnership established in 2004 between the Florida Museum of Natural History and the National 4-H organization and funded by the National Science Foundation.

The museum, which houses a significant lepidoptery collection and expertise, developed a curriculum and trained several 4H leaders, all members of their local communities, many without science backgrounds. These leaders then delivered training to their group or club, followed by a data collection field trip to an area of their county assigned by museum scientists. Those familiar with Citizen Science Projects will recognize this program format. Evaluation results of the original pilot project in thirteen counties in Florida demonstrated that in addition to science learning, the project delivered significant gains in science capital and other life skills.

More currently, in Dallas, Texas, the Perot Museum of Nature and Science is active in the community in two interesting ways. First, the museum circulates TECH trucks[9] to engage youth located in underrepresented neighborhoods in STEAM activities that can be reproduced at home. A free, bilingual program, The Whynaughts,[10] offers ten online episodes of STEM programming, much like a television program, in which child actors present science or natural history information and then frame an experiment for families to do together.

Moving beyond science museums, the National WWII Museum, harkening back to the scrapping efforts of students during World War II, developed Get in the Scrap,[11] a national service learning project for students in grades 4 to 8 about recycling and energy conservation. Serving schools and communities, the project connects student ecoactivism to the historic efforts of children to support the patriotic call for support during the war.

In a recent online NSF-funded conference Science Museum Futures,[12] a diverse group of museum and allied professionals discussed the future of science museums and innovative and sustainable ways of delivering on the museums' missions. Part of the conversation involved an intense discussion about the actual need for a physical space and the consideration that a science museum dedicated to its community might find itself more effective located in community spaces. Although no resolution was reached on the concept, it did underscore the benefits and utility of thinking "outside the box" of the museum building.

Learning is an evolutionary process, equipping us, individually and as a species, for survival and success. In an equitable world, all learners would have access to learning what they want and need, in the manner that works best for them. Museums, with their recently acquired (postpandemic) facility to move programs online, can also step into the community in real life and become more physically present and active in surrounding neighborhoods. In the ongoing search for relevance, becoming a more active part of the community may be an important part of the solution.

Figure 3.3.   Celebrating the Masters in WWII Studies graduates at the National WWII Museum, New Orleans, 2023. The program is a partnership between Arizona State University and the National WWII Museum. *Photo by Frank Aymami Photography. Image courtesy of the museum.*

3.4 Other Museums and Museum Associations

Museums have everything to gain by cooperation with other museums: this may involve *partnerships* with similar museums, or *collaborating* for marketing purposes with entirely dissimilar ones, in order to reach a wider audience and to appeal to philanthropists, foundations, and governments who increasingly want to see the impact of their support being maximized. It's an ecosystem principle—one that can involve mutually beneficial relationships between large and small museums, as well as between museums of similar size and collections.

In many cities or regions, museums have formed consortiums. In Richmond, Virginia, and Cleveland, Ohio, they have formed *cultural collaboratives* aimed at finding ways to economize through joint ordering of supplies or sharing of specialized staff.

Sharing exhibitions, either one-to-one or via area organizations such as a regional museums' association, a group of science centers, or children's museums in different cities, is a longstanding means of cooperation among museums. Sharing information to mitigate climate change, museums and cultural organizations have founded a US nonprofit, Environmental and Cultural Partners (ECP), to gather data, coordinate research, and accelerate climate action in the cultural sector.

The Solomon R. Guggenheim Museum Foundation in New York has led the way in sharing its collection with associated museums established for that purpose around the world. Following that lead, a consortium of nine French museums has entered into a long-term relationship with Abu Dhabi in the United Arab Emirates on long-term loans over a twenty-year period, while the "Louvre Abu Dhabi" builds its own collection.

In England, Tate has established branches at Liverpool and St. Ives in addition to its two London locations, to make its collections more accessible. Competition for acquisition of collections and donors persists—but even here collaboration has emerged, with museums sharing both the cost and display of a key acquisition when the work of art or historic artifact proves too expensive for one museum to afford on its own—it's the museum ecosystem that makes the acquisition possible.

Many museums and museum professionals relate to their colleague institutions through museum associations. At regional, state, provincial, and national levels these have been instrumental in the development of the profession. Their conferences, seminars, and publications are among the most important means of training and professional development for their members, both as institutions and as individuals. Some, like the American Alliance of Museums, have established accreditation or registration programs that have succeeded in raising professional standards for both institutions and individuals.

The International Council of Museums (ICOM) is the worldwide equivalent of a regional museum association. And in some countries, the national chapter of ICOM plays a similar role to that of regional museum association. For others, the specialized international committees of ICOM, such as the International Council on Conservation (ICC) or the International Association of Transportation and Communications Museums (IATM), are the vital link with fellow professionals or institutions with related concerns. The triennial conferences of ICOM, the annual meetings of its international committees; its journal, *Museum International*; and the many newsletters and publications of its committees; are for many the very lifeline of the profession.[13] ICOM's ethical standards and guidelines are also instrumental in supporting professional practices in many countries.

The influence of ICOM has been restricted in some countries by the practice of appointing only a few representative individuals to attend conferences, instead of recruiting members throughout the profession. Democratizing ICOM membership, and encouraging widespread participation in its committees through its publications, is of long-term importance in the development of the museum profession in these countries, along with the encouragement of national or regional museum associations. Professional development is very much tied to the existence of these organizations, whose conferences and publications provide a venue for the development of younger members of the profession.

> As the number and type of museums continue to grow and expand, so do the support organizations in the museum ecosystem.

As the number and type of museums continue to grow and expand, so do the support organizations in the museum ecosystem. The Association of African American Museums (AAAM) was established in the 1970s to be the voice of what was at the time an emerging museum type. Today AAAM and its affiliated institutions spans over three hundred sites and eight hundred members in the United States and abroad.[14] By definition, the International Coalitions of Sites of Conscience "is an association for the growing number of values-based museums including historic sites, and place-based memorials that prevent the erasure of crimes against humanity in order to ensure a more just and humane future."[15]

Science museums have an international support group with the European Network of Science Centres and Museums (ECSITE) and the Association of Science of Technology Centers (ASTC), while children's museums have two international organization, the Association of Children's Museums (ACM) based in Arlington, Virginia, while Hands-On is a European-based international organization that serves both independent standalone children's museums and children's galleries located in all types of museums.

The museum ecosystem features hundreds, and possibly thousands, of not-for-profit museum support organizations that provide data, information, exhibition exchange, training, and collegial support by the museum sector and for the museum sector in all its diversity. In March 2023, the United States continued to be the country with the most museums at 33,098, although depending on how others define a museum, a rough estimate is that our current museum ecosystem is composed of over ninety-five thousand museums across the globe.[16]

3.5 The Public Sector and the Plural Sector

Museums are inherently political institutions: history museums communicate the meanings of our past, art museums present works of art that often comment on the meaning or values of our personal and social lives, and science museums interpret what we think we know about the world around us.

> Museums are intensively involved in communicating values and ideologies about the meaning of their collections.

Museums are intensively involved in communicating values and ideologies about the meaning of their collections. These ideologies are usually implicit, but they can become explicit very quickly in a temporary exhibition on a politically sensitive subject—or one that suddenly becomes sensitive because of the content of the exhibition.

Museums are also "political" in the sense that they are very often funded by, or form part of, a public sector government service. Whether they are government line departments or at "arm's length" from government, independent charitable associations, or plural sector institutions with a mixed funding base, museums are very often dependent on government funding programs and policies, including myriad tax policies and government grant programs as well as zoning benefits from local government.

Museum management must therefore be concerned with the museum's position in relation to this government ecosystem: city, county, state, or province, and ultimately national government—not only to ministries or departments responsible for culture and heritage but also those concerned with tourism, education, and taxation. And if the museum's mandate touches on science, the military, transportation, or agriculture, these government departments may become important parts of the ecosystem as well.

In many jurisdictions, the ministry or department administering employment grants is among the most important to the museum. Managing the museum's relationship with government is a major responsibility of the museum director and trustees. Indeed, staff positions for "government and external relations" are often needed to help the director with this responsibility.

In some jurisdictions, one national, state, or provincial museum has been assigned responsibility for the administration of the general museum service or the distribution of grants to other museums. This often leads to perceived conflict of interest problems, at least in the eyes of the other museums, so that it is usually preferable to establish a separate entity for grants administration, and often for other centralized services as well.

In the United States, this is clearly seen in agencies like the Institute of Museum and Library Services (IMLS) and the many State Councils for the Arts and Humanities that are independent organizations with their own boards, which receive funding from government to distribute to arts organizations and museums.

In Europe, part of the ecosystem for museums includes many European Union agencies that boost museums and cultural institutions—including Creative Europe, Horizon Europe, and Digital Europe initiatives.

Such government line departments or quasi-governmental agencies responsible for museums have in many instances developed a high level of professionalism in assisting museums. Many have wide-ranging responsibilities for archaeological sites or architectural heritage preservation as well as museums. Some have established accreditation or registration programs that have been instrumental in encouraging or requiring museum trustees to ensure that their institutions meet professional standards.

Others, like the state museum services in Germany, provide consultants to assist museums technically. Most employ grants officers whose task is to ensure that public funds are effectively and efficiently spent in their constituent museums.

Other government agencies, such as the Canadian Heritage Information Network and the Canadian Conservation Institute in Ottawa, have established internationally recognized standards in their respective disciplines. Independent organizations—such as Collections Trust in the United

Kingdom and the Getty Conservation Institute in the United States—are also actively involved in research and standard setting that influence museums far outside their country's borders.

Museums in historic buildings may be concerned about meeting standards established by their own or other countries' national trusts or parks administrations, as well as international accords between governments respecting the conservation of historic sites. The United Nations Educational, Scientific and Cultural Organization (UNESCO) is another source of international standards through such mechanisms as controlling the status of World Heritage Sites.

In recent years many governments faced with fiscal restraints have moved to make museums more self-reliant in obtaining funds.

In recent years many governments faced with fiscal restraints have moved to make museums more self-reliant in obtaining funds. Some museums that were formerly free to the public have found admission charges necessary, while others, like Britain's national museums, have been given additional subsidy in order to allow them to offer free admission and encourage greater social inclusion. Many museums have been obliged by changes in government funding patterns to give much more attention to their shops, food services, and rental capability, and increasingly to seek donors or sponsorships in the private sector.

Managing such transitions and changes is often challenging and can be done much more effectively if the museum maintains a positive relationship with all relevant governments. In some cases governments at various levels (such as a city's parks department) can provide important help of a nonmonetary nature, such as providing buildings, grounds, and maintenance staff while the park or garden establishes an independent not-for-profit conservancy to manage visitor services and educational operations.

Another long-range concern is the government's attitude toward museum expansion or renovation. Growing collections are constantly generating the need for more space, and professional standards require upgrading of facilities. Politicians and government officials may view such tendencies with alarm, especially in times of fiscal restraint; yet in periods of high unemployment, especially in regions of chronic employment problems, the responsible development of museums or historic sites as cultural tourism attractions may be politically expedient, as well as a meaningful initiative, that can be launched with government support.

In many places, museums have become part of a determined government program to change the image as well as the economic basis of a community. Bilbao, Glasgow, and Salford are among examples usually cited, while French regional governments in Lorraine and Nord-Pas de Calais have established satellites for the Pompidou centre (in Metz) and Louvre (in Lens).

In the famous case of Bilbao, the success of the Museo Guggenheim Bilbao made it possible for the governments of the area to go further and support the expansion and renovation of the local fine arts museum and establish numerous museum projects.

Worldwide, it is clear that museums and their governments are closely related, and wise museum managers will pay close attention to this relationship. Maintaining an independent viewpoint in their exhibitions, publications, and other programs is a challenge that varies from country to country but is present everywhere. Respecting professional standards while sustaining good relations with all levels of government around the world requires an essential ingredient of great leaders—courage.

In some jurisdictions, relations with independent not-for-profit foundations and organizations supplement government support, while in others foundations may be more important than government. Museum research programs, such as field archaeology activities, are sometimes rooted in their relationships with universities. Others may be developed with special interest groups, such as an entomological society or a local historical association. Public programs may be developed with a broad range of groups, from farmers and Scout troops to Indigenous communities. Committed museum managers at all levels of staff should be continually exploring the museum's potential to extend its services by working closely with community organizations of all kinds.

In some cases, such cooperation may have important fund-raising implications for the museum.

This is especially true of working with foundations that have special interests. Some of these, like the Getty Foundation in the United States or the Calouste Gulbenkian Foundation in Portugal, have programs that are focused exclusively on museums, whereas others have broader educational or research objectives that the museum can meet. Museum managers need to be constantly aware of the prospects for working with national or international foundations of relevance to them. A project that is beyond the reach of a local museum may become realizable with the aid of an international foundation. Major US foundations like Kresge, Mellon, and Ford provide funding programs in such areas as collection development, capacity building, and diversity, equity, inclusion, and access. Collaborating with partners in the museum ecosystem requires networking. In her case study, Rosalia Vargas explains how to create networks that are sustainable.

> Collaborating with partners in the museum ecosystem requires networking.

How to Build a Sustainable Network

By Rosalia Vargas

The Portuguese National Agency for Scientific and Technological Culture has evolved into a network of twenty-two science centers located across the country called Ciência Viva.

It was started in 1996 and has grown into a complex ecosystem that includes partners at higher education institutions and local governments. This network serves as an essential link between knowledge emerging from the academy and a rootedness based on local power and experience.

Ciência Viva essentially acts as the conductor of a scientific cultural orchestra, continually adding new instruments to the performance and attempting to keep them in tune. Does this mean that all the elements of the network play to the same melody? Not at all. There is a lot of improvisation! Each center contributes to the enrichment of the overall network, and the various solos and dissonant tones make the network more attentive to new ideas and collaborations.

One of the network's founders and leaders, physicist and politician José Mariano Gago,[17] was once asked by a journalist about the number of centers that may be created or join the network: "How many?"

"As many as needed," he answered.

Indeed, the number of science centers in the Ciência Viva network is still growing—slowly and sustainably, because the creation of a science center is a complex and lengthy process, from the discussion of the content to the building in which its displays will be installed.

Let's examine a series of ten principles that we have developed that can lead to a sustainable and successful network.

The Ten Principles of Networking

1. Common Purpose (Building a Coherent Group)

A network must have a common goal, a purpose that unites its members. In the case of the Ciência Viva network, the common goal is to promote education and scientific culture in Portugal. It is a broad, general objective that gathers several initiatives into a larger mission, with each member contributing their unique piece to the overall puzzle—diversity brings harmony to the whole.

2. Diversity (Being Diverse While Being Equal)

It is crucial to get past the paradox that networks should only bring together affinities, similarities, and everything that creates connections—never what divides or what diverges.

The more equal, the better, right? Actually, no. In reality, new components must be introduced in a network, and the boundaries must be pushed almost to the point where it appears that borders have been crossed. In the Ciência Viva network, diversity is apparent in the different buildings that house these centers and their varied content offerings. There are Ciência Viva centers in prisons, churches, factories, mines, convents, and other formerly inaccessible locations that are now open to the public for new uses.

The themes of these science centers are also diverse: each is inspired by its structure, past use, or surrounding environment. The old monastery from the sixteenth century that now houses the Ciência Viva center in Estremoz (Alentejo, southern Portugal) is covered with enormous expanses of marble, and the center's exhibits are drawn from the geology, history, and abundance of marble in the area. One of the exhibits is a submarine—yellow, of course—representing the vast ocean that formerly existed in the now hot, occasionally parched Alentejo landscape. Anyone who is curious and visits one Ciência Viva center will find a reason to visit others because each of them is locally inspired and unique.

3. Scale (Not Too Small, But Not Too Big)

The number of science centers is undoubtedly important because scale is needed to create a network. Of course, there is a beginning: as soon as the first center was built and was successful, we felt encouraged to continue the project. A second center opened, but trying to create a network with only two contributors generated a cyclic system of exchange, alternating between the two and not leading to evolution. Then comes the third center, and the point of view is more diverse but still limited. Then with the fourth and the fifth, there are more reasons to gather its members together, which creates a surprising and rewarding dynamic. When the network passed beyond ten, we created scale, diversity, and, most importantly, cooperation.

4. Relevance (Their Role in Society)

A network is relevant if it appeals to the local population and shows an intrinsic aspiration to be known. At first, its focus is local but, as it is unique, it then expands its attraction nationwide and challenges numerous communities, always with inspiring stories to share.

For instance, a hydroelectric power plant in the riverbed served as the foundation for the Bragança Ciência Viva center (northeastern Portugal). The science center's power plant is a crucial component of its content, and it responds energetically to environmental cues like temperature, humidity, and weather. When people visit, they have the chance to learn about what was once there and how significant it was to the region. Simultaneously, the topic is increasingly relevant as society tries to become more environmentally aware and responsible.

5. Leadership (with Explicit Guidelines)

A healthy network of institutions functions like a neural network, which must maintain the activity of the synapses. In this sense, the network's leadership must be gentle yet consistent, watchful but empowering, and intense but reasonable. To lead a network is to uphold the active principle that bind it together, to care for it, to know about each node that makes it up, to recognize if it is weakening, and to always focus on the purpose for which it was founded, giving its members more control. Trust is the active concept that heals any sickness in the network, and that trust should flow from effective leadership.

6. Soft Power (Centralizing with Autonomy)

The cultural flavor that museums represent can be spiced up and improved by this ingredient. Building soft power requires a dash of imagination that—not always just metaphorically—invites us to a nice meal and a stimulating conversation at the table.

Policymakers, scientists, entrepreneurs, and artists can forge creative agreements that will improve services to the community around museums. Consider this a clear plan for forming alliances in a straightforward game of autonomy that can be won by developing a network that is rooted in trust, accountable to its users, and elective in nature. In this situation, soft power helps to support a democratic culture of power.

7. Innovation (Must Feed on Projects)

A network's ability to create and expand new projects—both in terms of quantity and quality—and its openness to cutting-edge technology are key indicators of how well the network will flourish. One indication, however, must be carefully monitored in order to determine whether a network is being developed on an innovative foundation: it is essential that the network's members are allowed to freely question one another in an atmosphere of open competition.

This innovation process is fueled both by external sources, like widely accepted scientific and technology practices, and by internal practices that emerge from team interactions.

For instance, in the Ciência Viva network, members are frequently taken aback by a project launched by other members that prompts them to wonder: "How come I had never considered that before? What a fantastic idea." A hint of healthy envy can inspire fresh innovation and hasten the adoption of new ideas by all network participants.

8. Credibility (Scientific Committee)

A network's credibility is based on a history of innovative and successful steps that have led to an accumulation of positive outcomes. A bylaw[18] that governs rights, duties, and obligations serves as the network's guiding text. It was created by the Ciência Viva National Agency after a cocreation process and ratified by all network members. Routine evaluations are regularly held, based on transparently communicated criteria. A bylaw and a regular evaluation are two essential aspects that allow the network to be viewed as a credible entity. A network should be demanding, flexible, and anchored in the people and institutions that ensure its present and future sustainability.

9. Sustainability (Support Received and Services Provided)

In every organization, but especially in a network, sustainability is a fundamental concept. It is crucial to discuss a network's financial health, which results from the commitment of all members to an active management that empowers business relationships with financial potential. The

Ciência Viva National Agency rules require transparency and fairness in the accounts that are presented and voted on at its members' biannual meetings. Sustainability also shows up in other contexts, such as in social or environmental spheres, which are just as crucial for the equilibrium of organizations. The institutions' strategic plans help to increase the network's sustainability in each of these areas.

10. Partnerships (Strong, Two Way, and Plural)

"Nobody knows enough to do everything alone" was a mantra of José Mariano Gago, the famed Portuguese physicist and former minister of science and higher education. He always encouraged us to cooperate and learn from others. The foundation of strong partnerships results from bringing together coalitions and sharing expertise. Partnerships with the scientific community, through universities, scientific institutes, with local governments, and with businesses are prioritized in the Ciência Viva network. Creating partnerships requires commitment from all these institutions.

These are the ten essential principles for creating, developing, and maintaining a network. Keeping the network active and relevant is an ongoing task requiring attention to detail. We have longevity on our side. The Ciência Viva network has now been in existence for more than two decades and is still expanding and growing—with each new meeting and conversation delivering an exchange of valued experiences and ideas.

Figure 3.4.   Pavilion of Knowledge, science center, and the headquarters of the Ciência Viva network of twenty-two science centers located throughout Portugal. *Photo by and courtesy of the Pavilion of Knowledge, Ciência Viva.*

3.6 Tourism

With tourism emerging at the turn of the last century as the world's largest industry, and with cultural tourism increasingly recognized as a dynamic sector of that industry, museums must take full advantage of their prominent roles as tourist attractions. For museums big and small, tourists may account for as much as 75 percent of visitors and an even higher percentage of visitor spending even when there is free admission. That is why the tourism industry—broadly defined as being part of the service sector that generates income to visited regions largely for the purpose of pleasure—needs to be seen as part of the museum ecosystem.

Of course, all museums in the world are in a state of change from the impact of COVID-19, after so many of those institutions had to endure a massive drop in attendance, or closure, for a period of weeks, months, or years. Many museums fought for their survival during the pandemic, and even those that did survive often had to absorb a huge amount of change. And many museum leaders and managers have reported using the pandemic downtime as a period to "reflect, reimagine, plan, and implement important changes" in order to reengage audiences when lockdowns were lifted. The move to digital was also sped up during COVID, with many major institutions investing in their Web platforms and social and digital resources, as ICOM reported during its multiple surveys of its member museums during and postpandemic.

> Directors should lose no opportunity to communicate to political and business leaders the potential or actual value of the museum's role in tourism.

Even relatively small museums can play a part in extending visitors' length of stay to a region of otherwise limited appeal, and directors should lose no opportunity to communicate to political and business leaders the potential or actual value of the museum's role in tourism.

Cooperation between museums and the tourism industry is therefore of vital importance to both. In general, staff in cultural institutions, including museums, have had limited understanding of—or even sympathy for—their tourist markets and often barely tolerate tourism operators. These operators in turn are often unaware of the realities facing museums and other cultural attractions on which they may be dependent for their livelihood. Wherever possible, museums should take the lead in bridging this gap, learning to work with tourism operators to mutual advantage.

Tourism has many motivators—visiting family or friends, sports, business, or shopping—but *cultural tourism* is among the strongest of them and can easily be combined with any or all of the others. Thus it is important for museums to seek ways to include themselves in the tourist industry—a discounted museum ticket or a special offer at the museum shop provided at hotel check-in can be beneficial for everyone, including the tourist!

Sustainable tourism is an important concept that is being developed in many of the more responsible tourist attraction centers. It begins from the recognition that tourism can be destructive of the very resource that attracts it—as perhaps most tellingly demonstrated at some of the world's great historical or archaeological sites. The imposition of special taxes on hotels, restaurants, or other businesses benefiting from tourism, and the provision of those taxes directly to those responsible for the preservation of the heritage, is one way that tourism and the cultural or heritage sectors can work together to ensure that tourism becomes a truly renewable resource industry. Dov Goldstein's case study describes how a new tourism attraction was added to one of the world's largest tourism destinations during the pandemic.

Reinventing a Heritage Site During a Pandemic

By Dov Goldstein

The Niagara Parks Power Station is a spectacular visitor destination in Niagara Falls, Canada, and one of the world's largest tourist attractions. The historic 1905-built hydroelectric power-generating plant reopened as a tourist attraction in 2022 with interactive exhibits, an immersive sound and light show, and large-scale industrial artifacts as well as a 2,200-foot-long tunnel that is 180 feet below the earth's surface and delivers visitors to the foot of Niagara Falls.

The fact that this unique visitor experience was created in just two years—and during a pandemic—illustrates what a team can accomplish through alignment on strategy, careful risk management, belief in an idea, and community pride.

The Niagara Parks Commission—the government agency responsible for the development and operations of this attraction—conceived and completed its planning for the project in the three years prior to COVID. Financing was secured and construction was set to begin just as the tourists at Niagara Falls were ordered home, and the rest of the world shuttered because of the pandemic.

Tourism is the lifeblood of the region, as well as the focus of the Parks Commission, and with the closing of international borders and the prospect of no visitors for the region's attractions, restaurants, and retail outlets, one could easily have imagined a postponement or even a shelving of the power station plan altogether.

Instead, the Niagara Parks Commission led by CEO David Adames and his team of directors, managers, and staff moved ahead with confidence and a steadfastness that continues to inspire, providing employment for many workers who would otherwise have been laid off.

Niagara Falls is one of the world's greatest natural wonders and premiere tourism destinations, and it consistently welcomed twelve million visitors annually to the Canadian Falls—prior to COVID—who animate and utilize its attractions, restaurants, theaters, casinos, and hotels in addition to its heritage sites, trails, monuments, museums, and unique immersive and interactive experiences.

In addition to its beauty and majesty, Niagara Falls continues to be an important and valuable source for hydroelectric power. In the late nineteenth century as this emerging technology proved to become a viable source of energy, hundreds of industries became operational in and around Niagara Falls, on both sides of the US-Canada border.

Engineers, scientists, and entrepreneurs had long sought to harness the energy of the Falls and the Niagara River, and by 1906, no less than four power plants were built in Niagara Falls, Ontario, serving tens of thousands of households, businesses, and industries in the Canadian province as well as in New York State.

While these power plants have been replaced with newer facilities that continue to produce clean, safe, and sustainable hydroelectric power, three of the four historic buildings became the responsibility of the Niagara Parks Commission, a provincial agency of the Ontario Ministry of Tourism, Culture, and Sport whose mandate is to be environmentally responsible as well as act as cultural stewards for the fifty-six-kilometer Niagara River corridor.

The last of the four power plants to close was the Rankine Generating Station. Decommissioned in 2006, this magnificent, beaux arts fortress-like building was left largely intact with all of its equipment, including the large-scale turbines used for generating electrical power. It was this station that Niagara Parks recognized as having great potential as a new attraction, and it has continued to inspire generations of employees who take enormous pride in its upkeep.

The Niagara Parks team, however, recognized a greater potential for the building than to simply maintain it. As Marcelo Gruosso, Niagara Parks chief operating officer stated, we can "take it off of our books from a multi-million-dollar liability to now becoming an asset that actually starts to generate some revenue."

Some background: Niagara Parks Commission operates seven visitor attractions, including multimedia, interactive, and immersive environments; zip lines and river cruises; two championship golf courses; five full-service restaurants; ten retail outlets; a butterfly conservatory; and numerous trails and gardens. It presides over seven heritage sites and museums, and additionally is responsible for maintenance of regional roads and parking, as well as transportation and police services.

Unlike most government agencies, Niagara Parks Commission is 100 percent self-funded. All of its revenue is earned—meaning its revenue is derived through admissions to its attractions; restaurants, and retail outlets; facility rentals; and various other related businesses. This self-funding model has instilled a great sense of entrepreneurship within the agency and its 280 employees.

With this in mind, between 2015 and 2017, Niagara Parks continued to do maintenance and repair work on the Rankine Generating Station. Throughout this period, the team uncovered multiple layers of the structure and discovered its tunnel or "tailrace" that diverted water to the station from the Niagara River and returned it back to the river at the base of the Falls. Unlike dams, these power stations returned clean water to the river, which is why this is a sustainable source of energy. When Gruosso and his team realized the tunnel was in reasonably good condition and potentially navigable, they were convinced of the attraction's extraordinary potential as a visitor experience.

The Niagara Parks Power Station was conceived of as a hybrid: part museum and part attraction—a paradigm that was new for the organization. Niagara Parks operates its museums, heritage sites, and attractions as separate and distinct entities. The museum component would demonstrate the authenticity while communicating the history and the site's many stories, as well as displaying artifacts. The attraction component would provide the entertainment factor that drives large visitation and admission revenue as a result.

As David Adames, explained, "The station links into both parts of our mandate. It's about balancing different elements. The wonderful thing about it is that it's a layered experience."

In 2019, after two years of project development including interpretive and business planning, design, and audience testing, the Niagara Parks Commission was prepared to seek project funding for the construction of its new attraction. With detailed business planning indicating a very strong future for the attraction, the self-funded agency secured financing via a loan with the Ontario Financing Authority, another provincial agency that manages the province's debt and borrowing program. With the anticipation of large visitorship and strong revenues based on Niagara Parks's projections, the loan would easily be paid off within ten years.

With the full support of the Niagara Parks Commission Board and the Provincial Ministry responsible for the commission, the loan was finalized and the team readied for construction. Then COVID hit, and almost overnight the Niagara Parks Commission went from its best year ever in fiscal year 2019 to a complete shutdown as of March 30, 2020. Closing the doors of the attractions, shops, and restaurants because of travel bans translated to a zero-revenue reality for the foreseeable future for Niagara and the agency.

The last thing most organizations would have done in this scenario would be to embark on a major capital project. It would have been much simpler and easier to retreat than push ahead and try to achieve the seemingly impossible. But that is precisely what CEO David Adames and his strong leadership team did.

Adames and his team communicated the vision and the plans to move forward and needed buy-in from the board and the entire Niagara Parks staff, which he received. Negotiations with the unions ensured representatives from essential trades were in place and willing to perform cross-functional duties, which were not in their regular job description.

Adames emphasized teamwork as crucial to the success of the project from all areas of staff, from engineering and marketing teams to finance and police. Everyone came together, demonstrating remarkable nimbleness and resilience to get the job done.

The all-hands-on-deck approach provided clarity on the power station's vision and plan but also translated into essential employment. The stark reality was that workers would have been laid off during the COVID shutdown had the province not been convinced to build. A green light for construction meant regular paychecks for staff, but it also provided focus, hope, and a sense of community. Further illustrating the Niagara Parks Commission's resolve and resourcefulness, the project also supplemented staff income by selling scrap metal no longer needed from the building.

David Adames and the entire Niagara Parks Commission knew they had proof of concept with the Niagara Parks Power Station: a unique combination of history, heritage, and attraction—wow factors that have helped it become Niagara's next great destination.

Figure 3.5.   The fully restored 1905 power-generating plant, Niagara Falls's newest cultural destination, brings to life the remarkable engineering feats of hydroelectric technology and the pioneers who created it. *Photo by and courtesy of the Niagara Parks Commission.*

Human Services

The museum ecosystem seems to benefit from the "winners" in a socioeconomic system characterized by a creative economy with government, foundation, and philanthropic support. What are the roles of museums for the suffering and marginalized in the ecosystem? Do museums provide shelter for the unhoused, warm space for cold days, and a cool place in extreme heat? In addition to providing students with programs that museums have determined are useful, do museums provide students with a place to do homework? Many public libraries answer yes to all the above, and yet few museums do.

> What are the roles of museums for the suffering and marginalized in the ecosystem?

Museums seem to occupy an exclusive niche in the social ecosystem—"not being everything to everyone." When we were writing *Cities, Museums and Soft Power*, we asked people working in human services to share their thoughts about how museums might help them in their work with their clients. This often drew a blank expression and the comment that "museums have nothing to do with us." The literature tells us that when museums have welcomed the disadvantaged and marginalized people, the experience was transformative for both parties—but these initiatives have not been promoted widely to the museum community.[19] It is to be hoped that in the coming decades, museum management will expand its role in the museum ecosystem to including caring, equity, and social justice.

3.7 Public Realm

The museum ecosystem includes the public realm, by which is meant places and spaces that are open and accessible to the general public. The COVID-19 pandemic demonstrated how very important these open spaces are for enjoyment, health, conversation, play, and exploration. Many museums have beautiful outdoor spaces as part of their property or grounds and nearby pocket parks and streetscapes. All these spaces are opportunities for activities, public art, and monuments—all of which spark conversation and controversy. Will the future of museums include more access to outdoor public spaces? It's a conversation worth having.

The essence of an ecosystem is sustainability. Creating and sustaining the right mix of relationships with a judicious balance of the museum's finite resources is a significant challenge at all levels of museum management. Understanding the extent and breadth of the museum ecosystem is a start.

> The essence of an ecosystem is sustainability.

Three levels of intensity may be distinguished among these relationships:

- Good professional practice is basic—participating in the relevant *museums association* or a marketing consortium focused on area attractions, for instance.

- More critical to the survival of the museum is the creation and maintenance of relationships related to *funding*—with governments, foundations, sponsors, and donors.

- The most advanced level is the establishment of *partnerships*—collaborations between institutions entered into for mutual benefit. These may be between museums sharing an exhibition, a museum and a school combining for an education program, or a *public-private partnership* designed to support the very establishment and operation of the museum itself.

In each instance it is vital to determine who the partners in your ecosystem are that will be most beneficial; how those relationships serve the museum's mission; what the impacts on staff, space, and budget will be; and whether those partnerships need to be exclusive.

> For a museum to thrive in the twenty-first century means acknowledging its place in a large and complex ecosystem, and the value it can offer.

Leaders and managers at any museum in the world need to be aware and learn more about all of the communities, partners, players, and forces in their ecosystems. As Yvonne Tang explains in her case study, for a museum to thrive in the twenty-first century means acknowledging its place in a large and complex ecosystem, and the value it can offer.

Comm(YOU)nity Matters

**By Yvonne Tang with Muna Faisal
Al Gurg and Terry Nyambe**

Until recently, most cultural institutions recognized their community primarily as those who share their specific story, their particular location, or their museum type. They generally included visitors who live nearby, who may have first attended with their grade school class or are "regulars" like people who conduct research at your institutions and engage with your collections, your expertise, your history, and your subject matter.

In the years surrounding the COVID pandemic, feelings of ostracization, imbalance, and insecurity were amplified. Institutions that previously relied heavily on visitation from school groups and tourists had to find ways to readjust when travel came to a standstill. Institutions that had scheduled openings or just opened had no way to bring in new audiences and gain stability. Voluntary and involuntary staff changes were constant for a variety of reasons. Doors closed or access was severely reduced. And no matter where you were in the world, we, as individuals and institutions, questioned our role(s) in social and racial injustices, traditional perspectives on learning, and maintaining colonialism and world-centricity. We felt the need for a greater and deeper connection with our visitors, and we needed to find ourselves within a world of diminishing resources.

What truly started to matter was caring and belonging. Finding, (re)connecting, and maintaining a community became of utmost importance.

Cultural institutions are a community at the core of a network of communities, an integral part of a multidimensional ecosystem of symbiotic relationships. Cultural institutions need to embrace a wider view of community that includes and adapts to the world today. It is a view of community that is regional and international, institution type and research focused, educational and entertaining. It is looking at community as your visitors and your neighbors, from the outside looking in. It is everyone who engages with you—online and onsite—the moment they visit your website, Google your name, enter your site, or buy a ticket online. It is also your staff, experts, partners, and sponsors from near and far. It is everyone who wants to be a part of your institution—the moment they apply to volunteer, put on your uniform, tell someone they work there, reach out to connect, or ask how they can help. Community is also thinking about how visitor experience can start from the inside and ripple outwards in exponential ways.

How can you foster community at your institution that is visitor forward?

First off, ask yourself—who is your community? Refocus and review who your community is. Ensure that you understand the various communities that you are serving, listen deeply to those you previously connected with, speak empathetically to those you haven't, and do it without stereotyping or undermining their capacities. Only then can you start making true connections and real relationships with your community.

- *Create a welcoming environment* that seamlessly anticipates the needs of visitors. Knowing your community then leads to creating spaces that the community identifies with and can use. Visitors who come for whatever range of reasons—your exhibits, a program, a celebration, for research, the bathrooms, the gift shop—should feel comfortable in your space. It encompasses staff and volunteers, so that they feel cared for and accepted, and thus exudes an inclusive atmosphere in all interactions.

- *Care* from within by prioritizing staff satisfaction, health, development, empowerment, and inclusion. Support their mental, physical, and emotional well-being. After all, they carry your morals and values as well as excitement and passion.

- *Cultivate a sense of belonging and a safe place* for learning, expression, and discord. Include staff and visitors in your story because they are a part of it. This will help them to see themselves reflected in your content, programs, and promotion.

- *Embrace multiple ways to tell stories.* Oral histories, intangible heritage, and multiple perspectives have always been prevalent, but in amplifying more voices, we must also be safekeepers of modern, remembered, and spoken histories. Develop spaces that are truly accessible, inclusive, and responsive to different ways of learning. People may thrive in testing, understanding process, and reading, while some may excel through sharing or listening, and others in visual cues or open-ended learning and experimentation.

- *Invest* in your community by providing learning opportunities, supporting local businesses, and communal growth. Community building is about embracing and building up around you, not just within. It should not be a one-way relationship but a symbiotic one, where there are collective benefits.

- *Reach out* to collaborate with scholars, leaders, partners, and other institutions (cultural organizations, education centers, or community groups) to *network and create stronger ties*. By fostering these relationships, you can generate shared resources, learnings, and benefits. They also bring their own entourage, their fans and followers, friends and families.

- *Consider* every interaction a potential for *your future everything*. Feeling like an integral part of a community resonates with potential donors, staff, partners, and visitors.

From our experiences and conversations with others, here are ten ways that museum management teams can incorporate community as an integral part of their work processes.

1. Shared Visioning

For new projects, establish a common vision by inviting a variety of voices at the outset. The act of early inclusion can be very impactful in creating a sense of shared ideation and gives participants a chance to be heard. This means working with staff across all levels and all departments, volunteers, subject experts, donors, sponsors, community members, and board members. It could be in the form of consultations, interviews, surveys, or workshops to gather insights and can be very powerful for both the individuals and the institution. A common vision at the outset is much more likely to lead to a positive collaboration and project outcome.

2. Collaboration and Cocreation

Ensure that departments have clear roles and responsibilities but encourage an integrative and collaborative workplace environment. Include a range of departments, community, and/or outside expertise in planning, development, implementation, and evaluation. Teamwork humanizes coworkers, creates relationships, amplifies individuals' strengths, and builds experiences together, regardless of each person's role or position within or external from your organization. Give individuals purpose while also giving your teams a connected sense of purpose and a concrete goal to work toward together.

3. Keep Communicating

The key to every great relationship is great communication, and when communities feel well listened to, they tend to start trusting those that have their interests at heart. Once you know your community, create spaces that the community identifies with. Share ideation and visioning and work together through development and implementation, even after opening. Your interactions must go beyond mere information and consultation into coimplementation of programs and projects. This is what yields a strong sense of belonging for members of the community. Let the community not only participate in creating content but be part of those telling others the stories about their cultures.

4. Empower Staff

Within your institution, staff should be encouraged to share new ideas, imagine, and cocreate with each other; have room for trial and error; and have the ability to test and experiment. Whether developing, mentoring, or directing staff, there should be room for trial and error that is judgment free and reflective. This creates opportunities for institutional improvement and, more importantly, for staff to feel seen, contribute, develop, and have a conduit to care about and share their passion for your institution.

5. Empower Youth

In many communities (and countries) young people are 50 percent of the population. They may not understand museums, but they have many skills that can flourish in your museum as paid staff, volunteers, and participants.

6. Amplify without Fear

No longer sites of top-down education and teaching, institutions should exponentially expand past experiences toward participation to highlight diverse faces and multiple perspectives, to be multilingual, and to magnify stories. Think outside the formal display and share "informal" histories like oral histories and community archives. Invite communities to work hand in hand with staff, lead with staff support, or take over altogether. Their ideas, passion, and expertise can add a different spark and perspective to your institution's planning and development. It may also build new audiences that you've never connected with before. Share in the unknown as well as the known—and acknowledge that there is always room for growth and opportunities for the future.

7. Build (and Maintain) Trust

Consider long-term relationship goals with your community. Establish ways that projects (exhibits, programming, marketing) can develop and grow within your institution as well as with those you've worked with. A children's program could grow to youth who develop their own program and become adults who are a part of your future. Perhaps allocate a percentage of your yearly operational costs to local community groups, firms, or organizations. Find stability in their presence, just as they can with yours. Show, in a multitude of ways, that your community is an integral part of your institution, and you will all benefit.

8. Empathize

Humans are multifaceted and complicated. Establish a variety of ways to care for each other. This means considering people's needs before, during, and after their engagement with your institution. This means providing experiences that are quiet, active, reflective, and participatory (but not all at once). This means providing comfortable seating (and tissues for crying), as well as a variety of ways to share collections and stories. And it means accessibility, allyship, and inclusion for all—visitors, staff, as well as yourself.

9. Make Events Matter

Rental and programming spaces bring in additional funding and create opportunities for new visitors to interact with your institution and your staff. If it's a community event, a wedding, birthday, or book launch, these could be people who don't or haven't come to your museum. Regardless of the event or experience, the moment people come through your doors and interact with you, that is your chance to create an impact. Think of new and innovative ways to bring people in—connect your vision and mission with wider education opportunities, programming ideas, community connections, and networking prospects. Staff sufficiently for a positive experience for visitors as well as your internal teams.

10. Celebrate Wins

Accomplishments on an institutional, organizational, individual, and community level should be celebrated. Visitors, volunteers, and staff of all levels should be praised for their part, however big or small. Often only sponsors, partners, and donors are thanked and acknowledged publicly. However, acknowledging individual and community contributions to large and small achievements can bolster a communal sense of satisfaction and pride.

We have collections of objects, art histories, and stories both tangible and intangible that are part of a communal human story that is still being written today. Without these communities, we would have and be nothing. We are all responsible for creating a multifaceted community in our institutions and we all have the potential to acknowledge and identify the "YOU" in community. This is how cultural institutions are responsible for finding what works—for you, your site, your institution, and the cultural community around you.

The authors gratefully acknowledge members of our museum and cultural community who made themselves available for informational interviews. Their institutional expertise and willingness to discuss their successes, failures, and ongoing projects helped to collectively shape this case study:

Ilana Altman, Coexecutive Director, The Bentway, Toronto, Canada

Jessica Ebanks, Community Engagement Officer, National Gallery of Cayman Islands

Lance Wheeler, Director of Exhibitions, National Center for Civil and Human Rights, Atlanta, Georgia, USA

Laura van Broekhoven, Director, Pitt Rivers Museum, Oxford University, Oxford, UK

Liwy Gracioso, Director, Museo Miraflores, Guatemala City, Guatemala

Orit Sarfaty, Special Projects and Business Development, Evergreen Brickworks, Toronto, Canada

Figure 3.6.   Children explore their history at the Etihad Museum in Dubai, which commemorates the unification of the United Arab Emirates in 1971. *Photo by Dubai Culture & Arts Authority. Image courtesy of Etihad Museum, Dubai Culture & Arts Authority.*

Chapter 4

WHERE

Location in a Digital World

By Ali Hossaini

Museums have proven resilient in the face of digital disruption.

Whether dedicated to art, science, or other subjects, museums have retained their position in society. Let us reflect on this achievement. Though longer in the making, the digital revolution arguably began with the World Wide Web in the early 1990s.

Since that decade, legions of digital disruptors have vanquished sector after sector, starting with creative industry. During the past thirty years, dominant institutions in music, publishing, radio, photography, cinema, television, and taste making have been utterly changed. As retail giants fell, pundits said the future belonged to "clicks not bricks." As of this writing, digital technologies continue to change stock markets, banking, government, and even money. Museums were an early target for disruptors.

There is no question that museums have changed with the times. They have adopted digital technologies, built digital capacity, and included digital experts in strategic planning. Some of the process is generational, as museum staff born after 1990 probably grew up with pervasive digital access.

Engaging with mobile media comes naturally to "digital natives," and museums often rely on specific cohorts to drive development. However, we should not expect digital natives to understand technological infrastructure, development, and workflow. Millions of people drive cars without understanding motors let alone roads, traffic lights, and the supply chains that deliver fuel.

Here's an interesting fact about museums in the digital age: museums have continually tried digital innovation, usually with few resources and little room to learn from failure. Most efforts have fallen flat, and, as a sector, museums can hardly claim digital leadership. Where museums have developed presence, for instance, in social media, they are small players relative to taste makers, commentators, and popular icons. What accounts for the resilience of museums?

Museums as Placemakers

Museums are placemakers extraordinaire. Among the principles cited by placemakers are uniqueness, locality, authenticity, and direct experience. Museums embody these factors, and they combine with strong brands. Being described as a museum confers a certain prestige.

> Museums collapse time and space, bringing remote eras and distant places into presence.

Museums are authoritative and edifying, yet they are also entertaining and offer strong retail experiences. One can count on museums for distinctive cards, gifts, and wrapping. Museums collapse time and space, bringing remote eras and distant places into presence. Museums engage all the senses, including the kinesthetic, and many are full-spectrum social destinations. As a favored destination for families and schools, museums evoke lifelong sentiment in adults. For locals and tourists, museums define the identity of neighborhoods, cities, and nations, and cascades of independent awareness building often accompanies their marketing campaigns. Museums will likely survive the metaverse.

Much of what I have written would be conjecture, except for the powerful experiment posed by COVID-19. As lockdowns stretched from months into years, tourism flatlined, and long-term plans sank. Revenue projections were meaningless. People flocked online for entertainment, socializing, and work. Offices have reorganized, and, as of this writing, commercial real estate, hospitality, and transportation continue to adapt to virtual society.

If an all-digital replacement for museums were waiting in the wings, it had no better window to grab minds and markets than lockdown. Yet, like Owariya, the Japanese soba shop founded in 1465,[1] museums have survived with few changes. Their survival strategy resembles that of Owariya: thrifty financial management and maintaining quality.

During lockdown, I was codirector of National Gallery X, a studio lab jointly operated by the United Kingdom's National Gallery and King's College London. One of the most salient pieces of learning speaks to power of tradition. In keeping with "snacking" habits formed before lockdown, the National Gallery had trimmed the length of its video offers. Lockdown afforded people leisure time, or time to edify themselves, and viewers requested longer videos. They missed lingering in galleries, absorbing interpretation, and the constant whisper of expertise, whether from curators, guides, or fellow visitors. As the pandemic receded, museums regained visitors.

What lessons can we take from this extraordinary resilience? I am not going to recommend that museums plod into the future. Societies experience generational as well as revolutionary change. If the metaverse ever happens—no predictions now—the foundations of placemaking may erode.

This chapter describes how museums can play to their strengths by developing digital leaders: museum natives not (simply) digital natives. Museums can use technology to become more efficient. They can also increase their social impact—come aligned with contemporary values— by using digital platforms to make collections more accessible and interpretation more diverse. Technology may not be a game changer for museums, but it can make them better at what they do. The chapter is organized into the following topics:

- Fundamentals of digital museum management

- Becoming more efficient

- Becoming more relevant

- Placemaking revisited

- Conclusion: planning for impact

> Technology may not be a game changer for museums, but it can make them better at what they do.

4.1 Visitor-Centrism

How did digital disruption happen? Did some people have a better understanding of technology, or was it something more profound? I assert the latter. One innovation stands out throughout the various digital revolutions, and technology is subordinate to it. It is user-centrism (or customer-centrism), a principle that translates into visitor-centrism for museums.

It might seem obvious that stores sell to customers, sport franchises cater to fans, and museums offer exhibitions. But many organizations operate by internal imperatives while leaving the client experience to frontline staff. Digital disruption happens when new entrants use technology to superserve constituencies, unlock new markets, or otherwise circumvent older systems. The rise of companies such as Amazon, AirBnB, and Uber is a prime example of how digital innovation shocked established industries by changing fundamental relationships with shoppers, travelers, and passengers.

User-centrism is both a value and organizing principle. What happens when this principle is applied within museums? How do we describe a visitor-centric museum? For this we might adopt the term omnichannel from retail. Like museums, stores have been the ultimate brick-and-mortar institutions. Mail order has been around since the nineteenth century when Sears pioneered remote sales, but remote retail became more vibrant in the 1990s when Amazon and others took the catalog online.

Today online media form a major sales channel, but the Internet is a double-edged sword. Price comparison has never been easier, and shoppers use mobile Internet to check competitors' prices within a retailer's walls. Rather than resist the trend, many stores decided to embrace new behaviors by offering public WiFi to customers. Shoppers are free to compare prices or even buy elsewhere, but WiFi also enables spontaneous deal making. It captures fine-grained data on individual customers, and retailers use it to build long-term relationships with shoppers.

As they adapted to digital behavior, retail strategists coined the phrase "omnichannel marketing" to describe a new approach: give customers what they want, when they want it, and how they want it, through every possible channel. But for retailers, omnichannel means more than 24/7 service on the Internet. It also means a relentless focus on the individual customer, and digitally driven companies have reorganized departments to achieve that goal. From R&D to sales, digital technologies address people as individuals. Omnichannel has moved from retail into sports and entertainment.

Both sectors generate large amounts of media that have moved from distinct channels like radio, television, and print onto a converged Internet. They also produce live events that engage audiences digitally in stadiums and performance halls. Omnichannel organizations move people seamlessly from computer to mobile to venues. Publishing systems are context aware, and they structure content according to the user's preferences, history, and location. Museums can do the same by putting visitors at the center of their plans.

4.2 Omnichannel Thinking

Digital change continues to operate at different rates depending on global region, nation, sector, organization, and even department. There's no way to create a distinct recipe for creating an omnichannel organization. But one thing is true everywhere: successful digital change requires activist managers. The following principles will help activist managers successfully deploy and adapt to the evolving digital landscape.

- Change is inevitable, so plan for change.

- Everything is networked.

- Build a nimble, responsive organization.

- Projects should be driven by strategy.

- Experiment constantly.

- Use data to validate and communicate.

- Consider online visitors equal to physical visitors.

Omnichannel thinking catalyzes certain kinds of change in your organization. Planning horizons shift closer to the present because development processes reiterate instead of cascading. Traits we first noticed in software development, which is always upgrading, are becoming characteristic of organizations. Dynamic, technology-driven markets inspire constant social and behavioral change. For the foreseeable future, new generations of hardware, software, and people will cast aside earlier assumptions.

Because change is constant, multidisciplinary teams are becoming the most effective way of quickly responding to markets. This approach, called "agile development" in engineering circles, emphasizes small steps with instant evaluation.

Each step of agile development assesses whether a particular approach is worth pursuing. Limited ambition and resources mean more risk can be built into the system without the possibility of catastrophic failure. This raises the rate, or productivity, of innovation because an agile team can both afford and learn from failure. In an agile environment, departmental barriers erode, and informal staff networks—knowledge sharing—are increasingly important. For some kinds of task, interdepartmental cooperation at the team level is complementing, or even replacing, linear, top-down management.

Omnichannel organizations move elements of R&D into operations. Experimentation becomes more acceptable, and the appetite for risk grows because small failures prevent larger ones. They often set aside a certain percentage of your budget for risk and reward staff who engage in fruitful failure, that is, projects that deliver insights while falling short of their objectives. Generalists who understand multiple arenas are important, and they move diagonally through organizations to cultivate projects that may grow in scope.

4.3 Digital Museum Management

Say you want to create an omnichannel museum. Transforming your organization in one pass is neither possible nor desirable. Instead, count on deploying change in phases, ideally by deploying projects that can, if successful, become standing programs. It is important to remember that you are engaged in engineering. Technical installations should be implemented systematically, and they proceed with the least grief when professionally planned and managed. Even the best managers require strategic oversight that is firmly rooted in organizational vision. You need to know what you are trying to accomplish, why you are doing it, and who benefits. Everything else follows.

Here are guidelines for incorporating omnichannel thinking into your organization's digital vision and development process.

1. Describe how the project advances your organization's strategy.

Every digital project should advance some element of your organization's mission, vision, values, or strategic plan. Answer the following questions.

- How does this project advance our organization's mission?

- Does the project support our organizational values?

- What strategic aims does the project achieve?

- Does the project support other initiatives?

2. Judge whether the project runs on your current infrastructure.

It is important to consider how your project fits into current and planned infrastructure. Review its full requirements, including connectivity and operations, to ensure you have accounted for future demands. Bear in mind that you may already possess the resources in your specification, particularly if it has been prepared by an outside party. Does it—or can it—utilize existing resources? Will new investments enhance current resources?

3. Convene a panel of stakeholders.

Identify the internal constituency for your project. Form a committee of interested parties to review, discuss, and revise the proposal. Convene your panel at key stages of development.

4. Coordinate the project with other initiatives.

Create a chart that projects the progress of current technical projects on a timeline. Identify resources required to execute, test, and launch a project to discover dependencies, bottlenecks, or conflicts.

5. Consider who is in charge.

When planning, upgrading, or managing digital strategies, museums must make a fundamental choice about how to develop IT infrastructure. You have a choice of developing a full IT department, outsourcing IT to an agency, or retaining an agency to support an undersized in-house team. Cloud services and remote access tools enable organizations to acquire sophisticated services at relatively low thresholds of cost and expertise. However, even agencies require internal management by at least one member of staff with digital expertise. Evaluation of budgets, impact, and work plans is best managed by an internal advocate who reports to the museum. Natalie MacLean's case study explains the importance of taking an even earlier step—assessing your organization's digital readiness.

Setting the Stage for Digital Transformation in Museums

By Natalie MacLean

Digital transformation in the museum sector has now been underway for decades, led by creative visionaries, innovative managers, and increasingly digitally literate audiences. The onset of the COVID-19 pandemic turned what was a slow drip to a tidal wave, as digital became the only method for program delivery. Museums broke the boundaries of what was previously thought to be possible with digital, creating inventive new programming that ranged from livestreamed talks to virtual exhibitions and interactive online galas. Digital programming and the use of technology had been a priority for some museums (especially those with the resources to pursue it), but overnight it became a requirement for all. This necessity led to a great deal of invention and no doubt opened minds to new digital possibilities, but it also exposed a dire need for the digital tools, infrastructure, and skills to make these prospects a reality. As museums move forward, it's important for them to prepare not only to use the technology available today but also to ready themselves to seize the opportunities of tomorrow.

"Digital readiness" describes how prepared an organization is to embrace new technologies and tools in service of operational efficiency, program delivery, and community engagement. It encompasses both the outward-facing digital presence and programming experienced by the public as well as the infrastructure, processes, skills, and partnerships that occur behind the scenes. Figure 4.1 illustrates how digital experiences are supported behind the scenes by a combination of digital strategies, staff skills, hardware, infrastructure, software, data, content, and more. As you can see, what is "below the waterline" enables digital engagement and is much larger than what is above. Just as with icebergs, there is more than meets the eye when it comes to digital in museums.

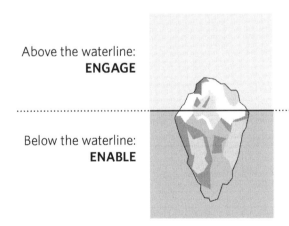

Above the waterline:
ENGAGE

- Content
- Website & Social Media
- Interactives & Touchscreens
- Screens & Projections
- Mobile Technology
- Kiosks
- Online Programming

Below the waterline:
ENABLE

- Digital Strategy
- Staff Skills & Knowledge, and Organizational Structure
- Connectivity
- Hardware & Infrastructure
- Systems & Software
- Collections, Data & Content Management

Figure 4.1.   Creating a Strong Foundation of Digital Readiness. *Lord Cultural Resources.*

To take full advantage of the "above the waterline" opportunities offered by digital tools and technologies, museums need a strong foundation of digital readiness. Without this strong foundation, museums may find their vision for digital engagement stymied by technological breakdowns, uneven adoption, and lack of internal skill.

This is the position Art Windsor Essex found themselves in during 2021 and 2022. Art Windsor Essex (or AWE) is a nonprofit art gallery focused on presenting the visual arts of Canada. Located in Windsor, Ontario, the gallery had recently undergone a strategic shift, emphasizing the power of art to open minds and hearts to new ideas. An important part of this revamped vision was the embrace of digital methods of audience engagement to connect with communities and create innovative programming. The onset of COVID-19 turned what was a developing practice into a present requirement, as gallery closures necessitated a shift to digital programming. Upon reopening, an interest in increased digital engagement continued, with an eye toward creating new and innovative experiences both in the gallery and throughout the community. As AWE tried to turn this bold digital vision into reality, they found themselves hitting multiple roadblocks.

One of the greatest frustrations AWE experienced in implementing new digital initiatives was related to infrastructure challenges. As part of an ongoing project to increase accessibility and enhance visitor experience, AWE was working with an external company to provide touchless video and audio content, accessed in the gallery using QR codes. These virtual tours gave visitors the opportunity to learn more about the works in the gallery and increased accessibility. However, the ability of visitors to access this exciting content was regularly hampered by poor cell phone service and unstable Wi-Fi throughout the gallery. This also created challenges for staff as they relied on the same networks to complete their day-to-day work. Forming a plan to address these issues was key to improving the current visitor experience and supporting future projects.

Another common challenge exemplified by AWE was the need to harness data, both for decision making and to enhance digital experiences. The ability to collect, understand, and analyze data is key for organizations hoping to better understand their performance and their audiences. At AWE, data was captured irregularly and did not flow throughout the organization, meaning it could not be used by staff to make decisions about programming or operations. Creating a data flowchart to identify what data is being generated, where it is shared within the organization, and what the gaps are is the first step in harnessing data in a museum.

Staff are a significant part of digital readiness, as they will be the ones who are required to adopt new technologies and create digital programming. They will also have to support audiences who may need assistance accessing new digital experiences, as well as troubleshoot any glitches that come up in multimedia installations. Although their skills and abilities using digital tools and technologies are important, even more critical is a digitally positive attitude. Transforming a museum to embrace digital technologies requires effort and a shift away from business as usual. For that transformation to be successful, it's important for staff to be aligned around both the need for digital transformation and the path by which it can be accomplished. The enthusiasm of staff is reflected in the programming they create, their adoption of new platforms and ways of working, and how they share new initiatives with the museum's audiences. Involving staff in the process, beginning at the research stage, throughout the planning, and in postproject evaluation can help build consensus and identify future barriers to success. Staff at AWE were excited about the possibilities of digital programming and were privy to tech glitches and visitor needs that would ultimately make or break future success. Their input was key to planning for and then implementing digital transformation.

One of the most important things a museum can do to increase digital readiness is to create a digital strategy, which outlines their digital vision, goals, and the objectives they will use to reach them. Digital strategies are particularly useful for organizations that are looking to make a significant step up in digital readiness—serving as a roadmap to transformation. Museums that have already achieved a suitable level of digital readiness may choose to integrate digital goals with their larger strategic planning process, but those who are just beginning their digital journeys or looking to achieve a specific digital outcome often need a distinct strategy. In the spring and summer of 2022, AWE undertook a digital strategic planning process, which culminated in a finalized digital strategy and implementation plan to lead the gallery through the next three years. Having a clear digital vision, as well as defined goals and objectives, informed budget allocations and has led to investments in technologies, tools, and expertise to support the gallery's future. By creating a plan for digital transformation, AWE has positioned itself to not only take advantage of the technologies available to the gallery today but also be more prepared to adopt the innovations of tomorrow.

4.4 Becoming More Effective

Planning for omnichannel starts by putting the visitor at the center of the planning process. Efficiencies follow priorities.

Whether reviewing a project brief or your mission statement, bear in mind that omnichannel services are organized around the needs of end users—the individuals they serve. Whether in retail or sports and entertainment, companies are giving people maximum information and maximum choice. As shop owners know, one size does not fit all, and smart technologies are making personalization the norm.

Once you have considered the needs of visitors, review your strategic plan. Where can digital services improve your organization? Virtually every activity can be performed more efficiently or more robustly with support from information technology (IT). Consider your entire workflow from acquisition to collections management to exhibitions, marketing, and visitor engagement. Interdependencies between digital projects are no less than the dependencies you encounter when managing your facilities and physical plant.

Yet, digital projects are often pursued on an ad hoc basis with no oversight from a senior manager or strategic plan. Efficiencies are strongest when IT and digital planning are integrated into every phase of your work.

The complexity of integrated digital planning is comparable to building. Architecture serves many roles. It is a symbol of your mission, a shelter for your collection, a lab for researchers, and an environment experienced by the visiting public. Digital channels are starting to fill these roles, and it might be easiest to think of them as a parallel universe that reflects, affects, and converges with the physical world. But the parallel worlds of online and physical experience are merging. Mobile phones are already ubiquitous, and they will increasingly be used to interact with physical places.

We are in a long-term transition in which more activities will take place in augmented environments that blend physical and digital experiences. Museums should start planning to take advantage of information-rich, personalized digital channels.

We are in a long-term transition in which more activities will take place in augmented environments that blend physical and digital experiences. Museums should start planning to take advantage of information-rich, personalized digital channels.

IT is the bedrock of the visitor-centric, omnichannel approach. The discipline incorporates computing, networking, and telecommunication resources into a system that supports professional activities. It follows that an important component of planning for omnichannel is to ensure you have a plan for IT service management (ITSM) within your museum.

The complexity of IT management grows with our reliance on digital systems, and an ITSM plan details how these systems will be maintained into the future. Activities supported by IT include:

- Collections management

- Analytics

- Donor development

- Marketing

- Ticketing

- Merchandise sales

- Exhibition

- Visitor interaction

- Member interaction

- PR/communications

Most museums have adopted digital practices for some or all of the previous list. There are still areas where much progress can be made, namely visitor circulation management, interpretation, and collections access.

The most basic method of visitor circulation management is to assign staff, possibly with counters, to observe and resolve bottlenecks. Cameras can be used for live observation or to create records for analysis. Today there is a simple method based on WiFi. Any mobile device that has WiFi turned on will signal its presence to a wireless router. (It does not need to be logged in.) WiFi systems can track the movement of devices to generate a heat map that shows the density of visitors.

This capability is called location awareness, and it can be used to track the movement of visitors through your building in real time or as a recording. By combining location awareness with location analytics, heat maps can form an inexpensive, accurate basis for circulation management. By analyzing the movement of visitors across time, museums can judge the popularity of exhibits, the effectiveness of signage, and the location of bottlenecks and other impediments to visitor flow. The system can then encourage visitors to avoid crowded areas or time entry into popular exhibits.

Interpretation and collections suffer from bottlenecks to access as well. The next section describes these bottlenecks, and it offers solutions based on digital access.

4.5 Becoming More Relevant

Museums are as relevant as ever. Neither museums nor the public has lost sight of their core tenet: museums exist to edify the public. Yet the edifice shows cracks. Starting with the Galleria Borghese in Rome, which admitted only "free men" and warned away malcontents, museums have always excluded certain populations. Even museums with free admission may present invisible barriers to entry. Some of these barriers may be unconscious while others may be planned.

In many cases, digital technologies can help museums welcome people by lowering barriers and encouraging participation. But digital technologies are not a panacea, and planners should always mitigate the digital divide that confounds people who cannot or will not embrace technological mediation. Like libraries, museums can offer multiple avenues for self-improvement.

Both society and scholarship have demonstrated the narrow perspective that informs many museums. This perspective determines what is collected, how it is exhibited (or not), and how it is interpreted.

For the purposes of this chapter, let us confine our discussion to how interpretation and access to collections affects public engagement. Objects in a museum tell many stories, and, by telling only one story, interpretation may alienate visitors who are either excluded or interested in other perspectives. Collections usually outstrip, sometimes by a massive percentage, a museum's exhibition space.

From Multiple Perspectives to Personalization

As with visitor circulation, much of the problem is physical. Floor space is limited. Wall space is limited. Only so many objects can be displayed, and interpretation has severe limits on words. Although accessibility has always been a problem, it is now widely acknowledged, and it is a problem that digital technology and the principles of omnichannel marketing can address.

As commercial vendors have found, digital media can expand the physical boundaries of a place. This can be done with WiFi and any number of techniques, for example, a QR code next to the object.

Instead of a single, generic message, interpretation can be unfolded into multiple perspectives.[2] Visitors can explore a variety of meanings, and they can save content for later. To adopt an omnichannel mindset, treat your building as a website.

Consider the features that enable personalization online: registration, preferences, sales, usage tracking, and social sharing. Digital functionality can activate your entire museum. It can be inserted wherever you have a point of contact with visitors, and it can also create new points of contact.

People are already using mobile phones in museums, and they probably expect free WiFi. You can enhance the museum experience by launching a splash screen (also called a captive portal) when they log into your WiFi. Rather than put generic terms of service, why not use your splash screen as a content hub that gets people excited about visiting? It can promote current events while serving as an access point for audio tours and rich, multilayered interpretation.

Omnichannel means projecting your museum's entire range of activities onto digital platforms. As the name implies, omnichannel integrates previously separate services and enables visitors to move among them. It might be helpful to compare omnichannel design to architecture. It takes architects and a host of planners, engineers, and designers to create a building. If they are successful, the building is a coherent whole composed of rooms, passages, and wayfinding features. Your digital infrastructure should do no less, and, when planning for digital organization, you should treat it as an extension of your architecture.

Digital technologies increase accessibility through personalization.

Digital technologies increase accessibility through personalization. The closest analogy is an observant guide who tailors experiences to the visitor. Supported by analytics, a set of mathematical tools that discern individual preferences, personalization can provide additional layers of service while deepening engagement. Registered visitors or members can transmit their preferences by swiping their phone over sensors.

Membership schemes deepen engagement while gathering valuable data about visitor interests. They also provide a clear opt-in to personalization that addresses privacy and security concerns.

Personalization can take advantage of the location awareness features discussed earlier. Visitors increasingly expect their phone to offer content relevant to their location. Museums are well positioned to take advantage of this trend. People wield mobiles freely in museums. They take photos of objects and interpretation, take selfies, or search for information. Museums can guide this behavior by engaging visitors through WiFi. It is now clear that selfies serve as valuable channels for promotion and visitor engagement.

However, where photography proves disruptive, museums could offer high-resolution images over WiFi and build selfie stations. While allowing people to search for information independently, location-aware WiFi could put museum interpretation and resources at the top of search.

Museums can also be sites for creative R&D. While most museums lack the capacity to conduct independent R&D, they can facilitate research by partnering with universities, technology companies, and government institutes. This research can run the spectrum from testing use cases for advanced systems to fundamental science facilitated by museum collections, expertise, or public engagement.

> While most museums lack the capacity to conduct independent R&D, they can facilitate research by partnering with universities, technology companies, and government institutes.

The past few decades have seen unwelcome disruption along with vast investments that have fizzled. Museums could extend their public mission to supporting the safe, productive deployment of technology. Virtual reality (VR) may be a case study for this argument.

Virtual Reality

VR takes digital media to their logical extreme. The best systems effortlessly track movements of head, hands, and body to transport individuals into simulated environments. Nature, architecture, and even video screens appear in virtual reality. Like museum architecture, virtual reality could be placemaking par excellence. While VR struggles to become a mass medium, museums could create virtual environments that bring objects to life. If headsets become popular at home, museums would be well prepared to extend the experience to everyone who can afford one.

Even if VR remains niche, it could become an important extension of museum programming. Some people cannot visit public buildings, and a traveling VR exhibition that includes headsets could open museum doors to people who are otherwise excluded.

Omnichannel engagement will evolve over time, but certain principles will remain consistent. It is important to bear these in mind when planning for change. To the greatest degree possible, combine digital services into the same IT infrastructure. It is easiest to give people a seamless experience when there are no seams.

> **Curators, content managers, and software developers should be in close contact.**

To achieve this, transcend departmental silos when planning digital projects. Curators, content managers, and software developers should be in close contact. Develop a unified, interoperable specification for databases and online publishing systems and make sure everyone has a voice in planning and operations. Become an advocate for sector-wide standards, especially for museums that share your mission. Standards make for savings in cost and efficiency, and they ease engagement with partners and visitors. As they travel from one museum to another, people will have a better experience if they already know how to use your services.

4.6 Placemaking Revisited

As we invest in digital platforms, we should reconsider the "clicks not bricks" logic that drove digital revolutions in other sectors. By pushing value online, digital technologies flattened the competitive landscape. A flat world opens avenues to exciting new services, but the resulting ecology also removes local advantage. By lowering natural barriers to competition, efficient digital networks encourage the dominance of megabrands over small organizations that thrive locally. Amazon, Google, and Facebook and a handful of other companies are undermining the diversity of their respective sectors.

Could we face a similar situation in the museum sector? Could a few superbrands become dominant digital destinations?

> **Almost perversely, digital empowerment of individuals creates a market that favors large commercial brands.**

At first museums adapted to digital technology by building websites. But the Web is a big place where audiences are elusive. Marketing imperatives are driving museum content to Google, Facebook, Twitter, and YouTube—firms driven by profit not mission. Almost perversely, digital empowerment of individuals creates a market that favors large commercial brands. Only a few organizations are large enough to push their own agenda in this environment. Social media drives aggregation, and aggregation drives consolidation.

Anyone who ignores commercial networks is left behind.

How can museums benefit from digital technology? Equally important, how can museums, especially smaller museums, exercise leadership in a world of megabrands? The former relies on adaptation—a process that is underway—but the latter relies on innovation. To state the obvious, innovation is doing what has not been done before. Where can museums blaze trails—ideally through a terrain that plays to their advantage?

Three factors stand out: mobility, sociability, and place.

- Mobility is well established but has far to go before innovation plateaus. The majority of online activity is already on mobile devices, and the introduction of 5G is triggering new generations of innovation.

- Social media underlie many disruptive trends, and their potential for future disruption is clear. Museums should keep a firm grip on their IP and reputation on social networks.

- Place may be the most unique strength of museums. Taken collectively the vast public investment in museums provides a counterweight to even the largest private companies.

> Taken collectively the vast public investment in museums provides a counterweight to even the largest private companies.

By developing these three factors, museums could lead the next wave of change, and they could introduce a new medium for engaging audiences: digital placemaking.

What would we want from a digital place?

Museums are beloved. They live in the centers of cities and the hearts of audiences who visit them for excellence in curation, presentation, and entertainment. Unfortunately, many museums are behind the technology curve and offer digital experiences that lag behind expectations being created elsewhere. By weaving digital technologies into the experience of buildings, exhibitions, and public gatherings, and by including visitors in the design of these experiences, museums can offer unique programs that play to their strengths.

The ingredients for digital placemaking are already in hand. The smartphones carried by most of their visitors are inherently social. Museums need to meet smartphone users halfway by engaging them in situ. Museums already possess the means to do so: public WiFi. At present WiFi is offered to visitors as a necessary free service where everyone goes their separate way.

Museums use WiFi to address people through a channel that is both intimate and public. Give people the Internet, but foreground interpretation and let them exit through the (digital) gift shop. Use WiFi to offer content throughout your museum and use location awareness to make it immediate and relevant. For instance, a deal on tickets to a blockbuster show, a call to share selfies with a dinosaur, or a live Q&A with the curator of sculpture.

The driving imperative behind mobility, sociability, and placemaking is choice. But being available on demand is not the only feature of digital experiences. It is personalized for individuals who form a relationship with the institution that offers specific content that makes them laugh or cry, answers questions, inspires creativity, or helps them understand a challenge. Museums should build on their knowledge of visitors to create personal interactions in public spaces.

Personalization means keeping visitors in control, and museums should remain bastions of choice. People typically walk into museums with companions. They speak to one another about whatever they choose, look at what interests them, eat when hungry, and rest when tired. Physical places support freedom, bridging, and bonding. They are places where you meet new people while connecting more deeply with the ones you know.

> Personalization means keeping visitors in control, and museums should remain bastions of choice.

Digital places should offer the same freedom.

By linking WiFi to content, collections, and relationship management systems, museums can combine the best of the physical and virtual experiences—creating flexible, interactive places that respond to people as individuals, couples, and groups.

But this is only the beginning. It is obvious that WiFi is a channel for personalized guides, apps, and interpretation. Is this sufficient to justify the investment necessary to create a digital place? The reality is we do not know what a digital place looks like, what it will do, and what benefits it will offer.

In parallel to other sectors that range from retail to government, the mature form of digital interaction is something that museum professionals and the broader world, including the visiting public, needs to create—ideally together—in coming years. Progress may come from unexpected quarters. A game may take the world by surprise, then leave models for more serious programs in its wake. Creative R&D can help museums shape the future.

There is little doubt that museums—and other organizations, some yet to be invented—will evolve new platforms for presenting artistic, scientific, and historical content. Smartphones are notoriously distracting, but new mobile platforms will be less intrusive, and they will coevolve with the Internet of Things. These emerging platforms will work particularly well for museums.

As museums use digital media to activate objects, people can collaborate with each other and museums to create unique experiences—which is the essence of placemaking. Rather than working solely online, digital leadership relies on a museum-centric strategy of clicks and bricks where investments align virtual spaces with physical places. Museums should consider themselves part of "systems and platforms"[3] where content generated by collections, exhibitions, researchers, educational programs, and even visitors is available globally. Digital placemaking can provide strategic guidelines for investments in cultural organizations that venture into the digital cloud but also draw people into beloved destinations.

By remembering the unique ingredient of place, and ensuring it drives digital strategy, museums can maintain their natural advantages in a world that offers a heady mix of disruption, misplaced optimism, and stunning opportunity.

4.7 Managing for Impact

Here we discuss how to judge whether the digital programs in your strategic plan are fit for your purpose. You should start by looking backward and forward at the project level. Too often digital projects are executed for their own sake, and these efforts often lack organizational impact. Many projects both past and future probably have digital components, and some may be completely digital. Examples of projects include:

- having your online store headline best sellers in the museum shop,

- installing video displays in your public spaces that update instantly with events and activities, and

- extending public WiFi system throughout your campus.

Get an overview of your internal capacity by prioritizing your projects. You can do this by developing a chart that ranks proposed projects according to cost, longevity, impact, and other criteria drawn from your mission. Charts help determine the priority, budget, and timescale of a project by giving an objective judgment of its value.

This evaluation process can be used to rank projects. Break out issues that are relevant and grade them 1 to 10, A to F, or any other scale that makes sense. Once you have assessed your museum's digital capacity, engage in the follow exercise:

1. Review your organization's vision statement and strategic plan. Do they recognize the connected world where museums are facilitators as well as authorities?

2. Compare your existing organization to your forward-looking vision. Map where your organization is in relation to your target and where it needs development. Answer the following questions to segment your plan and assess if it takes you closer to your aspirations.

   - Can your strategic plan adapt to evolving visitor expectations?

   - Does your plan promote current best practices in the cultural sector?

   - What sections need to be revised?

   - Where can change happen?

   - What projects may grow into standing programs?

   Map the priorities of your stakeholders. Where do they overlap to mutual benefit?

   Stakeholders may include the visiting public; scholars, scientists, and students; government and private funders; educational institutions; internal staff and contractors; or partners and sister organizations in the sector. And, importantly, your stakeholder map should include the nonvisiting public. Are there underrepresented demographics in your catchment? Can you use digital platforms to broaden your appeal, lower barriers, or otherwise serve people who avoid your doors?

3. Revise your strategic plan and incorporate digital practices where they can improve your organization. This can be done as an interim exercise if your long-term plan is set.

4. Do you have a strategy for ITSM? If not, work with qualified parties to develop a plan that includes the following topics:

   - Asset management

   - Problem management

   - Change management

   - Regulatory compliance

   - Digital security

5. Build in-house capacity. Too often organizations rely on one person's expertise. If recruiting is difficult in a competitive job market, ensure your digital experts train their colleagues.

Continuity is an issue that affects every level of organization from the department to the sector, and your efforts to retain knowledge even as staff move will benefit every museum stakeholder.

The Importance of Space and Place

By Gail Dexter Lord

We often hear it said that thanks to digital technology and artificial intelligence, distance is dead and that geography is history. As someone who travels a great deal, I can confirm that distance is not dead, and that place matters more than ever.

The concepts of "space and place" were brought to my attention in an unlikely location: the Microsoft campus in Redmond, Washington. I was conducting a workshop with some of the workers to get their views on how they might use a new art museum being planned for a nearby community. One of the participants said: "I spend all day working with a two-dimensional screen. When I get home, I relax in front of another screen. And for entertainment, I watch a bigger screen. For me, three-dimensional space is where I can be creative."

This goes a long way toward explaining why museum space matters so much to so many people today. Museum space is emphatically three-dimensional, punctuated by three-dimensional objects. It is a kinesthetic experience, during which our mere movement seems to change the space, and the place somehow changes us. We wander, we graze. Because this is an interpreted space—a place with assigned meanings—we may also be challenged to see things in a new way: to find our own way, figuratively, at least.

It's not only the prevalence of the screen that makes us appreciate space. It's also the increasing privatization of the public realm through advertising, shopping malls, and corporate office towers that dominate and direct not just our footsteps but our hearts and minds. The same shops, brand names, logos, and images punctuate urban space the world over. Derelict buildings, historic sites, and contested places have become increasingly important because here, at least, meanings and emotions have not been predetermined by the force of today's global economics but by the economics of the past that we struggle to understand or at least reimagine.

The contemporary artists creating site-specific works are the ones who have drawn our attention to the multiple meanings and complex identities of these spaces and places. In the early 1960s, Canadian artist Michael Snow created a two-dimensional cut-out figure, Walking Woman, in his New York Studio. Snow then proceeded to install her in various places and positions in lower Manhattan, installations that—temporarily, at least—reformed urban space. He filmed and photographed these interventions, and they were exhibited in New York. Within a short time, the Coca Cola Company began to incorporate photographs of a model in the pose of Walking Woman into its advertising in magazines and billboards, transforming her neutral dress into a red swimsuit and placing a carton of Coke in each hand. Today, Snow's Walking Woman can be found in art museums around the world as sculpture, and in his films and photographs, while the ad campaign has long since faded away.

Canadian artist Ken Lum has appropriated billboards to art. His massive work There Is No Place Like Home (177 feet wide by 32 feet high) was installed on the Karlsplatz in Vienna in December 2000 and January 2001. This work confronted issues of identity and the meaning of "home" in the capital city of a country that was polarized around immigration. Kunsthalle Wien, a noncollecting contemporary art museum, provided the space and financing for the project, which was seen by tens of thousands of people walking and driving by.

Shimon Attie is an American artist who photographs his interventions in cities to explore the layers of memory contained in urban spaces. In Berlin, for example, he used photographs of pre–World War II Jewish life in the city and projected them onto the very spots where they had been arrested for deportation, bringing ghostly images of victims of the Holocaust back to the scene of the crime. Attie then rephotographed them.[4]

For his most recent project, displayed at the Museum of Photography in Chicago in June 2004, Attie projected fragments of historical photographs (circa 1890-1920) of Roman Jews onto Rome's ancient ruins, within a few feet of the site where the original photographs were taken. He then made large-format photographs of the intervention; these vividly record the near past, the ancient past, and present objects like street signs, cars, and new construction.

Museums play a role in these projects as patrons, collectors, and communicators. The communications theorist Derek De Kerkhove characterizes the museum as "a cultural accelerator" because it accelerates our awareness of technological and social change, both by collecting objects that demonstrate change and by helping us to understand change through museum interpretation. Like the artists who help us see the particularity of place, the museum is an outsider—part of global culture and yet apart from it.

Museums and the "museum impulse" are helping to revive many places that were destroyed by war, deindustrialization, and urban renewal. In central Johannesburg—which was abandoned by many people and businesses when it became a truly African city after the defeat of Apartheid—the Johannesburg Development Agency committed to a process of renewal that preserves the past. One of its most important projects is Constitution Hill.

Constitution Hill is the home for the country's Constitutional Court—a magnificent contemporary building where one of the world's most progressive constitutions is tested by opening court proceedings so they are accessible to all. This is also the site of Johannesburg's notorious Old Fort Prison Complex, which has towered over the inner city since 1899. Rather than clear away the three jails (one for white male prisoners, one for black male prisoners, and one segregated for black and white women prisoners), the Development Agency, city, and province decided to restore and interpret them, so that "what was once a place of injustice and brutality would become a place of solidarity and democracy." This formerly closed no-go area of the city is now opened up. When the mixed-use precinct is complete, people will be able to walk through Constitution Hill to pass from one neighborhood to another. There is a public square and places to relax and chat under the trees, as well as event and education spaces. Within two years, there will also be a hotel, apartment buildings, and shops. The three prisons will remain a huge historic presence on the site—interpreted by both exhibits and tour guides.

WHERE: Location in a Digital World

On March 21, 2004, International Human Rights Day, the country celebrated the opening of both the Constitutional Court and the former Section Four prison where black men were detained in horrifying conditions without trial. In his remarks, South African president Thabo Mbeki described this renewed precinct as "the transition of a negative colonial space to a positive, creative one."

We have been privileged to work with Ochre Communications of Johannesburg to realize and operate this space in this place. Ochre Communications assembled a team of South African curators, historians, writers, filmmakers, and visual artists to create the interpretive strategy and the exhibits. Ochre invited museum designer Ralph Appelbaum to provide his insight into the project. The Ochre team conducted interviews with former prisoners and warders. They facilitated workshops in which ex-prisoners returned to the prisons, where they remembered the spaces, the horrors that occurred, and reclaimed the dignity they had lost. The prisoners reenacted many aspects of their experiences, which were filmed and incorporated into the exhibits in the cells, so that people today can better understand the Apartheid system.

Having access to this space has been a healing process for many visitors. Among the five hundred people who attended on the first open day were people who live high up in the neighboring apartment towers. They had seen the prisoners in the yard without really knowing what was happening inside.

Other visitors had friends and relatives who had been imprisoned there without trial. Now this former prison is an open space and a questioning place, interrogating what the term "criminal" means in an oppressive, colonial society.

The transformation of negative space into positive, creative space is increasingly important today. It represents a revolt, of sorts, against the homogenizing side of globalization—people creating places and spaces for telling their stories, for exploring the past, and producing their futures.

Yet globalization can also ease travel, compress distance and time through digital communication, and facilitate artists, designers, curators, and museums to play a decisive role in the discovery, preservation, and communication of stories and material evidence. People become better able to construct their own futures because they have the opportunity to see things in a new way.

Reprinted with permission from Curator *48, no. 1 (January 2005).*

Figure 4.2.   Shimon Attie's art reflects the multiplicity of meanings of place and time inherent in the museum experience. *Photo courtesy of the artist and Jack Shainman Gallery, New York.*

Chapter 5
WHO
Museum Staff

Museums are inherently social institutions operated by people who are inspired and organized to work together to achieve and sustain the museum's vision, mission, mandate, goals, and objectives.

The traditional organization of museum staff, still found in some older museums, was led by curatorial departments determined by the academic disciplines represented within the collection. Each department might have not only its own curators but also its own conservators, preparators, and technicians. Such an approach resulted in the identification some years ago of as many as forty-five different systems of documentation in use at that time in a large museum—now entirely changed, of course.

The organization of museum staff today usually responds to a wider range of functions than the curatorial and relieves the curator of responsibility for many administrative and programming functions. In figure 5.1 you can see six core museological functions as two sides of a triangle, or as two divergent directions, held together by management. There are inherent stresses in this model, which museum leadership must strive to make a creative rather than a destructive tension.

Each of the two divergent directions within the museum would contradict the other.

The safety, preservation, and documentation of the collection could best be accomplished in a building that was closed to the public, with large areas kept in the dark for most of the time; whereas the display, study, enjoyment, and dissemination of information about the collection takes us in the opposite direction, toward maximizing public access in brightly lit open displays, including hands-on programs where possible.

It is the task of leadership to steer these two divergent aspects of the museum's functions toward a positive and stimulating intersection. The triangle of museum functions suggests the organization of staff into three divisions—one concerned with the museum's assets, another with its programs, and the third with its administration.

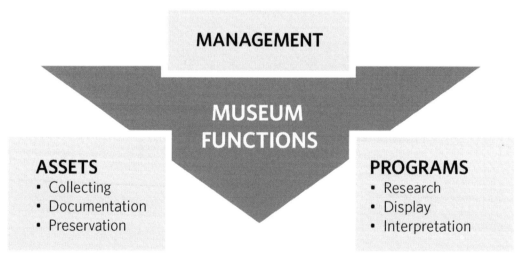

Figure 5.1. Triangle of Museum Functions. *Lord Cultural Resources.*

While the names of such divisions vary, this is the vocabulary commonly used:

- collections

- programs

- administration

Of course, there are other ways of organizing museum staff.

Some institutions group all the *content-related staff* together (collections, display, research, education, and programs), then *operations and administration personnel* (visitor services, retail, human resources, finance, information technology, and facilities), and cluster a third *external affairs* group (development, special events, communications, and marketing). The collection/programs/administration triangle of functions has the virtue of fitting all sizes of museums, from very small (where one to three people may be responsible for the three divisions) to very large institutions with many departments within each division.

This organization of museum functions into these three distinct "divisions" necessitates cross-divisional collaboration and team work throughout the museum because museum functions are interdependent. Limiting the "assets" division to collection management functions tends to relegate site and building operations and maintenance to the administrative division. Because the security division is concerned with site and building operation, it is often located there as well. This means that curators and conservators must rely on these administrative departments to control the environment and safety of their collections, and they need to establish ways of working effectively with administration. Conversely, security staff and building managers responsible for building systems need to collaborate closely with curators and conservators to maintain the conditions that the collections need. On the other hand, security staff generally have more contact with the public than curators and programmers—how can their experience be shared and enhanced?

Exhibitions are one of the principal activities or programs of most museums.[1] Several decades ago, they were almost exclusively developed and directed by curators. Exhibitions require significant participation by curators, researchers, content developers, registrars, and conservators from the collections division. Placing them in a public programs division has sometimes resulted in the creation of such anomalous positions as "curator of exhibitions," or exhibition departments where exhibition planners and designers work together but curators in the collections department are marginalized. The administrative division is also concerned with exhibition development, ranging from security implications through cost controls to sponsorship and the provision of retail stock specific to the exhibition in the museum shop. Educational and publications programs similarly require curatorial input and administrative controls. Multidepartmental collaboration for specific exhibitions, publications, technology, and public programs is needed to get the museum's work done.

There is no one "ideal" form of museum organization. It is the responsibility of the museum director/CEO working with the management team to develop the form of

> There is no one "ideal" form of museum organization.

museum organization that will be most effective in achieving the museum's vision, mission, and goals given its governance, financial realities, strategic plan, the museum's culture, organization,

Museums are cultural institutions that specialize in cultural content, have a complex culture of work, and are currently in dynamic change, including organizational change.

and its environment. In making organizational change, museum leadership and management must be cognizant of the impact on staff. The human resources department can be very helpful, as can specialist museum planners and change management consultants with museum experience. Museums are cultural institutions that specialize in cultural content, have a complex culture of work, and are currently in dynamic change, including organizational change.

5.1 Teamwork

Enabling staff to work together across departments and divisions to achieve museum functions is pervasive and significant enough to make teamwork a major theme of this chapter and this book.

Teamwork is especially challenging for museums because the staff represents an extraordinary diversity of specializations and qualifications: such as those with PhDs in various academic disciplines, writers who may come from the advertising and entertainment sectors, educators who have worked mainly with children, fund-raisers and government relations experts who are very corporate in style, accountants, building managers, and groundskeepers.

Some staff join museums because they love the past; others, because they want to change the future.

Some staff join museums because they love the past; others, because they want to change the future. Now add to that mix a culture that had been steeped in privilege, because historically many museum staff were those who could afford to work as volunteers or for minimal pay.

The professionalization of museums is less than one hundred years old. Now consider the social class boundaries of museums located in communities, open to the public but not really programmed *for* those communities. Instead their privileged staff leadership of decades past sees their audience as people similar to themselves—experts, collectors, and amateurs (in the best sense of the word), and tolerating, perhaps, educating the general public.

Consider too the racial bias and ethnocentrism that may persist in museums that hold collections that may have been stolen and looted through colonialism or that ignore collections owned by people who are not part of historic elites. Success in overcoming these historical realities and achieving museums' contemporary mission, vision, and goals depends both on staff teamwork and museum organization. Building a culture of belonging is therefore especially challenging for museums as Lisa Biagas explains.

Building a Culture of Belonging

By Dr. Lisa R. Biagas

In the United States and across the globe, 2020's social and racial unrest was a stark reminder of the purpose of arts and cultural institutions, specifically museums.

The COVID-19 pandemic, coupled with the dramatic racial injustices over the past few years—the murder of George Floyd, the rise in Asian hate crimes, and the attacks on places of worship—dramatically changed employee expectations of their workplaces and their fellow employees. The traumas and challenges outside the workplace caused some workers to rethink their employers' responses to these defining moments. Some wondered if museums are places for critical dialogue about histories and artistic and cultural preservation. Have they lived up to their ideals of connection and community? Organizational responses varied, but there has been an increase in museums looking for chief diversity officers to focus on initiatives regarding diversity, equity, access, and inclusion (DEAI) at their institutions.

What Is DEAI?

Diversity is the concept of acceptance and respect for individuals' unique differences. These differences can include multiple dimensions, such as ethnicity, gender, gender expression, sexual orientation, socioeconomic, age, beliefs, and lived experience. Achieving diversity entails assessing and questioning the makeup of an organization to ensure that multiple perspectives are represented.

Equity means crafting policies for the fair and consistent treatment of all individuals. It requires deliberate attention to removing implicit bias in recruitment, hiring, compensation, promotion, and retention practices.

Inclusion refers to the intentional, ongoing effort to ensure that all voices are heard and that all employees can be involved.

Accessibility gives everyone equitable access along the continuum of human ability and experience.

The Building Blocks to Belonging

The heart of DEAI goals is to foster belonging. The sense of belonging is an accumulation of everyday experiences that enables a person to feel psychologically safe to bring their whole, unique self to work. For BIPOC (Black, Indigenous, and People of Color) employees, belonging is not representation and goes beyond inclusion. It is the intrinsic human need to

> Belonging maximizes the organization's DEAI initiatives such that individuals are fully engaged, feel appreciated for their uniqueness, and secure that their contributions are valued.

feel welcome. Belonging maximizes the organization's DEAI initiatives such that individuals are fully engaged, feel appreciated for their uniqueness, and secure that their contributions are valued.

Each workplace is different, but there are a few key elements to building belonging.

- **Commitment and Strategy**

    A strategic plan with goals and objectives linked to diversity signals the importance to the organization. Strong and highly visible support from top management and board leadership with a written statement of commitment is vital. Rather than diversity goals being a different strategy or tactic, DEAI is embedded in all strategies, so there is a shared responsibility across the organization cascaded down through every employee and management level.

- **Diversity Advocate and Committee**

    The hire of a diversity advocate in the role of chief diversity officer or embedded in the role of chief people officer serving on the senior management sets the tone. This role prioritizes the organization's core values and designs the institutional DEAI programming.

    The creation of an employee committee focused on DEAI, which is responsible for helping to drive cultural change and inform policies and practices. Caution: Employers should be cognizant of the emotional toll on BIPOC employees who may be experiencing racial harm at work or home. It is not their sole responsibility to lead the charge. Allyship from persons who are not members of an underrepresented group helps alleviate the burden on BIPOC employees and helps to advance change.

- **Diversity Training**

    Diversity training increases participants' cultural competence—awareness, knowledge, and communication. Workshops should be customized for supervisors and managers responsible for setting the tone with their teams and supporting their employees. The training can help reduce and/or eliminate many barriers to workplace relationships, interactions, teamwork, and cohesion, such as *unconscious bias (also known as implicit bias)*. One way that unconscious biases can manifest is through microaggressions: subtle verbal or nonverbal insults or denigrating messages communicated toward a marginalized person, often by someone who may be well intentioned but unaware of the impact their words or actions have on the target. Microaggressions can be based on any aspect of a marginalized person's identity (for example, sexuality, religion, or gender).

- **Employee Resource Groups**

    Employee resource groups and affinity groups are community-building opportunities that bring coworkers together who have something in common. They come together and can share their experiences and recognize that they are not alone. This sharing helps to create a sense that there is emotional support from the organization because there is a connection to other employees like oneself, and one is not isolated or alone. Support from management for infrastructure and resources like a small budget is helpful to these types of groups. In addition, mentoring, scholarships, or other programs encourage greater access and participation for underrepresented employees.

- **Diversity Audit**

  A diversity audit examines the DEAI conditions of a workforce, which includes an unbiased review of its policies, procedures, and practices. Also, it can include a climate survey to study the employees' perceptions and perspectives on how it feels to work at an organization. A climate study can serve as a benchmark to measure institutional change over time.

The shift in focus from DEAI to belonging reflects the rapid societal changes over the past few years. It is not enough to craft culturally respectful policies and nurture a climate of inclusion if an organization treats these inflection points in society as "business as usual." Instead of fostering belonging, a museum's silence and inaction may indicate that they condone and tolerate hate and injustice or that the organizational values and diversity commitment statement are hollow and performative.

> The shift in focus from DEAI to belonging reflects the rapid societal changes over the past few years.

Today's workplace requires hard work on the DEAI initiatives and the courage to acknowledge that there is still work to combat racial and economic inequalities. After all, are not museums the perfect place to dialogue about our cultures and histories and their impact on society?

> After all, are not museums the perfect place to dialogue about our cultures and histories and their impact on society?

Figure 5.2.   Still life drawing class 2016. *Courtesy of the Pennsylvania Academy of the Fine Arts Philadelphia.*

5.2 Organizational Strategies

The following alternative organizational strategies highlight different methods museum management might use to overcome compartmentalization and facilitate teamwork among museum staff:

- Hierarchical pyramid

- Matrix organization

- Task forces

These models are by no means mutually exclusive and may be used in combination as needed to fulfill the museum's projects and plans. The organization chart may be constructed as a hierarchical pyramid, with matrix organization and/or task forces being introduced for specific functions or projects.

Hierarchical Pyramid

The *hierarchical pyramid* is the form of organization found in most museums around the world. Some might see this as a vestige of colonialism, others would see it as corporate, and still others appreciate the clarity of the structure and particularly stress the importance of the director/CEO being a museum professional. At a time when museums are increasingly sharing authority in an ecosystem model, it is perhaps the style of leadership as facilitation (discussed in chapter 1) rather than the organizational structure that needs to be stressed.

In a small museum, one or two persons may perform all functions. If only three or four can be hired, these functions must be distributed among them. In a larger, multidisciplinary museum, each division will have its own departments arranged to continue the hierarchy.

A fourth division, often called something like "external relations," is needed when the museum is engaged in civil society and large enough to sustain both the staff and the fourth major report to the director. Its responsibilities usually include:

- communications, information technology, the museum's website, and marketing (discussed in chapter 4);

- government relations, fund-raising, and membership (see chapter 7); and

- partnerships within the local, national, and international museum ecosystem (see chapter 3).

This fourth division in larger institutions reflects the more outward-looking civil society institutions that many museums have become, as well as their increasing dependence on multiple sources of funding, public, private, and philanthropic.

Here again, however, collections and public program divisions are also leaders in public engagement, so interdepartmental collaboration is essential.

Matrix Organization

A matrix is a format in which functions are arranged as axes of interaction.

Because administration serves the other two divisions, one application of *matrix organization* to museum management could be expressed in the matrix with the provision of administrative services indicated by the intersection of each administrative function with the other two divisions.

Another application of matrix organization to museum staff is the correlation of public programs and collection management staff. In the matrix organizations, curators, conservators, and the registrar are all involved with exhibitions, whereas only the curators normally have a continuing role in education and publications.

Combining the two matrices would give the image of a cube, with all three divisions shown as three interacting axes. The successful interaction of all three sides of the cube provides for an effective and efficient combination of the operational staff of a museum.

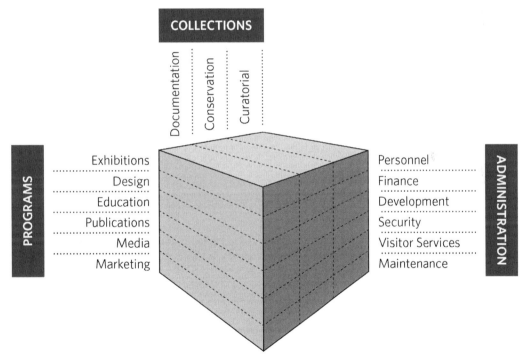

Figure 5.3.   Matrix of Museum Organization. *Lord Cultural Resources.*

Standing Committees and Task Forces

As the preceding section indicates, many museum activities, including such important ones as exhibition development, require the cooperation of departments from all divisions.

Interdepartmental cooperation can best be achieved by combining representatives of each department in *task forces* dedicated to particular time-limited projects, as well as *standing committees* for general functions that are not time limited.

Diversity, equity, and inclusion will be an interdisciplinary standing committee as this is an ongoing process that requires the attention and commitment of the entire museum staff. Some museums establish a department dedicated to DEAI or truth and reconciliation. Other museums establish both a department and a standing committee. All committees need to have terms of reference approved by the museum director that includes the goal, objectives composition, time frame, decision-making process, budget, and recording and reporting of decisions.

Exhibitions require both a standing committee to develop the ongoing exhibition program and exhibition task forces for specific exhibitions. The standing *exhibition committee* may meet quarterly, with participation from all departments, coordinating all concerned to the upcoming schedule, which will affect everyone, including maintenance, retail, security, and finance as well as the more obviously involved departments.

In addition to this standing committee there is a need for a specific *exhibition task force* for each major exhibition. This task force should combine the talents of all those responsible for the many aspects of the exhibition project,[2] such as:

Collection and content management

- Curatorial

- Research

- Conservation

- Documentation

Public programs

- Exhibitions

- Design

- Learning

- Publications

- Media

DEAI and truth and reconciliation

Administration

- Finance

- Human resources

- Development

- Building operations

Marketing

- Communications

- Security

- Visitor services

Each department should be asked to nominate its representative, deciding what skills are needed. Task forces present great opportunities for junior staff to participate so long as they are supported by experienced colleagues. Contracted participants—such as an exhibition designer engaged for that particular exhibition—should also be named to the task force.

The museum director should have final approval on the composition of the task force and should appoint the chairperson from among its members. Although the relevant curator might be the obvious nominee to chair many exhibition groups, the chair should reflect the objective of the project and the skills required.

Step one is to establish the *terms of reference for the task force* and its procedures.

The committee may begin meeting monthly, should have regular reports from all participants—so that security, for example, is not left to the last minute—and should increase the frequency of its meetings as opening day nears. Crediting the members of the committee on exhibition literature or signage is an excellent way to inspire dedication to an outstanding result.

Similar combinations of standing committees and specific task forces may be developed for projects in documentation, education, information technology, visitor services, and audience development. The standing committee on operations needs to meet weekly to review issues and match calendars, while the communications group should meet monthly to review marketing plans and changes needed in the museum's website.

The standing committee and task force system is a most useful way for museums to address their complex tasks, ensure that their professional expertise is well deployed, and provide opportunities for growth in individual staff members' responsibility and confidence.

Successful museum managers at all levels—from director to department heads—understand that in addition to staff members' professional qualifications and experience there is another key criterion for their success: the ability to work with others.

Good teamwork involves kindness, respect, inclusion, promising only what can be delivered, and meeting deadlines so that everyone can proceed with their part of the work.

Good teamwork involves kindness, respect, inclusion, promising only what can be delivered, and meeting deadlines so that everyone can proceed with their part of the work.

Teamwork can be learned but must first be consciously identified and understood as an essential feature of the working life of a museum professional. Teamwork requires good leaders, but it also requires responsible followers, willing to express differences of opinion, but dedicated to achieving the shared goal. Good museum managers find ways to recognize and reward effective teamwork.

5.3 Working Conditions

Once upon a time, some of the senior people who worked in museums were amateurs in the best sense of the word, and in some cases not even requiring payment for their work. Over the past century, museum staff have struggled to be recognized as a profession with commensurate working conditions and remuneration.

While in many parts of the world where museum employees have made significant advances in both pay and conditions of work, progress has been uneven. Many people who preserve and interpret the world's cultural and artistic heritage are still unable to earn more than a marginal wage, and they struggle with poor working conditions.

On the other hand, museum employees in many countries today are often graduates of museum training programs, sometimes with postgraduate degrees in addition to their original disciplines in the sciences, archaeology, history, or art history.

Conservators, registrars, and others are highly specialized experts in their fields. Directors and other administrators in some cases are accomplished museologists, and in others they have been attracted from the private sector as well as from senior academic positions.

Courses are available to assist curators to become museum directors. Museum associations, private foundations, and government agencies offer in-service training seminars and conferences so that museum professionals can keep abreast of current developments in all disciplines and management philosophies.

Online learning is a major tool of professional development that is only beginning to be fully exploited. Levels of compensation, at least in some of the larger institutions, are commensurate with the advancing levels of professionalism.

No matter how financially constrained the museum may be, it should recognize the value of its staff by adopting a *human resources policy* that addresses, within the museum's means, such issues as

- statutory regulations;

- salary;

- benefits;

- expense provisions;

- probationary period;

- hours of work and overtime;

- statutory holidays, vacation, sick leave, maternity or paternity leave, and leave of absence;

- training and professional development;

- support for racialized staff;

- intellectual property provisions;

- grievance and harassment procedures;

- performance reviews; and

- termination conditions.

Contracting (sometimes referred to as "contracting out") is often urged as an alternative to permanent employment by the museum.

This has worked well when it comes to functions such as catering, and some museums have used it successfully for retail, cleaning, maintenance, and security. However, the museum's concern for long-term preservation of its collection and for dependable security mean that there are limits to this approach.

Difficulties arise especially if the museum must subscribe to a government, university, or corporation policy to select the low bidder on every contract. The low bidder for a security contract may be the most dangerous for a museum! Low-bid security contracts often result in poorly paid, ill-trained, and indifferently motivated guards—with potentially disastrous consequences for the collection and a negative effect on visitors as well.

5.4 Diversity, Equity, Inclusion, Access, and Belonging

A very large part of the world today consists of multicultural and multiracial societies. This presents a great opportunity for many museums, which could benefit from a diversity of backgrounds and viewpoints among their personnel.

Yet many museums in these societies fall far short of reflecting this diversity on their boards, among their staff, and, not surprisingly, therefore, among their visitors as well. The need for *inclusion* of genders and socioeconomic, cultural, and racial groups is a responsibility of museums and other civic institutions, and it also offers an exciting potential for their growth in audience, research, and understanding of the collections and content.

A concerted effort is needed to provide for a diversity among museum employees that reflects the diversity of the museum's communities. Policies should be developed to encourage employment opportunities for visible cultural or linguistic minorities and to ensure promotion opportunities for all throughout the organization.

The goal should be to increase the number of visitors and to invigorate the creativity of the museums with the many perspectives and experiences that diversity brings. Experience has shown that this does not happen without the commitment of the board, CEO/director, and senior management vigorously encouraging diversity and inclusion at all levels.

> Museums that preserve and display the culture of living societies must be particularly concerned to include members of the descendant communities among their staff.

Museums that preserve and display the culture of living societies must be particularly concerned to include members of the descendant communities among their staff. This may require special training programs aimed at enhancing the opportunities for members of those communities to acquire professional or technical skills to complement their lived experience.

In South Africa over the past two decades there has been a particular challenge to develop such training programs for people who have only recently had the opportunity to take charge of the preservation and interpretation of their own culture. Elsewhere there is a pressing need for recruitment and training of local or national citizens in places where expatriates have been managing museums and other cultural institutions.

5.5 Working from Home

The COVID era propelled the world into a state of massive change, and this change included fundamental shifts in museum work and culture, with most museums having to close instantly, with almost no preparation, sending staff home to self-isolate.

During the COVID lockdowns of 2020, as most people from any profession were confined for weeks, or months, to their homes, many experienced something new: time to think, and in ways they never had before.

This profound psychological process led to large numbers of employees contemplating questions and issues related to the implications of structures of authority, both in their personal and professional spheres.

For museum employees, many profound questions arose, such as: Who sits on the board or is the executive of a museum? What is the discrepancy between management/leadership salaries and their own salaries? Who decides the scope and focus of exhibitions and which voices will tell those stories?

These concerns led other museum staff to conclude that regardless of salary discrepancies or power imbalances, their professional careers result in working with content and collections that they love and want to protect.

The professional and personal lives of millions of people changed during the COVID era, with "big questions" moving to the forefront.

At the same time, many museum employees were furloughed or lost their jobs permanently. Data is still being collected and analyzed about the long-terms effects of these job disruptions and losses on the museum sector. The American Alliance of Museums (AAM) was diligent in publishing information and analysis through its surveys of museums, during COVID and postpandemic.

One such survey reported that half of museums had reduced their staff by about 30 percent, while over 40 percent had lost income.[3] In 2021, UNESCO released its report on international museums and indicated a 70 percent drop in attendance and a 40 to 60 percent decline in revenue when compared to prepandemic numbers in 2019.[4]

Mental health was also an urgent issue for many employees, according to the AAM research. This shouldn't be surprising considering that most employees had to adapt to working from home for an extended time period, which included the comforts of this special arrangement, as well as how the work-from-home model impacted creativity, team morale, workflow, and mental health—especially for those who lived alone.

Postpandemic, the shift to a strong recovery for museums in the global north was underway, with significant assistance from government.

Diversity also became a leading priority at many museums emerging from the COVID era. George Floyd's murder in May 2020 brought the issue of antiblack racism to the forefront of the global media, and the Black Lives Matter movement shook the world even as the pandemic raged. In Canada, questions related to historical crimes against Indigenous peoples and the continuing power imbalance of those Indigenous communities within the larger national political arena took center stage in that country's psyche—in the wake of the Truth and Reconciliation report.[5] These issues were amplified with the horrific discovery of children's bodies buried on the grounds of historical residential schools in locations across Canada. These events completely changed the national discussion and debate.

At the other end of the spectrum, digital transformations, along with the embrace of new technologies, were used to connect museums to communities and ecosystems near and far.

Technological advances allowed for remote museum employees to work more efficiently as a team during COVID, but as museums reopened and called workers back to those shared physical offices, it is still unclear what the long-term impact of this prolonged work-from-home arrangement will be. At the moment, a hybrid model seems to be emerging, with some employees able to negotiate working from home for a portion of the week, while still maintaining partial "office" hours to directly interact in person with their peers and the museum community. Others, such as security guards and cleaners, do not have that choice. Questions of equity and social class remain.

The "hybrid" model is also being applied to the concept of brick-and-mortar institutions and their digital evolution. Many museums have created digital platforms for their collections and exhibitions to parallel their physical displays and services. This book devotes the entirety of chapter 4, written by digital expert Ali Hossaini, to the convergence of physical and digital museum realms.

5.6 Training and Professional Development

Training programs instruct employees in how to do their job, whereas *employee development programs* open up new opportunities for staff. Both may be mounted in-house, or may be provided by sponsoring (partially or fully) employee participation in courses elsewhere and online. These may be museum training programs from the introductory to the postgraduate level or courses in a wide variety of professional pursuits—technical or management skills that may be useful to museum staff members at all posts. Mentorship can be a very valuable form of training and development. Often it is helpful for staff members to have mentors outside the museum because they may be better able to discuss solutions to challenges in confidence.

Instituting a *training and development strategy* for staff has always been important, but it has become essential as museums meet the challenge of constant change, ranging from museum philosophy through technology to public expectations, diversity, and marketing requirements.

An important requirement of professional museum management is therefore to provide an "always be learning environment" that establishes general policies of support and can be related to the specific needs of each individual, from the director to the maintenance staff. The strategy, updated annually, should identify the training needs of the museum, including provision for planned changes in direction as well as the personal development plans of each individual, agreed in a consultative (and confidential) process of mutual identification of needs and resources. It is important for those responsible for human resources to ensure that there is an adequate budget for training and professional development and that personal development plans meet the institution's priorities as well as the career goals of the individual employees. Implementing such a strategy provides an outstanding opportunity to fulfill diversity policies.

One group that can benefit personally and professionally from a training and development strategy is the largest single sector of most museum staff: security guards. These very numerous employees are also very often the ones who have the most frequent and prolonged contact with visitors; it is therefore most important that museums ensure that they understand what they are guarding, as well as how to guard it, and that they see a future career for themselves within the institution.

Succession Planning—Diversity, Equity, Accessibility, and Inclusion (DEAI)

By Karen Carter

Planning for leadership change is never easy. In this time of heightened awareness around the need for more representation of diverse cultural communities on the leadership teams of museums, one would think this extra layer of thinking about succession planning should be front of mind. Following the murder of George Floyd many institutions added or ramped up their diversity, equity, accessibility, and inclusion (DEAI) policies. This case study provides some thinking about ways to better connect DEAI policies with some practical actions to help diversify leadership teams in your organization.

Hiring racialized staff at the entry or middle management levels is the easiest way for many organizations to show they are starting to do DEAI work. However, one key strategy is training staff with the goal of promoting them, in order to develop leadership positions across the museum over time.

This model is well established in the private sector and among many public sector service agencies—which set five- to ten-year strategic goals to fill staffing and representation gaps throughout organizations. Often these goals are aligned with budgets for training to boost expansion or other business outcomes. Investments in human resource development, though, are ever more important for talent recruitment and talent retention.

Mentorship is also a key means for museums and cultural organizations to ensure that leadership opportunities are passed on to the next generation. It is often thought that this approach is not viable due to budget limitations. I would argue that it is a matter of mindset because effective mentorship and training can be more cost effective—and less risky—than continuously hiring new leaders to achieve DEAI.

In their recent article Charlie Wall-Andrews and Owais Lightwala revealed that when Canada's largest cultural institutions are examined through the lens of gender and racial diversity at executive leadership positions, the findings are simply depressing. Their study found 94.3 percent of chief executives are white. They went on to highlight that the 2021 census indicates that 31.5 percent of Canadians identify as Indigenous, black, or racialized. Their article rightly asked: "How can you serve a public that you don't speak for?"[6]

I recently had the occasion to attend a meeting with the CEO of an organization that was interested in participating in our pilot BIPOC fellowship project. The BIPOC fellowship was established to help support BIPOC professionals to be successful in cultural leadership positions.

At the meeting, the CEO of the arts organization explained that they wanted to diversify their organization, and also noted that their staff included leadership team individuals who they suspected might be looking to leave or retire, but that the organization did not have a work culture that included succession planning. It was therefore missing out on the opportunity for training racialized mid-career or junior managers to grow into these soon-to-be-vacated leadership roles.

I suggested that the CEO speak to their leadership team about the need to diversify to better reflect society today and to ask team members confidentially if they would support the long-term legacy of the organization's growth by mentoring a BIPOC manager to replace them when they retire or leave. This way a potential retirement could become an opportunity to give back to the organization.

I did not go so far as mentioning the opportunity for this to become an internal mentorship program that would encourage mentors to develop their own leadership skills while supporting a colleague who would then be able to do the same for an emerging leader down the road.

This exchange led me to consider the need for a campaign to encourage the implementation of succession planning across the museum sector. An opportunity for expanding the work of BIPOC fellowship. It seems ironic that the museum sector—with its core external educational programs on offer—seems unable to support and implement such internal educational and professional development strategies.

In the private sector the motivation is the bottom line and shareholders returns. In the arts and cultural sectors, the bottom line is connected to our ability to remain relevant. Unfortunately, we are only beginning to see widespread tangible financial consequences to improve diversity of leadership from private and public sector funders.

Canada is on track to be populated by 40 percent Indigenous, black, and other racialized people by 2036. These numbers should also provide motivation. The ability to remain relevant in changing times is an important consideration as organizations contemplate their futures.

If you have successfully recruited talented, diverse people to your organization, you should have a plan for investing in them. If they are interested in staying with you for a long time to work with the museum to do better, the museum will have greater capacity to fulfill its mission, vision, and mandate—and everyone wins.

Figure 5.4. BAND Gallery and Cultural Centre Team's trip to Africville Museum in Halifax. *Image courtesy of Karen Carter.*

Performance Reviews

Performance reviews of all staff should be directed toward evaluation of both effectiveness and efficiency in the employee's accomplishment of museum functions in relation to the museum's strategic goals and departmental objectives. The priority and weight given to various factors should be adjusted annually according to current priorities. The employee should do a self-evaluation as part of the performance review, and all review records should be held in confidence.

The review should include both quantitative ratings and qualitative comments, and it should be linked to consideration of promotion and annual salary increments. The review should be done in consultation with the employee's immediate supervisor. The file on previous reviews, especially that of the previous year, should be reread by employee and supervisors participating in the review before each year's consultation.

The Role of Unions

Unions as a sector may be experiencing declining enrollment in the twenty-first century and are certainly looking for sectors where there is an opportunity for organization—and it turns out that the museum sector is ripe for unionization and collective bargaining, specifically because most museums have not advanced their compensation and safety practices at the rate of the private sector, and these areas are the expertise of unions and of concern to many workers at these cultural institutions.

In fact, in the United States, during COVID and postpandemic, there was a surge in unionization and worker organization at museums, including the Philadelphia Museum of Art, Boston's Museum of Fine Arts, the Whitney Museum of American Art, the Guggenheim, the Art Institute of Chicago, and the Museum of Contemporary Art in Los Angeles, according to a 2022 report from the *New York Times*.[7]

Podcasts dedicated to this bourgeoning sector have been created to support the energy of this new chapter of the cultural worker movement. And while the rise in museum unions is trending sharply upward, it is in deep contrast to the decline in national membership rates—from 50 percent of American workers in the 1950s to about 10 percent of the workforce in 2022.[8]

One major issue driving the museum momentum toward unionization is the growing gap between employee and CEO salaries, as well as the deep cuts that occurred during the pandemic—causing so many employees to wonder, "Am I next?"

In the realistic context of museums as (too often) relatively low-paid employment centers where professional development opportunities compensate somewhat for the low level of remuneration, *trade unions* may be seen as supportive forces in the workplace. In general, their pressure for higher pay can only benefit the profession, and they can be a powerful force for employment equity and improved training and development opportunities. Even where remuneration is appropriate to the professional qualifications of senior and middle management, there is often a need for such a force to upgrade the lower-level employees.

Unfortunately, trade unions are too often confined to the security staff, where confrontational policies on both sides can lead to the imposition of civil service or equivalent procedures that can result in inefficient operations. One government line department museum in Europe, for example, had to contend with extended lunch hours and breaks that necessitated doubling the number of guards required for its operation—a requirement that resulted in the regular closure of galleries to visitors.

Another difficulty often encountered, both for the museums and their unions, is the proliferation of multiple unions within one institution. The necessity to conclude separate collective bargaining agreements with several unions, often on different schedules, can challenge even the most dedicated human resources department—not to mention the complexities of multiple *grievance procedures*. If the union certification legislation in the museum's jurisdiction provides for separate unionization for guards, clerks, and technicians, for example, the museum may wish to encourage cooperation both among and with its unions to minimize the potentially harmful effects of more or less perpetual negotiations through coordination of agreement schedules and grievance procedures.

Unionized or not, museum personnel are sometimes concerned with the role of volunteers if these museum supporters appear to be supplanting staff positions in whole or in part. It is important to ensure that volunteer recruitment is aimed at tasks that are additional to those that the paid workforce can undertake. For instance, if the education department is mandated to train volunteer docents, interaction between the professional trainers and the volunteers should not be a problem, but if the volunteers are replacing former paid educators, there will almost certainly be strife.

Why Is Labor Organizing Growing in the Museum Sector?

By Gwendolyn Perry Davis

The recent news around labor issues in museums has been frequent and sometimes distressing. Job security, wages, health care, and other benefits are foremost in the decision criteria for new and established cultural workers. The concerns of museums workers in the twenty-first century are remarkably similar to those that unions have addressed on behalf of workers since the early 1800s.

In fact, as cultural workers, it is important to remind ourselves that organizing is not new to our sector either. In 1971, workers at the Museum of Modern Art in New York City organized into what is now MoMa Local 2110. Other museums have sought to address the perceived disparity in wages—and those who have had the opportunity to access those wages—for the past thirty years.

However, the collision of two important social events—the global pandemic that began in 2019 and 2020's clarion call for social justice—has led to the resurgence of organizing activity within museums. In hindsight, it is reasonable that the uncertainty of the past three years led workers to seek the resources to meet the basic needs for themselves and their families.

I spent my childhood in a union household. My father, a black man escaping the Jim Crow South and the back-breaking work of cotton picking, arrived in Chicago looking for safe and secure employment. He found it as a member of the union representing bus drivers and mechanics at the Chicago Transit Authority. If he was injured, our family would continue to receive some income. Our family also had access to basic medical and dental care that had never been available to my parents in their formative years. It was the individual desire for a better life and the ubiquity of union representation in government and quasi-government sectors that made this an easy choice for many families.

As I reflect on that experience and the requests of today's arts museum workers, I think frequently about the differences. Today,

- the current generation of museum workers is interested in the growth of the whole rather than the single individual. The educational model that many of these workers experienced were values of collaboration and participation. They are willing to collectively act to affect change, as we saw when they mobilized in the wake of the 2020 murder of George Floyd in Minneapolis, Minnesota.

- blue-collar workers like my father have left the workforce, having achieved a level of retirement security. Workers entering today's job market are able to choose between many more types of work, including desk jobs not typically represented by unions. As a result, the unions that have historically supported blue-collar jobs are experiencing declining membership.

- museums, for myriad structural reasons, have not substantively advanced issues of transparent compensation and safety practices at the pace of other industries.

Museum leadership has a responsibility to respond to staff concerns. The mission of contemporary art museums, in particular, is to support artists—especially living artists—and showcase creative practices that often confront the issues of our time. To achieve that mission fully, we must engage with the related concerns of the staff who make this work possible. I believe this looks like:

- Museum leadership thinking critically with its boards about governance issues. To ensure the integrity of the nonprofit sector (of which museums are part), the United States has laws that require that boards self-govern and appoint members to ensure the best interests of the museum are met. Museum staff work collaboratively with our board partners but are limited in their ability to change board membership. For many readers, this might be a surprise.

- Bringing creativity and innovation to museum-funding mechanisms. Many museums depend on financial support from their boards and other donors. I have often participated in conversations that suggest that museums must simply ask more people of color to support museums. This is a false equivalency that places undue burden on people of color. The wealth disparity between white and black Americans, for example, is so significant than it won't be resolved for decades, if ever.

- Become responsible for addressing issues of wage transparency and wage growth. I hear arts workers asking museum leadership to reduce the opacity around wage decisions, provide greater opportunities to grow into higher-paying museum positions, and offer employees more agency in planning their careers.

No museum is achieving these changes at the speed that our workers are requesting, but their smart and steady pressure is an important accountability tool. At the Museum of Contemporary Art Chicago (MCA), where I work, my team and I are committed to being accountable to our workers.

- In collaboration with our board, we have taken on more financial risk to ensure that our workers are paid in accordance with a transparent compensation philosophy that benchmarks salaries against similar positions in both the nonprofit and for-profit sectors (when possible) in similar-sized budget organizations in Chicago. The outcome is that we prioritize staff wages and benefits first when building our institutional budget. We have committed to an annual external review of all of our positions, not just a representative sample.

- We are committed to communicating with our staff about the issues that are important to them—such as wages, safety, and institutional decision making. We have reduced opacity around promotions by sharing criteria with all staff, not just managers. We post salary ranges on all open positions because, often, the best candidate is in-house. We share our compensation philosophy and model with all staff. We report on our institutional budget at quarterly staff meetings. We ensure that our budget, which is created in service of our three hundred thousand average annual visitors, is accessible. We address safety concerns proactively, whenever possible, and respond quickly to issues that our workers raise.

- We ensure that tasks and responsibilities align with staff job descriptions so that wages remain fair. If tasks and responsibilities increase temporarily, as they often do in a vibrant contemporary museum, we ensure that staff are compensated for additional work.

- We codesign training opportunities with our staff. We have a dedicated position—the associate director of employee engagement and training—that addresses employee growth.

- We host regular Discovery Forums, where museum leaders and staff gather in conversation around key institutional issues. We record these sessions for staff, creating a library of content that demonstrates our commitment to and accountability for reducing the information gap between board, leadership, and staff.

We are designing these actions to be sustainable and replicable, and I encourage other museum colleagues to join me. We can rethink and redesign legacy systems in support of a future workforce that will change the world.

Figure 5.5.   Redesigning legacy systems results in a more vibrant museum for staff and visitors alike.
Photo by T. McDonald Photography and image courtesy of Museum of Contemporary Art, Chicago.

5.7 Volunteers

Volunteers are vital to the life of many museums, especially those operated by nonprofit or charitable organizations. Some museum workers believe that volunteers are not cost-effective because they require too much staff time for training and evaluation. This can be the case if the volunteer program is not well organized and controlled. If properly constituted, however, a volunteer work force can simultaneously link the museum to its community and provide invaluable support to the museum.

Museums are at the heart of learning societies—all the more so as young people have to demonstrate experience to get their first job and as older people remain healthier longer. People of all ages are likely to have had multiple work experiences and may bring knowledge acquired in several different countries to the museum. Cultural institutions are best placed to leverage the talents of these accomplished individuals at all levels, but to do so they must put in place a well-conceived volunteer program. Although in smaller institutions a part-time volunteer coordinator may be sufficient to manage such a program, a full-time paid position is required for even medium-size museums to take sufficient advantage of this opportunity.

Operating a Volunteer Program

Museums in the startup stage of development are frequently governed by volunteers (the board), managed by a volunteer director, and operated by volunteers. This is a particularly challenging situation in which there are distinct roles and a hierarchy, but all are equally unpaid. It becomes even more challenging when the museum begins to raise enough funds to hire paid professional staff. In all stages of museum development and in all sizes of museums, it is important to be aware of the distinct roles and responsibilities of volunteers:

- Board members are volunteers who are engaged in governance.

- A volunteer director is engaged in management.

- Task volunteers are engaged in unpaid staff positions.

This section is concerned with this latter category of volunteers, who make important contributions to museums, including

- *information staff*, the most commonly encountered volunteer role (sometimes referred to by the word "docent") enabling the museum to provide guided tours to school parties and other groups, and providing information at the front desk and in galleries;

- *hosts*, from welcoming guests at reception areas and providing support at events;

- *retail sales*, making feasible museum shops that would otherwise not contribute significantly to museum revenue in smaller institutions;

- *research assistants*, undertaking systematic research tasks for which time would otherwise not be available;

- *library assistants*, undertaking time-consuming sorting and shelving in the museum library;

- *data entry assistants*, supporting the registrar with the conversion of manual to automated catalog entries; and

- *restoration technicians*, often enthusiastically at work in transportation museums, but requiring careful professional supervision.

Museums that utilize volunteers in these or other roles should address them as workers who are paid not with wages but with other rewards—of *personal and professional development* and of *social recognition*. The organization of volunteers must ensure that these rewards are attainable and relevant.

The first reward, *personal and professional development*, indicates that volunteers should be part of the museum's training and development strategy. A *volunteer coordinator* is essential. The volunteer coordinator (who may be paid or voluntary) should maintain a roster on which the training needs and development aspirations of each volunteer are recorded, and the museum should undertake to assist the volunteer in accessing this development—not financially but through providing training opportunities.

The second reward, *social recognition*, should be provided by the museum both on an ongoing day-to-day basis and in annual or seasonal social occasions that the senior staff and board members of the institution attend in order to present certificates or similar printed recognition of services rendered to the volunteers. The museum that understands the importance of volunteers will ensure that its senior staff and board members participate fully in such a recognition meeting and that virtually all volunteers are recognized for their contribution.

Recruitment of volunteers should be undertaken with the same care as recruitment of staff. Volunteer posts should be advertised with job descriptions and qualifications listed, and those interested should fill out a volunteer application form. A *volunteer manual* that links the museum's mission and mandate to the museum's volunteer policy and to practical details pertaining to the daily work of volunteers (such as provision for out-of-pocket expenses) should be made available to those expressing an interest. For museums with membership programs it is often recommended that only members can volunteer and that any volunteer committee must be part of the membership organization.

Interviews of potential volunteers should be aimed at determining the volunteer's interests, capability, and training needs as well as communicating the museum's requirements.

There are many different motivations for volunteering: people thinking about career changes, gaining credits for volunteer hours at work or school, and making friends. Special thought should be given to how volunteers can reflect the demographics of the communities the museum serves or wishes to serve such as youth, people of color, local residents, and the unemployed.

References should be taken and checked and health and criminal records investigated following the same personnel procedures as for any prospective employee. Less promising candidates should be politely declined in a letter thanking them for their interest. Some may be redirected to volunteering for tasks other than the post for which they applied.

Aspiring volunteers should then be offered a *volunteer agreement*, completed to fit the needs of the museum to their circumstances, committing them to particular days and times for a specified period. With fulfillment of this contract in view, the volunteer should be enrolled in the requisite training program, provided by the museum's education department or other qualified staff.

Such a program can be effective in recruiting, training, and maintaining in volunteers a commitment to the institution, while constantly developing volunteers' abilities and offering the rewards of learning, personal growth, and social recognition.

Interns

Interns are a source of mostly youthful energy, enthusiasm, and newly minted knowledge that can be invaluable to a museum department. These are usually recent graduates, sometimes still completing education programs, who are willing to work for low levels of remuneration in order to gain the experience of working in a museum and learning relevant skills. In some cases universities or other schools are willing to pay the intern a stipend and grant them credit for working in museums. If not assisted by their school, then interns should be paid by the museum. As with volunteers, it is important to ensure that interns are engaged on a clear contractual basis that is not threatening to fully paid employees, and that their status is transparent to all who will be working with them. A certain number may be hired for permanent positions, but it is important to ensure that all interns benefit from the experience of working in the museum, providing them with sufficient training and development opportunities appropriate to their time and role in the museum.

Museum management should be acutely aware of the rising cost of higher education and the burden of student debt when developing policies for the museum's internship program. The internship program, like the volunteer program, should reflect high standards of equity, inclusion, diversity, and social justice.

Chapter 6

HOW

Tools of Museum Management

Museums are dynamic organizations, simultaneously creating and responding to cultural change, which means that they are increasingly complex institutions to manage.

Chapters 6 and 7 address some of the tools that managers can use to lead their museum to thrive.

> We start at the very top of the organization, with the executive role, because if that isn't clear, everything else will eventually fall apart.

We start at the very top of the organization, with the executive role, because if that isn't clear, everything else will eventually fall apart. On a more positive note, if the executive function is clear and focused on mission, vision, values, and goals, the museum will have the best chance of succeeding, no matter the challenges ahead or the changing ecosystems.

Just what is the executive?

The organizational structure of museums is in constant change depending on the type and size of the museum and its location in the world. It's safe to say that most museums have a director who is the chief executive or chief executive officer (CEO). The director builds an executive team composed of the heads of key departments (for a small to mid-size museum) or deputy directors of divisions in larger museums.

Together, these positions comprise the "executive team," which is often referred to as "management." However, in larger museums management may refer to a much larger group including department heads who are not on the executive team.

6.1 The Executive Role

The executive role in museums requires both *management* and *leadership*: applying professional standards to doing the thing right (management), while inspiring the staff and board to do the right thing (leadership)—whether safeguarding heritage, ensuring that the public have physical and intellectual access, or challenging staff to be more effective at communicating and being creative in conducting their responsibilities.

The director's roles include planning, policy formulation, approving procedures, and developing and maintaining relations with other institutions. Some of the director's roles are in fact shared functions with the board of trustees or governing body. That is why it is often said that an effective director spends 50 percent of the time working with the board. This section reviews each of these executive roles. How they are implemented will influence all aspects of museum operations and in effect create the museum's *institutional culture*.

Planning

The director is responsible for the disposition of a wide range of resources including collections, content, buildings, people, and funds. Planning is the primary means for determining how these resources should be deployed, and developing a strategic plan is the most efficient way of organizing the overall planning function of a museum.

A *strategic plan* is a first-level tool that ideally aligns executive management, staff, board, and stakeholders with the mission and vision.[1] An effective strategic plan accomplishes this by coordinating the goals, objectives, and even the tasks to be accomplished for a three- to five-year period.

Successes and failures of the previous plan should be assessed as part of the initiation of this process. The overarching goal of a strategic plan is for the museum to be even more successful in meeting future challenges. In addition to their value for internal management, strategic plans are generally required for funding, sponsorship, and grant applications.

> A *strategic plan* is a first-level tool that ideally aligns executive management, staff, board, and stakeholders with the mission and vision.

> In addition to their value for internal management, strategic plans are generally required for funding, sponsorship, and grant applications.

Because long-range planning is a role shared by board and management, strategic plans are generally prepared by a committee of management, staff, and trustees led by the director, and often assisted by consultants.

It is important that all those who are expected to implement the strategic plan (that's everyone!) should be consulted in its preparation, feel they have participated in the resultant plan, and that their concerns and ideas have been taken into account. Thus, the entire museum (staff, board, and management) will have a sense of ownership in the plan.

Of course, not all ideas will make it into the final document, but the planning process should clarify why certain goals and objectives had priority over others, and the director should be prepared to explain and discuss these matters frankly with trustees, staff, and volunteers. Strategic plans that are imposed externally or from above without consultation are often resisted (if not merely shelved), whereas when strategic plans are formulated through consensus, there is the potential to elicit cooperation from all levels of the institution.

The term *strategic plan* describes both a type of plan and the process of creating that plan. At its best, this process involves determining the optimum future for an organization by studying its situation in a changing environment through the use of both external and internal consultation and research, including the following components:

- *Environmental Scans*—this process helps staff, board, and stakeholders understand the changes in society that are having the greatest impact on museums now and into the future.

- *External Consultations*—confidential interviews with cultural, political, business, and community leaders; "workshop" meetings with people who support or use the museum, such as donors, funders, teachers, and frequent visitors; and focus groups with those who do not use the museum. These consultations help planners understand the museum's public role, how it serves the community, where it fails, and how it can be improved.

- *Internal Consultation*—includes interviews and workshops with staff, volunteers, members, and trustees and helps in assessing the museum's strengths and weaknesses in relation to the museum's mission and the opportunities and threats it faces.

- *Retreats and workshops*—extended meetings at which trustees and senior staff consider long-range directions, opportunities, and challenges; review the foundation statements; and identify three to five strategic directions that can then be translated into goals. The destination of a strategic plan is alignment of the entire museum around strategic goals.

> The destination of a strategic plan is alignment of the entire museum around strategic goals.

- Based on these goals, specific quantitative objectives for each division or department, along with a budget and timetable, are developed by management and staff.

The strategic plan as a whole is then finalized by the board. After being finalized, it is implemented by the entire institution, and progress should be evaluated quarterly to ensure that the organization stays on target or that the plan is amended to reflect evolving circumstance.

The strategic plan is usually intended as guidance for a period of three to five years and may be the "ignition" for other planning activities—such as a master plan—if a major capital development is foreseen. Some institutions combine the two, with the strategic plan setting the overall qualitative direction and the master plan then applying its conclusions to an analysis of the museum's collection, content, space, or facility needs. (Much more detail on the strategic planning process plus case studies is provided by authors Gail Dexter Lord and Kate Markert in *The Manual of Strategic Planning for Cultural Organizations* [2017]).

> A *master plan* is more long term—usually in place for fifteen to twenty years—and more detailed than a strategic plan. It focuses on the museum's resource requirements of space, facilities, personnel, and funding, as well as the means for fulfilling them.

A *master plan* is more long term—usually in place for fifteen to twenty years—and more detailed than a strategic plan. It focuses on the museum's resource requirements of space, facilities, personnel, and funding, as well as the means for fulfilling them.[2]

Master plans include the following valuable components:

- *Institutional Plan*—addressing the museum's governance structure, its mission and mandate, and its relations with its entire institutional context or ecosystems including government, educational institutions, other museums, community organizations, private sector, and tourism.

- *Market Analysis*—comprising the results of visitor surveys as well as demographic and sociographic analyses of the community—resident, school, and tourist—aimed at identifying the museum's current and potential visitors both on-site and online.

- *Collection and Content Analysis*—projecting growth as well as present dimensions and directions of the museum's collecting activities, including current and desired levels of density of display and storage of the collections and issues of collection management and care.

- *Public Program Plan*—projecting the activities that the museum wishes to undertake or has been undertaking, ranging from exhibitions through interpretation of its collection to education, publications, extension services, outreach, and such visitor services public amenities as toilets, shops, or catering, in relation to the museum's target markets.

- *Staffing Requirements*—projecting requirements for human resources in order to operate the museum to meet the professional standards and community needs.

- *Facilities Needs*—deducing the space and facilities required for the collections and content in storage and on display, for the public programs and amenities, and for the needed support facilities and work spaces for staff.

- *Capital Cost Projection*—the amount needed to upgrade or build the requisite space, to provide furnishings and equipment, or to build the planned exhibits.

- *Attendance, Revenue, and Expense Projections*—forecasting all sources of income and categories of expenditure, with a view to identifying the need for subsidy or other fund-raising.

- *Funding Strategy*—meeting both capital and operating fund requirements from public, private, and self-generated sources.

- *Implementation Schedule*—propelling the museum from its present situation to the one outlined in the master plan.

The interconnectedness of the components outlined in this description demonstrate the benefits of completing the entire master plan.

For proposed new museums, relocations, or expansions, a *feasibility study* would cover some of the same ground as the master plan, except that it should conclude with a statement of the project's feasibility. This must be based on a set of assumptions about the quality and size of the proposed institution, its location, marketing, management, and freedom from debt.

Feasibility of museums is not the same as feasibility of a private sector project, where profit is the criterion. For public museums, it is usually a question of establishing the level of support (annual subsidies, grants, donations, endowments, sponsorships, or other fund-raising) that would be required beyond the potential for self-generated revenues, as well as sound judgment concerning the reliability of such annual financial support.

> Feasibility of museums is not the same as feasibility of a private sector project, where profit is the criterion.

Plans developed as a method of managing specific activities—such as exhibition plans, education plans, and marketing plans—are the shared responsibility of management and staff (not of management and board) and are discussed later in this chapter.

Policies

Plans are both a method and a tool of management directed primarily toward future accomplishment, while *policies* are instrumental to regulating both the fulfillment of present museum functions and the achievement of a desired future condition at the requisite level of quality. Both plans and policies should be aligned with the museum's mission, mandate, vision statements, and values.

> Both plans and policies should be aligned with the museum's mission, mandate, vision statements, and values.

Policies are formulated in order to ensure standards of quality and public accountability in the accomplishment of museum functions. They are therefore a shared responsibility of management and board, in which management through the director is responsible for policy formulation and for presentation of policy options to the board, while the trustees are responsible for ensuring that the policies are consistent with the museum's mission and goals, and that the institution has the resources needed to implement them.

The precise number and names of museum policies vary. Here is a check list of policies required by most museums:

- Collection policy, including acquisition, deaccessioning, and loan policies;

- Conservation policy, which may be included in a collection and content management policy;

- Documentation policy, another that may be part of the collection and content policy;

- Education policy;

- Exhibition policy;

- Human resources policy;

- Public access policy, including policy on access for the disabled;

- Communication policy, including the interpretation of the collection, but also extending to wayfinding in the building, graphics, Internet, and Web communications, marketing, and media;

- Research policy, which should also include policy on intellectual property;

- Security policy; and

- Visitor services or guest care policy

> Policies should identify the museum's goals in relation to each of these functions and should establish the level of quality to which the museum is committed in the implementation of its policies and plans.

Policies should identify the museum's goals in relation to each of these functions and should establish the level of quality to which the museum is committed in the implementation of its policies and plans. Because policies relate to ongoing functions, they should be drafted by the senior staff responsible—so that the chief of security, for instance, should be asked to draft the security policy—with the director serving as editor and joining in any revision required to align the policy with the museum's plans.

Policies should then be recommended by the director to the board and should not express professional standards that are unrealistic in terms of the museum's budget, space, technology, or staff limitations but should project attainable levels of excellence in each function, given the museum's mission and resources. They should be comprehensive, relating to all implications of the fulfillment of that function.

Once approved by the trustees, policy implementation becomes a staff responsibility, delegated to the respective managers for the policy area. However, trustees retain responsibility for monitoring the policies, so the director should report regularly to the board on their implementation, and with recommendations for policy changes—in order to ensure that no museum functions are neglected and that policies are more than wishful thinking.

Because many museums find that they need about ten to twelve policies, it is convenient to review and report on one policy per month: thus a board that meets monthly may consider a different policy document and a report on its implementation, along with any recommendations for changes, at each meeting. For example, collection policy in January, exhibition policy in February, security policy in March, and so on. This approach ensures that throughout a one-year period, all policies have been considered, reviewed, and changed if necessary. In this way the board retains an energetic role in the governance of museum functions, and policies remain relevant and implementable.

Procedures

A museum's procedures should reflect its established ways of doing things.

Many museum functions must be discharged in a systematic way—such as documentation of a new accession or security measures. The *procedures manual* is the main means of codifying and communicating the systematic means of conducting museum functions and related tasks.

Like policies, procedures are related to museum functions, but they are more specific and more quantified because they are linked to the attainment of specific quantitative objectives for those functions, whereas policies are related to longer-range qualitative goals.

> Like policies, procedures are related to museum functions, but they are more specific and more quantified because they are linked to the attainment of specific quantitative objectives for those functions.

The subject matter of procedures manuals may range from welcoming and ticketing procedures through documentation forms and condition reporting to security routines and—a particularly important one—an *emergency procedures manual*.

One area where procedures manuals should be used with special caution is in *visitor or guest services*. This is because each visitor is an individual, and the service required by that individual may or may not have been anticipated in the visitor service or customer care manual. Staff meeting guests—including security guards—should regularly be reminded that service to the individual visitor, as long as it is within the guidelines of the museum's policies, may override the strictures of a procedures manual.

Curatorial research, exhibition planning, and design are examples of other areas where procedures manuals may not be appropriate. Even here, however, there may be certain segments of the work that can best be accomplished by following a set routine that will most often obtain the level of quality desired. Library practices, for example, may benefit from being the subject of a procedures manual.

Procedures manuals are important tools that should be prepared by the responsible museum staff team, who may find that many manuals are required to provide guidance for all the activities occurring in that department. Procedures manuals are often simply a point form listing of steps that any employee, including new recruits, should follow in carrying out a specific activity, but they should always link those steps to the quality level articulated in the relevant policy. They should be consistent with that policy and should be reviewed and approved by the director, who should ensure that they will result in implementation of the policy.

Whenever the policy is changed, therefore, the procedures manual should be updated.

Reports

With policies and procedures in place, day-to-day management of the museum becomes somewhat easier.

However, this doesn't mean an institution can simply run on autopilot: attention must always be given to the myriad challenges, problems, and coordination issues that are constantly emerging. This is done through *reports* on all aspects of implementation.

> As the saying goes: "Management doesn't gets what it expects, it gets what it inspects."

As the saying goes: "Management doesn't get what it expects, it gets what it inspects." That's where reports fit in management's toolkit. Some reports are tools that record plans. Reports also help with evaluation of processes. Reports are tools and should therefore be concise and business like in their delivery of information and intelligence.

In the well-managed museum, reporting relationships and schedules for reports are clearly defined and understood at all levels. This means that each department head, and deputy director, should regularly be reviewing reports and summarizing them for their managers.

For instance, the admissions clerk should be reporting cash and attendance figures daily to the visitor services officer, who will be summarizing these reports weekly to the public programs officer, who in turn will prepare a monthly summary for the director, who will report on attendance quarterly to the board, which will issue an annual report based on these cumulative figures.

Reports should provide not just *quantitative data*—visitation, revenue, relative humidity variations, budget versus actual costs, acquisitions, donations, membership, and so forth—but should also provide a concise *qualitative analysis*—marketing impact, visitor satisfaction, progress in collection development, significance of research results, and so on.

The incisive ability to identify key factors in any area of museum activity relative to the museum's objectives for that function distinguishes outstanding staff members from the merely competent.

Management Method	Relevant to	Time Reference	Drafted by	Approval by
Plans	Mission, goals, and objectives	Future	Director and management	Trustees
Policies	Functions and goals	Present and future	Director and management	Trustees
Procedures	Functions and objectives	Immediate and present	Staff	Director
Reports	Fulfillment of functions	Recent, past and present	Staff	Managers and Director

Figure 6.1.   Museum Management Tools. *Lord Cultural Resources.*

Meetings, Meetings, Meetings

"Is this meeting necessary?"

Looking around a meeting room of a dozen staff members or trustees assembled for two hours, it is possible to calculate not only the *direct cost* of the meeting to the museum in person hours but also the *opportunity cost* as its participants are prevented from performing other functions while attending the meeting. The impact of email, Zoom calls, voicemail, and computerized messaging have both weakened and enhanced the tyranny of the meeting—depending on your perspective. But for management, the purpose of a meeting is actually quite specific: for example, is it about productivity or about the exhibition program?

It is unfortunately the case that many meetings are simply exercises in power or strategies for postponing decisions. It is management's job to ensure that meetings are productive by utilizing such simple tools as an *agenda* and *minutes*. If the meeting is virtual, via conference call or video, these tools are all the more important.

All participants in the meeting should be invited to contribute to the agenda in advance of the meeting. The purpose of a meeting is to share viewpoints and to gain collegial commitment to common purposes; this collegiality should begin with the agenda and continue throughout a truly participatory process of energized and focused discussion.

Minutes should be kept, preferably by someone who serves only that role in the meeting, with requirements for *action* indicated and allocated to individuals or groups in the margin. If all these actions point to the same person, it is obvious that the meeting was not necessary! Minutes should then be distributed within forty-eight hours of the meeting, with another forty-eight hours allowed for corrections so that the actions arising from the meeting may be readily implemented, and any agreements reached may become the basis for future action. Minutes should be understood as a planning and management tool, not as a passive record.

Communication

The meeting is just one of many communication tools.

Formal Communication

There are three degrees of formal communication among those concerned with the management of a museum: notification, consultation, and delegation.

Notification

Whenever a decision is taken, the museum manager must determine who needs to be *notified* of the decision.

For example, the decision to extend the time period of an exhibition, or simply to open the museum for an evening event, will almost certainly require notification of communications, visitor services, security staff, and probably food service, ticketing, and shop staff as well. Failure to notify all those affected by such decisions *promptly* is one of the cardinal sins in museum administration and one of the most common complaints of those who have to live with the consequences. Notification should not be casual but should be formally controlled and stated within the museum management system by official notification memoranda that must be dated, timed, and signed by the relevant museum officer.

Consultation

Consultation is a higher level of formal communication because it involves the opportunity costs of a meeting or some form of written input from those consulted.

Considering a possible decision, the museum manager must determine whether notification of that decision would be sufficient or whether it requires consultation with those affected before it can be taken. If consultation is thought to be worthwhile, the manager must truly *consult*—that is, to listen and take the ideas of those consulted on board.

A common management deficiency is to create the appearance of consultation when all that was really intended was notification. It adds the injury of wasting time to the insult of not listening to people's views and leads to cynicism among staff.

A common management deficiency is to create the appearance of consultation when all that was really intended was notification. It adds the injury of wasting time to the insult of not listening to people's views and leads to cynicism among staff.

Delegation

Delegation is perhaps the most important formal means of communication because it is most directly connected with accomplishing the museum's functions.

Delegation is perhaps the most important formal means of communication because it is most directly connected with accomplishing the museum's functions.

Like the other formal means of communication, it should not be done casually but should be made explicit by the delegating officer to the person to whom the task is delegated. Assumed or vaguely comprehended delegation is the root of many of the communications problems that afflict museum workers. Both delegators and delegatees should insist that the act of delegation be recorded, with the extent and limitations of the delegated responsibility made clear.

Informal Communication

Careful notification, consultation, and delegation may be of little use unless the museum culture also encourages a healthy climate of *informal communication*.

This involves an awareness of the art of *creative listening*, which starts with an understanding that listening is an active, rather than a passive, endeavor. Personnel at all levels, including trustees and volunteers, should be encouraged to understand that listening to each other is a creative task and that it is useful to "check back" with each other by saying, in effect, "What I hear you saying is . . ." Only when the original speaker confirms that what has been heard is what was said can we be sure that effective communication has occurred.

Above all, there must be sufficient motivation for individual *creativity*. In particular, it is vital to respect the need for creativity among curators and others concerned with developing exhibitions, education programs, publications, media, and special events, as well as those concerned with marketing them. Plans, policies, and procedures must *facilitate* creativity, not stifle it.

The effective museum manager should ensure that the corporate culture of communications in the museum is one that *welcomes* the original idea and that seeks to determine how it can be achieved, rather than why it can't be realized.

Email

In museums, as everywhere else, email in its many forms has revolutionized both formal and informal communications.

The workday and the workweek have been extended, as asynchronous digital communications can reach us at any time. We enjoy both the advantage and the disadvantage of being in contact immediately wherever we are—on vacation or attending a conference on the other side of the world. Mistakes that would have been caught and erased in the old days of signing letters and mailing them are now sent before they can be reconsidered, resulting in a chain of email corrections or qualifications to all concerned.

A digital communication protocol should be part of the museum's corporate culture including considerations of who is included on the "to line," the cc, and even the bcc, as well as language and working hours when replies are expected.

Copyright, intellectual property, and legal issues specific to museums should be addressed in an email protocol, along with requirements for saving or deleting messages.

6.2 Collections and Content Management

Collections and content are the defining attribute of museums—even for museums like science centers, children's museums, and "idea" museums—which often contain intangible collections such as music, stories, and ephemera.

This section begins by considering the role of the curator or keeper, then reviews the components of collection and content policy, and the steps toward forming a collection and content development strategy, before addressing the challenges of collection care, documentation, and conservation. The idea here is to understand why the museum collects material, and how that material should best be protected for future generations to learn from and enjoy. The following case study by Daniel Hammer demonstrates how the curatorial role can share authority with communities to the great benefit of research and public engagement.

Community in Curatorial Practice:
The Double Portrait

By Daniel Hammer

In 2021, The Historic New Orleans Collection (THNOC), a museum dedicated to the stewardship of the history and culture of New Orleans and the Gulf South, acquired a remarkable work of Louisiana art—an unusually large, pastel double portrait of two men, possibly a father and son, by Jules Lion (1810–1866), a nineteenth-century New Orleans artist noted for his important work in photography and lithography.

Lion, the first practitioner of photography in Louisiana, is identified in New Orleans City directories from the 1850s as a free man of color and has therefore long been understood as an important black artist. In more recent years, scholarship by art historian Sara M. Picard uses French records to argue that he was a French-born Jewish man who was somehow misidentified as a free man of color in the city directories due to his relationship with Charlotte Armantine Broyard, a free woman of color. The question of Lion's race has since become a matter of tense uncertainty in scholarly and cultural communities.

The double portrait dates to ca. 1845. Held privately since its creation, it began to acquire something of a public reputation in Louisiana when it was purchased in 1935 by the well-known folklorist and writer Lyle Saxon, who brought it from New Orleans to Melrose Plantation—at that time an artist colony where he lived—near Natchitoches, Louisiana.

During the middle half of the twentieth century, the piece stayed there, never moving, until 1975, when Saxon's friend, Francois Mignon, who inherited it from Saxon when he died in 1945, lent it to the groundbreaking American art curator Regenia A. Perry for the exhibition *Art Selections of Nineteenth-Century Afro-American Art* at the Metropolitan Museum of Art. Perry identified the sitters as Asher Moses Nathan, a successful New Orleans merchant of Jewish heritage born in Amsterdam in 1785, and his son Achille Lion (no relation to the artist). She described the piece as "the only portrait in 19th-century American art in which a white father openly displays affection for his biracial son."

The pastel was featured as the cover image on the exhibition catalog and, in subsequent years, gained a reputation of significance in art historical circles as it was used to illustrate numerous books and articles on African American art history and was included in additional exhibitions in museums around the country.

Meanwhile, absolute certainty about the identity of the sitters, particularly the younger man, eluded researchers, as well. According to THNOC chief curator Jason Wiese:

> There are several pieces of documentary evidence linking Achille Lion to Asher Moses Nathan, including an 1859 legislative act granting Nathan's adoption of the young man, then 22 years old; an 1862 oleographic will filed in Orleans Parish; and French notarial records related to Achille's sister, Anna. It is believed that Nathan was

Achille's biological father; THNOC staff researchers have established that Nathan was in France in 1826, less than a year before Achille's birth. The 1860 census identified Achille as a French broker living in the Fourth Ward [of New Orleans]. However, while the younger sitter is deliberately presented as having a darker complexion than the older man, neither the census nor local notarial records identify Achille Léon Lion as a man of color. Achille returned to Europe in mid-1861 and is not known to have ever come back to Louisiana. He died in Paris in 1916. He and his sister, Anna, were both legatees of Asher Nathan's estate.

Likewise, the provenance of the portrait is incomplete. According to Wiese, the ownership history of the portrait is unknown "between its circa-1845 creation and 1935, when New Orleans antiques dealer Albert Lieutaud wrote a letter to Lyle Saxon alerting him that the portrait had been brought to his Royal Street shop by an unidentified 'mulatto family.'"

In December 2021, the double portrait was offered for sale at auction in New Orleans. Keenly aware of the ambiguity present in three major components of the artwork's identification—the identity of the sitters, the biography of the artist, and the provenance—THNOC's acquisitions committee had to decide whether to propose that the institution bid.

Our holdings already included the most significant collection of daguerreotypes and lithographs by Jules Lion, and a traditional perspective on collecting may have therefore dictated that we should seek to acquire this magnificent pastel double portrait by Lion as a sort of capstone atop a tower of documentation of the oeuvre of an important artist. This, however, did not serve to justify the acquisition for the committee. In fact, our collections development policy specifically directs us not to pursue new acquisitions for the purpose of achieving some sort of poetic closure of a collecting theme:

> Although THNOC collects in Fine and Decorative Arts, the evaluation criteria should be based on the item's salience to the collective narratives of our community and how the item can be used in the telling of these stories. Although the quality of the work is an important criterion, the degree to which an artist or craftsman is represented or not represented in our holdings should not be a determining criterion for selection; nor is the degree to which the item represents an artistic style or movement.

It was rather the extent to which ambiguities of identity—inexorably drawn into the artist, sitters, and object itself—make this portrait salient "to the collective narratives of our community and how the item can be used in the telling of these stories" that the committee was most concerned with. More so than most objects, documents, or works of art, this portrait of what appears to be a mixed-race young man embracing an older white man by a possibly Franco-Jewish, possibly Afro-Franco artist, depending on which historic records you privilege, confronts the viewer head-on with the power that viewer has to choose to see what they want to see in a document of the past. It lays bare for the public the extent to which what we call history is not a series of objective facts but is rather the interpretation of the past that we, in the present, make through our intrinsically limited perspective.

The acquisitions committee therefore determined that we should seek to add this important artwork to our collection for the sake of ensuring that it be put to use for understanding the history of New Orleans *in* New Orleans, but if, and only if, we would be able to present it to the public not on our own but in partnership with other institutions whose mission it is to steward the history and culture of the specific communities whose history may or may not be represented in this artwork: the black community and Jewish community of New Orleans. Therefore, before making its recommendation, the committee reached out to leading museums in both communities to share with them our knowledge about the artwork, explain our interest, and inquire regarding their interest in partnering with us, should we acquire it.

Generously, the directors of Le Musée de Free People of Color (Le Musée) and the Museum of the Southern Jewish Experience (MSJE) pledged to partner with us on interpretive and research projects should we succeed in acquiring the portrait. These pledges gave us the confidence we needed to proceed. The acquisitions committee recommended that we bid at the auction, and our board of directors approved, with a bidding maximum that was greater than any amount we had paid to add an object to our collections in the history of our institution.

Upon our acquisition of the double portrait, we proceeded to build our partnership with Le Musée and MSJE. The first step was to introduce them to the artwork, begin to discuss our divergent perspectives on it, and explore together how we each thought the artwork connected with the interpretive focus of our respective museums and how it did not. We then proceeded to visit each other's museums and learn further about each of our unique missions and priorities. The goal became to find a way to begin to engage the public with this work of art that would be beneficial to each of our three museums, with a focus on driving joint visitor-ship and engagement. We waited to put the portrait on public display until we had a plan.

In June 2022, six months after the auction, we unveiled the portrait in THNOC's galleries with an extended label informing visitors about Le Musée and MSJE (including QR codes leading to their respective websites) and encouraging them to visit those museums. Likewise, Le Musée and MSJE displayed reproductions of the portrait in their galleries, with labels pointing their visitors toward us and the other partner.

Beyond this, we have continued to work on initiatives of mutual benefit, including shared internships, sharing of staff expertise, and ongoing planning for future joint programs and educational initiatives with the double portrait, all the while seeking to acknowledge and celebrate the things that differentiate us as institutions and the things that connect us.

Figure 6.2. Double portrait of two men, possibly father and son, by Jules Lion (1806–1866 and 1840–1850). Pastel on paper. THNOC 2021.0264. *Courtesy of The Historic New Orleans Collection.*

Role of the Curator

Despite the centrality of collections, the position of curator has been somewhat embattled in recent years.

This was originally due to the reorganization of museums, from curator-led departments to the more functional administration outlined in this manual, a tendency that has been intensified by the increasing emphasis on public programs and visitor services, and by the realization that exhibitions and other museum activities require input from many other professional disciplines and communities, as well as curatorial.

Yet with a greater emphasis on visitor-centered exhibitions and other public programs and services, the curator's role is even more important and should not be marginalized.

The intimate knowledge of a collection—whether it be mollusks, Monets, or mummies—is rooted in an ability to see, to make distinctions, and above all to make judgments about objects.

One of the difficulties with the role of the curator has been limited comprehension of its primary qualification and activity: *connoisseurship*. The intimate knowledge of a collection—whether it be mollusks, Monets, or mummies—is rooted in an ability to see, to make distinctions, and above all to make judgments about objects. This is connoisseurship, and it is as essential to a science, military, or transportation museum as it is to an art or philatelic collection. A scholar, however academically qualified, is not a curator; the curator is not simply a researcher and is not focused on written evidence, as many academics are, but roots their knowledge in the works of art, artifacts, specimens, or archival documents of that discipline.

Curatorial success at acquisitions requires inspiration, dedication, patience, opportunism, and a knowledge of sources that is both extensive and detailed.

The qualified curator brings such connoisseurship to the task of adding to the collection. Curatorial acquisition is a creative response to opportunity, disciplined by the necessities of the marketplace, the museum's acquisition budget, and the shape of the collection that the curator has (in most cases) inherited from predecessors. Curatorial success at acquisitions requires inspiration, dedication, patience, opportunism, and a knowledge of sources that is both extensive and detailed.

To sustain their abilities, curators need time for research. They need to research potential acquisitions, proposed exhibition subjects, and the knowledge base for publications or media productions that the museum wishes to undertake. Research may be done in the curator's office, in the museum library, in private galleries or artists' studios, among the communities that originated the objects, or on visits to other museums and private collections abroad. The most common complaint among curators of all kinds is the lack of time for consistent pursuit of research objectives.

Research is the unseen motor of all museum programs.

Research is the unseen motor of all museum programs.

Without adequate and accurate research, public programs can be misleading at best, and dead wrong at worst. Poorly researched acquisitions can litter the collection with irrelevant or unimportant examples—or worse, with copies or fakes. The most sophisticated high-tech multimedia programs depend on the quality and extent of the museum's research—some of them literally transposing the collection database into a publicly accessible format.

Because their responsibilities continually draw their attention to the museum's need for research, curators have devised various ways of finding time to undertake it.

One extreme strategy is to focus attention on a relatively narrow or even esoteric research program, often unrelated to the museum's programs, in some cases even unrelated to the collection. With this approach, the curator plays a minimal role in the public functions of the museum, in some cases publishing results of their research in academic journals unrelated to the museum's publications program.

The opposite strategy deeply involves curators in the museum's public programs, but as a result, they may be dragged from one research topic to another, usually in support of the exhibition program. For these curators it is difficult to find time for research on acquisitions, and their research work may become cursory, constantly moving from one exhibition topic to another.

Neither of these extremes is desirable, or necessary. The solution of an enlightened museum management is to support long-term curatorial research by establishing a *research policy* and by encouraging the development of *research plans*.

A museum's *research policy* should have the following components in this checklist:

1. Establish the museum's commitment to research in relation to the museum's mission and mandate.

2. Commit the museum to provide the personnel, time, library, travel budget, and other resources needed for effective research, commensurate with the museum's budget and other resources.

3. Resources—such as travel for fieldwork—is often contingent on the researcher getting grants to pay for them. The policy should articulate the extent and the limits of the museum's responsibility and encourage the individual researcher's role.

4. Address not only curatorial research but research by other staff members—conservators, education officers, and others—who will be expected to undertake research.

5. Outline the museum's policy toward outside researchers' use of museum facilities, whether they are visiting scholars studying the collection or secondary school students writing an essay.

6. Articulate the museum's position on copyright and intellectual property, usually making a distinction between the results of research done on museum time and personal research that some museum staff may undertake independently.

7. Most important, the research policy should insist that all museum-sponsored research, even if theoretical, should ultimately relate to museum collections or programs and must form part of the execution of a research plan by each individual researcher on staff.

Research plans prepared by museum personnel in response to their museum's research policy should include the following components on this checklist:

1. Individual research plans should be prepared by all museum staff members (not only curators) who wish to undertake museum-sponsored research.

2. The plan should indicate the relationship of the projected research to museum collection documentation or public programs.

3. The research plan should include a time framework for its accomplishment.

4. Research plans should be prepared annually, with a time framework likely to be in months or years.

5. Research plans should be drafted by the researcher, reviewed by the deputy director for that division, and approved by the museum's chief executive officer (usually the director).

The value of having both a research policy and research plans in place is that the museum management can then consider changes in research direction with due regard for the long-range implication of altering its research time commitments.

If, for example, the director decides that a new exhibition must be organized for next year, and therefore advises a curator to undertake the requisite research, that curator should respond with reference to their research plan, observing what effect the change in research direction will have on the objectives and timing of the formerly agreed research plan. A decision can then be made as to whether this alteration is in the long-term interests of the museum.

On the other hand, if a curator suggests a research plan that is not meaningfully related to the museum's collection documentation or public programming needs—but perhaps reflects their personal interests—the deputy director for collections management or the director can work with the curator to redirect the research so that it is of greater benefit to the institution.

Acquisitions

In view of the importance of collection and content development and the costs involved, many museum boards appoint an acquisitions committee from among their members.

Such a committee, which should meet with the relevant curator, is useful as a means of channeling trustees' efforts toward encouraging donations or bequests to the collection in accordance with the museum's collection development strategy.

Because acquisitions lead to increased operating costs and ultimately to space and facilities requirements, the acquisition committee should also function as a committee of recommendation for major acquisitions, defined as accessions above a certain monetary value.

The acquisitions committee should be empowered to approve acquisitions up to a certain value, but above that value its recommendations must go to the full board for approval. Collections committees with broader powers are not recommended because they inevitably become involved in day-to-day museum operations that should be delegated to the curatorial staff.

Collection Policy

The museum's chief instrument of collection management should be its *collection policy*. The clauses of a collection policy are based in the museum's mission and mandate. A comprehensive thirty-point collection policy checklist is included in appendix B.

The collection and content policy should be a public document that both the director and curator may invoke when necessary in the museum's dealings with prospective donors or vendors. It is most useful as a means to resist would-be long-term lenders, "all or nothing" donors, or well-meaning trustees whose proffered donations or bequests do not fit the museum's mandate. Marc Mayer's account of how the National Gallery of Canada developed and implemented a policy of integrating Indigenous art with all its collections demonstrates how collections can be at the very heart of dynamic change.

Integrating Indigenous Art at the National Gallery of Canada

By Marc Mayer

There was already a department of Indigenous art at the National Gallery of Canada when I took the reins in 2009. The department consisted of two curators and an intern, its own galleries in the contemporary wing, as well as five smaller galleries dedicated to Inuit art on the lower level.

Additionally, a series of historical and contemporary Indigenous works were shown in an extended special exhibition interwoven with the permanent collection in the galleries dedicated to Canadian art. Besides the contemporary works that had all been acquired, almost all the historical works were on long-term loan from other museums. My tenure, then, had a strong foundation upon which to grow this crucial aspect of visual arts culture in Canada: the multimillennial artistic legacy of the land's Indigenous Peoples.

Although things had improved considerably for Indigenous art at the National Gallery by 2009, including a named chair, Greg A. Hill, the Audain Senior Curator of Indigenous Art, to lead the department, we were still faced with serious impediments to equitable integration. The department was restricted to contemporary Canadian work, while the contemporary art department had an international mandate and benefited from a thorough historical in-house context afforded by the Canadian and international departments with their excellent permanent collections of historical art.

In order to give our public the best possible opportunity to appreciate the importance of Indigenous culture in Canada and beyond, we needed to raise the profile of Indigenous art in a meaningful way, including aiming for parity with departments. This meant internationalizing its activities and investing it with historical depth. The intent was to meet the aspirations of Indigenous audiences and artists and to create a deeper understanding around the influence of Indigenous art on other artistic forms, up to and including modernism. Canadian culture, after all, is a story of hybridization.

Two major initiatives that evolved between 2009 and 2019 provided the opportunities to meet those goals: the redesign and reinstallation of the Canadian permanent collection galleries, and the establishment of a biennial exhibition to showcase two years of Canadian art acquisitions.

The first initiative—the redesign and reinstallation—offered us a chance to tell the story of Indigenous art making in the country going back to "time immemorial" and to tell it alongside the story of the establishment of European culture on the same territory. The second initiative—the biennial—would show the best of contemporary Indigenous art made in Canada in the context of the best new art in the country. In both cases, we were convinced that the artistic and intellectual force, as well as the astonishing resilience of Indigenous art would be self-evident.

Working with staff and external experts, we developed a complex mandate for the Department of Indigenous Art expressed in the slogan: "Distinction and integration." Indigenous art would be treated separately, with its own home department to develop programming, publications, and acquisitions specific to Indigenous art. But it would also integrate its activities, both into the larger narrative of art making in Canada going back to prehistory, as well as under the big, diverse tent of international contemporary art. Such integration, however, was certainly not assimilation. It would happen on its own terms and under the authority of Indigenous curators.

The first step was to redraft the National Gallery collections policy in order to extend the acquisition mandate both to international Indigenous art and to historical work. As our immediate need for historical material was for the reinstallation of the Canadian Galleries, we decided to restrict such acquisitions to art that was made by peoples inhabiting the territory now known as Canada. After carefully explaining our long-term vision to the trustees, we were delighted when they agreed with us.[3]

To build international expertise, we took the bold step to organize a Documenta-style global exhibition of contemporary Indigenous art in Ottawa every five years. To achieve relevance beyond our borders, we formed an international network of advisors who would help us bring a large pool of remarkable international works to the gallery from which we could make acquisitions. Not insignificantly, the exhibition would also give Canada a leadership role in the field while building audiences for new Indigenous art.

Greg Hill assembled a strong project team and an equally impressive international network. He also convinced local venues to participate so that the exhibition was able to achieve a scale and a profile worthy of our ambitions. As the gallery and, indeed, Ottawa itself lies on unceded Algonquin territory, we invited the Algonquins to preside at the exhibition's inauguration, to be the diplomatic hosts of the events, and greet the many Indigenous artists visiting from all over the world.

These ceremonies were particularly moving to me, as I'm sure that they were to everyone who attended. We also gave the exhibition an Algonquin title: *Sakahàn*, or to ignite (a fire). I'm proud to say that the exhibition was an unqualified success on every level: the catalog is still a reference,[4] the collection was dramatically enriched, and the second quinquennial was equally strong, confirming the gallery's international reputation in the field.

The new biennial exhibition of recent acquisitions in contemporary art involved three departments: contemporary, Indigenous art, and photography. Conceived in the spirit of transparency, the complex show presented the acquisitions made by all three of those departments over the preceding two years, including gifts and commissions. Although not everything acquired could be shown, a full list of acquisitions was included in the catalog, which was deliberately designed to be useful to students and collectors. Each artist was represented by color photographs of their work in the exhibition, an artist's statement, and a notice by a relevant curator.[5]

Next came the reinstallation of the Canadian Galleries in time for the 2017 sesquicentennial of Canadian Confederation. This turned out to be the biggest challenge. The timeline was frighteningly short, our ambitions greater than our resources allowed, the Indigenous historical objects would have to be mostly borrowed and, therefore, were out of our control.

Cultural differences between the various curatorial departments involved caused frequent misunderstandings. How do you show two completely different perspectives in the same galleries? Which are the best works to tell these stories and how can we get them? How could we make sure that the reinstallation would be as useful, instructive, and inspirational for Indigenous audiences as they would be for everyone else? We decided that perhaps others could help answer these questions for us, so we devised a broad Indigenous consultation.

Working closely with Ruth Philips—an outside advisor to the board's acquisitions committee and a widely admired scholar of Indigenous art at local Carleton University—Greg Hill built another remarkably helpful group of advisors consisting of Indigenous elders, cultural leaders, and artists from across the country.

In a pair of two-day-long sessions, we listened to stories, histories, perspectives and advice, hopes, dreams, and, certainly, criticisms. As the director and CEO, I attended most of these meetings. Listening to this group was one of the most rewarding experiences I had at the gallery, hard as it often was, given Canada's sordid treatment of Indigenous peoples and their cultures. Not only did the advisors provide us with a wish list of the most important historical works we should consider, invaluable research that spanned the globe, they also helped us test and refine our ideas.

Here are some of the decisions that were made, based on those consultations:

- The permanent collection galleries would be renamed Canadian and Indigenous, rather than simply Canadian, respecting our motto "distinction and integration."

- We relaxed our innate museological obsession with chronology. If we could not secure a historical work for display in a relevant gallery, a contemporary work made in the same spirit would do. Also, as the survival and transformation of ancient cultures under colonization was a point we wished to drive home in the displays, the judicious inclusion of contemporary Indigenous art was practiced throughout the galleries.

- Labels for Indigenous work would be in three languages, English, French, and the traditional language of the maker.

- We would respect all ceremonial requirements for display, such as covering objects at night.

- We would not attempt to synthesize the various cultures into a single narrative but respect the different historical perspectives with an emphasis on the impact of history on material culture. For example, what effect did the government's Potlatch ban have on art making across Canada?

- Wary of overwhelming our audiences with didactic panels, we opted to tell the story with objects rather than words as much as possible, although each object would have an extended label. Nor did we shy away from using electronic media to supplement the story, such as videos showing seal hunting and hide preparation.

- We would spare no expense on nonreflecting vitrines to not visually disadvantage the Indigenous objects, especially in rooms dominated by well-lit and visually unobstructed paintings.

It seems that we got it right. The press response, notably from Indigenous journalists, was laudatory.[6] Our advisors expressed their heartfelt satisfaction with the results, which was particularly gratifying.

The main lesson that I drew from the success of our complex integration of Indigenous art into the National Gallery of Canada is that it needed to be as much a national effort as an institutional one. But there were other important lessons as well. Coordination and inclusion are more important than control. Artists working in the present can be a precious resource for understanding the past. Strict museological conventions are no longer sacrosanct to me. We also benefited from specialized, nonstaff educators from Indigenous communities and from philanthropists who helped us build Indigenous attendance through subsidized busing and educational outreach. Over all, the experience helped me to understand that, when it comes to living culture, we should always be open to questioning and testing institutional mindsets.

> Coordination and inclusion are more important than control. Artists working in the present can be a precious resource for understanding the past.

Figure 6.3.   Installation view of the entrance to the Canadian and Indigenous Galleries of the National Gallery of Canada, 2017. *Photo by the author.*

Collection and Content Development Strategy

Collections and content absorb two-thirds of a museum's operating budget and generate major long-range space and facilities needs that eventually require expansion and capital costs.[7] The development of a museum's collections is therefore a significant concern for management. A *collection development strategy* is the best tool.

A collection development strategy, to be drafted by the curator in consultation with the registrar and the conservator for approval by the director and the trustees, should begin with a *qualitative analysis* of the collection, which includes such features as

- the scope and range of the collection;

- international, national, or regional significance;

- outstanding pieces, representative or systematic character;

- uniqueness;

- representation of BIPOC, new immigrants, and formerly marginalized people;

- relevance to the museum's mission and the communities it serves;

- condition; and

- aesthetic quality.

The qualitative collection analysis should then proceed to consider the potential for enhancement of the collection through acquisition—which may be limited by sheer availability, the museum's acquisition budget, and other factors. This is because the purpose of the qualitative analysis in a collection development strategy is to project the trajectory of the collection's intended growth—where we are going, and how we will know when we get there (if ever).

The qualitative analysis should establish the museum's collecting horizon, and its qualitative priorities on the road to that horizon.

The collection development strategy should then proceed to a *quantitative* analysis that includes this checklist of components:

- The present size in numbers of objects of the collection as a whole and in all relevant categories, such as collection department, artifact type, historical period, materials (important for planning conservation needs), percentage registered and cataloged, and use classification—display, study, and reserve collections.

- The history of the growth of the collection in number of objects (not merely accession numbers) from as early in the museum's history as possible, again in relation to the same categories, and with both annual averages and the most recent *collection growth rate* computed, not in percentages (as is often erroneously advised) but in actual numbers of objects accessioned.

- The current *display/storage ratio* (by collection department if applicable), and curatorial recommendation of a more acceptable proportion if the present ratio is not satisfactory.

- Current *storage densities*—objects per square meter or square foot, or square meters or square feet per object, depending on the relative size of the objects in the collection (locomotives or postage stamps)—by object type or materials, together with the registrar's and conservator's recommendation of a more acceptable density if the present level is too crowded.

- Current *display densities*—again, objects per square meter or square foot, or square meters or square feet per object, whichever is more appropriate—in the permanent collection exhibition galleries, linked to an identification of the dominant display mode in that gallery (aesthetic, thematic, environmental, systematic, interactive, or hands-on).

A *design year* needs to be determined—the year by which the collection development strategy should be fulfilled—usually about twenty or twenty-five years in the future because projections beyond those limits are likely to be highly speculative.

Any factors anticipated to affect collection growth between now and the design year should be noted—an anticipated bequest, hiring an additional curator, or opening a new curatorial department, for instance—and their effect on the present collection growth.

Many curators find such projections difficult, but, in fact, past growth rates are likely to be indicative of future averages, with whatever qualifications may be due to developments that can be anticipated and gauged in proportion to past experience. Thus adjusted, the growth rate (again computed in actual numbers of objects, not as a percentage) may be projected to the design year, for the collection as a whole and for each collection department and material type.

The next variables to be determined are the preferred display/storage ratio and densities. In order to project these, the director and curators in consultation with the conservators, exhibitions officers, and designers (and sometimes a museum planning consultant) must decide on the most suitable and stimulating *display modes*:

- The *aesthetic* presentation of an art collection has a relatively low density—paintings and sculpture in a gallery with adequate viewing distance for visitors.

- A *thematic* presentation, linking objects contextually and interpreting groups of them together, is likely to be denser.

- *Environmental* exhibits (such as a furnished period room) will have still more objects per square meter or square foot.

- A *systematic* display mode, such as a visible storage gallery, provides the highest display densities, usually only about one-third less than the closed storage density for similar material.

Because the size of museum objects and the nature of museum displays varies so widely, each museum must determine its own density variables, and it may then undertake to increase public access to its collections by including at least some display modes of higher density (such as visible storage for suitable collections). Total display space may be distributed by percentage—so much gallery space for aesthetic displays, so much for thematic, and so on.

The collection and content development strategy may now project the museum's space and facility needs as far ahead as the design year, respecting the agreed growth rate, display/storage ratio, and display modes.

If the results of the collection and content development strategy are acceptable within the museum's present resources or anticipated capacity for growth, they may stand as the basis for a master plan; if not, it may be necessary to adjust expectations—either in the rate of acquisitions or in the intended plans for display.

If, for example, the collections are projected to grow by 40 percent over the next twenty years and if 5 percent of the collections are currently on display, it is unlikely that even an expanding museum can retain the "5 percent" display ratio at the end of that period—between now and then, of course, a building expansion can provide a higher proportion of objects on display, or alternatively a decision to make collections accessible online or to have an aggressive program of loaning collections to other museums—or a combination of the three!

Information Management

Information can be defined as "reduction of uncertainty."

For a museum, uncertainty about the meaning, status, or significance of objects in its collection amounts to a loss in their value because the museum must be certain enough of their meaning to display, publish, or in other ways communicate that meaning of those objects to the public. On the other hand, uncertainty can open the door to new research and improved understanding of objects that were identified based on false information or simple prejudice.

Retention and management of information is thus a central concern of all museums.

In many jurisdictions, the documentation of information about the museum's collection has historically been a curatorial function. In others, the position of *registrar* has evolved to specialize in managing the documentation base, even though the information usually originates with curators.

Given its commitment to the public dissemination of information about its collection, the management of that information is in many ways just as important to the museum as the management of the collection itself. Furthermore, the *documentation* of an object in the collection is of limited utility unless it can be related to the *location* of that object. The documentation of museum collections therefore means more than their mere registration or cataloging; it also means management of the location and movement of all objects in the collections. Hence, the registrar should be responsible for the museum stores and for loans and their insurance and must be involved in all exhibition planning, in addition to the management of information about the collection through the compilation of records and the provision of access to them.

Some would go further and suggest that museums are essentially about the distribution of information.

While the primacy of the object in the museum is indisputable, certainly the conversion of formerly manual records to computers, the digitization of automated data (including imaging), the provision of both staff and public access to the data, the possibilities of relating the database to other information systems within the museum, and the proliferation of databases as a means of sharing information within a museum and among institutions all point to the growing need for a more integrated approach to *information management*, of which documentation of the collection is only one important aspect. In some museums a director of communications has been put in charge of all verbal communication by the museum—oral, printed, or electronic.

There is a need for information management planning and the advantages to be gained from its integration across departments and divisions. Ticketing records, for instance, may be used as a mailing list for membership programs, a fund-raising campaign, and a volunteer recruitment drive, while media staff may need to convert the catalog entries for a group of objects into a visitor-friendly database for a visible storage exhibition.

When one considers, in addition to the staff responsible for them, the multiple *users* of these information systems—from curators' research of the collection catalog to providing public access for interactive and multimedia programs—the need for information management to coordinate the many persons involved becomes apparent.

It is also obvious that *task force* project teams (as described earlier in the book) are required to coordinate information management, with the registrar playing a leading role on these teams while focusing on documentation. Here again, a director of communications may be a key position providing leadership and coordination.

When the first edition of this manual was published in 1997, attention was focused on the possibilities for interinstitutional cooperation digitally, pointing to opportunities for sharing information *between* as well as within museums.

During the pandemic, the move to digital became urgent for museums and art organizations, as online access was key to staying connected to audiences and communities. And yet, in July 2020, a report by the Network of European Museum Organizations (NEMO) found that only 20 percent of museum collections were digitally accessible. There were two areas—education and research—that seemed to be driving museums to digitize collections.[8] The pandemic created a massive shift in the museum world's mindset toward digitization.

Today, the emphasis is much more on the provision of digital information to visitors in the museum and to users worldwide. Visitors are snapping digital pictures of museum exhibits—and their labels—with their mobile phones or using their iPhones to pick up and keep information that a few years ago would have been available to them only in a printed catalog. Virtual exhibitions are now routinely produced, either as part of a major physical exhibition in the museum or independently. Millions of users of the museum's digital programs now supplement the thousands or millions who actually visit the museum.

Technological literacy is therefore a must for museums as they adapt and integrate interpretative material with new media. Museums are able to leverage these forums as platforms for visitor engagement and promotion of institutional programs. Some examples include:

• digital features directly linked to curators' computers for real-time content updates;

• interactive opportunities through advanced radio frequency audience response technology;

- descriptive tours of permanent collections available on audio programs for the visually impaired;

- capability for visitors to "bookmark" images of selected objects during tours so that they can download, print, or email them to themselves after the tour; and

- podcasts with interpretative content and interviews available for download.

All of these developments are constantly impacting museum information systems and what is increasingly referred to as digital asset management (DAM). This is apparent in any institution where the registrar may have converted a card catalog or a registration book to a computer database only a few years ago—or in some cases may only be preparing to do so! Museums at whatever stage of automation need a sound data management policy and an information system plan.

The museum's DAM policy should include:

- Issues of intellectual property (IP) for all types of information—spoken, written, published, digital, and broadcast, within the institution and among its staff; a DAM system has a built-in capacity for IP management.

- Museum management's orientation to the use of its databases, or other dissemination of museum information, particularly images. The *digitization* of information, including imagery, has changed the way that we understand the concept of "reproduction" or "replication." The practical questions of encouraging open access to at least some parts of a museum's database and how to control such access (if control is either possible or desirable) should be addressed in the policy. Certainly there is an opportunity for broadening public access, but there are also risks of misuse of imagery; questions of copyright; and potential revenues, now or in the future, that should be addressed in the policy. For example, blockchain, more accurately called "distributed ledger," can be utilized for control of IP and also as a potential revenue stream based on micropayments. Contemporary art museums, where living artists may claim an interest in the information or the images, have a particularly acute challenge.

- The museum's commitment to documenting its collection accurately and comprehensively, retaining all pertinent information in an accessible format indefinitely, and providing public access as appropriate. Certain data—prices and insurance values, for instance—should be kept confidential, but visitor access to most other information—including nonvisitor access electronically—can be and is being provided, not only to scholars but also to the general interested public. The nature of knowledge about the collections—no longer the preserve of curators and registrars but accessible to all—and the nature of publication or dissemination of that knowledge have radically altered.

- Provision to update the DAM policy as technology, legislation, and the international flow of information evolve.

Having resolved, at least for the present, a satisfactory data policy, the museum should be able to develop an *information system plan*, possibly with the help of specialists in this field. Planning for an information system is most efficiently done after the conclusion of a strategic plan or master planning exercise that has identified all museum functions and priorities. This will form the basis for documentation procedures that are described in appendix C.

Public access to documentation is a growing field of applications. Visible storage has been made far more attractive because a simplified keyboard or touch-screen monitor can provide interested visitors with access to the museum's complete (or nearly complete) catalog information about the objects on view. The amount of information available to the visitor about a collection shown in this way is far greater than what could be communicated via a label and museum graphics in a contextual or aesthetic exhibition. Multimedia applications can animate such catalog data and bring it to life for visitors at all levels of familiarity with the subject matter. Virtual exhibitions can take that digital imaging and information to thousands of users worldwide, many of whom may never visit the museum.

The future is bright for museum information and information display systems.

This is an area where museums have already changed extensively and rapidly in recent years, and where the swift pace of change is expected to continue.

A strong DAM supports audience engagement by increasing engagement both online and at exhibitions. The former through the CMS (content management system used for Web publishing), the latter through the custom applications developed for exhibitions and in-house publishing (which likely runs off the same CMS used for the Web).

Digital management systems provide an exciting and engaging interface between the museum's knowledge base and its users. Some visitors may take home spoken interpretation, music, or pictures from an exhibition on their mobile phones, or use them to snap personal memories in the galleries. Virtual exhibitions are now regularly planned and presented as part of most major exhibition projects. Users far from the museum routinely access data and imagery from home.

The very nature of the museum as a public institution is being transformed. Yet the desire to see "the real thing" grows apace. Museum managers will have to be fully informed and aware of the manifold possibilities as the digital information age continues to transform us, and the ways we interact with our cultural ecosystems.

Preservation

Preservation of a museum collection entails the indefinite provision of security (considered as an aspect of facility management in section 7.2), and conservation, the subject of this section. A complete museum conservation program should comprise these four basic categories:

- preventive conservation,

- investigation and treatment,

- restoration, and

- conservation research.

In addition, the preparation and installation of museum objects for exhibitions—the work of the museum's *preparators*—should be closely integrated with that of the conservators.

Preventive Conservation

The aim of the conservator is to preserve the museum object and to slow any change in its original qualities as long as possible.

This is to be accomplished in the context of a public museum, which wishes to make the object visible to the public. Thus the conservation "ideal" of a black box with unvarying temperature and humidity and no light must be compromised to meet the needs of the visitors, and of staff who wish to study the object from time to time. A *conservation policy* should establish the long-range qualitative standards for this endeavor, particularly with regard to preventive conservation measures.

Over the past few decades conservators have increasingly shifted their emphasis from treatment of objects to concentrate on the prevention of deterioration by maintaining conditions as supportive as possible of the long-term intact survival of the museum object. *Preventive conservation* is the applied science of providing an environment that minimizes the object's deterioration in the public museum context. Its focus is on the following checklist of key environmental factors that are addressed in appendix D:

*   temperature and relative humidity,

*   air filtration,

*   light,

*   pests,

*   handling, and

*   emergency procedures.

Investigation and Treatment of Objects

Although preventive conservation has become an increasing concern, the investigation and treatment of museum objects with a view to preserving them is still an important part of the work of any museum conservation department. The conservation studio is the usual locus of this work, unless the objects in the collection are too large to be moved there.

Investigation and treatment may range from a *condition report*, mandatory if the object is to be loaned or taken from store onto display, through routine cleaning to extensive investigation and nonharmful tests of objects in order to determine treatments needed to conserve them, followed by treatments that are sometimes prolonged. These techniques can be extremely various, ranging from relining a painting on a "hot table" to preserving waterlogged wood by soaking it in tubs of polyethylene glycol over many months or years. Conservation laboratory equipment to undertake such investigation and treatment is highly specialized and is constantly subject to technological upgrade, so equipment budget allocations are a recurrent concern.

In larger museums specialized labs may be required for paper conservation, paintings, metals, archaeological materials, waterlogged wood, or other types of objects or materials in the collection. Collection storage rooms should similarly be organized by medium so that all works on paper may be stored together and all textiles and all metals enjoy the same dedicated RH and temperature settings.

Planning and management of this investigation and treatment is a challenging task of assigning priorities and attempting to maintain them, usually in the context of pressing demands for temporary exhibitions or loans that the museum wishes to make. A *conservation treatment plan* should be drafted by the chief conservator, and requests for variations from it should be considered in consultation with the deputy director for collection management and the director or curators. The museum can then balance the pressure of exhibition and loan needs with its long-range concern for the treatment needs of its collection.

Remember, some conservation treatments may be harmful to those undertaking them.

The laboratories must therefore be furnished with exhaust devices to eliminate harmful chemicals from the atmosphere, and the museum's first-aid center, including eyewash and shower facilities, should be adjacent to the laboratories in the event of splashes or other accidents.

Restoration

While conservation treatment is focused on the preservation of the object, or at least on slowing down its deterioration, the *restoration* of museum objects is aimed at returning them to a previous condition—either an original state or some other condition that is preferred, usually for purposes of display. This activity needs to be controlled by both a *restoration policy* and a carefully considered *restoration procedures manual*.

The museum's restoration policy should clarify its philosophical intent in restoring objects. It should make clear that lacunae in the original object must generally remain visible (by painting them with a neutral color, for instance) rather than attempting to conceal or fabricate them as if the object were intact. This policy is extremely important for retaining both the integrity of the collection and the trust of the visitor, who will recognize that the museum has taken pains in restoring the object to allow him or her to distinguish what is original from what has been supplied in the conservator's laboratory.

One important principle common to most conservation treatment and restoration policies is *to do nothing that is irreversible*. This entails written and photographic documentation of treatments in detail and prior investigation of how to remove or undo treatments if this should become necessary in future.

Restoration policy and procedures manuals are particularly important in institutions where volunteers participate in restoration work—as commonly encountered in transportation and military museums, or in agricultural museums and heritage villages.

The well-meaning intentions of such volunteers are sometimes directed toward "restoring" vehicles or machinery to a "band-box" finish that they never had when in use. The restoration procedures manual should require them to proceed with work only under professional supervision, following a step-by-step plan written by the responsible curator or conservator. Documentation of each step in the restoration process, by photographic and written reports, is also of the utmost importance where volunteers are involved.

Exhibit Preparation

Preparators (sometimes simply called technicians) belong to one of the more underrated professional groups in the museum. Yet their work in preparing museum objects for display or loan and installing, dismounting, and returning them to stores brings together both the conservation and public aspects of the museum in specific relation to the collection.

Preparators should be encouraged to work closely with the conservators, especially in ensuring that all support materials used in display or storage are pretested or are known to be safe. If they have mount-making abilities—creating the supports for artifacts, specimens, or works of art—they can save the museum much time and money if they are given time to do this highly specialized but essential work.

Now that we've examined how to manage the museum's collection and content, let's move on to the truly exciting experience of showing it to the public in a creative and engaging manner, which should spark new ideas, connections, and curiosity among the communities who visit.

6.3 The Experience

The visitor experience encompasses all those activities that touch the museum's guests, whether inside the building, on the grounds, in the neighborhood, far away through traveling exhibitions, and even at home, school, or work—through publications, products, and virtual experiences.

There are so many touch points that the museum experience merits a book of its own![9]

> Museums are often thought of as "learning organizations," but unlike the vast majority of learning organizations they neither require nor confer qualifications. Instead, museums only ask that people be interested and curious to know more about what is on offer.

Museums are often thought of as "learning organizations," but unlike the vast majority of learning organizations they neither require nor confer qualifications. Instead, museums only ask that people be interested and curious to know more about what is on offer.

Realistically, though, there of course are some qualifications and barriers—an admission fee (although many museums are now free), a feeling of belonging (challenging to instill because many museums are viewed as exclusive clubs), and the confidence to enter museum spaces that can be viewed as intimidating, especially to marginalized and racialized people.

Recently, museum managers have been giving a lot of thought and research into overcoming those barriers and changing how their institutions engage with new audiences.

Crisis Can Lead to Opportunity

The crises of the pandemic and antiracism/social justice movements have challenged museum management with how to balance the museum's mission and the needs of communities often facing board and stakeholder opposition on the grounds of "We can't be all things to all people" and "Stick to our core mission of art . . . science, etc."

Another challenge is creating a framework so that creativity and innovation flourish. Museum management has tools to guide experiences toward success, such as continual evaluation through surveys of visitors, participants, and nonattenders; hiring and retaining team members and talent who are not only content experts, designers, and educators but also empathetic communicators; as well as inclusive teams trained in conversation, observation, and collaboration.

Inspiring Creativity

Creativity is the "wow" factor that sparks the visitor experience whether for pleasure, discovery, learning, or all three.

It's the inspiration of a museum guide making a historical story come alive today, the surprise a curator conjures by juxtaposing paintings from different cultures never before seen together in the same gallery, the new meaning that an immersive theater confers on the discovery of the human genome, the wonder of visible electricity when an experiment creates an arc of light, or the haunting and magical sounds that whales utter to each other.

All human beings are creative, which is why it's up to museum management to sustain creativity among staff (despite the daily grind) as well as in the visitors' experiences.

> All human beings are creative, which is why it's up to museum management to sustain creativity among staff (despite the daily grind) as well as in the visitors' experiences.

Seven Types of Experience to Choose From

This section reviews the role of management in creating and sustaining seven types of museum experience and introduces some of the tools management can use to keep them fresh and community-centric.

- Exhibitions

- Interpretation

- Learning

- Engagement

- Communication

- Marketing

- Visitor services

These seven functions may be located in one department or distributed among several departments depending on the history of the museum or its priorities. In any case, it is crucial that staff working in these functional areas collaborate in teams to be effective.

Exhibitions, Excitement, and Engagement

Exhibitions are the museum's most well-known and main forum for interacting and engaging with the public. Indeed, the public most often judges the success or failure of a museum by its exhibition program. An exhibition policy and the exhibition development process are two important tools for managing a creative and visitor-responsive exhibition program—and museum managers need to use both of them for maximum success.

Exhibition Policy Flows from Leadership

The *exhibition policy*, which is formulated by the museum's leadership, is the principal management tool for establishing the following checklist:

- the objectives of the exhibition program;

- the philosophy of presentation; and

- the number, frequency, size, and scope of temporary exhibitions.

It is equally important for the staff and the museum's supporters to understand the *objectives* of the exhibition program—for example, the particular balance between scholarship and visitor attraction; the relative emphasis on exhibitions of local, regional, national, and international significance; the role of research in the exhibition program; and the degree to which the museum endeavors to increase public access to its collections through rotation and special exhibitions.

Balancing the Modes of Presentation

There are many different exhibition *philosophies or modes of presentation* used in exhibitions that tend to define the experience.

The many choices of modes of presentation are summarized shortly. Some museums use only one mode (such as contemplation, for example), while others apply many modes. The decision on which modes of exhibition to use is not a policy on which the board or governing authority passes judgment. It is a professional decision by museum management in conversation with staff, based on balancing the mission, visitor experience, and community need.

Here we offer a checklist of seven successful modes of presentation for management to consider when trying to strike this ideal balance:

1. **Contemplative or "Aesthetic" Mode:** In this mode of presentation, museum specimens, artifacts, or works of art are presented for contemplation, with the intention of enhancing the visitor's affective experience of the object. This approach is most common in art museums and galleries, but it is used to good effect in many other types of museums to evoke a sense of wonder or awe, as, for example, in the dramatic display of a piece of moon rock in a science museum.

2. **Thematic or Contextual Mode:** In this mode objects are grouped together to show their relationships with each other, while graphics and computers or other interpretive devices place them in their social, historical, cultural, or scientific context. Exhibits in this mode are

commonly found in archaeology, history, and natural history museums—and most recently in art museums as well.

3. **Environmental Settings:** Room settings or large-scale walk-in dioramas of natural environments re-create or evoke the time and place in which the artifacts or specimens displayed in them were originally found. This mode is almost universally found in historic houses and decorative arts museums, as well as in many natural history museums.

4. **Systematic Mode:** The comprehensive display of museum objects to demonstrate type variations or a range of comparable specimens was the dominant form of museum exhibition in the Victorian period. Today it is found in *visible storage* installations, which offer a systematic display of all or most of the objects of a particular medium or type in the museum's collection, accompanied by computer terminals where the entire catalog entry on each object is keyed to the display by a simple numerical guide to the shelf and individual object.

5. **Interactive:** This mode of display involves the visitor in dialogue with the exhibit. Touchscreen computers utilizing multimedia technology have been particularly effective not only in helping visitors to explore scientific principles in science centers or design principles in design museums but also in allowing them to explore the image catalogs of the entire art collections of many art museums today.

6. **Hands-On:** This mode of display encourages visitors to learn through physical, kinesthetic experience. Mechanical and physical devices can be very effective, especially in the children's (or family) gallery of any museum—demonstrating color mixing in an art museum, the lever in a science museum, or how sails are hoisted in a maritime history museum, for instance. Once the exclusive mode of science centers and children's museums, today many types of museums offer *touch tables* or *discovery boxes* where visitors of all ages can feel the weight of an ancient bronze or touch the glaze on a Korean ceramic, where duplicates, secondary examples, or replicas are used.

7. **Immersive:** The entire museum is an immersive experience! In addition, immersive exhibits in one gallery or in a suite of galleries may be designed to produce a three-dimensional visual and sound experience of art, science, history, or geography—any subject. This approach, first developed for world's fairs, is especially effective for delivering concise messages in a powerful 360-degree format while the visitors retain the freedom to walk through at their own pace.

Multiple Perspectives and Sharing Authority

Underlying the contemporary approach to museum exhibition is a fundamental shift away from the idea of the museum as representing absolute authority in its field to an understanding that the museum presents and interprets facts, concepts, or theories that are sometimes contentious or even contradictory and may reflect the convictions of various experts including communities of use and descendant communities, as well as those of the curators. To be a pluralistic institution implies multiple voices, and this is a key management decision.

Underlying the contemporary approach to museum exhibition is a fundamental shift away from the idea of the museum as representing absolute authority in its field.

Another fundamental shift is the idea of moving away from the museum as a closed institution where curators know all to an open one that invites both the specialist and the broad public to contribute their knowledge and information. This has the greatest impact on exhibition planning, but there may also be a visible effect in the galleries, and on museum websites, where visitors may be invited to record their comments on the exhibits in graphic or electronic form. The museum's exhibition policy should set out the commitment to consult with communities of origin, while museum procedures should set out the guidelines on issues of authority and openness for museum staff in addressing these complex matters during the exhibition development and design process.

How Temporary Is Temporary?

Temporary Exhibition Policy: The sources, number, duration, frequency, size, and scope of temporary exhibitions are all cause for continual debate among museums. How many exhibitions of local significance, how many of regional import, of national importance, and of global origin and character will vary with the type and specific situation of each museum.

Balancing a regional artists' association's annual exhibition with shows of greater range—or replacing one with another—can be a controversial decision.

Many museums offer too many changing exhibitions, leaving the staff too little time for other activities and not allowing the public time to communicate news of the exhibition by word of mouth, the most powerful form of publicity if it is given time to have effect. The duration of travelling shows is often too short, due to constraints imposed by lenders, but the museum's own temporary exhibitions should be planned for longer stays so that they can be effectively marketed.

Blockbuster or Bust?

Size and scope are still more controversial, with continual dire warnings of the "end of blockbusters," despite their continuing popularity. Its advocates point to the great opportunities that the *blockbuster* offers for scholarship as well as audience development, whereas its detractors complain of the drain on staff and the distraction from other aspects of the museum's mission. Meanwhile such large major exhibitions remain one of the great attractions museums can offer to their public.

Many new museums and expansions have been fueled by the desire of their stakeholders to participate in the world of these major international shows. Here are five guidelines that may be useful in evaluating whether a blockbuster (or major) exhibition is worth doing:

- Re-presentation of artifacts and/or works of art as a result of new research. This may offer a juxtaposition of works not often seen together or a new thesis about the artist, the group, or the theme.

- A transformation experience: in other words, surprise and discovery of new attitudes, values, or appreciation of meanings. This is the essential visitor experience that exhibitions can deliver.

- A self-directed experience. Visitors may choose an audio or human guide, but the possibility of a self-directed experience is always there.

- Engagement of visitors of all types: scholars, learners, artists and people in the art business, relaxation seekers, escapists, cultural tourists, first-time visitors, or diligent students.

- Transparency as to the sources of the exhibition's viewpoint. As a medium of representation, the exhibition is actually ill-suited to the omniscient presenter (even though we have been accustomed to this approach in the past). Exhibitions are more suited to a multiplicity of voices.

An exhibition policy should provide the goal for the changing exhibition program consistent with the museum's mission and vision. However, guidance on the number, type, and content of exhibitions is a professional decision based on procedures (including, for example, conservation schedules, research priorities, and community input). The cost of the exhibition program is significant enough that it will be decided by the governing authority; however it should be presented as an annual or multiyear program. The board does not decide on the content of specific exhibitions.

The two-year chart in figure 6.4 is a useful tool for discussing the exhibition plan and budget with the governing authority and for monitoring the exhibition plan as it evolves to ensure an appropriate balance is maintained. The column at the left indicates whether the content of the exhibition (whatever its origin) is local, regional, national, or international in character. The types of exhibition for a notional regional museum are ranged across the top as an example.

This generic example is for a museum with a strong regional history mission, mandate, and collection. The plan is for a robust nineteen exhibitions over a two-year period in which ten are based on the museum's own textile and works on paper collections. Six small exhibitions would focus on new acquisitions, current research, and items of local or regional significance from the collection. Over the two-year period the museum will mount four larger exhibitions on broader themes, two on local and two on regional subjects. The museum will also borrow five larger exhibitions over this two-year period, three of which will have national or global reference, providing the community with a "window on the world." Toward the end of this two-year period, staff should evaluate the program, and the director should recommend changes if it is felt that a greater or lesser number of exhibitions of the various types is required, or if there is a demand for more exhibitions of global or national scope.

Scope	Rotation	Small	Thematic	Loan
Local		3	2	
Regional	4	3	2	2
National				2
Global				1

Figure 6.4. Sample Two-Year Exhibition Schedule for a Regional Museum. *Lord Cultural Resources.*

An exhibition is a medium of communication that is the museum's main method of connecting with the public. To communicate effectively through such a social medium requires all the resources of the museum—and often involves resources from outside as well.

An exhibition is a medium of communication that is the museum's main method of connecting with the public. To communicate effectively through such a social medium requires all the resources of the museum—and often involves resources from outside as well. Its exhibition development process is the method that the museum employs to coordinate all these resources so that exhibitions open on time, within budget, and to the desired level of quality. This case study from the famed Rijksmuseum demonstrates exciting new approaches.

Engaging Young Imaginations at the Rijksmuseum

By Annemies Broekgaarden

Amsterdam's Rijksmuseum is one of the world's most respected museums of art and history.

With a superb collection of over a million works of art, its permanent presentation features more than eight thousand objects in eighty rooms. These cover a period spanning from the Middle Ages to the twentieth century in chronological displays that combine paintings, sculpture, applied art, and historical objects. Together they tell the story of Dutch art and history. Over the years, millions of visitors have seen these amazing collections, attracted by the largest number of Rembrandts on display anywhere, alongside Dutch Masters such as Johannes Vermeer, Frans Hals, Rachel Ruysch, and Vincent Van Gogh.

The Rijksmuseum reopened in 2013, following an intense, ten-year restoration process. In the course of that decade, the museum took time to reinvent itself, a process in which I was privileged to be involved starting in December 2008. Our aim was to change gears: rather than offer a traditional museum experience presenting objects for display, we would transform into an open museum, making every visitor feel welcome. *Education became a priority*. As head of public engagement and education and part of the museum's management team, my job was to develop the education department to meet these new objectives. Having identified our common values, we then formulated the museum's new DNA:

- Authenticity—always starting with an authentic object or story

- Quality—striving for the highest quality

- Personal—giving visitors a personal experience (preferably with a person as intermediary)

- Innovative—innovating and staying innovative in every way

- Clear and simple—remaining accessible to everyone

Our goal was transparent: to strive for an open, accessible museum catering to all audiences. Realizing this has been our ongoing challenge.

Since I joined the museum, *school pupils and families with children* have become key audiences for the museum. Schools play a vital role because pupils are the museum's most inclusive audience. Every child in the Netherlands goes to school, and our aim is for every schoolchild in the Netherlands to visit our museum at least once. We are proud to share that school visits have grown from 30,000 in 2009 to 200,000 in 2019. Moreover, most of these children have taken part in a guided program. In 2019 we welcomed 480,000 children and our school programs are highly regarded.

How did we *reduce the barriers for schoolchildren*?

Our expertise is based on research results. As we learned how to connect with teachers and pupils, we realized that the following were crucial:

- to offer curriculum-based programs, preferably programs that supplement lessons in the classroom;

- to reduce costs as much as possible;

- to provide (inter)active programs because children learn by doing;

- to provide free transport facilities; and

- to make programs fun.

We have implemented these lessons and continue to work with teachers to develop our programs further. The result is that teachers can now use these programs in the classroom. We also work with partners such as ThiemeMeulenhoff, one of the country's leading educational publishers. Some programs now link directly to online content and where the museum component adds value, we develop lessons together. This, along with our team of eighty skilled museum guides and twelve professional actors, has resulted in a much deeper engagement with schools.

Creating a museum that acts as an attractive place for families with children to spend their free time is a bigger challenge. For many years, despite our best efforts, parents thought of the museum as an unattractive destination for a family visit. Unlike schools, where art is part of the curriculum, parents who decide to visit a museum have to make that decision on their own, which means that those who haven't been raised to enjoy culture are less likely to bring their children to a museum.

How Did We Make the Museum More Attractive for Families and Children?

Everyone working at the museum should be educated on the importance of families and children as a main audience: from the directors and the management team to security personnel, public services, and the marketing department. Like adults, children want to feel welcome as visitors, and they need tools to connect with our collections and stories—tools that engage their needs and interests. A key aspect, therefore, is to be aware of what children find appealing—and this can vary enormously between the ages of four and twelve. We relied on research to help us make informed changes to our museum, and our research has enabled us to embrace the following lessons:

- Take the needs of families into account and respond by developing age-specific tools and programs to help visitors connect with art and history.

- Grant free entrance/tickets up to the age of eighteen.

- Invest in educational programs and policies and in training museum staff, security personnel, and public service colleagues to help them understand families and their needs.

- Install a family desk to specifically help families visiting the museum with children.

- Provide a space to rest, where visitors can consume their own food and drink.

- Accept that children are energetic and create awareness for this among the museum staff.

- Provide hands-on programs to stimulate curiosity—learning to see by doing.

- Personal guidance provides a better experience.

- Develop marketing plans to inform potential visitors about our programs and create special events.

- Develop children's programs in consultation with children and those who bring them to the museum.

- Provide opportunities for intergenerational learning.

Over the past ten years we have developed a range of products and programs to enable families with children to access and enjoy our collections and exhibitions. The result: an independent board of children judged the Rijksmuseum as *child-friendly*, with a score of 8.3 out of 10.

We also developed an innovative educational center, Teekenschool, with art workshops and an interactive space hosting a unique theatrical program for children. All Teekenschool programs involve "learning to see by doing," and a visit to the museum is always part of the program.

An Exhibition for Children in Family Groups or with Caregivers

We are proud that our family audience is growing, and we have decided to take our mission one step further. In June 2023, after the Vermeer exhibition closed, our entire exhibition wing of one thousand square meters, began hosting a family exhibition titled "Mission Masterpiece," focusing on our eight years and older audience. Families will be able to learn more about our collections by taking part in activities and will discover more about an aspect of the museum where art meets science.

The exhibition deals with fundamental questions such as: When is an object a masterpiece? Why does a museum take this object into its collection? When do you display the object in the museum? Scientific research, the children learn, helps to answer these questions.

Although it's a vital aspect of the Rijksmuseum's work, visitors are seldom aware of our involvement in scientific research, even though it plays a crucial part in expanding our understanding of the museum collection and history. Restoration, for example, is based on extensive technical research. With our state-of-the-art technology, we lead the way in conservation and scientific development.

"Mission Masterpiece" is a hands-on learning challenge for children and adults, who must solve research questions by examining six carefully selected real objects that they examine with different research techniques. By doing so, the visitors are able to answer questions such as: Is this crown made of gold? Are the gems on the crown real gems? Is this ceramic object still in one piece? Is this painting a real Vermeer?"

The idea is for participants to learn about specific objects through technical analysis, learning to use methods such as ultraviolet spectroscopy, macro XRF, and dendrochronology. After the process of technical analysis they can decide whether the object is a masterpiece worth presenting in the museum.

Visitor Research and the Importance of the Narrative

The exhibition was developed based on visitor research by Motivaction and regular testing with children (and their parents or caregivers) in different age groups. We also used the many years of experience with our Teekenschool program "Sporenonderzoek," a track-and-trace program inviting children to learn how to investigate whether a painting is a genuine Rembrandt.

By becoming involved in research themselves, participants gain a new awareness of the reasons why an object is a masterpiece. It also gives them the sense of looking behind the scenes. A narrative developed by an award-winning children's author and an immersive environment experience makes the concept challenging and fun. The narrative also gives context and a sense of urgency to the mission.

Mission Masterpiece—The Research Challenge

Children and their parents move through the exhibition together, entering a transition room where a reporter asks for help with her mission to discover masterpieces in the collection storage vault. All visitors are issued a lab coat and a badge when entering the research area.

The six rooms of the research area each present one of the six objects that play a central role in the exhibition and six research stations where the group (a maximum of five visitors per group) will conduct their research. The results are noted on the badge with pencil, and a "help line" can be activated by a QR code.

In the final room the group is asked to present one ultimate masterpiece to the reporter on a screen and the visitor and the artwork become part of a new artwork that the reporter presents in our Gallery of Honour. By means of a QR code this video can be downloaded and shared by social media.

Website and Publication

As we will limit the amount of text in the exhibition, children and the adults accompanying them can visit the website for more information. By means of film, the items researched will be explained in a playful and humorful way and the site will also contain "puzzles" to acquaint the children even more with research if they are interested. The publication that will be developed with the exhibition is done with a specialized publishing company producing high-quality "puzzle books."

Realization and Partnerships

This exhibition—which we will call a research challenge—was developed with a designer specializing in creating interactive exhibitions for children, and it is a joint project with NEMO Science Museum. We thought it was an advantage to have a partner who specialized in translating scientific research into accessible, hands-on experiences for kids.

"Mission Masterpiece" was a unique project for the Rijksmuseum, and as far as we know, no national art museum has ever dedicated an entire exhibition wing to a show for children.

We developed the exhibition together with Northern Light, a design company that creates interactive exhibitions for families together with Irma Boom Office who is responsible for the graphic and visual design.

We look forward to analyzing the results of how "Mission Masterpiece" attracted new audiences and how it contributed to more awareness of our national collections among children. We also hope to increase the profile and value of scientific research in museums and to make children—as well as adults—aware that objects can be masterpieces for a variety of different reasons.

Figure 6.5.   Rijksmuseum and NEMO Science Museum invite children and their families to investigate real works of art. *Photo by Olivier Middendorp. Courtesy of Rijksmuseum.*

A Dynamic Yet Balanced Approach

These three types of exhibition committees require great facilitation skills by museum management—but they are all needed to ensure a dynamic yet balanced approach: the standing exhibition committee, exhibition task force, and advisory committees.

1. Standing Exhibition Committee

Composed of staff representing all departments (because everyone is affected by the exhibition schedule), the standing exhibition committee meets monthly—or at least quarterly—to review the upcoming schedule and the results of recent exhibitions. This committee, which reports to the director, should also recommend members of exhibition task forces for specific major shows being planned. The director or a designate chairs this committee, and it is the director who has the final decision-making role in deciding whether or not to proceed with a particular exhibition.

2. Exhibition Task Force

For all major exhibitions, whether originated by the museum or borrowed, there should be a specific task force project team that combines the talents of all those responsible for the many aspects of the exhibition project. Each team should include representatives of the following functions in the museum:

Collection Management

- curatorial

- conservation

- documentation

Public Programs

- exhibitions

- design

- education

- publications

- website

Administration

- finance

- development

- security

- visitor services

- marketing

Exhibition task force project teams are project oriented and nonhierarchical. In selecting personnel to serve on a particular task force, therefore, department heads should take account of the knowledge and ability of each staff member rather than their position or title alone. Where outside contractors are involved—in exhibition design, for example—they should also participate in the exhibition task force meetings.

> Exhibition task force project teams are project oriented and nonhierarchical . . . department heads should take account of the knowledge and ability of each staff member rather than their position or title alone.

Department heads should recommend their representatives to each exhibition task force, but the director should have final approval of the composition of the project team and should appoint its chairperson and project manager. Although the relevant curator may be the obvious choice to chair an exhibition, in some cases the exhibition department representative, an educator, or a conservator may be a suitable choice. While the chairperson may be responsible for the content of the exhibition, a separate *project manager* will be needed for larger exhibitions and may be an experienced consultant contracted from outside the museum. The director delegates penulti-mate decision making on the budget and schedule to the task force. The chairperson and the project manager report to the standing exhibition committee and the director, who is an ex officio member of the task force and may join its meetings at any time to review progress.

Depending on the exhibition timeline, the team might begin by meeting monthly but will need to meet more frequently as opening day approaches. Regular reports from all participants should be heard at each meeting—so that security concerns, for example, are not left to the last minute. The project team is the forum for staff ideas and creativity, so all staff should feel welcome to present ideas and suggestions on the exhibition to the project team. Crediting the members of the team on exhibition literature and a graphic in the gallery is a good way to inspire dedication to an outstanding result.

The challenges experienced by exhibition task force project teams are legendary: the members of the team are required not only to bring their own professional expertise to the table but also to be skilled in working cross-functionally and to understand the needs of all other disciplines, usually under time and budget pressures. The team leader needs to be both a skilled facilitator and a determined project manager. These are *not* necessarily the same abilities required to achieve a PhD in art history or paleontology, nor to be a talented exhibition designer. Training in teamwork is often required, and an experienced project manager contracted from outside the staff may be the best way to achieve the result everyone wants to see.

3. Advisory Committees

These are often established when the museum does not have all the in-house expertise needed for an exhibition. These may be committees of academics, collectors, and scholars in the field of the exhibition whose knowledge will enhance the quality of the show. Or they may be an advisory group based in the community of interest relevant to the exhibition, locally or globally, who can ensure that the exhibition responds to the cultural experience and community sensitivities.

Exhibitions of First Nations and Indigenous people, and their belongings, which were often looted and misinterpreted by museums, require significant engagement from Indigenous curators and the descendant communities. Marc Mayer's case study on how First Nations and Indigenous art was integrated into the Canadian National Gallery's permanent exhibitions and into its development of two major international Indigenous exhibitions offers an informative description of these processes.

Exhibitions on a specific culture, or controversial or difficult subjects like slavery, antiblack racism, or migration, for instance, could involve members of the communities directly involved as well as experts in those subjects to ensure that multiple perspectives are represented. The results can be significant in ensuring enthusiastic participation by that community to share their stories, lend their collections, and participate as guests.

Advisory committees often also involve the museum in divergent views of what is significant about a culture or in contentious accounts of history. The key to successful advisory committees is often the director's personal commitment and involvement and always a sincere intention not merely to listen but to implement suggestions or to explain why not, and to achieve consensus concerning other solutions.

The Exhibition Process

Where do exhibition ideas come from? The director's leadership, curatorial research, and suggestions of the educators are among frequent in-house sources. Community conversations and understanding of communities needs are also great sources for exhibition ideas. The museum should care about the ideas of all its staff including security guards who have the most contact with the public; here again conversation is an effective way to gather their ideas. Some museums conduct surveys of their visitors, attendees at events, and through their contact lists. A suggestion box in the lobby, and on the museum's website, inviting exhibition suggestions, is also recommended. And of course many exhibition ideas come from outside the museum, from the *zeitgeist* of current interests and concerns.

Just how the exhibition evolves from a vague idea to opening day will differ from museum to museum. Figure 6.6 represents the general process that is then described in appendix E.

Communication versus Interpretation

> The term *interpretation* is somewhat misleading because it suggests that the "language" of museum objects is somehow "foreign" and needs to be "translated."

Interpretation is the term used to describe the ways that the museum *communicates* with the public about its collections and research activities. The term *interpretation* is somewhat misleading because it suggests that the "language" of museum objects is somehow "foreign" and needs to be "translated"—which is essentially one-way communication—whereas museums should be about two-way communication between the museum and the public, including orientation, way-finding, labels, and provision of information—both internal and external.

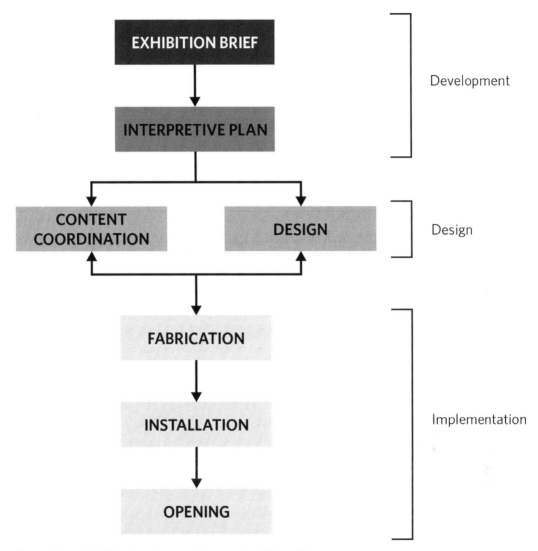

Figure 6.6. Exhibition Development Process. *Lord Cultural Resources.*

The job of museum management is to formulate a communication policy for board approval that guides where, when, and how the museum communicates. Museum staff prepares communication processes and protocols that ensure consistency, professionalism, and appropriate approvals.

Visitor Orientation

Visitor orientation is of two types; unfortunately, museums tend to undervalue both of them:

- *Physical orientation* is informing visitors about where they are, the visitor services available and in what languages, what there is to see and do, and how and where to find those experiences.

- *Intellectual orientation* is clarifying what the museum is about and the many ways to explore it so that guests are enabled to make informed choices about their visit. For example, should they follow the prescribed visitor route, or is there a quick highlights tour? A special family gallery? Is there a resource center for visitors who prefer to cover fewer subject areas in more depth?

Visitor studies and common sense indicate that guests who spend most of their time lost or looking for the toilets or who are not sure what is on offer in the various galleries do not get as much from the exhibits as those who know their way around. Not surprisingly, being lost or uncertain increases the "I don't belong here" feeling and discourages repeat visits. Informing visitors at the outset about services such as coatroom, rest areas, restaurant, shop, toilets, baby change areas, first aid, use of wheelchairs and strollers, and the role of guards and information staff helps all visitors, especially first-timers, to feel at ease.

> If they do not understand the full range of the museum's exhibits and programs, they may leave mistakenly thinking, "We've done that," rather than, "There's so much more to see and do, we must come back."

The quality of orientation also impacts the museum's revenue stream. If visitors are not aware at the beginning of the visit that there is a pleasant café on the roof, they may not make time for it. If they do not understand the full range of the museum's exhibits and programs, they may leave mistakenly thinking, "We've done that," rather than, "There's so much more to see and do, we must come back."

Once museum management and staff grasp the importance that orientation adds to the quality of the visitor experience, visitor orientation can often be improved. For example:

- If there is not enough room in the lobby, consider that posters outside the building can begin to communicate the museum's philosophy and what is inside.

- Use all possible means to communicate the visitor's choices, such as informational signage, interactive kiosks, the information desk, pamphlets, and floor maps.

- Develop a consistent way-finding system, starting outside and with directional signing throughout the museum's public spaces, and link signing with print and audiovisual materials.

- Train all frontline staff in the importance of helping visitors find their way and encourage staff to report back to management on the problems they learn from visitors—and then do something to solve the problems.

- Use the auditorium for intellectual orientation, where a short audiovisual presentation of six to ten minutes can tell the core story of the museum.

Labels

"Labels are the foot soldiers in the museum wars," is how one curator described the centrality of labels. "Wars" may be an apt description of the label-writing process in many museums. As with exhibition development, each museum develops its own procedure for writing label and panel text. The museum's interpretation policy should guide

- the names or themes of galleries;

- the size of label or text panel;

- the type of information to be provided (date, artist/inventor, provenance, accession number, gift, description, uses, donor, and the like);

- the tone (authoritative, pluralist, objective?); and

- the style (everyday language or technical terms?).

The museum's label-writing procedure establishes

- the word limits;

- type size and color;

- placement; and

- writing and approval procedures.

The label text process generally starts with the curator responsible for a particular gallery or exhibit. Next, the education department reviews it from the visitor perspective, and the publications department edits for style. The curator provides final sign-off on the text, while the director is usually the court of last resort. But the entire process should be controlled by the interpretation policy and a procedures manual.

Provide Valuable Information

We are living in an information age, when museum visitors both online and onsite seem to have an insatiable thirst for more information.

We are also living in a disinformation age in which people have difficulty separating fact from fiction and truth from lies. Fortunately, museums continue to have a higher level of trust than other public sources of information.[10] This means that it is even more important than in the past for the museum's presentation and distribution of information be well considered, consistent, carefully fact-checked, and checked for cultural sensitivity. All staff need communication training because they will all at some point be asked by the public for information, usually through one of these ways:

> Museums continue to have a higher level of trust than other public sources of information.

- The information desk is the front line for information. The staff or volunteers are prepared to respond to questions ranging from where to catch the bus to where a specific painting is to be found. Larger museums place information desks throughout the museum as well as at the entrances.

- Information staff or volunteers may be positioned at desks or may roam the galleries wearing shirts that say "Ask Me." Science centers, which can provide these interpreters with white lab coats, have been best at this type of information provision (which is, of course, labor intensive), but they are invaluable wherever they are employed, and whatever shirt or jacket they wear. This is an excellent role for well-trained volunteers.

- Interactive information centers provide visitors with a range and depth of information convenient to the galleries.

- The library may be fully accessible to the public or open at special times or by appointment. Very often museum libraries are unnecessarily restricted to staff when they would be of great value to the limited number of visitors who wish to explore the subject matter of the museum in greater depth.

- Computers and multimedia terminals, installed in or near galleries to provide contextual information; access to some card catalog data on objects; or simulation exercises and games to explain processes, concepts, and principles. These are a valuable component of visible storage galleries, keyed to a number code shown on the shelves so that visitors can instantly access the museum's catalog information (except for insurance or security data) for each individual object in a dense display, affording access to a large range of that part of the museum's collection.

- Audio guides, personal device tours, and QR codes, for both special exhibitions and permanent collections, are evolving from the rentable wands into systems linked to iPods or mobile phones. Audio systems are particularly important for highly popular exhibits like famous paintings because they make it possible for large numbers of people to view them without crowding around to read a label. The content and tone of the scripts for these guides should, like the labels and graphics, reflect the museum's communication policy even when created by a contractor.

- Tours, lectures, and demonstrations. Because of their interpersonal quality, these tried and true methods continue to be the preferred way for many visitors and museum interpreters to communicate. Most museums offer a range of tours and lectures by docents (paid or volunteers), along with occasional lectures by specialists. In history, science, and children's museums, there may be demonstrators (sometimes costumed) and interpreters on hand to explain the exhibits.

Languages and Universal Design

The languages in which information will be available and *"universal design"* for special physical, hearing, and visual needs are all part of the policy.

In a globalized world, museums should communicate not only in the main languages spoken in the community but also related to collections and stories on display—especially Indigenous collections.

Where there are several official languages, as in Switzerland, Belgium, Wales, or Canada, many museums are required to provide all interpretation in multiple languages, including signage, labels, publications, and guided tours. In the many regions and communities that are culturally diverse, but where there is only one official language, the museum should provide leaflets, guidebooks, information paddles, and directional signs in the main minority languages. Label text may be made available on broadsheets in many languages as well as in large-print size for the visually impaired and for older visitors. Directional signs and floor plans in the minority languages are particularly important for reasons of public safety if they include emergency exit instructions. The museum should ensure that at least one member of its information staff who is able to communicate in the main languages spoken in the community is on duty at all times.

Tourism, particularly cultural tourism, has become such a major factor, not only for museums but for their governments, that museums that attract or hope to attract a high proportion of tourist visitors should consider providing services in the four or five main tourist languages. The main orientation, directional signs, and information leaflets should be prominently displayed in these languages, with translations of label text, guidebooks, and catalogs available for sale in the shop and for consultation at information desks and in study and rest areas. Guided tours should be available in various languages and for special needs groups, including the visually impaired. Digital audio guides can be adjusted to meet the needs of the hearing impaired and can be made available in numerous languages.

Planning for physically, visually, or hearing impaired persons should guide all aspects of museum design, not only the toilets and circulation routes, which should be barrier free and wide enough to accommodate wheelchairs. *Universal design* is the term that has been used to refer to ensuring that all aspects of a museum or an exhibition encourage access by all visitors, whatever their limitations.

Despite the challenges of information and disinformation, centralized management of the museum's communication services is rare in museums.

Typically, information desks are managed by visitor services or the communication department, while tours and lectures are organized by the education department, and the library is its own department; meanwhile, label writing, audio guide, and multimedia production are happening in many different places. Should there be one "interpretation" or "communications" department in the public programs or operations division, or is there a virtue in having a multiplicity of departments providing information? Because many departments communicate with the public, it may make the most sense to create a standing interdepartmental communication team that includes representatives from all departments, with a mandate to implement the museum's communication policy and coordinate the growing number of communication initiatives that will—as long as the museum staff is visitor responsive and creative—keep emerging everywhere.

The Learning Museum

Museums are redefining their role as public educational institutions. One of the signs of this realignment is a change in nomenclature from the generic "Education" to the more directed title, "Learning," which suggests not only that the interest is focused on the learner (rather than the educator) but also that the museum is a learning institution, and that there is learning on the part of the staff as much as on the part of the visitor. For a fuller treatment of this new approach to learning, see *The Manual of Museum Learning*.[11]

School Groups

School parties usually comprise from 15 to 25 percent of museum attendance, introducing many young people to museums and performing a valuable service for school systems. There is an increasing emphasis on relating the school museum visit to curriculum, learning objectives, and educational attainment targets. Cutbacks in school budgets have made museum bus trips harder to justify. Museum education departments are obliged to work more and more closely with teachers and curriculum advisors to integrate their programs with the needs of the schools. Some of the tools being developed include:

- *Advisory committees* in which museum educators work with teachers and community advisory committees to ensure that the themes, classes, and workshops they present are relevant, up-to-date, and meet the children's needs in the specific context of that museum's community. This is particularly important in marginalized communities.

- *Teacher resource centers* have been established where teachers can borrow materials to use in the classroom to better prepare students for the visit and for follow-up activities. This resource center may also provide training workshops for teachers. Some museum training programs confer state accreditation for the teacher.

- *Secondment to the museum* of staff from the school system is a good way to facilitate close coordination and mutual understanding. A cross-appointment of a teacher who works half time in the museum and half time coordinating school visits is ideal.

- *School–museum liaison officers* connect with all other teachers in that school, passing on information about new exhibitions or other programs that will be of interest to them. A semi-annual meeting of these liaison teachers at the beginning of each school term is an excellent way of ensuring that the museum's learning opportunities are not being missed.

- *Student volunteers, interns, and students* on co-op or work-study programs provide invaluable training opportunities and keep the museum in touch with young people.

- *The museum's website* can create a more integral relationship between museums and schools. Students can access museum collections and information about them and even consult museum curators from their classroom.

- *Museum schools* are the result of establishing partnerships with schools, with lessons taught in the galleries, often with special attention to science, art, or whatever is the subject matter of the museum.

Many museums rely on volunteers to guide school visits and activities so that staff educators may focus on program development, training, and evaluation to ensure a growing level of quality. While a dedicated corps of volunteers is a tremendous asset for the museum, the challenge is in attracting volunteers who are able to respond to the interests of an increasingly diverse population, particularly in urban schools. Many museum education departments are working with community advisory committees to develop strategies to meet this challenge.

To cover the costs of school programs, museums may contract with school systems to receive an annual allocation for a specific service. Some museums have a per-student charge that varies with the cost of the program, depending on whether an educator has to accompany the class or not. Other museums offer school programs free of charge in recognition of their local, state, or national government grants, which may be conditional on such a service. Many museums are developing partnerships with the private sector to provide free or low-cost school visits, especially for areas where schools and families may not have sufficient means to pay.

Adult and Family Learning Programs

Museums offer informal education, which, with the exception of guided tours, consists of *self-directed learning.*

The goal should be *affective* rather than cognitive learning, aimed at affecting visitors' interests, attitudes, or valuations rather than imparting information. This means that organized education programs should respond to people's interests and abilities and thus will vary widely, including workshops, courses, lectures, films, concerts, family activities, tours, seminars, symposia, and artists in residence. Some of these programs, such as a concert or film series, may be presented and perceived primarily as entertainment rather than as education, learning can be fun!

> The goal should be *affective* rather than cognitive learning, aimed at affecting visitors' interests, attitudes, or valuations rather than imparting information.

Programs like the highly popular "sleepovers" at science centers when children participate in an overnight program of learning activities that includes sleeping in the galleries and breakfast in the café the next morning. Families with young children are particularly eager for learning opportunities near home. Meeting the needs of this group is especially important because studies show that children who participate in cultural activities with their family are most likely to be participants as adults. Museum "Saturday Morning Classes" (some of which date to the early years of the twentieth century) are a good example: they are still going strong in many communities and being extended to summer and holiday museum camps.

Today, museum education departments are reaching an even wider family audience through special education galleries with a variety of exhibits and hands-on activities for school groups on weekdays and for families on weekends and holidays. In her case study, Annemies Broekgaarden, head of public engagement and education at the Rijksmuseum in Amsterdam, describes a major new hands-on gallery for families and children.

The cost of providing public education activities, with or without nominal charges to the schools, is often covered by user fees, corporate sponsorship, and project grants from government agencies and private foundations. It is usually not possible for museums to recover all that they expend on their learning programs. Frederic Bertley shows that by taking museum learning outside the museum can engage both audiences and funders.

Scaling Science Education by Scaling the Museum Walls

By Frederic Bertley

In general, museums are defined as physical buildings wherein artifacts, documents, art, sculptures, photographs, bio species, and now digital phenomena are displayed for audience consumption. Grander than this monolithic, almost sterile, definition of museums, however, is the larger landscape of experience.

Every museum is part of that larger landscape of cultural institutions, which, in their simplest form exist to provide some kind of enlightening cultural experience for their guests. At our Center of Science and Industry (COSI), we learned that by scaling our own walls, we could extend our own efforts to community scale. This transformation, when taken to community scale, leads to a more educated and cultured citizenry and community.

This is why the notion of the "Museum Ecosystem" becomes exceptionally important. To keep pace with current technology, museums need to migrate toward a hybrid construct wherein cultural experiences are provided within *and* without the walls of their physical establishments. This means that museums need to migrate from place-based visits only to space-based experiences.

Indeed, museums need to evolved from simply being an address on a given street or avenue to a more engaged cultural institution that extends far beyond our walls in order to fully connect with the community. An effective migration into that deeper "Museum Ecosystem" will result in a more robust and relevant impact for communities and people—where they live, learn, and lounge. This approach will enable museums to become a relevant vehicle of content creation, curation, and dissemination unrestricted by a brick-and-mortar approach.

Here are some successful examples that we've learned from at the Center of Science and Industry, and helped us effectively reach out beyond our museum walls. These programs and experiences can be ideated, customized, developed, and executed in any science museum or cultural institution regardless of size, budget, or mission.

Curating Community Connected Science Festival

Originating several decades ago in Europe, science festivals were developed as a way to build community around science and engineering to ultimately increase awareness and comfort about science, engineering, technology, and math (STEM). The proliferation of science festivals in the United States has been exciting, with festivals ranging from smaller, one-day events to larger, multiday programs, showcasing everything from cutting-edge lectures to hands-on, engaging, and experiential offerings for people of all ages, backgrounds, and scientific acuity.

Six years ago, COSI embarked on the creation of the COSI Science Festival (CSF) for our Central Ohio region. Through an elaborate matrix of partners, including corporate, public, private, education, and not-for-profit organizations, COSI created a comprehensive, inclusive, community-driven festival that ensures all are welcome and everyone will be engaged. With a geographic reach drawing from eighteen cities spread across six counties, and an impact of reaching more than fifty thousand participants, our festival event also has an online presence and digital impact in all fifty US states.

To effectively take science to the community, COSI partnered with elected officials (senators, congresspersons, mayors) from every city and district in Ohio and engaged their constituents to codesign science experiences relevant and customized to their micro-communities. As such, we developed over one hundred events in various places including, but not limited to, neighborhoods, community centers, YMCAs, schools, churches, synagogues, other nonprofits, restaurants, small businesses, large companies, and municipal parks throughout Central Ohio. We "brought science" and our museum to these communities. Programs include: Star Parties, Bioblitz, Youth Programs, Exhibition Booths, STEM Stars, The Big Science Celebration, and many other community-curated STEM engagement opportunities.

Walking the Talk with a Digital Footprint

With the growing concern of science communication and the importance of having trusted spaces to acquire content, we created two modalities for bringing science communication to an audience beyond our walls.

The first is a prime-time, magazine-style television show called *QED with Dr. B.*, and the second is an animated series of three- to five-minute videos called *Dr. B. in 3*. The television show, *QED with Dr. B.*,[12] was developed in partnership with PBS, while the *Dr. B. in 3* animated series was conceived, developed, and executed entirely in-house.[13]

Collectively these programs have won numerous awards, including five Emmys, for their capacity to reach audiences outside of the museum and communicate science in an engaging and easily digestible manner. Moreover, the creative media programs provide cutting-edge, understandable science content for a wide spectrum of individuals and diverse audiences. Many of our viewers, due to geographic, financial, or other reasons, have never come to our physical COSI building, but they regularly consume our digital content from these two programs and therein, from their testimonials, have built an identity with and appreciation for our museum.

Boxed-In: Creating a Learning Laboratory

Our physical doors were closed for fifteen months due to the pandemic. Like many other museums and organizations, this unplanned closure forced upon us the question: How does the institution remain relevant as a traditional museum if your doors are closed? Luckily, for us at COSI, we were already engaged in an important, but prescient, thought experiment: "What would COSI be without its bricks and mortar?" With this question on the forefront of our minds, we were poised to create relevant, engaging, and accessible museum-curated experiences for our guests, donors, and the public at large. Second, while the pandemic did not cause the educational gap within various communities and along socioeconomic lines, it certainly exacerbated it. STEM fields fared the worst here, as the educational gap was most pronounced in STEM subjects.

To help provide assistance during our museum closure, and understanding that guests could not come to COSI for a visit, we would put COSI into a box! Therein was the birth of our STEM-interactive COSI CONNECTS Kits for the K–12 landscape.[14] Each STEM kit was a topic-specific box with five different hands-on activities mapped to the Ohio Science Learning Standards as well as the Next Generation Science Standards (NGSS). Moreover, the content for our science kits was developed in partnership with experts from various organizations and entities. For example, the Nature Kit was developed with the Ohio Department of Natural Resources (ODNR); Space Kit—NASA; Energy Kit—USDOE; Engineering Kit—Honda; Hyperloop Kit—Virgin Hyperloop; and Water Kit—EPA.

In addition, to help address the aforementioned underserved K–12 population, we created a version of the STEM kit called the "Learning Lunchbox"[15] and partnered with agencies to ensure kids in more science-challenged zip codes had free access to this resource.

The name "Learning Lunchbox" references some of our early partners, food pantries, with whom we would provide our science kits alongside their food provisions. We have since expanded our distribution partners to include schools, libraries, and community centers. We also distribute our Learning Lunchboxes alongside social services including foster care, recovery centers, and homeless shelters.

The impact of this latter work was measured and analyzed by Harvard Business School, where a case study report was generated espousing our effective model of STEM education engagement as a social good. The outcomes and impact of these kit distribution programs have been outstanding and have allowed COSI to deliver our science education mission to the most vulnerable communities, who might not otherwise visit our museum or be exposed to the COSI brand.

All of these successes have been made possible by and in concert with public and private partners, underscoring the power of partnerships. Overall, our suite of "Boxed Learning Laboratories" has been a true extension and growth opportunity for COSI and other science museums specifically, as well as cultural institutions in general.

Additional Great Outcomes Reaching Out Beyond the Walls: Diversity, Equity, and Sustainability

In our modern world, science is everywhere; and as such, science is for everyone. This necessitates a reframing of who should have access to science literacy, as well as the opportunity to leverage the promise of STEM careers.

Democratizing access to STEM education and removing stereotypes and prejudices that sometimes haunt the scientific community are critical to the assurance of a healthy, just, and fair society. Moreover, the greater the population that participates in the science enterprise ensures a larger pool of individuals from which is drawn the next generation of great scientists, engineers, and persons who may transform our very world with amazing discoveries or inventions.

This is exemplified in one of COSI's signature programs, *The Color of Science*, which exposes K–12 students as well as the lay public to women and persons of color who are scientists and engineers, living in your own communities.[16] In fact, there is a built-in social justice component to supporting and promoting the notion that science is for everyone—and this is especially true offsite of our campuses.

Two very important outcomes of reaching beyond your walls is the capacity to significantly improve on the diversity of your institution's audience. While progress has been made within the museum landscape to engage more diverse individuals and communities, there often exists a "sterility of brick-and-mortar institutions" and a sense of "that place is not for me." By reaching out beyond the walls and engaging audiences in their communities, in their homes, in their microenvironments of assembly, there is a more natural feeling of belonging, appreciation, and recognition that the content and brand of *your* museum is indeed for *them* too.

In addition, by diversifying your audience, expanding your base, and reaching far and wide outside of your building, there is the additional impact on sustainability. Our capacity to fund-raise dramatically increases as individual donors, corporations, foundations, and government agencies have evolved to appreciate inclusivity, accessibility, and engagement of previously marginalized communities. Demonstrating a measurable impact by being more inclusive in your institution's outreach efforts, and sustaining these efforts through long-term engagement, presents an attractive case for support.

In summary, during the twenty-first century, cultural institutions, including science museums, are charged with providing experiences for guests to ultimately elevate their cultural vocabulary and hopefully positively impact their humanity. This construct, especially in the competitive macroenvironment of instant access to information by way of our ubiquitous digital tools, should not be limited to our museum buildings alone. Museums, especially science centers that provide indelible experiences around STEM, must migrate from place based to space based and engage, inspire, and transform lives in local and distal communities. Success in these outreach and engagement efforts will result in a more robust and relevant impact, diversity audiences, and positively affect the bottom line. As cultural institutions, if we fail at being more than our edifices, we may wind up in a "museum for museums."

Figure 6.7. COSI Connects Kit Distribution at Space Center Houston. *Photo by Kevin Michael Seymour. Courtesy of Center of Science and Industry (COSI).*

The Pluralist Museum

Just as the term *museum education* is being replaced by the more inclusive concept of *museum learning*, the traditional word *outreach* (meaning working outside the museum's walls) is seen as a limiting idea implying a sense of "us and them." Increasingly, museum program staff seek to *engage* communities of interest and geographical, nearby communities.

Particularly for museums that have grasped their pluralist society role, extension and engagement programs may be instrumental to asserting a stronger connection in the community. Relatively intensive levels of staff effort are often involved in providing such programs. Recently, many museums have joined popular social networking sites and have experienced significant success engaging nontraditional audiences, especially young adults.

There is now a need for young, technologically savvy museum program staff who in turn need management support in setting objectives and in facilitating their initiatives within the framework of the museum's mission. Dr. Frederic Bertley, CEO of the COSI Science Center in Columbus, Ohio, expands on these ideas in his case study on "Scaling the Museum Walls."

Making museums engaging and accessible via television, the Web, and presence where people live and work is increasingly important not only to fulfilling the museum's mission but to the sustainability of museums in society.

Whether public engagement is inviting local families to a special community evening at the museum, celebrating the Day of the Dead and other culturally specific festivals, providing after-school study halls, or hosting monthly events for singles, pluralist objectives cannot be accomplished in one event or one year: it's a way of museum life led by management.

Publications and Products

The museum's publications and product development are also management tools. They provide information about the museum collections, services, and research to visitors and to an expanded audience of the interested public that is not able to visit but may consult the museum's publications in libraries or purchase them in bookshops or over the museum website.

The range of publications and products may include exhibition catalogs; guidebooks; catalogs of the collection; books; children's books and games; teacher packs; leaflets and brochures; postcards, posters, and prints; fashion and jewelery items based on the collection. Museums may publish scholarly journals, magazines, membership newsletters, and occasional research papers.

Museum publishing has entered the multimedia age with considerable imagination and creativity. Videos as well as other online, digital multimedia offerings are often available from major museums, in some cases providing images of entire exhibitions or collections as well as information about them. The high cost of quality publication has led museums to forge partnerships with the private sector for both print and digital media. While some museums have their own imprint, many publish books and catalogs with academic publishers; French museums routinely make agreements for special issues of commercial art and culture magazines on featured exhibitions.

DAM is a major challenge for museum management. Should they sell the rights to their content to private sector agencies or maintain control in their own hands, or is there a middle ground that provides new source revenue as well as a creative use of a valuable museum asset and appropriate levels of museum control?

Marketing and Branding

The term "museum marketing" may seem discordant, and references to actual and potential visitors as "market segments" perhaps seems even more so, when considering that current museum practice is to speak to people as guests, participants, and stakeholders. However, marketing is a tool of management. And museum managers need to apply marketing data and strategies to the objective of increasing attendance.

Marketing is an integral part of the museum's communication with the public—and it may indeed be a department within a communications division. Because it is focused on the public, museum marketing should be closely allied with public programs, but it is frequently found in the museum's administration division—in departments such as communications or development—and it may be contracted.

Wherever the marketing function lives on the museum's organization chart, the management of marketing will be important to the entire institution: curators are interested in how well an exhibition is attended, the development director knows that an increase in membership and donations accompanies high levels of public awareness, and the finance officer sees a substantial difference in the bottom line when attendance is up. This means that marketing projects are prime candidates for blame when things don't work out. Good management pays attention to marketing, assuring that it is integrated in all public activities and focuses on

- identifying the museum's present and potential markets connected to audiences, and communicating effectively with them;

- advocating within the museum for the continual improvement of the museum's services—because an improved product is the most effective form of marketing—to meet the needs of people in these market segments so that they will visit the museum and return; and

- increasing attendance and visitor-generated revenues.

Research on cultural participation and museum attendance in various countries tells us that between 27 and 35 percent of the adult population may normally be expected to attend a museum at some time.

The frequency of attendance will vary greatly, from those who visit more than ten times a year and are likely to be members and supporters to those who visit occasionally, mostly as tourists.

The typical characteristics of frequent museum visitors are that they have higher education and income than the general population—although it's worth noting that education is a far more significant determinant than income—and that women attend more frequently than men.

The prime age for attendance varies with museum type: for example, science centers and children's museums attract young families, while art galleries appeal to young singles and adults over forty-five. Attendance previously tended to decline after sixty, but this is changing as the population ages in better health, and museums become more attuned to improving facilities for elders as well as for continuing education and lifelong learning.

Within these broad groups of visitors and nonvisitors, there are many specific *market segments*, relatively homogeneous sectors of the population that share common demographic, geographic, and behavioral or lifestyle patterns. Through its marketing strategy, the museum can influence their attendance patterns, as explained in appendix F.

Branding

"If you don't decide on your brand, others will do it for you," the saying suggests.

The default brand of museums that fail to demonstrate value is all too often "a community attic" or "the belongings of dead people."

By constructing a brand based on delivery of the museum's mission and vision, management can focus public perception and enhance appreciation of the museum in the public sphere. Of course, it ultimately depends on the product—the quality of service that the museum is providing—and the positioning of the museum (its mandate).

Recent decades have seen intensive activity by some of the world's leading museums to build global brands. The Solomon R. Guggenheim Foundation was foremost, extending its brand to link great architecture with contemporary art. Starting from its signature 1959 Frank Lloyd Wright landmark building in New York, it created a branded international system with the equally remarkable architecture of Frank Gehry in Bilbao (1997) and extending the brand still farther to another Gehry building, the Guggenheim Abu Dhabi. The Louvre, which is the most attended museum in the world (with 7.7 million visitors in 2022), developed over two hundred years and has created a global brand through recurring loan agreements with the High Museum in Atlanta, a branch for northern France at Lens, and leading the consortium of French museums into long-term agreements for planning and loans for the Louvre Abu Dhabi and mega projects in Saudi Arabia.[17] In Britain, the single name "Tate" has been focused as the brand not only of the successful Tate Modern (with 3.8 million visitors in 2022) and Tate Britain (with 3 million visitors in 2022) in London as well as its branches in Liverpool and St. Ives, but also through media and a boat along the Thames that links Tate Britain with Tate Modern.

These major museums have learned to "valorize" their brands.

The motivation is certainly at least partly to enhance their capacity to generate both earned and especially contributed income. But it is also a strategy to expand their Eurocentric collections in an effort to understand the historic and contemporary expressions of formerly colonized cultures. Donations, sponsorship, annual giving agreements, and even government subsidies are responsive to this globalization and effort at "soft power."

Branding is an important tool of museum management. It is said to be the "promise" of an organization or product delivers, strengthening public awareness of its benefits to society. Awareness can be enhanced by various means, such as

- marketing campaigns, specifically "awareness campaigns";

- website—and digital presence outside the museum's own site;

- advertising;

- public relations;

- festivals and events; and

- mutually beneficial relations with the museum ecosystem.

For a museum, a brand awareness campaign would be directed at stimulating awareness of the contribution the museum is making to society, communities, and people. It is ultimately the quality of the actual service being delivered and the values behind the exhibitions, educational programs, and activities that the museum is providing at home and abroad that are the true motors driving its brand. The museum logo, wordmark, tagline graphics, and the control of its presentation, the images associated with it, and the ways in which it is used in various media and events are *in support of* the brand. They are *not* the brand. The successful museum managers of institutions of all kinds and sizes are leaders not only in developing better and more conscious control of their museum's brand, but also communicating it.

Visitor Services

Visitor services, including admissions, retail and food services, rentals, and general visitor care, greatly influence the quality of the visitor experience and communicate the museum's attitude toward the public.

These services are often managed by administrative departments, although the staff, whether full or part time, salaried, contract, or voluntary, have more personal involvement and communication with visitors than many other museum workers. They offer a wealth of frequently untapped information about the museum's visitors and their needs. And to do their job well, they need extensive training, monitoring, and evaluation.

Museums that are truly visitor-responsive have redefined the role of frontline staff from being vaguely "administrative" to asserting a very conscious approach to "visitor services," creating a new working environment that integrates visitor services staff fully into the museum profession. Where this has not been done, visitors often suffer from ill-informed admission clerks, bored security guards, and undistinguished food services. When museum management has made the commitment to integration and equity for frontline staff, everyone benefits!

Chapter 7

HOW

Managing Infrastructure

Museums may be located on a university campus, in a city park, a busy downtown street, a historic battlefield, or a heritage village. Museums are also finding their way into mixed-use facilities, like condominiums or hotels and even within suburban shopping malls. And there are museums without walls and nomadic museums too.

> Museum management plays a leadership role in the development of space and facilities plans for museums as well as operating them.

Museum buildings may be contemporary creations designed by leading or emerging architects or heritage structures painstakingly preserved, or a combination of both. There is a widespread myth that old buildings automatically make good museums, and also that great architects make great museums. Neither is necessarily true, although either may be made so by careful planning and informed decision making. Readers may be wondering at this point what management has to do with it. Isn't this the job of the architect? Museum management plays a leadership role in the development of space and facilities plans for museums as well as operating them. These are the subjects of this chapter.

7.1 Facility Planning By Sean Stanwick

In some cases, new museums are brought to life through the dedicated planning and fundraising of impassioned stakeholders and committed governments. In other cases, museums grow beyond their bounds as a result of one of their essential activities—collecting. Museum buildings are also continuously being expanded or upgraded because of changing audience expectations and the impact of technological change: with increasing frequency tourists are joining residents with ever higher expectations of the museum experience, intensified by social media and international travel. Continually evolving technologies, economic pressures, and social change also impact decisions about how to adapt museum space and facilities, whether for a new building, an addition, or internal modifications.

All of these factors result in a constant, ongoing process of growth in the number, size, and complexity of museums. In fact, museum buildings are among the more complex of building types and

> Museum buildings are among the more complex of building types and among the costliest to construct.

among the costliest to construct. As a result, they are inevitably products of compromise, as budget and technical requirements are mutually adjusted. As museum planners, we see all too often museum projects that begin with high aspirations and goals yet do not fulfill the expectations of those who use them. This is usually from lack of planning.

The planning of museum buildings, their expansion, relocation, or renovation, is a process that must be executed carefully in order to ensure that it meets the needs of the museum profession to care for the collection and serves the museum's visitors and its community needs as creatively as possible.

Eight Factors of Facility Planning

Taking the time to plan the facility before consulting architects, designers, or others is the first step toward building, expanding, renovating, or relocating a museum successfully. This type of planning is often called briefing or programming, and its result is termed a *functional brief* or a *functional program*. A preliminary but also very valuable document in the planning process may be termed a *facility strategy*. It may be surprising to learn that this is not the job of architects and engineers (although they may be very helpful) but the responsibility of museum management, as can be seen from this list of eight key factors impacting museum facility requirements.

1. **Design Year:** One of the fundamental decisions at the outset of a facility planning process is to determine the design year, which may be defined as the last year for which the facilities being planned are to be adequate. It may seem paradoxical to begin by determining the year in which the plans being made will be insufficient, but in fact it is necessary to draw a horizon or limit on the extent of collection growth, exhibition space expansion, attendance increases, or other factors that may determine the size and character of the additional space needed. For many projects, the design year is set at fifteen to twenty years—because opening day of the new or expanded facility is usually five years after the planning period, and because growth of collections and other resources cannot reasonably be projected after that length of time.

2. **Visitors:** Both qualitative and quantitative analysis of the museum's present visitors (if the museum is already open) help to determine visitor needs in the facility. Surveys and tracking studies may be helpful in developing this analysis, remembering to consult physically challenged visitors, teachers with school groups, tour bus providers, and other groups as well as general visitors.

3. **Market:** Still more important is to understand the visitors of the future—the potential market—again both quantitatively and qualitatively, so that the new facility might reach out beyond the present attendance group to serve a broader public. The analysis may aim at identifying priority markets for a new facility or the new audiences attainable after an expansion, renovation, or relocation. The decision to take advantage of such opportunities is, of course, dependent on the museum's mission, vision, and mandate.

4. **Collection and Content Development:** The heart of the museum is its collection of works of art, artifacts, specimens, and nontangible collections such as stories, music, and ways of life. A thorough analysis, not only of its present size and character, but especially of its anticipated growth, along with decisions about how much to display and the ways to display it, is essential. Provisions for adequate storage, security, and collection and content care are also vital considerations in the museum facility planning process.

5. **Public Programs and Activities:** Museums appear to be about objects but are really about people. What do we plan to do in the museum? For what activities must we provide? The museum's exhibitions, its approach to the interpretation of its collections, with all the technological potential now available; its education programs; its publications and media productions; its extension and community programs; and the amenities to be provided to guests, including shops and food services, all have important implications for the facility strategy. Often neglected—the unseen heart of the museum's public programs—is *research* within the museum, not only for staff but also for Indigenous people, descendant communities, and community collaborators who have invaluable knowledge to share that is the museum's lifeline.

6. **Museum Ecosystem:** Another key factor in the facility strategy is the determination of the museum's relationship with its many constituencies, including government, educational institutions, other museums, residents, artists, descendant communities, the tourist

industry, and potential donors or sponsors. Although these issues are usually considered more deeply in the context of strategic or master planning (which is why it is a good idea to have completed both prior to initiating the facility strategy process!), they are equally important for facility planning because the needs that they generate require space and facilities. If, for example, the museum is to become more independent of government, or more responsible for generating its own funds, it is likely to require more and better-located retail space, food services, and function rooms. If it is to offer programs in partnership with the school district, it may require additional facilities to be designed and built with input from the schools.

7. **Institutional Plan:** Another often neglected area is determining or reconsidering the museum's mission, its mandate, and its purpose, as well as its mode of governance and the structures through which it is administered. Although these again are produced as part of a strategic or master plan, in fact this information directly affects the priorities of the facility strategy, especially as it becomes apparent that not all the space and facilities that are desired can be accommodated or afforded.

8. **Operational Business Plan:** Decisions regarding various operational models for a new or expanded museum will have a direct impact on the viability and sustainability of the institution for many years to come. Conducting a business planning process simultaneously with the programming effort will allow an institution to explore a range of operational models and develop operational assumptions that balance economic realities with space needs; for example, the right sizing of temporary galleries needs to be balanced against the annual cost of hosting temporary shows, which in turn impact not only up-front capital costs but also long-term operational expenses.

Planning for staff, space, and facilities is sometimes approached—especially by engineers—primarily in terms of meeting relevant *building code* requirements for fire protection, health, safety, and the needs of the physically challenged. Compliance with code is, of course, important, but facilities planning should also be seized by museum management and the board as an opportunity to fulfill the museum's mission more fully than before—or perhaps even to reconsider that mission. Meeting internationally accepted museum standards of environmental control, lighting, and security may, for example, be instrumental in enabling the museum to organize or borrow major exhibitions.

> Museum managers also need to consider the fundamental question of the degree of *access to the collections and content* that they wish to provide to the public.

Museum managers also need to consider the fundamental question of the degree of *access to the collections and content* that they wish to provide to the public. Again and again, unplanned museum building projects proceed without examination of this basic issue. Many museums exhibit only 5 to 15 percent of their collections, and there have been instances of museums concluding capital expansion projects with a *lower* percentage of their collections on display.

Another consideration is whether to continue, expand, initiate, or eliminate offsite collection storage and how much to make available at the main site. Offsite storage is appealing in that it allows an institution to safely store its items in less expensive facilities. However, issues often arise with the duplication of space, coordinating frequency of transport but more importantly access and proximity. Offsite locations tend to have a strong gravitational attraction in that they draw other functions to their location. Conservation, research and education, curatorial staff, and even the public all want to be near the collections, and so museum managers must often have to balance the needs of collection access with the economic realities of operating two sites. There is a very exciting current trend to have publicly visible storage both onsite and offsite.

Once all possibilities have been considered, the museum's requirements for staff, space, and facilities can be translated into monetary needs—for both capital construction and long-term operating costs and revenues.

Site Selection

Site selection and site expansion are often part of museum planning, and management must be involved because site involves both community and ecosystem. Some of the key factors are

- availability;

- access;

- audience development potential;

- cost of acquisition and development, balanced by funding opportunities;

- security considerations;

- building type (if it is a question of renovation of an existing structure);

- size and layout of site or existing structures;

- parking and public transportation;

- visibility;

- compatibility of neighboring facilities; and

- contribution to local plans and needs.

Each factor should be weighted before it is evaluated—that is, each factor is given a "weight" value in terms of its importance to the museum. This is multiplied by its evaluation to give a total rating for that factor, and then there will be a total for each site option.

If funding is possible only for some sites but is crucial to the enterprise, then that factor must be given a heavy weight. On the other hand, a security issue may be so alarming that it outweighs all other factors, so security must be assigned an appropriate weight. Another is zoning. Often cities that cannot afford to provide funds or tax relief to museums can make a great contribution in terms of zoning.

A question frequently asked is whether renovation of a historic building is preferable to a new purpose-built structure, or vice versa. The answer must always be specific to the comparison being made. Renovation is sometimes less expensive, but the unknowns of an existing building, particularly in older or heritage structures, can also drive the cost up to become comparable or even more than building new. If this happens, the governing body of the museum may find themselves regretting the decision to renovate, as they try to cope with inadequate spaces, awkward corridors, multiple floor levels, and insufficient space to maneuver outside lifts or elevators.

Very often the preservation of a historic building for which no other use is feasible may be given as justification for preferring renovated space. This may be praiseworthy from the viewpoint of architectural preservation—and that preservation may indeed be part of the museum's own mission—but the justification should be recognized as unrelated to the functional requirements of the museum, so that the costs in both capital outlay and operations may be considered as well.

The Facility Planning Teams

Who Is to Undertake Facility Planning?

The governing body and director establish the *building committee* both to raise money and to guide the process by establishing and monitoring the policy and budgetary framework for the project. The museum's director and board chair provide leadership. And it is essential for the museum to name a *project manager*. The building project manager may be already on staff—but if so, must be relieved of other duties while assuming the project management role; alternatively, project management skills may be contracted for the life of the capital project only. The process of museum facility planning and programming is often facilitated by specialized museum planning consultants who work with all these personnel to achieve the optimal result. Even with professional museum planners and an experienced project manager, it is vital to involve the staff—all those who will have to provide services to the collection and to the public—in the new facility. Museum facility planning is very much a collaborative team effort.

> Museum facility planning is very much a collaborative team effort.

The most important step in organizing the museum's forces to address a capital project is therefore to establish both a museum project team and a building team, which usually includes a building design team.

- The *museum project team* comprises museum personnel who address the various museum functions affected by the capital development—curatorial concerns, conservation, security, revenue generation, and many more. This team should be led by the museum planner, whether a professional consultant specializing in this area or an appointed member of the museum staff. The museum project team's task is to ensure that the museum's requirements are clearly stated and that those requirements are met by the architects, engineers, and contractors. The cost consultant (or quantity surveyor) should also meet with this team to ensure that the cost implications of their requirements are made clear.

- The *building team* includes the architect, engineers, landscape architects, and other technical specialists needed, along with the contractor and the construction manager. Their task is to answer the requirements of the museum project team with technical drawings and specifications. Decision leaders on the building and museum project teams become the "combined project team" chaired by the project manager. This group meets continually throughout the process. In addition to the professional teams, the museum may create advisory committees to involve neighbors and communities of interest—the ecosystem!

Figure 7.1 outlines the organization of the various team members that will likely be involved or required during the planning process.

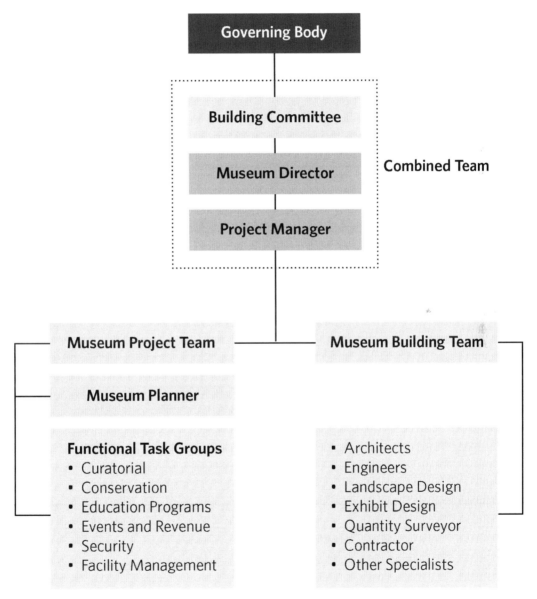

Figure 7.1. Project Planning Team. *Lord Cultural Resources.*

The Role of the Architect

Many museum professionals, and trustees, assume that planning a museum is "a building problem" and therefore can only be solved by an architect. There is no question that the architect has an important role to play—but the architect may not always fully understand how a museum functions, both for the public and for collections.

Determining the functional requirements of a museum is ultimately a job that is best done by museum professionals, before the architect begins work. Calling the architect too soon is the most common error in the museum facility planning process. It should be noted, however, that a collaborative approach among museum planners staff and the architect can bring value to the process. Having the architects participate in the initial planning meetings will enable them to fully understand the early decisions that were made and why. And vice versa, having museum planners involved during the design phase will ensure that those early museum-specific requirement are maintained throughout the entire process.

When quantifying important museum-critical requirements, or raising issues relating to functionality, museum directors and curators may be told, "It's too early." Usually this is when the museum director is pointing out a missing feature or function.

When the director or curator asks about these features, the architect sometimes assures everyone that these are concept sketches and that it's "too early" to get into that kind of detail. This is a fair point, as the concept presentation is often the first time a director or curator will see the design, and the architects are most likely testing initial ideas for reaction.

However, it is also the point in the design process when early ideas can very easily become *baked* into a scheme or lost forever. It's therefore important to have a functional program that records needs and functions so that in several months it is not "too late" to make changes. We call this the "it's too early; it's too late syndrome"—one to be avoided!

Hiring the Architect

Whether it be at the outset of the project or after the completion of a functional program, hiring the architect is one of the single most important decisions the museum building team will make, impacting not only the quality of the building but also financial and moral support.

The hiring process could be via open tender, competition, limited selection, or by invitation. Regardless, selecting the right architect to implement the museum's vision is a critical decision that will have an impact on the success of the project for years to come. This is particularly relevant for projects procured via competition, as it will very likely attract many submissions from a range of qualified professionals.

Hiring a museum planning professional to be actively involved in the architect selection process can help alleviate some of the complexities and stress. Roles for the museum planner in this capacity can include the following checklist of tasks:

- Review and comment on the expression of interest/request for proposal/competition documents prior to release

- Review and comment on the architect's submissions

- Make recommendations on which candidates to shortlist for interview

- Participate in the architect interviews as an informed but impartial advisor

- Review design competition submissions

- Make recommendations to help lead to the winning team

The interview process is also a highly valuable tool in assessing the suitability of an architect. A useful approach is to consider the initial RFP process as a way to demonstrate capability and technical knowledge. The interview, on the other hand, is an opportunity to explore the balance between experience and "chemistry"—the intangible foundation for successful working relationships.

An architect's portfolio will determine if they have the requisite experience; your conversations with them should determine if they are the right fit for the museum. When interviewing candidates, one might embrace a strategy that intentionally avoids questions that will solicit predictable results and instead ask questions that explore their interest in engaging with the museum and its supporters. Ideally the right architect should guide the museum team through a rewarding creative experience that is based on a *transformational partnership* rather than a *transactional exchange of services.*

> Ideally the right architect should guide the museum team through a rewarding creative experience that is based on a *transformational partnership* rather than a *transactional exchange of services.*

Ultimately, the goal is to find an architect who has the skills, process, and vision to create the legacy project most clients are looking for. Their approach should raise the architectural bar while delivering value for every project dollar. To gain insight into their thinking, consider forward-looking, insightful questions, such as:

- Rather than highlighting previous work for other clients, ask prospects to "describe how their past work can advance the goals of your project." Experience has shown that winning firms describe the relevance of their work to your project, while others focus only on past efforts.

- Approach and vision are unique to each team and should be the differentiator. Questions like "How will you help us turn our aspirations into reality?" will tell you if they are interested in bringing hidden opportunities to light.

- It is important to also assess your expected level of involvement during the design process. Their choice of words is a key indicator of how they see you in the design process. Language such as "we will design *for* you" versus "we will design *with* you" will identify whether prospects will engage in partnered dialogue or will make their own assumptions.

Clients may also choose to procure an architectural team via a design competition, either by open call or invitation. The competition can be managed by the client, but given the complexity it is usually overseen by a professional management firm who can help with the creation of the competition brief and management of the submissions on behalf of the client.

The competition brief will often contain well-developed project mission and vision statements, an initial program of spaces, and the required sizes, functional adjacencies, information on the site, collection data, initial interpretive or thematic concepts, and terms of reference, among other items. It may also include a financial reward (stipend) for shortlisted teams to cover a portion of the internal pursuit costs incurred by participating firms. The process often starts with an initial expression of interest to determine basic qualifications, and then shortlisted firms are invited to proceed to the final design round.

Competitions generally use design as a way to identify the most qualified firm, sometimes touted as a vehicle to encourage lesser-known firms to demonstrate a creative approach to a particular problem. While this is generally true, clients should be aware that competitions require a significant amount of management on the part of the client and even more so on the part of design teams who often spend many more hours than the stipend will cover to complete the design submission.

The Functional Program

The sequence of events in the facility planning process for museums should begin from a strategic or master plan, which should be agreed on or updated as required, in order to place the capital project in context, in relation to the museum's mission, mandate, and objectives.

Beyond a strategic plan, a capital project requires the collection and content analysis, development strategy, public programming plan, market analysis, and marketing strategy, which are all part of a master plan. If it is a new museum, this may be called a feasibility study, culminating in a conclusion about the relative feasibility of a museum or other facility.

With the strategic and master plan establishing the institutional goals and the collection, programming, and marketing objectives, it is finally possible, preferably with the aid of experienced museum planners or programmers, to draft the key document that is referred to as the functional program.

A functional program is written in language that the museum's trustees, management, and staff can understand because it provides requirements, not specifications.

A functional program is written in language that the museum's trustees, management, and staff can understand because it provides requirements, not specifications. It will continually be updated throughout the process as priorities change with budget and other realities. A checklist of components contained in a functional program is available in appendix G.

The Need for a Functional Program
By Barry Lord

I was invited with a group of museum professionals to review three sets of architectural drawings and models for the expansion of a venerable museum in continental Europe. The collection featured medieval and Renaissance oak and other wood furniture and carvings, housed in a 1950s structure with a massive floor-to-ceiling window wall along all of the galleries. With that much glass, environmental controls were quite impossible: the curator told me that on a humid summer afternoon one could hear a concert in the galleries—the squeaking of the joints of furniture!

The three sets of shortlisted architectural plans and models (for which the museum had paid) all provided a mixture of temporary exhibition galleries, a members' lounge, a pedagogical center, a restaurant, and many other attractions. But what was to be done with the permanent collection? I was advised that the plan was to build all these new facilities and then to renovate the existing building with whatever funds remained. But in fact, this was the only time in twenty years when the museum would have the funds to accomplish any substantial physical improvement, and their money would all be spent by the time they completed the addition, so that nothing would be left for the permanent collection galleries.

When the time came to make comments on the architects' plans, I had to say that I chose none of the three. The architects were all disappointed, but I reassured them that it was not their fault. No one had asked the right questions, so none of the architects could give the right answer. No one had recognized that the museum's highest priority had to be the preservation of its collection and that this need should have been at the center of the brief given to the competing architects. I could only recommend that the museum reconsider its brief before beginning over again with the architects—which I understand was subsequently done. Such a functional brief was what was needed.

Cost of Facility Planning

The cost of facility planning is often considered to be high, but this is usually because it has not yet been put in the perspective of the cost of the capital project as a whole. Many museums are cash poor, even at the beginning of major capital projects, and are often reluctant to allocate money to planning when it could be used to "get on with the job." Yet the entire planning and programming process usually costs no more than 1 percent of the total project value. Even taken together with the cost of the ongoing review of the architects' and engineers' drawings and specifications throughout the design process, total costs are likely to reach only 1.5 percent. The costs should be seen as the initial 1.5 percent spent to ensure that the remaining 98.5 percent is well used. The costs of the architect's or contractor's change orders may be much more substantial if not guided by good planning.

The cost of the entire period throughout which the museum planners should be meeting with the architects and engineers to review their schematic and detailed designs and specifications will vary according to architectural billing practices throughout the world, but it is usually only about 12.5 percent of the total project value, including the 1.5 percent for planning and programming. It is during this planning and design phase that the opportunities to make changes are still relatively inexpensive—before we hear, "It's too late!"

7.2 Site and Building Operations by Barry Lord, updated by Robert LaMarre

The operation of museum sites and buildings involves three functions:

- managing daily operations,

- maintenance and repair, and

- security.

Following a discussion of these three functions, this section will conclude with a consideration of the ways in which museums can put an environmental consciousness to work.

Managing Daily Operations

Managing the operations of a museum site and building requires the correlation of six major factors, usually prioritized as follows:

1. health and safety of visitors, staff, and others;

2. security and preservation of the collection;

3. comfort and convenience of visitors;

4. facilitation of staff requirements;

5. preservation of the building; and

6. sustainability, environmental conservation, and energy savings.

If the building is a historic structure, the fifth priority is likely to become the third, ahead of visitors and staff. If the historic building is more important than the collection it contains, the fifth priority may even be second, ahead of the collection as well. The operation of a museum site and building may be seen as an art of balancing all these concerns, some of which will be mutually exclusive at times. It is helpful if the operations manager or building engineer makes clear the priorities, not only in general but also with reference to specific directives or practices.

Both *monitoring* and *control* functions are required to manage these five factors. In addition to the operations manager, the conservators and those responsible for public programming should have input on the standards to be achieved and should receive regular reports on actual conditions. The cooperation of those responsible for building operations with those responsible for the collections and those concerned with visitor services is vital to the smooth functioning of the museum, and may require the intervention of senior staff from time to time to ensure efficient collaboration. Regular meetings, perhaps monthly, are perhaps well advised.

The inherent conflict that is often observed between preservation of the collection and preservation of the building should be acknowledged, with priorities clearly understood by all. The collection manager's goal of maintaining a constant relative humidity (RH), in temperate zones usually at 50 percent, plus or minus 3 percent at 20–21°C (68–70°F), with as little variation as possible, may present a difficult challenge to the building engineer, especially in historic structures, if the external RH is varying widely, from 90 percent in midsummer to 20 percent in midwinter, for example. Air barriers to stop conditioned air from entering the structural envelope and vapor barriers of 4 ml polyethylene with a recommended permeability rating of 0.04–0.08 perms must be carefully designed and installed. Failure to do so can harm the building fabric and may be signaled by such symptoms as efflorescence on the museum walls.

Air circulation is a function where the needs of the collection and the public must sometimes be adjusted. The outside air dampers should be of fixed volume design, controlled by a timer set to admit the minimum acceptable volume of fresh air during public hours, and to close at other times. Carbon dioxide (CO_2) monitors that adjust the volume of outside air to the human use of the space are expensive but repay their costs many times over in day-to-day operating efficiencies—given the particular concerns of the museum for conditioning the air in its buildings.

Nowhere is the collection/public contradiction more apparent than in questions of windows and glazing *(fenestration)*. Museum visitors like windows because they provide orientation, views to outside, and daylight. Both architects and many museum professionals believe that skylights are attractive features in a museum gallery, due to a preference for natural light, especially in art museums. Entire walls of glass are common in contemporary architecture. Windows in galleries are *not* recommended, and in historic structures are usually blocked (in such a way as to ensure that the window blocks are not visible on a historic facade). But skylights over galleries are commonly found in both historic and new structures. Glass walls provide an even greater challenge; while they provide orientation to the outdoors, they make it expensive and environmentally unfriendly to control RH and temperature and may make it impossible to see information on digital media.

> Nowhere is the collection/ public contradiction more apparent than in questions of windows and glazing *(fenestration)*.

All these openings in the museum wall and ceiling challenge the ability of even the most reputable building engineers. Others find that solutions that work in temperate climates, such as the ingenious arrangement of louvers and computerized environmental controls in the area under the skylights above the Neue Pinakothek galleries in Munich, may not work nearly as well in harsher climates of greater extremes.

All fenestration should be triple paned, with at least 0.5 inch (1.3 cm) between panes; laminated glass or Plexiglas should be used with an ultraviolet filtration capability of reducing UV rays to less than ten microwatts per lumen, and with a polycarbonate outer layer for security. Louvers, operated by hand or photocell, are needed to ensure that the sun's rays enter the gallery indirectly, and the area below the skylight may have to be housed separately from the gallery (with another layer of glass as its floor and the gallery's ceiling to prevent condensation).

Museums in tropical climates have the added challenge that most of the professional literature is focused on temperate zone conditions. Artifacts or specimens of tropical origin have a different hydroscopic capacity.

Energy-saving approaches using lower-technology methods to control the environment, with the added attraction of cost saving, may be adopted wherever possible, but with a cautionary note about their possible impacts on the collections or on the museum's ability to borrow exhibitions. Conservators may prescribe greater ranges of fluctuation in conditions affecting the collections. For instance, the engineer may be advised to allow a minor and gradual seasonal variation from the RH standard for a controlled period of the museum's operating hours.

The effect of such variations may be limited, however, by the fact that museum buildings and/or individual galleries and select collection spaces must meet not merely the requirements of the institution itself but also those of actual or potential *lenders*. The need to maintain the highest standards in the temporary exhibition galleries twenty-four hours per day year-round—or at least to maintain the capability to achieve these standards when needed to meet the demands of lenders—is the ultimate criterion determining the operating performance requirements of many museum heating, ventilating, and air-conditioning (HVAC) systems. And if that capability must be provided for the temporary exhibition gallery, it may be more cost effective on an overall project basis to provide it for all the collection zones.

Maintaining a recognized performance standard of 50 percent RH, plus or minus 3 percent RH at 20–21°C (68–70°F), year-round requires vigilance but may not represent a major challenge in a purpose-built new facility planned, designed, and constructed to accommodate that capability in a more temperate climate zone. In a historic structure, or in any building not constructed to maintain such a standard, it may be difficult or impossible, especially in a more extreme environment or climate zone such as those prevalent in the Arabian Gulf. Given agreement from collections managers, setting a more flexible target of 55 percent RH standard may be the best compromise possible, and even then it may nonetheless be necessary in a historic structure to adjust the humidity settings each month for a three-month gradual transition period each spring and fall, allowing a fluctuation from 40 percent RH in the winter to 55 percent in the summer, and a commensurate temperature swing from 21 to 24°C (70–75°F) and back during the same three months.

Given a facility's fully tested capability to achieve its required HVAC performance standard as set by the museum's chief conservator, it is important for those responsible for the facility's operation to insist that they can and must be attained.

Contemporary building management systems (BMS), which allow continuous recording and display of temperature and RH sensors in all installed areas and programmable control capabilities, and the related HVAC equipment deployed in the museum can be decisive in facilitating achievement of the required standards, when planned, installed, tested, commissioned, regularly calibrated, and operated in accordance with both the BMS and HVAC mechanical systems manufacturer's instructions. It is essential for those responsible for a facility's operations to understand and ensure that both the sensor- and IT-driven BMS and mechanically driven HVAC physical plant/equipment each have their own respective operating and preventative maintenance regimens to be diligently maintained and regularly tested, which may require the support of external service providers.

Redundancy is an important consideration in planning and operating a museum building system. By "redundancy" we mean the capability for building systems to sustain operation despite malfunction or power outage to the regularly operating equipment. This need not mean that the museum must maintain 200 percent of its heating, ventilating, and air-conditioning equipment requirements; it may be sufficient to have about 130–140 percent because normal usage is likely to require only about 65–70 percent of capacity at any one time in a professionally planned system. Redundant power capability and dedicated and supervised security telephone lines are also important for security as well as preventive conservation purposes, as may be BMS system presets with programmed anomaly detection and alarm capability.

Once the standards for both regular operations and redundancy capacity have been determined and the equipment installed, much of the site and building operations schedule can be regularized in procedures manuals. Although initial operating manuals may be the final documentary product required of the building and HVAC systems contractors, the museum director and the conservators especially should ensure that these manuals and the priorities they manifest are consistent with museum policies and that all installed systems have been fully commissioned and tested to the required performance standards. Simple procedural errors, such as leaving exterior doors of the building open to waft outside air through a foyer directly into expensively conditioned galleries, have been observed even in otherwise sophisticated institutions—the reason being that no one had explained the museum's requirements and the reasons for them to the attendants or shop clerks who opened the doors for human comfort or convenience.

The loading dock and the shipping and receiving bay are areas where staff procedures may transgress not only museum policy but also the reasons why sensitive and expensive equipment was provided in the first place. One useful way of ensuring that roll-up loading doors are not left open too long is to install interlocking mechanisms on the two sets of roll-up doors, one at the outside vehicular access to the museum, and the other at the interior access from the shipping and receiving bay to the area where crating and uncrating may take place, such that if one door is open the other must be closed or locked. A separate personnel door beside the shipping door is also important, ideally with a security station controlling access to both, hopefully with the help of closed-circuit television and intercom system, so that delivery personnel can be identified before either door is opened.

Cooperation between security staff and building operations personnel is crucial to the well-managed museum. Both should be fully familiar with the policies and procedures of the other, and regular meetings between the chief of security and the operations manager or building

Cooperation between security staff and building operations personnel is crucial to the well-managed museum.

engineer can be rewarded by greater efficiencies in operation as well as assured security. It is particularly important that both departments are fully informed of such events as the delivery of incoming exhibitions or the shipment of outgoing collections. As one example of required procedures, the operations manager should also have a sign-off arrangement with the registrar or curators to ensure that no artifacts, specimens, or works of art enter or leave the building unless authorized.

When planning, designing, and constructing new facilities and major renovations, best practice suggests that no such development should be undertaken without including a BMS room if not already present in the facility. The flexibility of contemporary BMS systems allow a wide range of both monitoring capabilities possibly including, depending on the installation, networked sensors located inside individual display or storage cases. Conservators' hygrothermographs, with their styluses recording temperature and RH on graph paper drums, when properly operated, maintained, and calibrated, may offer a reliable secondary record of RH and temperature performance within a given air space.

Environmental sustainability and energy savings is top of mind due to the climate crisis.

The sixth priority, environmental sustainability and energy savings, is top of mind due to the climate crisis. This is usually challenging for museums, which are inherently an energy-inefficient building type.

Environmental conservation, climate change, and increasing energy costs are all combining to encourage the development of green strategies for the construction and operation of museums.

Green strategies may most likely be of two kinds:

- strategies to promote sustainable environments, and

- strategies to promote energy savings.

These goals and others may be combined, and in each case higher capital costs may be offset through operational savings. Energy-saving options that do not compromise the collection environment should be encouraged, and each strategy should be considered in a cost-benefit analysis, weighing the potential for operating savings against the certainty of higher capital cost. The positive internal and public regard generated through consistent and visible efforts to promote and implement sustainability as a core value of museum operations may provide a less tangible but nonetheless measurable benefit.

Energy consumed by HVAC systems in managing relative humidity and temperature levels to "precision control" tolerances twenty-four hours per day year-round is the main reason why museum buildings are seldom exemplary green buildings. In addition, the reliance on artificial instead of natural light means that museum electrical and heating loads, which also in turn increase cooling requirements, are bound to be higher than ideal. While supplementary building insulation and airtightness measures can be very effective initiatives to facilitate overall energy savings, supplementary systems-related measures must recognize that preservation of sensitive collections must always take priority over energy saving.

All aspects and impacts of any proposed energy-saving devices or practices must be considered in deciding whether to introduce them. For example, energy-saving measures such as "free cooling" or airside economizers that are often used in other building types to lower energy consumption may not be effective for museums as the money saved in cooling costs may be lost due to the increased load on the particulate and gaseous filters and the humidifiers. It is also very difficult to provide a stable RH when utilizing free cooling.

Some other energy-saving measures that *are* recommended for consideration include the following:

- Waterside economizers, which have proven effective for museum use despite the initial higher capital investment.

- Multiple types of chillers, such as a high-efficiency standard chiller for the most economic production of chilled water, combined with a double bundle heat recovery chiller for the provision of "free" reheat energy for RH control, combined with a reversible cycle chiller (heat pump) for heat production in the winter and additional cooling capacity during the summer.

- Air exhausted from the building via the HVAC system (but not via exhaust systems from restrooms or other spaces) could be put through a heat recovery device to capture sensible and latent heat for the tempering of the outdoor air being brought into the building.

- A dedicated HVAC unit in the outdoor air duct could further temper this makeup air before being distributed to HVAC units serving specific spaces throughout the institution, thereby lessening the load on each of these units and allowing them to be more efficiently sized.

- The use of carbon dioxide (CO_2) sensors to control the quantity of outdoor air being brought into the building, instead of purging the space with a fixed amount of outdoor air all the time, has already been recommended. The sensor minimizes the exchange of the relatively expensive conditioned air when the galleries are empty during closed hours, or scantily attended during slack times, but responds to crowds at an exhibition opening or other event by increasing the frequency and volume of air exchange. Such a sensor requires an additional capital cost but one that earns its keep in subsequent energy savings.

- The provision of airlocks at entrances either as vestibules or as revolving doors is energy efficient and can help to prevent the entry of dust, gaseous pollutants, and pests into the building. The two airlock doors of the vestibule should be at least ten feet (three meters) apart, so that the one door closes before the other can be opened.

- With the high reliance on electricity in many museums to provide cooling, air movement, lighting, and vertical circulation, and because a significant portion of this load is present twenty-four hours per day, it may be possible to use *cogeneration*; this would involve providing an electrical generator to produce electricity for the operation of chillers and other electrical equipment, with the heat from the generator engine used for controlling RH by providing reheat energy and for winter heating where needed. Where readily available, use of exterior chilled water supply system, while maintaining required redundancy capabilities for the museum, may be encouraged, especially in extreme climate zones, such as those present in the Arabian Gulf or other tropical locations.

- In the near future, fuel cells (hydrogen and oxygen combined to produce electricity, heat, and water) may be commercially available.

- Building materials have a finite life, with known time spans for each material used, after which replacement will be necessary. The *recyclability* of each material could be used as a criterion in making the choice of materials during construction or renovation. For example, linoleum with a linseed oil base would score higher in the recyclability category than vinyl or tile flooring.

Lifecycle costing of the building during its planning and design will help to make the museum itself, as well as its community, more sustainable.

Museums can be designed to last for a century, with materials and equipment designed for replacement at defined times, such as every twenty-five or fifty years. *Lifecycle costing* of the building during its planning and design will help to make the museum itself, as well as its community, more sustainable.

In response to supporting a client museum's particular sustainability objectives for a new facility, Lord Cultural Resources's consultants have recently undertaken a detailed comparison of requirements and potential opportunities associated with updating standards from the American Society of Heating, Refrigerating and Air-Conditioning Engineers' (ASHRAE) 2011 edition, with those of their latest 2019 edition. Key findings of this analysis suggest that a tiered approach to optimizing museum building standards in different collections spaces may be advisable to support building sustainability and energy costs savings through adherence to ASHRAE 2019, while also leaving the door open to future loans from highly demanding/prestigious institutions that may require more strict adherence to the generally higher ASHRAE 2011 performance standard.

Maintenance and Repair

The cleaning of museum buildings is another area where building operations come into contact with the needs of both collections and the visiting public. Clear lines of demarcation must be drawn between building maintenance and collection care responsibilities, especially if there are open displays or large artifacts or specimens that are easily accessible to cleaners. This is particularly important if cleaning staff are on contract and so do not report directly to museum management. A detailed new staff training regimen should be implemented and a cleaning manual should be strictly enforced, including details of materials and equipment to be used, degrees of access to and within areas holding collections, and so on.

Museum concrete should include a hardening agent, and all surfaces should be *sealed*, including those above false ceilings. This is not only to prevent concrete dust from falling but especially to prevent it from entering the air circulation system. All other surfaces should be painted.

Vacuums should be central systems vented to the outdoors, or may be portable *high-efficiency particulate air filter* (HEPA) vacuums, which boast a dust-capture efficiency of 99.97 percent. Carpentry workshops and any other dust-producing workrooms should be vented outdoors, and care should be taken in planning the air-circulation system to ensure that dusty air from such work stations is not recirculated.

The correct replacement of air filters is another task that requires a carefully drafted procedures manual. The bank of filters, measured by the ASHRAE atmospheric dust spot efficiency test section of ASHRAE test 52-76, should provide 25–30 percent prefilter capacity, 40–85 percent medium-efficiency filters, and 90–95 percent afterfilters. Activated charcoal filters are recommended for the filtration of gaseous pollutants. Each filter should be provided with its own manometer to indicate any drop in pressure, and these should be monitored individually, with each filter changed as necessary.

Cleaning materials and techniques should be reviewed and approved by conservators, and maintenance personnel should be included in training sessions aimed at familiarizing them with the requirements of the collection. Similarly, public expectations and those of the staff providing visitor services should be made clear so that performance evaluation of cleaners can be based on compliance with museum procedures manuals and specific public needs.

The replacement of lamps is a routine but critically necessary activity that requires a procedures manual written in consultation with the curators and conservators. There is little use in a museum policy requiring a low level of ultraviolet radiation (under ten microwatts per lumen) if the maintenance worker replaces the lamps in the gallery with fluorescent tubes that do not have the built-in levels of UV protection or discards the sleeves that were supposed to control the UV emission levels along with the first generation of tubes. Similarly, the maintenance worker needs to know precisely which lamps are needed in which orientation in each display, or the effects contrived by lighting consultants may be lost after the first change of lamps.

An important principle of museum facilities planning is to provide access for repair personnel that does not require them to pass through or past collection zones. Much repair may be done after hours, so it is a simple security precaution (and puts far less responsibility on the shoulders of the repair workers) if replacements or repairs can be done without walking through or past galleries or collection stores. If the layout of the building makes such a provision impossible, it is necessary to accompany repair and replacement personnel at all times.

Deferral of maintenance and repair is a chronic problem in museums. Budgets for upkeep or improvements always appear to be easier to postpone than others, with the result that relatively minor maintenance requirements become progressively more serious until they result in major disasters and capital

> Deferral of maintenance and repair is a chronic problem in museums.

costs for complete replacement. Such deferrals may also weaken the security system. An assiduous management should seek to avoid such long-run inefficiencies by maintaining regular budget commitments for maintenance and repairs. A *preventive maintenance* program is also critical to enhancing sustainability.

The repair and replacement of exhibits provides an interesting question for museum managers: How much should the museum undertake directly, and how much should be contracted out? Some museums, particularly in continental Europe, traditionally have had exhibit designers or even architects on staff, as well as extensive workshops where new exhibits could be built and old ones repaired or replaced. The result in some cases was a "house style" of exhibits—for better or worse. Today, many museum managers prefer to contract exhibit design, choosing a different designer for each project, thereby reducing their workshop needs to the minimum. Even framing may be seen to be more cost-effective if done on contract rather than dedicating space, facilities, and trained staff to a function that is required only intermittently; however, insurance implications of having to send art and artifacts outside the building for even minor work should also be considered. For many museums the solution is to provide both a "clean workshop" (in Zone C) for framing, mount making, and routine cleaning of objects in the collection or on loan, and a "dirty workshop" (in Zone D) for carpentry, spray painting, or other exhibition preparation work without collections present.

The advent of electronic, video, and computerized exhibition components, especially in science centers or children's museums, points to another need: the requirement for relatively quick and easy replacement parts on hand, with weekend as well as weekday staff trained to fix exhibits before too much "down time" accumulates. Failure to provide for such replacements results in too many of the "Sorry, this exhibit is not working today" signs that frustrate the museum public, especially those who are one-time visitors. Admission charges have been one important factor in stimulating museums to ensure that malfunctioning exhibits are quickly repaired or replaced. It has also led many to calculate the anticipated "life span" of exhibits, and the projected cost of their upkeep, when preparing an exhibition plan. Video art and other time-based media art are the challenges for art museums, especially when the technology of the period in which the artwork was produced is no longer manufactured.

Security

Planning and managing security for museums is an undertaking of primary importance and should be the new museum director's first concern in a new posting. "Security" here refers to the entire range of activities concerned with the protection of the public, staff, and others in the museum, and the protection of the collections from all threats to them.

Like building operations, security affects and is affected by both the collections and public activities aspects of the museum, so that the head of security should meet regularly with those responsible for these functions, as well as with the operations manager, to ensure that security provisions are effectively in place at all times. The security head should also meet regularly (at least annually) with local police, fire, and hospital officials to ensure that the museum is up-to-date with current practices in these jurisdictions and to acquaint them with the museum building's layout and recent or proposed changes to it.

Security is an area where policy and procedures manuals should be utilized fully and updated regularly. The management of security includes an ongoing process of planning and policy formulation and review of procedures manuals to update them to accord with present realities. A security policy should include:

- risk analysis;

- health and safety precautions;

- insurance coverage and valuation procedures;

- security equipment, present and recommended; and

- emergency procedures manual.

These are discussed in more detail in appendix H.

Journey to the Green Museum

By Sarah Sutton and Elizabeth Wylie

Going green is a journey, not a destination.

Today, the public is increasingly aware of the climate crisis, and museums are making the connection that environmentally sustainable practice is mission work. The growth in green action between our 2008 book *The Green Museum: A Primer on Environmental Practice* and the second edition[1] in 2013 was so significant that we presented hundreds more examples of museums applying sustainable practices: from energy, water, and land use to food service, waste management, programming, and everything in between, including endowment investments.

Since 2013, there has been exponential growth in the fundamental understanding that climate change is an existential threat. Cultural institutions are understood to be uniquely positioned to message and model mitigation and adaptation strategies. Connecting this work with community, district, and regional efforts is critical for greater efficacy. To that end, funders are now awake to these opportunities and are sponsoring projects to push the needle on the kind of collective and large-scale action needed to make a difference in the climate crisis. Museums and the cultural sector are fully a part of the Bloomberg Philanthropies–funded America is All In, a coalition of five thousand communities, businesses, and institutions committed to cutting US emissions in half by 2030 and reaching net zero by 2050. Both NEH and the Helen Frankenthaler Foundation's Climate Initiative have focused on capital funding for energy efficiency and to date have funded work at hundreds of museums, and the IMLS-funded Culture Over Carbon research study (2021–2023) has created the cultural sector's first in-depth energy use analysis and the first estimate of the sector's energy impacts on climate. What gets measured gets done, as the popular saying goes. In climate work, having a baseline is a critical component of planning, designing, and implementing reductions in resource use.

There are so many more examples and emerging data sets[2] available, we thought the strongest contribution to this museum management manual would be to reintroduce and reinforce ideas about sustainability statements, principles, and policies as important bedrock actions that undergird measurement, monitoring, planning, implementation, and, importantly—so the work can be scaled-up—connecting with community, district, and regional efforts.

So which comes first: statements, policies, or practice? It is less about what comes first and more about what will take your organization where you want to go. If your museum has some sustainability experience, it tends to be easier to create the statement, policies, and plans that guide your work. Without some experience, writing statements can be challenging, so developing baseline measurements of energy, water, and waste can help you define next steps. This is critical to creating a vision and developing the plan and policies that lead the institution along its green journey. Wherever you are in your green journey, when you want to develop a greater vision and more complete plan, the practice of back-casting may help you: if your vision is for a sustainable organization, then begin by defining what that would "look" like, and then work back through the actions and achievements that will lead to that future.

Your *sustainability or climate statement* is the key to moving from "guerrilla green" to strategic green. While some of your first actions may be the "low-hanging fruit," significant change will come once you identify and schedule sustainable activities that support your mission and align with your strategic plan. The idea is to position your museum for success over the long haul, to prepare for the continuous journey.

As with any *institutional statement*, there is no correct way to present your sustainability statement. Start by examining other sustainability statements and adapt them to your specific situation. Your sustainability statement could say, "We actively choose environmentally sustainable, climate-friendly practices that create the healthy environment our employees and visitors expect and deserve, and our collections require." Perhaps your vision or value statement identifies community engagement: "Climate-smart practices—in programs and operations—demonstrate our commitment to our community not just through programs, but by institutional behavior." A bolder statement would be: "Climate change is a threat to our community and institution. Everyone is responsible for taking action. The museum is taking action by decarbonizing its operations, engaging the public in climate smart-activities, and contributing to community climate resilience."

To put that statement into practice most effectively, the manager of environmental services, the green team, or a sustainability consultant then articulates *principles* to guide choices for each new step of the green journey. These principles support thoughtful decision making to conserve resources, manage risk, inform others, and create the best sustainable solutions for each situation.

Museums have *policies* for collections, communications, security, and learning (to name just a few), but in developing sustainability policies they are far behind colleges and universities and many corporations. Policies on environmental sustainability are now an expectation for all types of organizations. These policies institutionalize behavior by providing vision and frameworks, defining process, identifying goals and evaluation methods, and delegating authority. You may create a policy that stands alone, or one that is woven into existing policies. What matters is providing a responsive framework for decision-making. Folks need not reinvent the wheel, find one you like and tweak it for your own institution.

Spend some time reading policies for colleges and universities and for museums.[3] Consider the scope and format, review the action plans and performance metrics, and consider the kinds of ripple effects sustainability decisions have on all aspects of your organization, from mission and finances to products and visitor engagement. Develop the policy in draft form, plan to finalize it in six months, then yearly to update it. Like your other policies, one on environmental sustainability will be unique to your institution but will have components in common with other museums. Your institution will have its own needs, culture, and environment to consider, and so you will create your own format for a policy. What is important is that you create the policy and attend to it as conditions evolve. Appropriate components of an institutional policy on environmental sustainability include the following:

- Guiding principle

- Explanation of authority and oversight

- Supporting documents

- Baseline information

- Explanation of goals, metrics, and timelines

- Budget

The environmental sustainability of your museum is a mission-based decision; implementation should come from mission-driven decisions daily. So what is your mission-related position on sustainability? "We really need to take a much stronger leadership role in inspiring the public to make changes in the way they live and operate," says Richard V. Piacentini of the Phipps Conservatory and Botanical Gardens. "If we're concerned about saving biodiversity and saving the planet, we can't be islands. People come to our facilities for inspiration and learning; they are ready for us to lead by example."

The Madison Children's Museum (MCM) was an early leader in this work and continues that role today as project director of Caretakers of Wonder, an IMLS-funded National Leadership Grant (2022–2024) that blends strategic operational initiatives with the creation of a developmental framework for climate change engagement for children (ages zero to eight) and the adults who care about them. The grant's network of nine museums in four bioregions around the country means the project results can be disseminated and adopted rapidly and widely. The museum owns and operates a green building and has chosen to weave green practice throughout the institution.[4] The museum states its sustainability commitment this way: "We focus on children, including their future. We are committed to being a sustainable organization, balancing economic, social, and environmental factors to help ensure that we meet our present needs, while enabling future generations to meet their needs. We empower and equip children to actively shape the world they will inherit." To get at the "how," the museum states, as educational and community leaders, we will

- integrate the principles of sustainability into all major business decisions;

- seek strategic collaborations;

- evaluate and reduce the environmental impacts of our operations; and

- design and develop our products, services, and materials with the long-term health of our children and community in mind.

Conclusion

Policy development and implementation require full participation by the board and staff leadership, with understanding of all-staff ramifications. Developing this policy is not a one-person job; it is an institution's job—or it must be if it is going to work. Be clear who has decision-making authority, who is responsible for oversight, and what the mechanisms are for ongoing training for staff and volunteers. This section is where you should identify broadly your evaluation methods and goals. Knowing that the supporting documents provide more detail allows you the flexibility to update those documents without changing the main body of the plan.

The baseline information is the collection of energy and water audit information and historical use data, as well as the design and age of your buildings and systems. Trust us, this will take more time to collect than you realize, but it is more than worth the effort.

Your goals and the timeline for achieving them should be repeated here and treated in detail, along with how to benchmark progress and evaluate success. Action plans implement policy. If your green team has a sustainability action plan, it will be a significant part of the institution's overarching action plan.

And your budget: it shouldn't really wait until the end of the document to appear because it is a critical resource for much of what you must achieve, but not every part can come first. Provide a narrative with your budget for how you calculate return on investment, or what you assume for energy and water cost fluctuation, or for inflation.

Does a particular green element positively affect mission-related public value, directly or indirectly? If you answer yes to either question, then the green option becomes highly desirable. It is no longer a question of whether to go green, it's a question of what, when, and how quickly.

When you look across your institution, using metrics to examine energy and water use, as well as your waste stream, start making connections between the environmental impact of your museum and the impact of your staff, your neighbors, your town, and your region. The collective impact hits home, and the list of things to do to conserve, to collaborate with others, and to educate about what you are doing grows.

It is a long list. It is an important list. It can be overwhelming, but give yourself a break: no one knows it all. The field of environmental sustainability is expanding so rapidly, and new research is coming out so frequently that no one person or institution is going to know it all. If we all share our knowledge and experience, we can all make progress. We have to; this may be one of the most important to-do lists in the museum field.

Reprinted with minor modifications by and permission of the authors of *The Green Museum: A Primer on Environmental Practice* (Rowman & Littlefield, 2013).

7.3 Financial Management By Javier Jimenez Fernandez-Figares

Museum management is responsible for a wide range of functions, including financial management.

For museums operated by independent, not-for-profit organizations, financial management has always been a central concern.

Over the past few decades, with governments around the world emphasizing increased self-reliance, even for museums that are wholly integrated with their own line departments, ensuring the financial well-being of the museum has become a major responsibility for museum management.

As a result, major national museums such as the Louvre (Paris) and the Prado (Madrid) have consolidated new legal frameworks to achieve greater operational and funding autonomy. The job descriptions and qualifications of museum directors increasingly focus on their capability to manage the finances of the institution, especially their fund-raising abilities. Their challenge is to provide for the institution's financial needs while maintaining its creativity, scholarship, and intellectual independence.

Directors and trustees must ensure that the mission is paramount and that the museum's financial arrangements support it, not the other way around. In other words, the balance between market-driven and mission-driven activities should be properly calibrated. For this reason, this section on financial management follows all others, rather than preceding them. The appearance of losing sight of these priorities can diminish public trust in museums and question the very need to devote public resources to them.

> Directors and trustees must ensure that the mission is paramount and that the museum's financial arrangements support it, not the other way around.

This section begins with revenue generation and is followed by controlling expenditures—adequately insuring the museum's assets to protect the institution against loss, while financial planning and budgeting can ensure a positive future in the long term and effective monitoring during the annual cycle.

Revenue Generation

Many museum administrations used to be considered (and used to consider themselves) primarily as cost centers, expending government funds to provide public services. As a result of increasing private wealth and decreasing government revenues as well as the increasing number of museums, museums throughout the world have been challenged to generate nongovernmental revenue.

Earned Revenue

Earned revenue refers to the museum's capacity to generate revenue from its operations, in contrast with government funding, endowments, sponsorship, and donations, all of which may be termed *contributed revenue* and are external sources of revenue. Earned revenue includes the following sources of funding, most of which derive from services to visitors. As museums think of creative ways to monetize their offerings and assets, new sources of earned revenue will be developed in addition to the following:

- admissions

- retail sales

- food services

- memberships

- rentals

- films, performances, and special events

- educational programs

- publications and media

- contracted services

- intellectual property rights, licensing, and franchises

- digital programs

Admission Strategy

Charging for admission to public museums has been and remains an issue of controversy.

The argument put by opponents to charging is that museums are a public service and should be financed by taxes to maximize accessibility. Advocates of charging observe that the quality of museum service often improves when staff and visitors know that admission is being charged, and that relatively affluent tourists who often account for half of museum visitors do not contribute to the cost of free museums, which are borne by the taxes imposed on residents of their host communities.

The imposition of admission charges on formerly free museums, generally, has an immediate negative public perception and a decline in attendance of approximately one-third, which is sometimes (but by no means always) recovered over the following five to ten years, depending on the extent to which the museum follows up their introduction of charges with exhibitions and other programming of wider appeal, enhanced marketing, and other strategies to boost attendance levels.

Conversely, the experience of going free after having had admission charges has historically resulted in attendance increases of 50 percent or more, as seen in the United Kingdom or China after the implementation of nationwide free admission policies for national museums.

There continues to be much research and debate on the impact of charging on the demographic characteristics of visitors. Despite the general perception that low-income and marginalized people will experience admission charges as a barrier to attendance, research in North America and Europe consistently shows that, in fact, other factors like lack of interest, location and distance, or insufficient information can be much more decisive factors. Free or low-cost admission in and of itself does not guarantee broad public participation in the museum—therefore *both* charging and noncharging museums must examine how they communicate with the public, whether they are welcoming to the diversity of people in various communities and what their programs have to offer to their residents and tourists. Because there are many ways to charge and many ways not to charge—as will be seen—what is needed is an *admission strategy* appropriate to the specific situation of each museum.

> Because there are many ways to charge and many ways not to charge—as will be seen—what is needed is an *admission strategy* appropriate to the specific situation of each museum.

The importance of admission revenue on the museum's finances is often overvalued: most museums that charge find that 10–20 percent of their total revenue can be derived from this source, but not more. Admission rates must be appropriately comparable to those for other attractions in the area and are usually scaled for adults, seniors, children, families, and groups.

It is important to reduce the cost for those visitors who visit more than once in a given year—*repeat visitors*—and ways of doing so include: offering free entry to members, free or discounted entry for everyone on particular days or at times of the day when demand is low, tickets that are valid for reentry during a certain period of time, or a reduced rate based on postal code (ranging from the district to the state or province level) to benefit the local community.

Another admission strategy is to charge only for special exhibitions and events and to offer free admission to the exhibition of the permanent collection. This option has proven successful in many jurisdictions around the world, both in maintaining revenue and in providing a free, basic level of museum service to both tourists and residents—who are granted free access to *their* collections.

In some circumstances, this strategy may result in higher levels of income from the retail shop, programs, and food services because of higher foot traffic in the museum than if there were a general admission charge and fewer first-time and repeat visitors.

A briefly popular strategy of "suggested admission fee" among museums in major metropolitan areas of North America is losing favor. A suggested amount—closer in concept to a donation than to an admission fee—theoretically allows visitors to adjust the cost of admission to their economic capacity.

However, the number of museum goers willing to pay the recommended amount has sharply declined over the past few years, and many of them are tourists. Often the more savvy museum goers (statistically of higher education and higher income) are the ones who feel entitled not to pay, while the low-income visitors are the ones who end up paying. For instance, in 2018 the Metropolitan Museum of Art changed its fifty-year-old policy of a suggested admission price of USD $25 to a mandatory admission fee of the same amount for all non–New York State residents.

Ticketing—whether paid or free—offers an opportunity for data analytics and visitor profiling that is fundamental to understanding attendance patterns and visitor preferences. This has been enhanced with the use of digital bookings—which also allow for timed slots for crowd control and dynamic pricing—as well as the creation of user accounts to enroll in programs and events.

Of course, any such usage of personal data must comply with data protection laws and should also be consistent with the museum's code of ethics, reflecting the museum's commitment to respect its visitors' privacy.

Retail Sales

While admission charges may remain debatable, little controversy attends the almost universal provision of museum retail shops, which are not only a revenue source but an integral part of the museum experience. The shop offers visitors an opportunity to take home a product that will remind them of their museum visit and will provide further opportunity for study and entertainment; therefore the quality and educational value of the retail offerings should be consistent with the mission and goals of the museum.

Most museum shop initiatives have proven successful, so that retail sales remain one of the most consistent of the museum's revenue options without discouraging attendance. Cost of sales is generally in the range of 50–60 percent of total sales, leaving a gross margin of 40–50 percent. Taking staffing and other overhead into account leaves a net profit of 10–20 percent of gross sales. Gift shop operations often contribute 5–10 percent of total museum revenues. Smaller museums make their shops cost-effective by combining volunteer retail clerks with paid retail managers.

Even if the shop is not profitable, there is still a case to be made that it contributes to making the museum a *destination*. Shops can provide an anchor to the visit and extend the length of stay by contributing to the array of potential things to do. They can also help diversify the types of visitors in the building by attracting individuals motivated primarily by the shop—who then have the potential to spill into other areas of the museum. Visitors expect retail to be part of their overall cultural and entertainment experiences, so this becomes another service that the museum can provide.

Museums are increasingly extending their retail operations through such means as

- online sales, the largest growth area, both on the museums' own websites and through online retailers;

- satellite and pop-up shops, elsewhere in the same city (often in airports, shopping malls, or during seasonal events) as well as in other cities and countries, for example MoMA Design Stores in Japan and Hong Kong;

- placement of the museum product line in other museum shops and in suitable commercial outlets; and

- collaboration with major brands and licensed products.

Spending per visitor varies widely by the size of the shop and the type of museum. A larger shop usually results in higher sales per visitor but often in lower sales per square foot or square meter; but a shop that is too small in a well-attended museum may actually result in lower revenue at the busiest times because visitors will perceive it to be too crowded and so will avoid it.

Revenues in all museum types can be much higher if the stock is well matched to the market and the attraction (preferably changed for each major temporary exhibition) and if the shop is well located and advertised. Sales at art museums tend to have a higher dollar value as they often resemble higher-end design and concept stores, while science or children's museums will focus more on educational products and toys.

Location is critical to museum shops, as in all retailing. Facility planning should provide for a shop that is visible to visitors entering the museum and inescapable to those leaving. The shop should also be visible to passersby and, ideally, accessible to shoppers who are not even visiting the museum (if this can be arranged while respecting museum security). The ideal museum shop is positioned

> Facility planning should provide for a shop that is visible to visitors entering the museum and inescapable to those leaving.

so that it can open and close independently of the museum, maintaining additional hours to those of the museum if necessary in order to meet market demand or to match special events.

Most museum shops combine a site-specific line of publications, media products, reproductions, and concept store gifts with a more generic stock of books, toys, jewelry, crafts, and other creations that are more or less unique in that community, and may provide an important sales outlet for local artists or artisans while connecting visitors more deeply to the local traditions. *Production for sale* by museum demonstrators on industrial heritage properties—such as ceramics produced at a historic pottery—can be an attractive addition to interpretation at a living history site. Decisions on new stock should involve the marketing team for the perspective of likely appeal to various market segments, as well as curators for approval on aesthetic as well as intellectual grounds. The curators and the director should approve all reproductions or replicas made of objects in the collection, which are often undistinguishable to the average visitor from the actual historic object and can be very popular.

Some museum shops have made themselves more effective by changing their stock significantly for each temporary exhibition, keeping the stock relevant to the current exhibitions. To do so, of course, the retail manager must be a part of the exhibition planning process. Even more common now are shops specific to temporary exhibitions, usually located immediately at the end of the temporary exhibition galleries. Specialized shops or pop ups dedicated to particular permanent collection exhibitions or iconic artifacts have also become commonly accepted practice in many museums. New museums or expansions are now designed with a provision for such ancillary retail spaces.

Most museums continue to operate their shops directly, in order to maximize income, maintain quality control, and provide an individually different retail character associated with their institution. Outsourcing is another option for those who find retail a distraction from the core mission of the museum: there are specialized museum retail agencies that can operate the shop on behalf of the museum. These agencies are able to achieve cost savings by bulk ordering of stock and supplies, and they can service online orders directly, while undertaking to allow for the individual differentiation that is important to a successful museum shop specific to the character of its host institution.

Food Services

Unlike shops, museum-operated cafeterias and restaurants generally do not produce significant levels of income for the museum. The museum director and the food services manager must understand the objectives of the food service (visitor comfort, extending the length of stay, becoming a destination) and attempt to ensure that it does not lose money (although many museum-operated food services do lose money when all relevant staffing and overhead costs are attributed to them).

While many museums operate their shops directly, most prefer to contract or "concession" food services and to receive either a share of proceeds from the contractor (concessionaire) or a rental fee or both. The reason is that food service is a business type with a high rate of failure and logistics that have little in common with those of museum operations, requiring a particular expertise and economies of scale that are generally not achievable in museums. Accordingly, many food service companies will bargain for a very low (or even no) rate of return to the museum, with the condition that they must be the exclusive or preferred caterers for special events and rentals in the museum.

> While many museums operate their shops directly, most prefer to contract or "concession" food services.

Thus the contractors or concessionaires aim to achieve economies of scale by operating several food services throughout the building or the campus (if the museum is part of a larger cultural complex) and especially by catering for special events and rentals. This can be a satisfactory arrangement as long as the museum maintains a quality control provision in the contract, whereby the museum may cancel the contract, after appropriate notice, if quality does not meet the museum's standards over a stated period of time. Quality control is a crucial contract provision because a poor or overpriced lunch or an unsatisfactory snack can outweigh an otherwise outstanding museum experience or event in the minds of many museum visitors and supporters. This quality control provision should address not only cooking, ambience, and customer service but also type of food, nutrition and health standards, and the use of proximity products, as opposed to strictly market-driven savings in food quality. The contractor and the museum should agree in the contract on policy regarding the type of food to be offered and whether the menu needs to align with the identity of the museum—El Museo del Barrio (New York) has a strategy to partner with restaurant operators who will offer dishes representative of the museum's Latinx collection and identity.

Many food service contractors will aim to provide catering for rentals of museum facilities by outside agencies as well as for special events. However, the museum may be in a more flexible and accessible position for rentals if it allows outside caterers to bring in their own caterers for rental events. In most situations the museum offers the contractor's catering service as an option, possibly at a discount, but also allows those renting their facilities to bring in their own caterers if they prefer.

Most smaller museums find that a good-quality cafe with a light snack service, with or without a warming kitchen to heat precooked meals, is sufficient for their visitors and for after-hours rentals. Larger institutions may offer a full restaurant as well. Some very busy museums have evolved three levels of service—a café for light refreshments, a full service restaurant, and a fine dining option (sometimes with views, often led by renowned chefs). The various options are likely to have different customer targets, providers, operators, as well as different opening hours. MAS in Antwerp (Belgium) offers three eating options: casual Café STORM on the ground level (popular with nearby offices and passersby, as well as museum visitors), bring-your-own picnic at the rooftop (with the possibility to borrow a blanket from the museum if you forgot it), and three-star Michelin restaurant Zilte.

As with the museum shop, the location of the museum food services dramatically affects its profitability. Many art museums like to include a courtyard, where sculpture can be enjoyed by diners seated outdoors in temperate weather, or at least viewed from behind glass during the winter. More important commercially is a location that facilitates access after museum hours, if there is a market for that level of food service in that location. The museum's lavatories, or a separate set of washroom facilities for diners, must also be accessible if the café is to be open after the museum's public hours.

If a museum is located in a commercial area with convenient access to food services, it may choose not to invest its capital resources in a food service area but to develop admission policies that encourage visitors to use neighboring restaurants and cafés and to reenter the museum as often as they wish on the day of their visit. This is often helpful in establishing good relations with nearby restaurants and retailers and may help to justify needed governmental support because the museum's policy promotes economic development and income from tax-paying private businesses. The nearby restaurants and their operators may then be encouraged to become corporate or individual members or sponsors.

The museum must also provide for its other food service needs:

- refreshments for exhibition openings and other special events,

- food services for a multipurpose hall or party room (especially if rentals are involved),

- a school lunch area for school groups, and

- light refreshments for the staffroom and the members' lounge.

In providing all of these services, care must be taken to ensure that food supplies and garbage circulation routes do not cross areas or use corridors in which the collection is held or moved. Refreshments for exhibition openings should ideally not be served in the galleries themselves but in an adjacent multipurpose public area that does not hold artifacts, specimens, or works of art—if such space is available; if not the lobby may function in this way, as is the case at the Ayala Museum in Manila (the Philippines).

Still another space provision that is often found advisable, particularly for museums that receive a large number of school groups, is a *school lunchroom*. Many museums find that a dedicated space for this purpose frees their cafés from large numbers of low-spending and potentially loud school children, and enables them to bring their own boxed or bagged lunches. The area allocated for school lunchrooms need not be exclusive for that use—instead it can be a multipurpose space that becomes a revenue earner through rentals and events, or an education suite that doubles up as lunchroom when required.

Memberships

Memberships have features of earned revenue, in as much as they are a museum service (that is, member benefits) that the public is willing to pay for; and of contributed revenue, in that they can be understood as a form of individual philanthropy for those wishing to support the organization.

As a result, membership revenue may be found under both categories in museums' financial accounts, although are increasingly found more under contributed revenue. We treat it as earned revenue for the purposes of this *Manual* because much of the membership program's success depends on how it is packaged and marketed to visitors (as revenue from its "operations"), acknowledging that for some readers and institutions it might be better classified under contributed revenue.

Museums that are line departments of governments, universities, or corporations usually do not offer memberships, although some have established "Friends" organizations. Memberships are most common among independent nonprofit institutions, where they serve more importantly as a means of organizing and retaining loyal support groups, in contrast to their function as a secondary source of revenue. Nevertheless, building and sustaining a strong membership plants healthy roots into the community for any cultural institution, so that even governmental museums would do well to consider such a program.

In the not so distant past many museum directors expected membership fees to cover only the cost of providing services to members. Today many museums are becoming much more ambitious about their membership programs, both as a source of revenue and as a means of extending their support from the traditional base of high-income individuals and corporations, to one that reflects the social, economic, and cultural diversity of the community.

There are two types of museum members depending on their motivation:

1.   the relatively small number who join out of loyalty to the institution or interest in its specialization and

2.   the much larger group who are attracted to join by the advertised advantages of belonging.

For the first mentioned group, those who join in order to support the mission of the institution or to participate in its specialized field of interest, the membership is seen more as a form of philanthropy, civic pride, or personal interest, and these motivations should also be recognized and appreciated. Charges for upper-level memberships in this category may be higher, but the costs of serving these members, paradoxically, may be relatively lower.

Membership of the latter group is built and maintained by offering tangible benefits geared to the interests of frequent visitors, supporters, and donors such as

*   free admission to museums or changing exhibitions that otherwise charge for admission;

*   free or reduced admission to major charged exhibitions;

*   discounts at the museum shop, for charged programs or for rentals;

*   a regular newsletter;

*   invitations to exhibition openings or other events;

*   priority access to museum activities and programs (members of many major museums are given the opportunity to purchase tickets to special exhibitions that are often sold out ahead of the general public); and

- special activities like travel expeditions guided by museum experts and behind-the-scenes tours of the museum by curators.

When the direct and indirect costs of these value-for-money memberships are calculated relative to the revenues earned, many museums find that they actually do not make money from them. Travel expeditions, however, are often large earners when well managed. Moreover, memberships motivated solely by value for money often end once the perceived benefits cease and are harder to retain: the number of basic-level members at free art museums can be completely dependent on the strength of the special exhibition schedule; children's museum memberships are usually discontinued once the children in the family reach an age at which they are no longer interested in attending. Nevertheless, it may be very worthwhile for the museum to maintain such a membership program in order to demonstrate to funding entities and donors the extent of the museum's support. Membership is often the first step in a ladder leading to philanthropy.

In the case of institutions that offer free admission, the number of basic-level members is almost completely dependent on the strength of the special exhibition schedule. If special exhibitions are separately ticketed and are popular (that is, are sold out at peak times), members will be motivated by the potential ticket discount to those exhibitions, and also by benefits such as priority bookings. Membership and marketing staff should continue to test various offers and strategies in addition to the obvious economic incentive provided by free or reduced entry into a popular charged special exhibition.

In order to attract both types of motivation, categories of membership may include individual adults, couples, seniors, students, and families, but they may also provide several donor and corporate membership levels on a graduated scale of increasing support with attendant benefits or exclusivity privileges. Corporate membership at higher cost levels should include benefits (such as free or reduced admission) for the member company's employees, both as a means of creating a closer relationship with the corporation and as a means of expanding the museum's audience. Corporate or donor memberships at the higher cost levels may also rate invitations to exclusive events and reduced rental costs for corporate hospitality or opportunities to sponsor exhibitions or events.

Rentals

The rental of museum space—lobbies, theaters, meeting rooms, multipurpose event rooms, open air gardens and rooftops, or even some galleries—to groups or companies who wish to associate their event or their image with the museum has become a major source of self-generated revenue. Museums are highly desirable rental venues on account of their iconic architecture and location, and their positive perception in collective imagination.

This practice depends upon well-located attractive spaces for rental with access outside the museum's open hours as well as during visiting times, usually with movable chairs and tables stored nearby and with handy food services. Because museums require these multipurpose space for their own exhibition openings, special events, or receptions, it becomes attractive for them to rent these rooms as well. Flexibility is key—multiple seating or standing configurations, walls that can be partitioned to reduce or enlarge the venue, broad audiovisual projection capabilities including immersive technologies—as are the spatial adjacencies to other museum functions: a storage room to keep movable furniture, the lobby for access and gathering, theater or auditorium facilities, and the galleries to enable it to be used for exhibition openings. Food services and refreshments of adequate quality are crucial, as is access to the museum's public toilets.

Museums tend to charge for the use of their facilities based on the duration of the event (including preparations before and after), which normally spans between one hour, a half day, or a full day. The most straightforward operational model is for the museum to provide the empty space and for the user to take care of security and janitorial services, furnishing and equipment rental, event production, as well as catering.

Museums should be careful not to charge below the going rate for comparable rentals in their communities because this would be effectively providing a subsidy and undercutting commercial operators in that area.

On the contrary, museum rentals should be priced at the high end of the market, at "carriage trade" rates, because their competitive advantage is to offer the prestige of association with a leading cultural institution. The exception is provision of such facilities to specialist groups or community organizations primarily as a public service; this often means charging a reduced rental rate (as compared to the rate to for-profit entities) to accredited organizations. For example, El Museo del Barrio in New York makes its theater facilities available to local community groups at a discounted rate and ensures a minimum number of calendar days are blocked for this type of space rentals (versus commercial productions).

> Museums must define clear policies with regard to the types of events that are admissible within their premises to ensure compatibility with their mission and identity.

Museums must define clear policies with regard to the types of events that are admissible within their premises to ensure compatibility with their mission and identity. Although weddings and birthday parties are often disallowed, institutions with attractive gardens or heritage buildings and grounds onsite may consider weddings a lucrative source of revenue; children's museums can make good use of a school lunchroom or classrooms by allowing birthday parties, while establishing a closer connection with their target audiences.

Museums should also establish conservation and security requirements in the rental contracts to prevent wear and tear on the fabric of the building and risks to collections, as well as the range of admissible rental hours to avoid competing for space with their mission-driven programs.

Multimedia, Performing Arts, and Special Events

Multimedia programs and performing arts presentations, such as dance and theater, increasingly complement a museum's exhibitions and contribute to diversifying audiences. Special events may be of any kind, including festivals during holidays. Some smaller museums welcome half their visitors on a dozen special event days during the year, for which special admission rates may be charged.

The capacity to offer such attractions is, of course, dependent on the provision of adequate facilities. For many museums, a lecture auditorium with digital projection equipment is sufficient. Again, access after the museum galleries' opening hours is important to make such facilities cost-effective. If evening programs of two and a half hours or more are planned, it is best to provide the comfort of fixed seating to theater standard on a raked floor rather than just movable chairs on a flat floor. Automated convertible seating systems are also available on the market to enhance flexibility, although they are more expensive to install and maintain.

A significant planning decision affecting museum operations is whether the auditorium or lecture theater is also to be used for the museum's orientation program or other multimedia experiences. Trying to combine both functions in one space can lead to operational problems and to oversizing or undersizing, so in many cases consideration must be given to providing two facilities—a multipurpose, flexible space or black box for the orientation, smaller format presentations, and immersive experiences; and a separate (and usually larger) lecture theater for more formal film, music, theater, or lecture programs.

On the other hand, some museums have observed that their theaters are the most underutilized spaces in their buildings. Particularly today, when audiovisual programs are available in many media and formats accessible at home, it can be more difficult to attract audiences. Right sizing the auditorium, particularly in the case of fixed seating, is important to avoid half empty venues on a regular basis.

Some larger museums and science centers have had success with large-screen theaters, such as IMAX or IMAX DOME. However, the "wow" effect of these big-screen showings has somewhat diminished over the past couple of decades, partly as a result of the availability of large-screen home entertainment systems with surround sound and partly due to the adaptation of these formats to regular Hollywood films and the ubiquity of the large-screen theaters, especially since the digitalization of the formerly cumbersome film format.

Simulators, augmented reality, and virtual reality have added another dimension to museum exhibitions, which can form yet another revenue center if an additional fee is charged for their use. This adaptation of technology to the needs of the museum industry was pioneered by science centers and military and aviation museums and has extended nowadays to all museum types. Some museums rent dedicated handheld devices or provide fixed stations with custom-made hardware and software, while others develop apps that can be downloaded to the visitors' handheld devices. For example, Casa Batlló in Barcelona rents custom-made tablets that provide several augmented reality itineraries throughout that particular historic Gaudí building and transport visitors to a different era (digitally).

Still other entertainment formats are available to museums. Digitally programmed planetaria are attractive features at science centers and may be utilized for presenting laser shows with popular music as well. Multimedia theater programs, including such features as moving screens and computerized lighting effects, with or without live actors or animatronic figures, can be developed—sometimes called "4D theater" if they incorporate such special effects as misting, smoke, scents, and simulator chair movements. These are usually part of the "destination experience," specific to the story the museum has to tell.

Another option is live theater, which may be attractive for a summer season, when student actors are available, or as part of an employment grant scheme. Historic sites may opt for first-person interpretation, in which costumed actors play their parts in period clothing and answer visitors' questions from within the time and space limitations of the historic setting.

If possible, in institutions where admission is charged, all such feature attractions should be included in the general price of admission, but it may be preferable, depending on their scale and location, to present them as additional cost features, on offer at the original point of sale when the museum admission is purchased.

In the case of special events and festivals it is likely that the museum facilities will not be able to accommodate the larger number of participants that can concentrate at a given time. Similarly, regular museum staff might be insufficient to provide the necessary level of service. For these types of large-scale events, it is recommended to partner with other community agents and organizations and to activate the outdoor spaces of the museum when possible, including the neighboring plazas, streets, and other public spaces. The necessary permits, agreements, and extended insurance coverage should be in place.

Learning Programs, Publications, and Media

Learning programs are usually considered as cost centers, especially if the museum provides guided tours free of charge or cultural programs at affordable rates for the benefit of the community as part of its mandate. In such cases, the museum often receives a government subsidy, foundation grant, or corporate sponsorship that is partially or wholly justified by its educational service and mission-driven nature.

However, in some instances, educational services can also be revenue centers in themselves. Museums may contract with schools to provide a certain number of guided tours to designated classes or charge school parties a special admissions rate. Sometimes admission is free for school parties but charged when museum staff provide special programs or guided tours. Some museums have time-sharing agreements with school boards or local authorities, whereby school parties have exclusive access during certain hours (certain mornings, for instance) when the museum is not open to the general public; the museum provides guided tours or other educational programs during those hours and receives a set fee from the school board or educational authority. Teacher training programs may also generate revenue.

Separate entrances with turnouts for school buses are often provided for school tours so that they may come and go safely without interfering with other visitors. Separate cloakrooms and a school lunchroom are also helpful, with the lunchroom doing double duty as a multipurpose rentable space for events on weekends or evenings. Classrooms have become common and may be useful for orientation prior to a visit or for discussion afterward, as long as both museum staff and schoolteachers remember that the museum is the ideal setting for informal, not formal, learning and that the affective learning that the museum can provide can be experienced best in the galleries, not in a classroom. A hands-on learning lab equipped with computer workstations or lab equipment may be a better model for the educational space than a classroom.

Adult education lectures, workshops, or seminars may be a revenue source and are usually more successful in museums if they are offered as series or courses. Such series can also be a means of building membership or recruiting volunteers. An auditorium or classroom with digital projection facilities and a sound system is usually sufficient for this level of programming.

Some art museums have studios in which they can teach both fine and applied arts, ranging from informal weekend or evening sessions for families (often booked well in advance) to more structured courses for every level of serious interest in the arts. Artists' demonstrations and artists in residence can be accommodated in the same studios, or the spaces can be made available for rent when not in use for classes.

Travel programs with museum staff as expert guides can also be revenue generators. This might work particularly well in the case of museums conducting field work beyond its walls (archaeological or natural history museum projects, for example), or in the case of historic sites.

The COVID-19 pandemic consolidated a growing trend toward digital media and online learning programs, which are generally delivered via the museum's website, or in partnership with an online platform such as Coursera. Online programs are often more difficult to monetize than in-person programs because the public has gotten used to having infinite free content available online, and the costs of producing digital content are not negligible. Some museums have been successful in partnering with formal education institutions to offer accredited learning courses, such as the National World War II Museum in New Orleans, which offers an online master's in World War II studies in partnership with the Arizona State University Online.

The publication of catalogs and books about museum collections and exhibitions has long been a source of revenue for museums, although in many instances print runs were not related to the foreseeable target market, resulting in massive, long-term storage requirements for unsold copies. Such publications about collections and exhibitions are often complementary to ad hoc museum apps—which allow visitors to scan artifacts with QR codes and create their own digital collection for free—and to digitized collection repositories, either on the museum's websites or on external platforms such as Google Arts Project.

The development of digitized media has put a premium on the museum's control of the imagery of its collection—an issue that is particularly important for art museums but also to other science and history institutions. Considerations of control over subsequent usage of the imagery, along with copyright (or copyleft) provisions, may lead museum directors to be cautious about leasing rights to digitized images of objects in their collections, while remaining positive about extending their images and information to new and much larger audiences through these media. The balance between providing free and universal accessibility to a museum's digitized collection (a model that the Rijksmuseum in Amsterdam embraced with its online creation tool Rijksstudio) or taking a more restrictive approach to the use of collection images remains an institution's decision.

Charging for the use of museum sites, buildings, or collections in film, television, or advertising is another revenue source that although hard to project in advance is worth considering. Museums need policies that set differential rates for educational films, entertainment, or advertising. These should take into consideration not only rights to the imagery and safeguards concerning ethical uses of it but also the real costs to the museums of providing access to the filmmakers—particularly having to close down parts of the building during opening hours.

Contracted and Consulting Services, Franchising, and Licensing

Museums themselves may undertake contracts to provide research, consulting or technical services to other museums, to government agencies, or to the private sector. Traditionally, some museums have been mandated to provide archaeological services within their geographical areas or natural history curators to identify pests for appropriate regional agencies or municipalities. The field has evolved substantially in the past two decades.

In what is both a cultural diplomacy effort and revenue source, national museums such as the British Museum, the Louvre Museum, the Hermitage Museum, and Centre Pompidou have embarked on lucrative international licensing agreements by which their brand is "leased" to new institutions in other countries, alongside a full suite of support services from consulting to managerial support, long-term collection loans, and temporary exhibition contracts.

This formula allows their "clients" to take a shortcut to address a lack of collections of their own and a lack of brand recognition of an otherwise unknown new museum in a city that wants to be put on the "cultural tourism map." The best-known example of this is the Louvre Abu Dhabi, in Saadiyat Island.

Museum conservation departments, in individual institutions or within regional museum services, have attempted to offer conservation services on contract to other museums and to private collectors. These have sometimes been moderately successful, although the type of equipment, personnel, and practice required for such a regional service is likely to be quite different from what the conservation department normally provides.

One difficulty with all such contracts is that they divert time and attention away from museum priorities toward the imperatives of the revenue-generating contract. Another more fundamental challenge to museum management in the provision of such services under contract is to preserve the spirit of shared scholarship and freedom of access to information that has always been a hallmark of museums.

> As museum managers strive to develop more revenue sources . . . it is important that they ensure that academic freedom of information about the collection is not forfeited in the process.

As museum managers strive to develop more revenue sources by tendering for contracts for research or other services, it is important that they ensure that academic freedom of information about the collection is not forfeited in the process.

A related service that at one time was considered very problematic is to "rent" storage space for private collectors and other institutions within a museum's spare back of house facilities. Museums can ensure conservation and security standards that most corporate and private storage facilities cannot. Institutions like the Depot Boijmans Van Beuningen in Rotterdam make some of their storage modules available for rent to individuals and corporations.

With regard to intellectual property and licensing, some museums have explored industrial and commercial applications to the outputs of their research and creative processes and the intersection between disciplines.

Contributed Revenue

Contributed revenue is given by others in support of the museum's mission. Therefore, despite the current emphasis on earned revenue, contributed revenue remains of the utmost importance, including

- government funding,

- grants,

- endowments,

- sponsorship, and

- donations.

Government Funding

Governments at all levels contribute to the financial support of museums for a wide variety of reasons, but principally because they provide four main services:

1. **Preservation of the collective heritage:** Any community of people, whether they constitute a nation, a state, a province, a county, or a municipality, inherits a *natural heritage*—the land, air, and waters they inhabit or use—and a *cultural heritage*—the archaeology and history of their ancestors and those who came before their ancestors in the place or wherever their history has taken them. They are constantly adding to their cultural heritage, as well as affecting their natural heritage. If they are or have become multicultural populations, the collective heritage will be accordingly diverse. Museums are charged with the preservation of the entire collective heritage, past and present, natural and cultural. Government subsidy is justified primarily by museums' fulfillment of this vital function.

2. **Education:** Museums are a most effective means of informal education of the public, especially in the values and meaning of the collective heritage, both natural and cultural. Informal education is an important adjunct to formal education institutions, not only because it makes abstract lessons concrete, but even more so because it provides affective rather than merely cognitive learning. Affective learning is far more important in conveying and retaining values than mere cognitive comprehension of them, it can unite generations with widely differing formal educational backgrounds in the common experience of an exhibition or demonstration.

3. **Cultural tourism:** Museums are a key driver of tourism to the city or region. Cultural tourism is the most dynamic sector of this vital industry, even in countries whose tourist appeal has relied on the now universally suspect "sun, sea, and sand." Governments must find ways to redirect taxes levied on this industry to make tourism a renewable resource. Providing subsidies to museums is one way of contributing toward the preservation of the natural and cultural heritage, the principal resource for the cultural tourism industry. It may also (as in the Arabian Gulf nations) facilitate the acquisition or the long-term or short-term loan of important works of art or whole exhibitions that can act as a magnet to cultural tourists.

4. **Social cohesion, social capital:** A more deep-seated reason for government funding of museums is the contribution these institutions make to the creation of what economists call social capital. This is the intangible but invaluable force of social cohesion that gives people shared learning and enjoyable experiences in stable public institutions—a particularly important function of museums and other public cultural attractions in a fast-changing world often dominated by commercial interests. This is certainly one of the motivations that has led many so-called emerging nations to establish national and other museums. These institutions provide a public forum in which common values may be presented or challenged, common interests pursued, general public knowledge enhanced, or multiple cultures displayed and interpreted on an equal basis.

> This is the intangible but invaluable force of social cohesion that gives people shared learning and enjoyable experiences in stable public institutions.

As governments and people continue to reevaluate the role of government, we may expect that the reasons for supporting museums may change, and the degree of support may also change. In China, for example, the central government over the past two decades placed a strong and increasing emphasis on opening new museums throughout the country to compensate for a historic deficit of this type of institution, thereby stimulating the development of the sector and increasing its museum budget exponentially.

> For whatever combination of reasons, government subsidy remains the most important *single source* of revenue for most museums around the world.

For whatever combination of reasons, government subsidy remains the most important *single source* of revenue for most museums around the world. It accounts for 80–90 percent of many national, provincial, and state museums' revenue, particularly in Europe and Asia, and for 40–60 percent of all museum revenues, even in many countries (such as Britain or Canada) where museums have become active in increasing earned revenue. In the United States, however, its importance has been declining in the past few decades: whereas support from all government levels was at a 39 percent average in 1989, by 2006 it had dropped by 15 percent to a national average of 24 percent, according to the Museum Financial Information Survey by the American Alliance of Museums. A current analysis of the market suggests that following the 2008–2012 Great Recession and the COVID-19 pandemic, government support has continued to drop.

To what extent should governments subsidize museums?

The Lord study for what was then the UK Office of Arts and Libraries, *The Cost of Collecting*, indicated that about 67 percent of all museum expenditure could be directly and indirectly attributed to care of the museums' collections.[5] The figure for American museums is somewhat lower, at about 56 percent. One might take the view, therefore, that government subsidy or a combination of government subsidy and revenue from endowments should amount to approximately 55–70 percent of museum budgets if the collective heritage is to be preserved for future generations. A government with high educational priorities could go further, providing an additional 10–15 percent to ensure that the museum fulfills its educational objectives for the population. However, the reality in most of the world is that government funding has been reduced from that level in the 1970s to between 25 and 50 percent today.

Another approach is to look at it from a tax contributions perspective. According to the American Alliance of Museums (AAM), the economic activity of museums generates over $12 billion in tax revenue, one-third of it going to state and local governments; each job created by the museum sector results in $16,495 in additional tax revenue; and museums and other nonprofit cultural organizations return more than $5 in tax revenue for every $1 they receive in funding from all levels of government.

In some jurisdictions, generous government assistance has been instrumental in stimulating higher standards of professionalism among museums. Annual contributions have been made contingent by some governments on the recipient museums' adoption of desired policies or the preparation of long-term plans. In some cases these requirements have been imposed directly by government cultural or heritage departments, in others by agencies established or encouraged by governments to impose registration or accreditation schemes, compliance with which then becomes a criterion in deciding whether to grant subsidies at all, or subsidies above a certain minimal subsistence level. The overall effect of such requirements has been positive for the recipient museums and for the museum profession.

Cities may be very generous by providing grants in lieu of taxes or making museums exempts from property and other taxes. Providing zoning or other planning incentives can have value far exceeding a grant.

While government line department museums and some "arm's length" institutions may receive government subsidies, independent, nonprofit associations—and some arm's length and government line department museums as well—are more likely to receive government support in the form of *grants*. Grants are distinguished from subsidies in that they are not an assured allocation but are subject to application by the recipient museums to programs that have defined goals and objectives. Another significant difference is that museums need to provide a proportionate level of funding of their own, fostering entrepreneurship. In some countries, lotteries are the sources or administrators of grants. Private foundations also award grants to museums.

Grants may be of two types:

1. **Operating grants:** These are grant programs that provide contributions to museums annually, so they are similar to subsidies, except that the recipient museums must apply for them and often cannot predict the amount of the annual grant. These are often made subject to their recipients' compliance with professional standards, which may be indicated on the application form. Funds granted for operating purposes may usually be expended on a wide range of activities or for any running costs.

2. **Project grants:** These are grant programs that have specific objectives and therefore make funds available for particular purposes. Although some of these may be museum specific, others may arise from agencies, government departments, or foundations with very different concerns; among the most common are employment grants. Funds provided under these programs must be expended on the projects for which they have been approved, and separate project accounts are usually required. An example of this is the Mellon, Ford, Getty, and Terra Foundations 2023 grant "Advancing Latinx Art in Museums" (ALAM). The funding partners committed a combined $5 million to the initiative, which will provide ten grants of $500,000 to institutions in support of the creation and formalization of ten permanent early and mid-career curatorial positions with expertise in Latinx art.

In many museums the preparation of grant applications has become a specialized function within the development office or by contractors. The person responsible for this function needs to meet with the museum personnel who will execute the programs or projects seeking funding before preparing the application, to ensure that all costs—in time, space, personnel, facilities, and materials, as well as money—have been considered. Failing to allow for the cost of administering successful grant applications is one of the more common errors of overenthusiastic museum managers.

> In many museums the preparation of grant applications has become a specialized function within the development office or by contractors.

Grant projects also need to be carefully correlated with the museum's long-term policies and priorities. Winning a grant from a government employment program is of little value if it conflicts with the museum's personnel policies or requires far more time for training than is justified by the progress realized on a museum project. Even more important is to ensure that grants are secured because they accord with museum priorities rather than allowing grant programs to determine the museum's programs.

Some government departments administer grant programs directly, whereas others establish agencies, such as the National Endowment for the Arts, the National Endowment for the Humanities, the National Science Foundation, or the Institute of Museum and Library Services in the United States. Some of these specialized agencies have been instrumental in stimulating higher levels of professionalism among recipient museums.

> Private philanthropic foundations are increasingly important sources of grant aid.

Private philanthropic foundations are increasingly important sources of grant aid. Some, like the Gulbenkian Foundation, the Getty Foundation, the Pew Charitable Trusts, the Mellon Foundation, or the Ford Foundation, have major programs specific to museums, whereas many have more general cultural or educational objectives that museums can fulfill.

A significant trend in both operating grant and project grant programs in recent years has been *evaluation by outcomes* rather than more narrowly defined functional or project objectives. Not satisfied with merely recording that the museum continues in operation or that the funded museum learning program served the requisite number of children, evaluation by outcomes seeks to determine what difference the funded program made in the world. The application forms for such grants typically require the applicant to articulate social or cultural outcomes in advance, thereby encouraging activities that are more broadly or communally focused rather than being limited to operational priorities.

Endowments

Many museum managers in countries where the government is the main source of museum income have the impression that their museums largely pay for themselves through earned revenues. This is rarely true. A more important aspect of US museum funding is the tradition of philanthropy through *endowments*.

An endowment fund is an investment portfolio of a charitable and nonprofit institution with the initial capital deriving from tax-deductible donations. These endowments are not spent directly on museum activities but are invested, with a percentage of the interest earned by the investments being devoted to the museum's operating costs. Investment decisions may be made by a special committee of trustees with expertise in that area or investment counselors. Average revenue from endowments accounts for around 11 percent of US museum operating budgets; botanical gardens and art museums have traditionally had the largest endowments.

In museums with current or planned endowment funds, raising contributions to the endowment becomes an important aspect of fund-raising in itself. Museum trustees and members in particular should be encouraged to make donations or bequests to the endowment as the most effective way of helping the museum achieve financial stability in the long term.

The best opportunity to raise contributions to unrestricted endowment funds that may be used for operations arises during capital development campaigns, when endowment requirements can be presented as part of the overall development need. The difficulty in raising endowment funds is that they appear to be too long term and too diffuse in application, so that potential donors do not feel in control of, or responsible for, the results of their philanthropy. For this reason there are restricted endowment funds with specific aims and uses, such as acquisitions.

Maintaining endowment funds means resisting the temptation to utilize all of the interest earned, or even to bite into the capital, in times of need. It also means being ready to see the endowment fluctuate along with economic cycles: during the 2008 recession, the Metropolitan Museum of Art's endowment lost an estimated $800 million, representing 28 percent of its value at the time.[6] The professional endowment fund manager will advise the museum on the appropriate draw. As for utilizing the capital, this is almost always counterproductive because it strongly discourages future donors to the endowment fund at the same time as it diminishes the capital on which interest can be earned.

Despite the advantages of the endowment model, few countries outside North America see a significant representation of this revenue stream among their museums. The reasons are twofold: less confidence in the financial system by institutions and the public, and lack of sufficient tax incentives to encourage contributions for such types of funds.

Sponsorship

Sponsorship of exhibitions and other museum programs, particularly learning programs, is one of the most productive ways in which the private sector can be involved in museums. Unfortunately, some advocates of government cutbacks have formed the notion that such sponsorships can somehow supplant grants and subsidies. Even where sponsorships are fully engaged, this is never true, particularly as most corporate sponsors' contributions are contingent on the museum continuing to receive government support.

Nevertheless, private sector sponsorship has taken its place as a significant revenue source, particularly as it can be combined with corporate memberships. Museums should prepare sponsorship policies that articulate the institutional mission and values and ensure that control over the content and style of exhibitions or other programs is retained by the museum. Company executives are usually relieved to learn of such provisions because they ensure that the sponsorship does not risk subsequent public criticism for alleged interference. Acknowledgments of sponsors' contributions should include a statement of the museum's responsibility for, and control of, all issues of content.

The museum management should consider the sponsor as a partner and aim to develop mutually beneficial relationships. Sponsorships are most often provided for major special exhibitions that attract a large audience, thereby realizing the greatest "return" on the company's "investment." That being said, museums should avoid tailoring their exhibitions and cultural program exclusively to what the market will sponsor best. They should preserve their artistic independence and propose content that may be provoking, politically incorrect, or that sparks critical thinking. However, the temptation to program more commercial content that will be appealing to corporate brands has proven to be hard to resist and is often referred to as a "privatization trend." It needs to be pointed out that all types of funding may have implicit or explicit strings attached. This is why the museum's operational statements—mission, mandate, vision, and values—are so important, and that the governing body and staff are committed to maintain them. Recent controversies about museum board members reflect concern that they have conflicts of interest that could prevent them from making decisions consistent with those foundational statements and values.

Growing numbers of companies regard contributions to museums as part of their public relations or marketing strategy rather than as philanthropy. Museums can respond to this orientation (which usually places significantly larger amounts of funding at their disposal) by targeting potential sponsor companies with interests in the content of museum projects or with a marketing focus on the target market for specific exhibitions or other programs. Thus companies with products or services directed at children and their parents may be interested in sponsoring a children's gallery or an educational program, while others may be particularly drawn to a program directed at encouraging multicultural participation in the museum.

Donations

Gifts and bequests of artifacts, specimens, or works of art, and related donations of money by relatively wealthy individuals, have historically been responsible for the development of many major museums. For the most part these were made before the donations earned significant tax advantages for the donors; rather, this kind of philanthropy aimed to establish a lasting memorial that would have cultural and educational value for many years to come.

Such donors still exist, and it is very much in the interest of museums to seek their support where it is available. Income tax deductions for donations to museums in the form of acquisitions or cash remain an attraction in some jurisdictions, but have been substantially reduced in others. Another motivation may be to reduce or escape capital gains taxes or estate duties or to comply with cultural property export and import legislation, which usually restricts sales abroad and makes donations to national institutions more attractive.

However, it should be noted that collection donations have also skewed museum collections so that in art and history, for example, art and artifacts by women, people of color, Indigenous people, and poor and working persons of all genders and backgrounds have been underrepresented. This has limited the subjects of museum exhibitions and museum research. Many potential donors of such important material would not benefit from tax incentives and may not think of a museum as a logical place to memorialize their values. Museum directors and staff need to develop programs to recalibrate donations and to reach out to a broader base of donors to achieve a more pluralist approach including nonprofit social organizations and trade unions.

In some countries museums are more successful in attracting donations of goods or services from corporations rather than asking for money. Such donations in kind may be especially valuable at a time of capital development, whether of new buildings, new facilities, or renewed exhibitions. Computer or audiovisual hardware and software are other frequent donations in kind.

An important consideration for both museum and donor to understand is that donations or bequests of acquisitions convey to the museum the *liability* of caring for the donated material. The donation of a collection, or even of a few works of art, artifacts, specimens, or archival materials, should be accompanied by a cash contribution to the museum's operating funds for the care of the donated material. These funds will be expended on providing the storage areas, display space, security, conservation, documentation, curatorial research, and many other costs associated with the addition of the donation to the museum's collection. The larger the collection donated, the more important such financial support of the museum's running costs becomes.

Proposed donations of acquisitions should be acknowledged with temporary receipts while under consideration. The permanent receipt for an accepted gift or bequest must make clear that the transfer of ownership is total and in perpetuity and is unconditional.

Under no circumstances should the museum be persuaded to accept donations with strings attached, such as stipulations that the donation should be placed on permanent display, or that it cannot be loaned to other museums. If such arrangements have been inherited, the museum should move to renegotiate them with the heirs or executors if possible. Such commitments can hamper the museum's scope of operations severely, especially its ability to change displays or to participate in loan exhibitions, and dissolving such constraints is not easy, as the trustees of the Barnes Foundation in Pennsylvania or the Burrell Collection in Glasgow can attest. Refusing donations with such conditions attached takes courage, but accepting them inevitably circumscribes the institution's long-range development.

There is a trend for wealthy individuals and corporations to establish their own museums, as opposed to donating collections or resources to existing institutions. Some recent examples include museums founded by philanthropists Eli and Edythe Broad (the Broad Art Museum at Michigan State University and the Broad in downtown Los Angeles), or bank foundations like Fundación BBVA (Madrid) who decided to open their own permanent cultural facilities after years of sponsoring major museums. Whether this represents less availability of resources to established museums, or even competition for other contributed revenue sources such as grants, remains to be seen.

Another trend that digitization has enabled is crowdfunding. This mechanism allows fundraisers to collect money from many people via online platforms and generally works best for small and medium one-time projects. Colchester Museums (England) launched a crowdfunding campaign in 2022 among local people to bring to life its new exhibition Wicked Spirits? Witchcraft + Magic at Colchester Castle. With over two hundred donors, the campaign exceeded the £15,000 target.[7]

Fund-Raising Campaigns

Fund-raising campaigns are the means of organizing donations. They range from once-in-a-lifetime capital fund-raising drives to annual solicitations, but usually follow a similar pattern.

First is forming a *fund-raising committee*. Raising money is a social enterprise and is best undertaken by a committee of people who can be convinced that it is not only valuable but necessary to raise the required funds because they believe in the institution, project, or programs for which the funds are to be raised. Each member should join the committee by making whatever donation he or she can afford; the trustee or development officer forming the committee should determine in advance the amounts each committee member might donate and invite them to join with a suggestion of a suitable amount.

Committee members who have not contributed appropriately themselves cannot convince others to do so, but those who have already contributed are usually strongly motivated to persuade others to join them. In addition to their willingness to give according to their means, committee members should be selected as representative of the groups who are considered to be the most likely donors—if a certain industry has a special interest in the museum or the exhibition, for instance, then a leading person in that industry should serve on the committee so that he or she can lead the campaign industry-wide.

The committee may also wish to appoint professional fund-raising consultants and to agree on a campaign budget and goal. Both of these amounts may be determined by consultants who specialize in conducting fund-raising feasibility studies. Fund-raising consultants can be helpful in providing planning and sound advice, especially about realistic objectives, but unfortunately they cannot do the work of the committee, who must undertake the actual fund-raising themselves.

Second, the *case statement* must be drafted. The first rule of fund-raising is "If you don't ask, you don't get." But the museum must be sure that the use to which the funds will be put is made clear, not only in terms of what will be done with the money but, more importantly, why the museum needs the funds. This is usually articulated in a case statement, in which the museum management makes the case for the project, or for the continuation of the programs to be funded. Drafting a persuasive case statement and publishing it attractively is crucial to a successful fund-raising campaign.

The fund-raising plan must identify an adequate but realistic goal, the anticipated groups of *donors*, and attainable amounts to be sought from each group, adding up to the overall goal. Remembering that people give money to other people (*not* to projects or causes), the plan should also identify the volunteer *fund-raisers*, pairing those who will ask with those who it is hoped will give. Transparency and ethical philanthropy have become more important in recent years as certain industries are no longer welcomed by many museums. The phrase "ethical consumption of culture" has been used to describe this cultural shift. Each museum governing body will make decisions about what meets their operations statements and values with respect to fund-raising. Considerations of pluralism—by which is meant organizations in the private sectors of mid- to small-scale and representing a variety of perspectives and purposes—may be helpful in making these decisions and setting goals.[8]

Next, *pacesetting donations* are acquired. Up to 80–90 percent of the target amount is often donated by only 10 percent of donors. The campaign should begin with this relatively quiet phase in which key donors are approached with the case statement, with a view to obtaining pacesetting donations—amounts that can then be cited when approaching subsequent donors in that group.

Naming rights are often tied to pacesetting donations. Buildings, wings, galleries, or display cases may be named for donors at specific value levels. It is most important that these rights be determined in the fund-raising plan at the outset, with the values required for each level of naming determined in proportion to the total amount needed. Giving away major naming rights early in a campaign for too little is a common error.

The *public campaign*, a well-published campaign to secure relatively small amounts from a large number of donors (often realizing only 5–10 percent of the total to be raised), complete with fund-raising events, should follow after the pacesetting contributions have been secured, as the rest of the private donations are being made. The value of this part of the campaign is to engage with stakeholders and the broad public that is part of the museum ecosystem.

The *collecting of pledges* is set up. Many campaigns seek *pledges* of amounts to be given over time. Wherever possible, automatic payment methods such as postdated checks, standing orders, covenants, direct debits, or charge card commitments should be arranged, but however it is organized, it is crucial that the campaign includes a schedule for the collection of the money pledged.

Finally, the *donors are thanked*. It is vital for the museum to acknowledge donors in a suitable way—which might range from throwing a party in celebration of a successful campaign to erecting a plaque in acknowledgment of a major donor. Small contributions must receive acknowledgment and the museum's thanks in some tangible way.

Operating Expenses

A common mistake when planning a new institution is to disregard the fact that museums are expensive to run on a daily basis and that there is an eternal need to incur operating expenses! Most project managers focus on the capital expenditure needs (CAPEX) and ignore the operating expenses (OPEX); the former are key to successfully starting up a museum, but the latter will determine if the institution is able to survive well beyond opening day. Planning for long-term financial sustainability is key, and that involves developing a realistic business plan, annual budgeting efforts, as well as controlling expenses.

> A common mistake when planning a new institution is to disregard the fact that museums are expensive to run on a daily basis.

The operating costs listed in museum budgets and financial reports can usually be classified according to the following main line items:

- salaries and benefits;

- occupancy costs;

- curatorial and conservation costs;

- exhibitions and other public activity costs;

- marketing expenses; and

- administrative costs.

Salaries and Benefits

Museums are labor-intensive institutions. Salary and benefit packages vary widely, with a few larger institutions offering very attractive compensation levels but most museum staff suffering from below-average salaries and wages relative to other professions. Despite the relatively low wages often paid to each employee, salaries and benefits often amount to 50–60 percent of total operating costs in collecting institutions with curatorial and conservation responsibilities typically requiring a higher percentage than noncollecting science centers or children's museums. Proportions even higher than that—ranging up to or even above 70 percent—are common enough, particularly in some government line department museums in countries where civil service pay levels are subject to annual increments while government budget allocations for museums remain static or are being reduced. Proportions higher than 65 percent may be regarded as unhealthy because they leave too little money in the rest of the budget for the staff to accomplish museum goals and objectives of the budget allocated to staff costs. A target of 55–60 percent might be taken as an attainable goal for many institutions, except in those government line departments. The benefits proportion in many countries accounts for 20–25 percent of total employment costs, although it ranges as high as 40–50 percent in some.

Occupancy Costs

By "occupancy costs" we mean expenses incurred by the operation of the museum's site and buildings. These may include rent or taxes (if applicable), utilities, groundskeeping, cleaning, maintenance and repairs, the operation of security systems, and insurance on the building, but not the cost of major renovations, which is a capital expense. Maintaining environmental controls and security to museum standards is expensive, and utility costs have increased substantially with rising energy costs in recent years, so occupancy costs in museums usually account for 15–20 percent of total expenses, unless some functions are being provided by the museum's governing body as part of a centralized government or university campus service.

Curatorial and Conservation Costs

Most collecting institutions should aim to reserve around 5 percent of their total budget for direct collection management costs other than salaries. Lesser reserves are often encountered, usually indicating neglect of this important resource. Yet these direct curatorial and conservation expenses are by no means all the costs of maintaining a collection. They do *not* include acquisitions costs (which are not part of the operating budget), nor the wide range of wages (all the security guards, for instance) made necessary by the collection, nor the indirect administrative and building occupancy costs connected with maintaining a museum-quality environment for the collection. Lord's pioneering study of the total costs of collection care in one hundred British museums, *The Cost of Collecting* (1989), indicated that when salaries and benefits were included in the allocation to collection-related functions, fully 38 percent of the museum's budgets were both directly and indirectly linked to collections care, and that when allowance was made for the indirect costs of administration and building operation that were due to the museum's retention of collections, the total climbed to about 66.5 percent, which, with the median cost of acquisitions added, rose still further to approximately 69 percent of all museum expenditure. No wonder museum budgets have been squeezed as core government funding has declined well below the historic levels in the 60–80 percent range.

Despite the fact that the 2022 ICOM definition of a museum includes collecting and conserving (among other functions), many of the new museums being planned in the global south have very few collections to start with—or none at all. This is because some of these new museums are driven by other needs such as national building, education, tourism, and urban development.

The classic "kunsthalles," which are temporary exhibition venues, also lack permanent collections. In both cases, curatorial and conservation costs are likely to be very low, while other line items such as exhibitions and public programming may be larger in relative terms than for collecting institutions.

Exhibitions and Other Public Programming Costs

Museums serving the public with a lively and well-researched program of exhibitions, education, and other activities should aim to reserve between 10 and 20 percent of their running costs for the nonsalary costs of such activities. When the proportion is lower than this, the museum is usually failing to serve its visitors. Because some of these public activities may be revenue generating, it is likely to be in the museum's immediate financial interests, as well as serving its broader concerns with fulfilling its mission, to allocate adequate resources to these ends. The percentage allocated will depend on the frequency and scale of exhibitions and programs (blockbuster exhibitions are more costly to produce or borrow than regular exhibitions) and the degree to which the museum wishes to provide a changing schedule of activities to reach a broad diversity of audiences or maximize repeat visitation.

From time to time some museum directors undertake to reduce their institutions' commitments to exhibitions, especially to large and expensive blockbusters, in favor of redirecting their discretionary budgets to collections research, presentation, and care. Such a reallocation is often counseled by curators and conservators, who find their priorities continually warped by the demands of the exhibition schedule. Predictions of "the end of the age of blockbusters" have thus far proved to be premature. Incremental changes in the display or interpretation of the permanent collection are seldom sufficient to elicit the broad community interest that an important exhibition can; one viable strategy that Tate Britain pioneered is to transform an annual rehang of the permanent collection into a major exhibition in itself, with an opening and focused marketing. A judicious mix of temporary exhibitions and permanent collection research and care remains the best formula, however difficult it may be to sustain the correct balance between them.

Public programming expenses also include the cost of museum learning programs, often the Cinderella of the budget cycle, used to justify grant applications but often neglected with lower salaries and nonsalary allocations than are really needed to provide a quality service. Special events budgets are another important component, often requiring expenditure but resulting in a substantial proportion of the museum's attendance on a relatively few days or through a holiday season.

Marketing Expenses

Failing to provide adequate funds for marketing is the most common lapse encountered in museum budgets. Many museums spend far less per visitor than a comparable commercial attraction would, with predictable results.

The target for a sound museum marketing budget should be at least 5 percent of the institution's total operating costs. The budget can get closer to 10 percent in the case of a new museum that needs to create basic awareness of its existence. The cost of marketing for the new museum's opening, which is a significant predictor of success, needs to be included in the capital campaign budget.

Administrative Costs

These are the routine operating costs of communications, bookkeeping, auditing, and other professional fees; office supplies; and other expenses, for which 5 percent or more of the budget should be reserved.

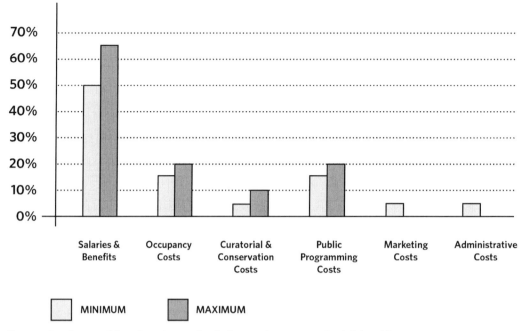

70% ....
60% ....
50% ....
40% ....
30% ....
20% ....
10% ....
0%

Salaries &	Occupancy	Curatorial &	Public	Marketing	Administrative
Benefits	Costs	Conservation	Programming	Costs	Costs
		Costs	Costs		

☐ MINIMUM   ▨ MAXIMUM

Figure 7.2.   Range of Cost Distribution for Collecting Institutions. *Lord Cultural Resources.*

Insurance costs are included under administrative costs. In most museums the registrar is responsible for maintaining insurance on the permanent collection and on incoming and outgoing loans, while the chief of security and the operations officer and building engineer are concerned with insuring the building and equipment, and the finance officer takes care of liability coverage. Museums generally require insurance of five kinds: insurance on the collection, insurance on buildings, insurance on equipment, liability insurance, and insurance on loans.

Controlling Expenditure

Given the challenge of combining the many sources of revenue listed previously—or the equally demanding challenge of living within the constraints of a government line department budget— museum managers need to keep close control of their expenditure.

In addition to administering the annual budget, as outlined further shortly, the museum's director and the finance officer may facilitate such control by establishing *financial responsibility levels* for each position in the organization. Each financially responsible museum officer should have an authorization level, below which each is authorized to commit the museum's resources. Departmental commitments above that amount must be referred to the next higher responsibility level or beyond. Within his or her responsibility level, each officer should be empowered to make requisitions, which should be directed through the finance office. Actual *purchase orders* should be issued only by the finance office and should be countersigned by both the relevant department head and the finance officer.

Museum *contracts* with suppliers of all kinds—from exhibit fabrication to cleaning or food service—should be administered according to a tendering or bidding policy that meets the standards of the governing body and those of granting authorities from which the museum has received, or hopes to receive, funding. Given these constraints, museum management should, if possible, avoid commitments to automatic selection of the lowest bidder. Very often—in security services or exhibit design, for example—it is crucial that the museum be free to select higher bidders in order to ensure that museum standards are maintained.

Monitoring departmental expenses against the budget throughout the year is now usually carried out by referring to a dashboard that shows *variances* from projected expenditures to date. Variance statements should be reviewed with departmental officers monthly, with reports to the chief executive officer on any that exceed a preset level of tolerance—say, 10–15 percent. Very often, such variances may be due to unforeseen opportunities, so they need not necessarily be viewed with alarm; however, a plan for congruence with budget projections should always be in the hands of the director and the finance officer. These often involve balancing underexpenditure in one department, or one section of one department, against overexpenditure in another; again, such changes may represent an entirely positive adjustment of plans as they are recorded and agreed upon by all concerned and fed into the budget cycle.

Museums in most countries are exempt from many taxes, usually because they are either government agencies or charitable organizations. Many are able to reclaim value-added taxes or sales taxes. In the United States, museums are now taxed on unrelated business income arising from revenue-producing activities that are not directly the result of their core operations as nonprofit or charitable organizations. For example, museum shop proceeds from the sales of items not directly related to the museum collections may be subject to tax. As a result, it is common to find two separate legal entities under a museum's governance structure: a limited liability company to deal with commercial activities, and a nonprofit organization for the mission-driven ones.

Financial Planning and Budgets

Financial planning refers to the exercise by which future revenue and expense targets are projected and linked to strategic priorities and staffing requirements. Financial planning can take the form of an annual cycle—drafting and monitoring the museum budget within a fiscal year—or a business plan that looks at a multiannual horizon (generally three to five years into the future) and that will materialize in subsequent annual budgets.

A budget is a plan with money attached. An annual budget attaches monetary values to the year's goals, which are the quantified short-term applications to the budget year of the museum's longer-range qualitative objectives. There should be a discernible continuity from the goals and objectives of the museum's long-range strategic plan through the objectives of this year's action plan to the amounts allocated in this year's budget. In recommending the budget to the museum's governing body, the director should be able to demonstrate this continuity.

Specifically the director should point to *variances*, the fluctuations in allocations due to the influence of the museum's current action plan goals. Some governments require *zero-base budgeting*, which requires museum managers within their line departments to justify each allocation in relation to the programs it makes possible, as if it had no history. In most museums, however, many allocations are assumed to continue because those functions must be sustained, and it is only the variances—the increases or reductions in these amounts—that are of interest.

In practice, budgeting is usually done departmentally, but budgets may also be organized by program, objective, or function:

- The *departmental* approach is the most common: each department is asked to review its past year's allocations, adjust for current objectives and tasks, and recommend next year's figures.

- Alternatively or additionally, budgeting can be by *program*: each department identifies the programs or services it is providing and allocates funds to each in accordance with the priority or emphasis given to that activity in the current year's plans.

- Budgeting by *objective* can be a useful review process, in which fluctuations in the current year's proposed allocations are evaluated in relation to the objectives identified in the museum's strategic plan and the outcomes they are intended to achieve.

- *Goals* of the current action plan should be reflected in the fluctuations of allocations; checking budget changes against agreed goals or longer-range objectives should be a part of every budgeting process.

- It is also useful to review allocations in terms of the fundamental museum *functions*. How much of the museum's financial resources are dedicated to collecting? How much to documentation, preservation, research, display, or interpretation? How much is going to administration? The answers can be revealing and can point to a need for changes in the balance of allocations, in view of the museum's mission and strategic plan.

Museums may budget for various funds and purposes:

- Operating budget: the annual revenue and expenditure for the museum's collection care, public activities program, and operation of its site and building

- Acquisition funds: the amount retained for purchasing objects for the collection or for the expenses associated with acquisitions

- Endowment funds: usually donated moneys that are invested, with all or only a portion of the interest earned being spent, either on operations (in the case of "unrestricted funds") or for specific purposes such as acquisitions, exhibitions, or a lecture series ("restricted funds")

- Capital budget: an amount retained for planned development of the museum's site or buildings, such as renovation, relocation, new construction, or exhibition renewal

- Grant projects: government or foundation grants often require separate accounting of the projects their contribution is meant to support

- Reserves: amounts retained for contingencies or for future development projects

The operating budget should be the end result of an annual budgeting process. This should be a constant cycle, with the progression to next year's budget beginning immediately after this year's has been approved. Figure 7.3 suggests a year-round approach to budget generation by quarter.

Monitoring the current year's actual revenues and expenditures in relation to budget allocations is important both as a means of control within the present year and as a vital part of the preparation of the coming year's budget. Figures should be refined in accuracy as the budget

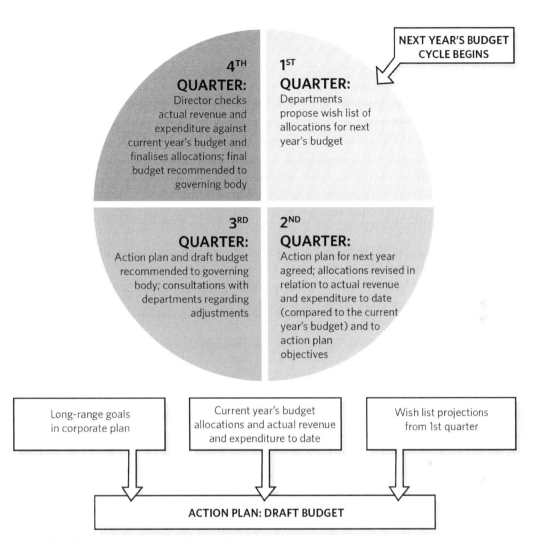

Figure 7.3.   The Budget Cycle. *Lord Cultural Resources.*

cycle proceeds and as one cycle succeeds another, reflecting the museum's experience of the current year's figures and any deficits or overages to be carried forward. As soon as the budget is approved, of course, it becomes the subject of that ongoing monitoring, as the next budget preparation cycle begins.

Long-Term Financial Sustainability

Despite their widespread success and growing public, and notwithstanding the list of revenue sources described earlier, museums almost everywhere are struggling to cope with government cutbacks on cultural funding and demands that they should be more self-reliant and less dependent on subsidy.

Although relatively few museums have closed for financial reasons, many are obliged to postpone important tasks, and some are closed to the public for several hours or days each week.

The financial constraints on museums in the long term can only be increased by the fact that one of their primary activities—collecting—results in constantly growing demands on space and facilities. Hence even financially healthy museums are constantly faced with capital fund requirements for expansion, renovation, or relocation.

> Another dimension of museums' financial crisis is rooted in their very success with the public.

Another dimension of museums' financial crisis is rooted in their very success with the public. Visitors, better informed than ever by travel and media, are constantly raising their expectations of exhibitions, technology, and even museum shops. In an effort to meet rising expectations, museums constantly need fresh development capital and the requisite additional operating funds.

Trustees and museum directors, therefore, have the responsibility to rise above the constant scramble to meet current operating, capital, and acquisition costs in order to plan the long-term financial future of their institutions. This may be addressed as part of the strategic planning process or when the corporate plan is being reviewed. The principles of such a long-term financial plan may be suggested here as a useful conclusion to this consideration of the financial management of museums:

- The museum's long-term financial plan should aim to secure financial *stability* for the institution. Whenever possible, government, corporate, or university funding should be put on an assured rather than a contingent basis, as a regular allocation rather than being dependent on grants. This may require strenuous representation to government or other funding sources.

- Where appropriate, a government-operated museum should become, and should endeavor to remain, part of the institutional framework of *education*, another area that is subject to government cutbacks, but one that, in the long term, will experience continuity of funding.

- Trustees and senior museum staff should promote the museum as a vital part of the *cultural tourism* industry and lobby to make tourism a renewable resource through taxes on tourism operators or an equivalent arrangement that channels part of the revenue from tourism back to institutions like museums that are its fundamental resource.

- Recent research has demonstrated that museums are key to public health and social cohesion. This has resulted in such programs as doctors providing prescriptions for museum visits, with the cost paid by the health service. Museums should consider advocating for funding support from public health bodies.

- An *endowment fund*, or some equivalent form of return on investments, should be established. Donors should be persuaded to address the long-term interests of the institution so that contributions and especially bequests may be made to such a fund. Providing for a growing proportion of the museum's needs with the interest earned by such a fund is one way to secure greater financial independence.

- A *visitor engagement program* should extend the museum's appeal to those sectors of the community that are currently underrepresented among museum visitors. Government or other support should be sought to institute such a program and should then lead the museum to a still more widespread base in the community, which in turn can serve as the foundation of further funding. In the long term, this financial sustainability of museums is inextricably linked to providing broad-based meaningful service to the community.

- Because the museum is a knowledge-based institution in the "knowledge economy" of an "information age," the plan should give careful consideration to the museum's ability to gain funding through intellectual property initiatives and digital programs while making its collections broadly available to the public, as new media for education and entertainment continue to be developed. Beyond a digital assets strategy, this points to careful consideration of the best use of the *brand* that the museum has established over the years.

- Whenever the governing body determines that a new or larger building, renovation, or expansion may be needed, or may even be considered essential to the museum's financial future, it is imperative that careful financial planning of the implications of the relocated or expanded facilities should be undertaken in a feasibility study or business plan, in addition to whatever facility planning, architecture, or design is to be done. Capital cost projections should always be accompanied by operating cost and revenue implications in a carefully considered business plan for any changes to the museum's physical plant. All too often the relative ease of raising capital funds prevents decision makers from considering alternatives such as long-term loans of collection to museums lacking collections and other partnerships.

- Museums should consider expanding their financial focus beyond the traditional government and corporate sectors. The pluralist model of society identifies that balance of public sector, private sector, and the not-for-profit/civil society sectors are essential for a healthy society. Could greater inclusion of this plural sector lead to a more balanced financial model as well as increased diversity in collections, content, and audiences?

Museum finances are a complex amalgam of external and internal forces, including macroeconomic trends, major shifts in social values, and changing values of museum staff and communities. Financial management is a central concern of museum management, staff, and the board—as much philosophy and values as it is "number crunching."

How Museums Can Matter More

By Sandra Jackson-Dumont

> The museum of the twenty-first century is one that sits in the world, is of the world, and is engaged in the world—not one that sits as a box to collect the world.

The museum of the twenty-first century is one that sits in the world, is of the world, and is engaged in the world—not one that sits as a box to collect the world. While museums will always be places to see art and artifacts, the challenge is to make them places where we experience the act of *seeing* differently.

How can we ensure that the museum as a platform or concept platform can help us understand issues and ideas from different vantage points? This exchange of perspectives was once the intellectual "social work" of museum educators, public programmers, and community engagement specialists. Once considered child's play, this concern for public engagement and meaning making is now at the center of museum discourse. To the extent that this change makes museums more inclusive and equitable, we're long overdue.

Beginning in 2020, the world experienced a pandemic and what has been referred to as a racial reckoning. The convergence of those two acts created a mirror for museums and their workers to reflect on their relevance, their purpose, and their practice. This was not only a reality check, it was a mortality check: What do I need to change? Who do I need to make amends with? What is missing? How can I make things better? And most importantly, what is my purpose?

These conditions immediately put museums in the world and of the world. To participate in the moment at hand, museums had to muscle up on their skills and competences.

There's now a generation of directors, curators, and educators who are systematically shifting museums toward urgent relevancy. We need to figure out how museums remain active in the social-emotional psychology of the public. Museums became more relevant to me when they became a part of my daily discourse. When you find yourself not going to a museum merely for an opening event, or for a tourist moment, but going because that's where the *actual conversation is happening*—that means something.

Museums matter more, and become better, *when they put people at the heart of their mission.* I mean *all* people to be considered in the ecosystem of participants. We need critical, inclusive leadership that expects museums to be at the nexus of the experiential, the intellectual, the social, and the diverse.

Of course, museums need to hire people who come to the institution with specializations in any given area of work. Those specialists should be experts that also center on diversity, equity, inclusion, and accessibility in their practices. Institutions must do more than offer workshops about diversity. They need to implement the learning into policy *and* practice and address a sense of belonging. Leaders must define elevated expectations and behaviors, to clarify the thoughts and practices that need to abound in an institution. At the Lucas Museum of Narrative Art, our core strategy is framed through the lenses of diversity, equity, inclusion, accessibility, and the sense of belonging.

One might ask, "What about the objects?" Of course. But that ought to go without saying, especially because museums clearly state, "We collect, conserve, study, and exhibit," et cetera. But that's not a mission. It's a list of extremely critical tasks. The question is not, "Is the object important?" but instead, "What is the *purpose* of collecting, conserving, studying, and exhibiting?" For whom are we doing these things? The answer is, "For the people."

I'm going to offer you two quotations from James Baldwin:

> The world changes according to the way people see it, and if you alter, even by a millimeter, the way a person looks at reality, then you can change it.

Baldwin wrote that quote about literature, but we can apply it to many other things as well: visual art, music, education, and certainly museums. If you work in an art museum, these are words to live by. The inequities, the financial pressures, and the sheer maddening inertia that can sometimes abound in museums can lead you into cynicism.

But if cultural workers truly believe that the art museum container and the presence of *art can alter the way people look at reality*, then there is promise in what Baldwin points out so aptly—when perception changes, then there's a chance for reality to change.

I call this the moonshot of the Lucas Museum: the art of storytelling can connect us to shape a more just society. So for us the idea is that museums and art must matter because the stake are so high. This is intentional and highly considered work.

> The art of storytelling can connect us to shape a more just society.

This second quotation from James Baldwin offers the beginning of an explanation for how art can lead to change:

> I can't be a pessimist because I'm alive. To be a pessimist means that you have agreed that human life is an academic matter.

So there it is. I am alive. You are alive. And our lives, in this world we share, are urgently *real*. We must not be persuaded that our lives and our art, at best, are objects of academic interest. I am going to propose that transformation can happen, and does happen, when museums begin their work from the optimistic viewpoint of *caring about how we live*.

In practical terms, what could that mean? To start with, it might mean going beyond worrying about how museums can make their collections, exhibitions, or programs relevant. Instead, flip that question, and we might start by asking ourselves, "What makes a *life* relevant?"

That's a question all museums face, whether they know it or not. It is, at minimum, an implied question—because if you want your museum to live up to its best possibilities, it needs to contribute to supporting healthy communities.

You see what happens when you start by asking, "What makes a life relevant?" You wind up calling into question so many structures and power dynamics, including the assumption that one's thinking and work ought to proceed from a *deficiency-based* model—a model in which you step forward to provide people with things *you* think they lack. But what if you don't make that assumption? Imagine behaving as if everyone's life is urgently real, and therefore begin from an *asset-based* model—a model in which you recognize that the people you want to talk with, whoever they are, bring their own assets to the table: their life experience, language, their resources and frame of reference, their sense of humor and critical intelligence.

To be clear: I'm not proposing, as some people do, that all the public really wants is to be made to feel welcome. I am not proposing that the main thing we should do is ask communities what they want and then try to give it to them. Because that might *sound* generous and open-minded, but not so secretly it's just another deficiency-based approach, where we assume we're here to supply cultural riches to people who are lacking. People have culture. Period, end of sentence.

What is the rigor in that assumption? If we think we're giving people something, don't we want to give them our *best*? We want to consider varied viewpoints, make it deep and considered, tether it to people, places, and objects that can sustain long-term thought and lasting, powerful emotion and action. It's too easy to say, "Let's ask people what they want, and make them feel welcome, and that will be the end of our job."

When it comes to museums, I think we need to do something harder but much more rewarding. We need to show people why we believe these artworks are urgent and real—as James Baldwin said, not simply an academic matter. And having done that, we need to risk engaging with people's responses. Not just accepting whatever those responses might be, as if it's all the same, but *listening*, and then working to bring the conversation to the next level, and the next. As I stated at the beginning of this case study, in order to stay relevant, the museum of the twenty-first century must be engaged in the world and deeply engaged with people—not just one that sits as a box to collect the world. Years ago, I saw a sign that said, "Speak the truth and point to hope." I'm extremely hopeful about the future because I think that people are being more honest and brave.

Figure 7.4.   Lucas Museum park rendering. *Image courtesy of the Lucas Museum of Narrative Art.*

AFTERWORD

Museums are in dynamic change.

The new internationally adopted museum definition spells change—a proactive, community-based approach that fosters accessibility, diversity, and sustainability.

People are engaging with museum content as never before. Rapid advances in technology further intensify the dynamic of change because the museum experience is everywhere, all the time and all at once.

It's also a time of deep reflection on how two hundred years of hierarchy, compartmentalization, exclusion, and secrecy can be transformed into more caring organizations that engage with many perspectives in a spirit of openness.

The movement to repatriate artifacts, works of art, and specimens that were looted, purchased under duress, or stolen through colonialism and war has intensified, with positive learning potential for everyone.

Museum staff are becoming partners with management in formulating the values that inspire how people work together to create and communicate meaning from the evidence and stories that museums preserve, research, and display.

New governance models are emerging. It is no longer a matter of government versus independent not-for-profit museums—governance is more frequently a hybrid of the two models, creating a new dynamic between public and private accountabilities.

Hybridity is also part of dynamic change with staff working from home as well as from their offices, the museum floor, and with communities.

As those readers engaged in and with museums know—this dynamic change sometimes feels like it has arrived at a breaking point.

Climate change challenges the very survival of institutions that have depended on the "wow effect" of edifices that are expensive to build and even more costly to sustain. What are the new methods of museology that will be environmentally friendly? And where will this innovation come from? What will the global north learn from the global south where museum growth is most needed and most likely?

Collection expansion is a source of both dynamism and disaster. Collections—whether tangible or intangible—will grow because human understanding grows and because so much human experience and research has been previously excluded due to prejudice and ethnocentrism.

How will the global museum profession balance growth with the reality that most museums display and use less than 10 percent of their holdings? Why not open their bursting storerooms to make artifacts, specimens, and works of art available on long-term loan or gift to the thousands of museums that want them? The vast majority of museums and communities in the global south possess solely local collections because they lack the wealth and power to make international acquisitions, not because they lack the interest.

Museums are one of the most successful social means of communication because they are among the public's most trusted institutions. Through the generations, they have transformed from private treasure chambers, to the scholar's study, to public institutions of self-directed learning and discovery.

Dynamic change creates the conditions for new solutions to old problems and new ideas for the future.

For what is the
museum if not people?

Hopefully, this *Manual* will help current and future generations of museum management to do both. For what is the museum if not people?

—Gail Dexter Lord, 2024

ACKNOWLEDGMENTS

Preparing this third edition of *The Manual of Museum Management* has been a journey through museology shared with my late husband Barry Lord with whom I coauthored the first two editions and who is on every page of this edition.

Our text had its origins in our certificate course on museum organization and management many years ago for the Ontario Museums Association. The course and its text traveled with us through seminars, courses, and presentations to museum professionals—including museum training programs organized by universities and museum associations in Canada, England, Austria, Spain, Serbia, Turkey, Hong Kong, Singapore, Korea, China, and Russia.

Thank you to the many students and colleagues whose questions, challenges, and insights over the years stimulated the development of the course and eventually the content of this third edition of the *Manual*.

Originally launched by the Stationery Office in London, *The Manual of Museum Management* was first published as a book in the United States and this new edition with Rowman & Littlefield Publishers is being released as part of a series of Lord Books on museum ideas and practice.

This third edition also reflects our continuing international experience in the development and management of museums large and small in our role as consultants to museum professionals and trustees in sixty countries around the world. Grateful acknowledgment is therefore due to the many clients and colleagues for their creativity, resourcefulness, and professionalism, which it is hoped this volume sufficiently reflects.

Special thanks are due to the thirty authors of the case studies, which are new to this edition and bring the book to life. Each contributor is an inspiring museum leader whose work gave me the courage to address museum management in this time of dynamic change for the sector. Thanks are also due to the photographers for the illustrations in the case studies. Thank you to the museums who gave us permission to share their foundation statements.

I am grateful to my colleagues and thought leaders at Lord Cultural Resources. Some have contributed case studies or chapters; all have expanded my thinking through our creative, collaborative daily work—especially through the traumatic COVID-19 years we all shared.

And my thanks to the friends and colleagues whose thankless tasks included reviewing, debating and sympathizing: our daughter Beth Lord; dear friends Marta Braun, Daniel Drache, T. M. Glass, Michael Hirsh, and Natalie Davis; and museum colleagues Ali Hossaini, Tim Johnson, Joy Bailey-Bryant, Kathleen Brown, Dov Goldstein, Hamida Ghafour, and Matthew Rowe.

The commitment of "the book team" provided astonishing energy for this project.

Mira Ovanin, who is not only an executive assistant but also an executive intelligence, coordinated the many parts of the *Manual* including the case studies, permissions, further reading section, and illustrations as well as my writing and consulting schedules. I am indebted to her keen eye and extensive reading that finds just the right reference for an idea and corrects me when needed. Thanks to Isabella Rivera for her research support and organization of the glossary, foundation statements, and further reading section.

Gratitude and admiration for our designer Michelle Selmen who lifts all our spirits with the inspired cover and page design while preparing the manuscript for the publisher.

Charles Harmon, senior executive editor of Rowman & Littlefield, is both a friend and publisher. His confidence in me and Barry and Lord Books is valued by us all.

Special appreciation is due to Naomi Minkoff, production editor at Rowman & Littlefied, for her diligence and care during the editorial process. Thanks to Charles and his entire team at Roman & Littlefield for making this *Manual* a reality.

Finally, a very special thank you to Joshua Knelman, who joined the book team late as our much-needed editor. He established order in chaos, came up with the storyline, and insisted that less is always more, where readability is concerned.

Thank you to our readers including present and future museum managers—for what is a manual but the practitioners? And what is a museum but the people?

—Gail Dexter Lord, 2024

APPENDICES

APPENDIX A
Museum Foundation Statements

Chapter 2 explains why foundation statements are key for the effective management of museums and how they are developed. This selection of recent foundation statements is organized under the following headings: Mission Statements, Vision Statements, Mandate Statements, and Values. Thank you to the museums that granted permission to reprint their statements in this *Manual*.

Mission Statements

Museum of Fine Arts of Montreal—Montreal, Quebec (May 2023)

The Montreal Museum of Fine Arts was founded on and has continued to develop thanks to the generosity of multiple generations of Montrealers. Its mission is to acquire, conserve, study, interpret, and present significant works of art from around the world and from every era, in the hope that members of its community and all Museum visitors may benefit from the transformative powers of art.

Ciência Viva—Lisbon, Portugal, 2021

Active citizenship based on scientific knowledge.

Longwood Garden—Kennett Square, Pennsylvania (2019)

Longwood Gardens is the living legacy of Pierre S. du Pont, bringing joy and inspiration to everyone through the beauty of nature, conservation, and learning.

Oakland Museum of California—Oakland, California (2013)

OMCA inspires Californians to create a more vibrant future for themselves and their communities.

V&A—London, United Kingdom (2021)

Our mission is to be recognized as the world's leading museum of art, design, and performance, and to enrich people's lives by promoting research, knowledge, and enjoyment of the designed world to the widest possible audience.

Rijksmuseum—Amsterdam, Netherlands (2013)

At the Rijksmuseum, art and history take on new meaning for a broad-based, contemporary national and international audience.

As a national institute, the Rijksmuseum offers a representative overview of Dutch art and history from the Middle Ages onwards, and of major aspects of European and Asian art.

The Rijksmuseum keeps, manages, conserves, restores, researches, prepares, collects, publishes, and presents artistic and historical objects, both on its own premises and elsewhere.

Museum of Islamic Art, Qatar—Doha, Qatar (2008)

MIA sheds light on our origins to illuminate our future. Through safeguarding masterpiece collections of Islamic art and showcasing extraordinary exhibitions, MIA shares knowledge while spreading curiosity, understanding, and joy.

Tenement Museum—New York, New York (2018)

We aim to build an inclusive and expansive American identity and believe that the exploration of our complex history—one with moments of both inclusion and exclusion—helps prepare us to recognize and discuss today's complex issues with empathy and nuance.

National Museum of African American Music—Nashville, Tennessee (2016/2017)

Mission statement: to educate the world, preserve the legacy, and celebrate the central role African Americans play in creating the American soundtrack.

Smithsonian—Washington, DC (2023)

The increase and diffusion of knowledge.

Woodland Cultural Centre—Brantford, Ontario (2023)

Our mission is to protect, promote, interpret, and present the Hodinohsho:ni worldview.

Oneida Nation Museum—Da Pere, Wisconsin (2017)

The mission of the Oneida Nation Museum is to provide accurate information about the Oneida and Iroquois culture, history, and nationhood. This is accomplished by developing, preserving, and expanding resources and collections, and by providing exhibits and other educational programming. The Museum also displays and promotes Iroquois artwork. The Oneida Nation Museum shall provide a unique and enlightening experience that can be interpreted to all ages for the next seven generations.

Vision Statements

Museum of Fine Arts of Montreal—Montreal, Quebec (May 2023)

The Montreal Museum of Fine Arts aspires to become a leading hub of art, community, and conversation; a place where all feel welcome, and where new ways of thinking about art and art history inspire diverse audiences to come together and imagine a more inclusive, accessible, and just world.

Ciência Viva—Lisbon, Portugal, 2021

We inspire and mobilize through science. This is our identity.

And we can't do it alone: we count on schools, universities and research units, museums and science centers, municipalities, associations, and other bodies working in this area.

New Britannia Mine Museum—British Columbia, Canada (2023)

Britannia Mine Museum delivers an entertaining world class experience that encourages an informed understanding of mining and its impact on the environment, communities, and sustainability.

Woodland Cultural Centre—Brantford, Ontario (2023)

As a center of excellence, Woodland Cultural Centre envisions a future where Hodinohsho:ni people will speak their language, know and practice their culture, and share their history.

Smithsonian—Washington, DC (2023)

Through our unparalleled collections and research capabilities, and the insight and creativity we foster through art, history, and culture, the Smithsonian strives to provide Americans and the world with the tools and information they need to forge our shared future.

Oneida Nation Museum—Da Pere, Wisconsin (2017)

A Nation of strong families built on Tsiʔniyukwalihó·tʌ and a strong economy.

Mandate Statements

New-York Historical Society—New York, New York (2021/2022)

Experience 400 years of history through groundbreaking exhibitions, outstanding collections, immersive films, and thought-provoking conversations among renowned historians and public figures at the New-York Historical Society, New York's first museum. A great destination for history since 1804, the Museum and the Patricia D. Klingenstein Library convey the stories of the city and nation's diverse populations, expanding our understanding of who we are as Americans and how we came to be.

Museum of Fine Arts, Houston—Houston, Texas (2016)

Houston has been hailed as America's most diverse city, a reflection of how the nation will look in just a few decades. By its nature, the Museum of Fine Arts, Houston, along with the Glassell School of Art and the two house museums—Bayou Bend Collection and Gardens, and Rienzi— embodies the character of this city through the Museum's staff, visitors, mission, programs, and collections.

National Museum of African American Music—Nashville, Tennessee (2016/2017)

The National Museum of African American Music is the premier global destination for music lovers of all generations that inspires, educates, and transforms your appreciation of American music.

Woodland Cultural Centre—Brantford, Ontario (2023)

We will achieve our mission and vision by:

Facilitating Indigenous and non-Indigenous understanding by providing education opportunities, producing innovative exhibitions, promoting local artists, and creating language resources;

Inspiring and engaging communities through the accessibility of the collection for present and future generations;

Fostering relationships with community-based organizations, academia, and cultural institutions to produce multi-disciplinary programming, strengthen oral traditions and language retention, and renewal of contemporary and traditional artistic practices;

Ensuring accurate documentation, education, and promotion of the values, practices, language, national treasures, and articles of Indigenous peoples; and

Honoring Residential School survivors by ensuring Indigenous voices and perspectives are leading and defining reconciliation efforts.

Values Statements

MacKenzie Art Gallery—Regina, Canada (2013)

As the board, staff, and volunteers of the MacKenzie, we:

Represent the MacKenzie to the best of our ability at all times.

Celebrate one another's successes, work toward shared goals, and recognize the unique value of each member of the team.

Are stewards of an enduring and ever-deepening public trust rooted in our Permanent Collection, in the legacy of our predecessors, and in the achievements of the present.

Welcome the community to the Gallery with the highest standards of hospitality and share our passion for the arts with creativity and innovation.

Work with the highest professional standards, accountable for our decisions and actions, and responding with creativity and innovation to opportunities that will benefit the Gallery.

Believe passionately that art transforms us and advances knowledge and our understanding of the world around us.

Believe that artists and their engagement with our visitors are indispensable to the success of the MacKenzie.

Research, exhibit, and celebrate the past, present, and future of the Indigenous peoples in collaboration with contemporary Indigenous creators, knowledge keepers, and publics.

Are proud to take the work of Saskatchewan artists to the national and international stage and to bring the art of Canada and the world to Saskatchewan.

Ciência Viva—Lisbon, Portugal, 2021

We believe in social progress based on curiosity, creativity, critical thinking, and the involvement of everyone.

Museum of Science—Boston, Massachusetts (2020)

Our Values

Everyone: We are everyone's Museum. We pursue equity and celebrate every person for who they are. We foster an inclusive environment in which we value and respect diversity.

Service: We serve our colleagues and community. We hold ourselves accountable to be a trustworthy public resource, and to support a sustainable, just, and evidence-based future.

Learning: We love learning. We are curious about the world and want to share our joy and wonder with others. We value open minds and recognize that everyone has more to explore, discover, and create.

Connection: We find strength in connections. We collaborate across communities, organizations, and disciplines to make science relevant and accessible to all.

Boldness: We dream big. We boldly push ourselves forward, pursuing new ideas and challenges. We experiment and learn from our failures as we seek to inspire purpose, spark imagination, and encourage hope.

Minnesota Museum of American Art—Saint Paul, Minnesota (2015)

Values

Bold: We dare to respond to complex truths and envision a hopeful future.

Engaging: We build participation through fun and stimulating artistic experiences.

Relevant: We question, listen, and exchange ideas with our diverse communities.

Inclusive: We strive to make the Museum welcoming and accessible to all.

Respectful: We seek authentic relationships and act thoughtfully and transparently with resources in our care.

Portland Art Museum—Portland, Oregon (2015)

The Portland Art Museum strives to be an inclusive institution that facilitates respectful dialogue, debate, and the free exchange of ideas. With a deep commitment to artists—past and present—and freedom of expression, the Museum and PAM CUT's collections, programs, and staff aspire to reveal the beauty and complexities of the world, and create a deeper understanding of our shared humanity. We are a Museum for all, inviting everyone to connect with art through their own experiences, voices, and personal journeys. The following core values guide the Portland Art Museum:

Creativity

The arts are at the core of our humanity, representing a timeless human impulse.

Connection

The arts touch us and connect us across time, geography, and cultural differences, shedding light on how humans interact with their world.

Equity

To fulfill our mission, our commitment to equity means including, serving, resourcing, validating, and centering our colleagues and community members of color on an institutional and individual level.

Learning

The arts open us to diverse ideas and ways of knowing ourselves, our community, and our world.

Accessibility

The arts must be economically, intellectually, and physically accessible to everyone.

Accountability

Transparency and careful stewardship of resources—including collections, staff, facilities, and investments—are essential for mission fulfillment now and in the future.

Connecticut River Museum—Essex, Connecticut (2022)

Our Values

Embracing Stewardship

Dedicated to Excellence

- We follow professional standards of quality and excellence in all our programs, our collections, and exhibitions.

- We explore topics and stories in an inclusive, diverse, and equitable manner, mindful of their relevance for contemporary issues and with a view to engage with new audiences.

- We collaborate with other organizations, groups, and communities that share our values in order to broaden the experience of our audiences.

- We encourage academic institutions, such as universities and research centers, to use our archives and collections for academic study and research.

- We strive to maintain our accreditation by the American Alliance of Museums.

Embracing Openness and Innovation

- Our Museum acts as a community, a "learning campus," where we engage with our audiences in new and creative ways to create long-lasting relationships.

- We experiment with content designed to build bridges from the past to the present and into the future, ready to provoke, challenge, educate, and inspire, while demonstrating creativity, ingenuity, and innovation.

- New technologies and platforms are an integral part of our strategies. These tools serve to enhance visitor experience and to extend our reach, bringing our stories to diverse audiences without geographical or physical limitations, or time constraints.

Dedicated to Diversity, Equity, Accessibility, and Inclusion

- We endorse staff, board, and volunteer recruitment policies that reflect the diversity of the communities we serve.

- We foster cultural competence among staff and board.

- We address financial barriers to facilitate access to our Museum for all.

- We reach out to diverse communities and encourage access to the Museum for people of all backgrounds.

- We facilitate access for people with disabilities.

- Our collections and exhibitions, and our children and adult educational programs reflect a comprehensive understanding of history, adequately reflecting minorities and underrepresented groups in society.

Dedicated to Sustainable Development

- As a Museum on the Connecticut River, we are an integral part of its environment and embrace our responsibility as stewards of our property, including the riverfront.

- We contribute to sustainable development on all levels, including through our educational programs and exhibitions.

- We protect our historic buildings and collections from the effects of climate change, especially flooding, and storm damage.

- We join efforts to help fight invasive species and pollution in the River, and support other initiatives designed to preserve and protect the River and its environs for future generations.

- We strive to minimize the negative environmental impact of our Museum. This includes the choice of goods for our gift shop, food and beverages for visitors, and the use of technologies we operate on our premises.

Committed to Personal Values

- As trustees, staff, and volunteers we are united in our commitment to further the mission of our Museum.

- We fulfill our respective tasks with integrity, honesty, enthusiasm, and respect for one another.

Being a Good Neighbor

- We act as a community center.

- We seek cooperation with local partners, institutions, and businesses on all levels.

- We highlight local products and artifacts in our gift shop.

Woodland Cultural Centre—Brantford, Ontario (2023)

The core values that guide WCC in its work are the cornerstone principles of the Great Law of Peace, an integral resource in Hodinohsho:ni philosophy, ways of knowing and conduct:

Skén:nen—peace (resolution, love, gratitude)

The WCC recognizes that language is an important part of every stage of our lives, from the celebration of our birth to the Funeral Rites when we've gone home, but also the moments in between.

The WCC builds an environment of kindness, as a safe space where we as First Nations people draw strength from our identity, spirituality, cultural practices, and our communities.

The WCC agrees to approach issues with a good mind, fostering an atmosphere of open communication and understanding.

WCC promotes cultural humility by demonstrating respect and support for the cultural diversity of our member communities, Indigenous peoples, and others. We will deliberate and plan by taking into account everyone's situation and being sensitive to how different communities work.

Three indigenous women traditionally dressed standing in the grass

Ka'nikonhrí:yo—good mind (commitment, respect, responsibility)

The WCC practices high standards of excellence and stewardship, promoting extensive research of cultural, historical, and theoretical discourse that contributes to Indigenous Art History.

The WCC has a responsibility to protect and promote the tangible, intangible, natural, and cultural heritage, incorporating Indigenous knowledge and holistic approaches.

The WCC values truth, which is demonstrated through openness, honesty, acceptance, and trust. We will work in compliance with rules we've set for ourselves, and uphold our commitments to each other, ensuring accountability to each other and the communities we serve.

The WCC ensures intergenerational care and respect for elders, children and earth—our past, our future, and what sustains us as a people.

Ka'satsténshsera—power/strength, to get things done (generosity, collective thinking)

The WCC uses wise practices, community input, and traditional knowledge in their endeavors.

The WCC fosters an atmosphere of open communication and understanding that encourages lifelong learning not only for both Indigenous and non-Indigenous people/patrons/learners.

The WCC encourages empowerment and interdependence by supporting, mentoring and teaching each other.

The WCC addresses issues in a timely manner, conducting ourselves with integrity and functioning as an effective and efficient business.

APPENDIX B
Collection Policy Checklist

This appendix outlines how to maintain a responsible collection policy, with an easy to use and comprehensive thirty-point checklist.

1. The museum's commitment to maintaining the collection as a *public trust*—for which it will provide conscientious care indefinitely—should be declared. The status of the collection as a public trust means that the public has entrusted it to the care of the museum's board and staff, who have the responsibility to preserve and present it for public study and enjoyment.

2. The range and limits of the collection related to the museum's mission and mandate should be defined.

3. Usually the policy establishes beginning and end dates (if it is a historical collection), the geographical range (if relevant), and the materials (for example, ceramics or glass) to be collected.

4. A qualitative statement of the objective of the collection should be stated: an art collection may be said to be restricted to *outstanding* examples, whereas a natural science collection may aspire to be *comprehensive* or *systematic*. A history museum's collection may aim at a *representative* sample of a particular period. Some historical collections are centered on exceptional items related to great events or individuals, whereas others focus on objects typical of their time and place. The collection of a museum in a heritage building may be restricted to objects that were actually used in the building, or may extend to objects of the type used there.

5. The policy may also determine whether artifacts must have been *made* in a particular district or era or merely *used* in that place or period, or both.

6. Natural history collections that aspire to be systematic must be further specified as to whether they will include merely one example of each species, whether they include definitive *type specimens*, or whether they aim at an example of each stage of development of each species.

7. The *criteria* for inclusion in the collection should be specified. These go beyond the foregoing general statements of the collection's range and quality to identify such particular requirements as

   - size,

   - demonstrated authenticity,

   - an established provenance,

   - the legal issue of clear title, and

- either display condition or a condition that the museum has the resources to restore and maintain.

8. Monetary value levels requiring different levels of approval—curatorial, acquisitions committee, or acquisitions committee recommendation to the board for approval—should be specified.

9. Criteria may also distinguish between objects for different parts of the collection. For example, original documents, tapes, and other media related to the subject matter of the museum may belong in the museum's *archives*, but material in print or other media that is collected only because it provides information about the rest of the collection will be found in the museum *library*.

10. Approved *acquisition methods* should be specified, which may include gifts, bequests, purchases, fieldwork, deposits from other museums, and acceptance of acquisitions from government programs or agencies responsible for cultural property protection.

11. The collection policy should establish the museum's position on *ownership* of the collection, including acquisition procedures for donations (gift agreements) and purchases (receipt requirements). Usually the collection policy disallows gifts "with strings attached" and requires that donations must be transferred wholly and entirely, without qualification as to the museum's use of the acquisition.

12. The museum's policy with regard to tax deductions for donations of objects to the collection should be articulated in this document. This should be written to comply with the legal requirements of the country, province, or state in which the museum is located, identifying who can determine evaluations (not the curators but an independent evaluator), and under what circumstances the museum will provide tax deductible receipts, if it is qualified to do so.

13. *Ethical* commitments of the museum and its trustees with regard to acquisitions should be included, such as the museum's commitment to international conventions, national laws, or treaties, including policy regarding objects from Indigenous cultures and policy regarding the repatriation or restitution of objects to their origins.

14. Ethical guidelines adopted by the trustees regarding potential conflicts of interest with their own or staff personal collecting activities (as discussed in chapter 2) should also be included in the collection policy.

15. There should be a statement of the purposes for which objects may be collected, leading to a classification by purpose, usually including

   - a *display collection* acquired for exhibition and interpretation purposes,

   - a *study collection* acquired for purposes of comparative or analytical research (such as archaeological shards from a museum dig or zoological specimens in spirit jars), and

   - a *reserve collection*, which may consist of objects pending assignment to either of the first two classifications, duplicate or secondary examples assigned to hands-on educational programs or objects pending deaccessioning.

16. The collection policy should indicate that the display collection and study collection are to be preserved indefinitely, whereas some of the items in the reserve collection may not be.

17. Some museums acquire a *contemporary collection* of the potential artifacts of tomorrow (while they are still inexpensive and plentiful) and hold these items in reserve for a period of years (say, twenty), after which they may be either transferred to the display or study collections, or deaccessioned.

18. The reserve collection may also be used for unwanted objects that the museum is sometimes obliged to accept, at least temporarily, as part of a donation that includes other objects needed for the display or study collections; if possible, the donor should be persuaded to give only the desired pieces, but when faced with an "all or nothing" offer, it is convenient to assign the unwanted objects to the reserve collection (as long as this is explained to the donor and recorded in the gift agreement), so that the museum need not make the commitment of long-term preservation of unsuitable material. Objects in educational hands-on collections, which may be seen as part of the reserve collection, will deteriorate from repeated handling and are thus not going to be preserved indefinitely. This is why it is useful for the collection policy to state the museum's commitment to preservation of the display and study collections, while allowing for the reserve collection to be subject sooner or later to deaccessioning.

19. The museum's policy on *deaccessioning* should be included in the collection policy as a means of collection management. Although some would resist any such inclusion, it is far better to have a sound policy in place than to pretend that the museum will never need to dispose of unwanted items.

20. Certain objects—or the entire display and study collections—may be declared exempt from deaccessioning in perpetuity, with deaccessioning restricted to items in the reserve collection alone.

21. The deaccessioning section of the collection policy should make it clear that in general the museum collects objects only for their indefinite preservation, and therefore that deaccessioning is to be regarded as an exceptional activity. Both the International Council of Museums and many countries' museum associations have published suitably cautious statements on deaccessioning, which may be quoted: "There must always be a strong presumption against the disposal of specimens to which a museum has assumed formal title," as the ICOM Code of Ethics puts it.

22. Criteria for consideration for deaccessioning should be listed, including

    • objects that do not fit the museum's mandate,

    • objects that have been found to be spurious,

    • objects acquired illegally or unethically,

    • objects due for repatriation or restitution to their origins,

    • duplicates that are inferior to more recently acquired examples, and

    • objects in a condition that is not cost-effective to restore.

23. The steps to be taken in the event of deaccessioning should be spelled out, providing rules such as the following:

- Only curators can initiate deaccessioning.

- The process must be fully documented with the reasons for deaccessioning according to this policy fully recorded.

- The museum's information about the deaccessioned object must be retained.

- Approval procedures for deaccessioning should always involve the director and may also require the attention of the trustees.

24. Acceptable options for disposition of deaccessioned items should be indicated, with alternatives listed as the following:

- A sequence of "first refusals" should be laid out aimed at keeping the object in the public domain, if possible within the country, state, province, county, or municipality.

- Destruction of objects should be done only by curators in the presence of the director and recorded.

- In the event of sale, any revenues from the disposition of deaccessioned objects must be used only for new acquisitions or collection care—never for the museum's operating costs.

25. The museum's policy on *loans* should be included in the collection policy, distinguishing between long-term loans or *deposits* of items from other museums or collections and short-term loans (both incoming and outgoing) for temporary exhibitions:

- The clause on *long-term incoming loans* is usually written to persuade prospective long-term lenders to become donors instead and may go as far as to forbid long-term loans from individuals entirely, while admitting the possibility of deposits from other collections or museums (which will be restricted by their own collection policies and therefore only able to deposit objects on long-term loan).

- For *short-term outgoing loans* it is usual to identify the approvals required (such as registrar and curator for most, but the director or even the board for some objects, with still others never to be loaned), to specify that the museum will lend objects only to institutions able to provide an equivalent level of environmental and security protection and insurance, and to require that the borrowing institution fill out a satisfactory *facility assessment* form and provide condition reports at each packing and unpacking point. The policy may also require that couriers must accompany certain loans to supervise their installation and demounting.

26. The museum's policy on *appraisals* usually protects curators from being asked for monetary evaluations, especially if tax deductions for potential donations are involved. Sometimes curators may appraise up to a certain market value, with higher values being referred elsewhere.

27. Procedures for *documentation* of the collection are usually included in collection management policies, describing the entire process from arrival of the object in the museum (possibly with a temporary receipt while it is under consideration) through the numbering system and information fields to be captured for each item, requirements for gift agreements or receipts, procedures for multiple objects within one accession, and the responsibility of the registrar to record collection movement, loans, and relocations from storage to display or back again. This may be extensive enough to justify a separate *documentation policy*.

28. A collection management policy usually also addresses *conservation*, requiring a condition report for each new acquisition and the subsequent maintenance of such reports throughout the object's life in the museum, and providing that any treatment of the object will be recorded. This section may also require that a conservator's recommendation be considered prior to acquisition to ensure that the object meets the museum's requirements that its collections be either in display condition or in a state that can be cost-effectively restored. The policy may state the museum's objectives in conservation—whether simply to retard the object's deterioration optimally or to return it to a specific prior condition, for instance. As with documentation, larger museums are likely to find it preferable to elaborate a separate but related *conservation policy*.

29. The museum's commitment to the *security* of its collections should be articulated in a collection management policy. This security section of the policy may incorporate a *risk management strategy* that identifies threats to the collection and the measures that the museum takes to meet them. For example, this section might include a commitment to two-hour firewalls and doors on the collection storage rooms, the conditions under which the museum will place its collections under sprinklers (at home or on loan), or the staff levels permitted to enter the collection storage rooms or to handle the collections.

30. *Insurance* provisions are an important section of a collection management policy. In some countries, government museum collections are self-insured. Some offer indemnity programs according to which the government will cover the cost of any harm or loss, making insurance for international exhibitions unnecessary up to a preagreed value—but only if the institution qualifies for the program. More generally, the policy should identify the range of insurance coverage and conditions affecting the collection, including third-party liability, deductible levels of reimbursement for loss or damage, inventory requirements, and the museum's procedure for recording insured values, reviewing and changing them regularly, and communicating current values to its insurers.

APPENDIX C
Information System Plans, Documentation, and Cataloging

This appendix outlines an approach for managing information system plans, with special attention to the areas of documentation and cataloging.

- An information system plan begins with a list of all information-related functions.

- It then determines which components can be efficiently integrated in the near future, ensuring as far as possible the necessary compatibility of systems so that further links can be forged later.

- An *information model* may be devised, showing in graphic form the current tasks and consequent information flow and desired improvements in these patterns. Merging of software programs is likely to be involved here.

- It should then be possible, with some specialist consultant assistance, to list functional requirements of the information system and use these as a guideline to preparing specifications for both hardware and software.

- Costs—in terms of training and development as well as money—must also be calculated, and the plan may have to be adjusted to realistic parameters—although the potential of sponsorship by hardware or software companies should not be discounted.

With both an information policy and an information system plan in place, the registrar may need to upgrade the *documentation procedures manuals* to ensure that they are compatible with the entire system.

Procedures manuals are usually important for both registration and cataloging. In addition to the steps involved in making a satisfactory record of a new accession, these manuals must provide very explicit instructions for the catalogers and data entry clerks who will be using them.

The steps in the registration procedures manual should include at least this checklist:

- *entry* of identification, source, and history in a secure and permanent file

- *numbering* of both object and record

- *acknowledgment* to the source of the acquisition

- formal *transfer of title* by gift agreement or receipt

- addition of the object to the museum's *insurance* coverage

- an initial *condition report* by the conservator

- the initial *location* record for the object

Although a wide variety of registration systems have been employed throughout the museum world—forty-five different ones were found to be in use at the Victoria and Albert Museum when it commenced automation of its records many years ago—most museums today register acquisitions by means of what is called the three-part numbering system. It comprises

- a three-digit number referring to the year of acquisition—009, for example;

- a period and a number referring to the number of the acquisition in the present year—so that 009.13 refers to the thirteenth accession made in 2009;

- another period and a number referring to the object within that accession—so that 009.13.4 refers to the fourth object donated by the source of the thirteenth accession of 2009; and

- if necessary, a lower-case letter designating part of an object, so that 009.13.4a might refer to a teapot, while 009.13.4b might refer to its lid.

A numerical system that is unrelated to any object categories has been found to be most durable for collections of all kinds.

Some collections may need to correlate it with other conventions. There is an international registration system for stamps, for example, and archaeological collections may need to correlate finds with the universal geographical site reference system. Many natural history collections find it preferable both to document and to organize their holdings by genus and species, while coins are classified by country, ruler, material, denomination, and date.

Others may have inherited a historic system that remains viable—although any system must admit of infinite change, as the conceptual bases of classifications of objects of all kinds are continually evolving. Thus, it has not proved useful to base a documentation system on the periods of art history, for example, because the very basis for the period classifications is questioned and revised from time to time by the discipline itself.

Remember to take great care when numbering any object. Numbers may be applied to very small objects, or ones where all surfaces are of equivalent aesthetic importance, by means of tags. Unbleached cotton labels may be discreetly sewn into costumes. For most other objects, numbers may be applied on the base or in a comparable inconspicuous place in varnished drawing ink on an acetone base coat; conservators recommend that the base coat should include a 20 percent Paraloid B72 solution and that the area where numbers are applied must have adequate ventilation for the safety of those working there.

The registration procedures manual should detail the numbering process and recommend suitable places for locating numbers uniformly on the type of objects in that museum's collection. *Bar codes* introduced a more permanent method of tagging objects, now increasingly in use in museums, and now Radio Frequency Identification (RFID) tags are smaller, more robust, and easier to attach than bar codes, and they can be detected without visual inspection.

The documentation procedures manuals should also refer to the museum's *location tracking* method. This should be initiated at registration with the *entry documentation* and maintained for each acquisition throughout its retention in the museum, regardless of when or whether it is subsequently cataloged. The manual must determine who is allowed to move objects in the collection and what procedures they must follow, to ensure that others will be able to find the objects subsequently.

All storage and display locations should be codified for easy reference. In the event of loans, the manuals should provide an approved *exit documentation* procedure, which must be checked by security officers as well as collection management personnel.

Maintaining a sound location tracking practice is essential for the success of a collection *inventory*, which is vital to security as well as to collection management. Government line department museums may be expected to meet auditors' requirements for inventory of their collections. But all museums should undertake inventories in regular rotation, with every object, even in large collections, being checked at least once every few years. Insurance policies may require regular inventories.

Cataloging is a more extensive recording process than registration, and many museums that keep up-to-date with their registration have a backlog in cataloging. While registration records a limited number of data fields—name and function of the object, its source and provenance, place and date of its origin, its materials, and a brief description, for instance—the museum catalog aims to record a full sense of its significance in relation to other objects in the collection, in other collections, and in the world at large.

While the registrar and data entry clerks may be able to register an object with input from the curator, the catalog entry should be fundamentally a curatorial concern. It should include references to relevant literature and reproductions—much of which may be standardized for groups of similar objects. Developing a comprehensive catalog of a collection is a museum's major responsibility that should not be forever postponed due to the deadlines of temporary exhibitions or the opportunities to add still more acquisitions.

The *automation* of collection records often throws a spotlight on hitherto little-known lacunae in the museum's catalog. Early endeavors to transfer records to computers attempted complete catalogs, trying to record comprehensive information about a necessarily restricted number of objects; experience has shown that entry of only a few key fields from the registration records for a large number of objects is far more efficient and effective, as long as the system allows further information to be added in the future. In this way the registration records and the eventual complete catalog can be integrated in one automated system.

The *nomenclature* used to record museum objects has become an important subject in itself, particularly as computer word-search programs facilitate access for everyone, from curators to visiting scholars and schoolchildren.

Standardizing terminology internationally, not only for technical terms but for color references, for example, will help to smooth global access to the world's growing collections database. Some disciplines, such as the natural sciences, have inherited conventions such as the genus and species classifications, whereas others are still in the process of development. In Britain the *Social History and Industrial Classification* published by the University of Sheffield in 1983 may be helpful for collections of that kind, while in the United States *The Revised Nomenclature for Museum Cataloguing* published by the American Association for State and Local History in 1988 (based on the earlier edition by Chenhall) is almost universally employed for historical collections of artifacts—but some Australian museums have found it necessary to develop their own standard guide for their historical collections.

Many software programs designed for museum registrars' use are available. Some museums that chose their systems many years ago subsequently had difficulty in acquiring imaging capability or providing public access and had to reconvert. Waiting for the ideal software or upgrade is not a solution, however; instead, the registrar or curators, often with specialist consultant advice, should undertake systematic development of an information system plan to ensure that all possible specifications have been considered and should then either make a commitment to the best system on offer or may prefer to develop a program unique to the museum's needs but compatible with as broad a range of applications as possible. The capacity of some computer programs to accommodate nonalphabetic languages may also be important—for Asian art and archaeology collections, for example.

Data entry to convert manual records to computer software programs has been labor intensive. One major British museum reported that trained workers there could input only seven one-thousand-character records per hour from cards or book entries. Such data entry almost always involved reconfiguring the original record into the format required for the computer. Merging or migrating from one computer program to another today is much less challenging, at least in terms of person hours. Although this work is largely accomplished in many major institutions, it is important to remember that it is still underway in many smaller museums and those in developing countries.

Digitized *imaging* is another important step in the upgrading of museum records. In many cases this has required rephotographing an entire collection. The benefits for both the museum's documentation system and interpretation of the collection to the museum public are usually sufficient, however, to justify such an undertaking. Advances in digital photography have made the manipulation of images so much more effective for all museum purposes. *Digital asset management* (DAM) programs are needed to optimize use of both word and image data, including possible leasing for other uses.

APPENDIX D
The Challenges of Preventative Conservation

The climate crisis, which is now understood as a threat to human existence, is causing museums and the public to question many of the assumptions underlying the concepts of preventative conservation, which is itself a relatively new idea and practice.

The reasons for rethinking are costs both financial and environmental. This is especially the case for the global south, which has fewer museums than the global north and is where museum growth is wanted and meaningful.

At the same time, it is the global south and marginalized communities in the global north that are most negatively impacted by the twin costs of the climate crisis. We can therefore expect change and innovation in preventative conservation. Let us hope it does not require a return to the "glass case museums" of seventy-five years ago, which was the dominant method of preventative conservation.

Temperature and relative humidity: These two climatic factors are closely interrelated; relative humidity (RH) is the ratio, expressed as a percentage, of the absolute humidity of sampled air to that of air saturated with water at the same temperature. Organic materials respond to fluctuations in temperature and relative humidity, especially the latter. Continued fluctuation results in a weakening of the organic material. Textiles, paper, leather, and wood are among the objects commonly found in museum collections that are particularly susceptible to such deterioration, which can present special difficulties in objects of mixed organic and inorganic materials. If RH is too high for too long, mildew and mold are additional hazards, along with corrosion of metals.

The standard for environmental conditions for many museum collections of organic or mixed materials in temperate zones is usually a diurnal constant of 50 percent RH plus or minus 5 percent year-round at 20–21°C (68–70°F) plus or minus 0.5°C in winter, which may be modulated upward by 0.5°C per month to 22–24°C (72–75°F) in summer. For new buildings constructed to withstand such conditions, especially in a temperate maritime climate, this standard need not present a major problem; for historic buildings, or other structures not built to sustain such a standard, especially in continental climates, 55 percent RH is likely to be the best that can be maintained, or it may be necessary to adjust humidity from 55 percent in summer to 40 percent in winter by three monthly 5 percent steps in RH settings each spring and fall. If engineers still find such limits constrictive or the museum finds their maintenance too expensive, allowance can be made for wider variations for, say, 5-10 percent of operating hours during a year, with the standard maintained for the rest of the year. Metal and paper collections require a lower RH, around 40 percent, while collections that have originated in the tropics may have a higher hydroscopic content and may require 65 percent RH.

Once the standards are agreed upon, it is the conservators' responsibility to monitor these environmental conditions closely—traditionally with psychrometers or hygrothermographs, but more commonly today through computerized building management systems (BMS) by digital means of recording RH and temperature. Monitors should be positioned to record conditions at all levels of galleries and stores and in major display cases. Simultaneous records should be kept of outside climate conditions and of internal spaces that do not benefit from the museum's heating, ventilating, and air-conditioning (HVAC) controls designed to maintain this collection environment. Zones that do not normally contain collections may be maintained at human comfort levels for those who work in or use them.

The climate controls are usually maintained by a ducted air-handling system that provides heated or cooled and humidified or dehumidified air as required. Unmodified replacement air is normally kept to a minimum, and building engineers must provide not only insulation but also a vapor barrier of 0.04-0.08 perms to prevent water vapor from dampening the insulation, and an air barrier to stop air from leaking into the fabric of the building from the interior. Fenestration, if present at all, should be triple paned, with panes at least 1.3 centimeters apart, and skylights, if present, may be buffered with an area that provides a halfway zone between the exterior climate and that in the galleries or stores. Section 3.4 indicates some of the challenges related to the building that arise from the climate control requirements of preventive conservation.

Air filtration: Dust and air pollution are other environmental factors affecting the condition of the object, which are especially obnoxious in the industrial or high-traffic areas where many museums are located. Fortunately these can be controlled with an appropriate system of filters—ideally a 25-30 percent efficiency prefilter (according to the American Society of Heating, Refrigeration and Air Conditioning Engineers' [ASHRAE] dust spot efficiency test section, ASHRAE test 52-76), followed by a medium 40-85 percent efficiency filter, and a 90-95 percent afterfilter. This bank of filters should be positioned so that both outside and recirculated internal air passes through it. (Electronic air filters should not be used because the ozone they generate can be harmful to the collection.) For gaseous pollutants, the standard test is to place polished metal "coupons" around the museum for long periods of time and then to analyze any corrosion products that form on them. Activated charcoal filters are preferred to eliminate or reduce air pollution.

Light: Deterioration of color due to natural or artificial light is another concern of conservators. An ability to set light levels at 50 lux (5 footcandles [fc]) is essential for exhibitions of works on paper, drawings and watercolors, feathers, and other light-sensitive organic materials. A level of 150-200 lux (15-20 fc) is usually recommended for oil or acrylic paintings and other moderately sensitive objects, while ceramics, glass, stone, and most metals are among the items that are not particularly light sensitive and can therefore sustain 300 lux (30 fc), resulting in a *contrast ratio* of 6:1 from the most brightly to the most dimly illuminated object on display. The challenge for architects and lighting designers is not just that these levels must be maintained in dedicated galleries (50 lux or 5 fc in a photography gallery, for instance) but that in a gallery that will be showing works in all media, they must be attained side by side in many instances.

A prime concern is the duration of exposure, with conservators recommending withdrawal of light-sensitive items as necessary to keep lux hours down; *rotation* of objects on display should accordingly be planned into all exhibitions containing works on paper or textiles, and the number of hours exposed to light should be carefully controlled. Standards ranging from a maximum of 120,000 lux hours to 50,000 lux hours have been proposed for highly sensitive 50-lux (5 fc) items, such as works on paper or textiles; for its Turner paintings in the Clore Gallery, Tate Britain aims to restrict annual exposure to 500,000 lux hours per annum, at a constant of 100 lux (10 fc).

Ultraviolet light is another concern, with standards recently dropped to <10 microwatts per lumen from the previous level of 75, due to technical improvements in the UV filters built into fluorescent light tubes or made available as film or laminations for window glass. The choice of both fluorescent tubes and incandescent lamps—and now the availability of fiber optics—provide the conservator, the curator, and the exhibit designer with a wide range of illumination possibilities, and although many aesthetic factors (such as a color rendering index minimum of 85) may be considered, the preventive conservation requirements of lux and UV control must be paramount.

Pests: Rodents and insect pests are among the enemies of the conservator. Good housekeeping is the best defense against them. Poisons and chemical treatments are also of value but must be mitigated by consideration for any effects they may have on the object. Fumigation of new accessions used to be widespread in museums but has been found to be highly problematic due to risks to staff and the consequent need for licensing of operators in many jurisdictions. An *anoxic isolation chamber*, using nitrous oxide for instance, is an effective and less noxious way of eliminating insect pests.

Handling: The preventive conservator should be concerned with the training of all museum personnel who will be allowed to handle artifacts. They should develop procedures manuals that prescribe safe practices for handling, movement, and installation. The use of unbleached cotton or white gloves, for example, should be prescribed for all artifacts except for a small class of items (such as intricately carved lacquer, for example) where it is not well advised; handling and installation techniques designed to sustain support for the object at all times should be made relevant to the needs of each collection and the materials in it. Dusting or cleaning procedures must be detailed, along with instructions on who is to undertake such work at what level. Requirements for museum vehicles, vans, and dollies should also be specified in the manual, ensuring padding where necessary to protect works of art, artifacts, specimens, or archival materials in transit. If the museum has a costume collection, storage, display, and handling procedures are likely to be very particular and detailed in the manual.

Emergency procedures: Conservators should confer closely with the chief of security to ensure that the effects of emergency procedures on the collection are fully considered. For example, conservators should ensure that the appropriate type of sprinkler system is installed and that procedures in the event of sprinkler discharge are well understood by those whose actions will affect the collection. A fire, flood, earthquake, hurricane, or tornado will equally be the conservators' concern. The chief conservator should certainly be a member of the emergency action team.

APPENDIX E
Exhibitions: From Concept to Evaluation

This appendix outlines how to manage the development of exhibitions, from initial concept to evaluation. When the idea for a museum exhibition has received some tentative level of interest and support among the museum leadership, it may then be developed by its proponents into a concept plan that articulates the following:

- exhibition objectives in relation to the museum's exhibition policy;

- scholarly significance of the exhibition and research or documentation required;

- visitor and/or community interest;

- what the exhibition will look like and the amount of gallery space required;

- a general indication of the type of artifacts, works of art, or specimens available in the museum's collections, with reference to their present condition and need for conservation;

- sources of potential loans and the likely availability of those;

- potential use of media and potential for a parallel virtual exhibition on the museum's website;

- initial cost range;

- potential sources of funding or sponsorship; and

- initial projection of schedule.

This *concept plan* should be submitted by the exhibition's proponents to the standing exhibition committee, who may recommend it to the director for a go/no-go decision. If the initial cost projection is very high, but the exhibition is considered to be desirable, the concept plan may be given to the development director to seek a sponsor for all or part of the cost. The development director is likely to ask for preliminary *renderings* or even a *model* that suggests what the exhibition will look like, even at this early stage, in order to interest potential sponsors.

Formative evaluation can begin at this stage and may be sustained throughout the following stages. The term means, quite simply, evaluation while the exhibition is taking shape or forming. It is intended to ensure that the exhibition works from the visitors' perspective. One useful approach is to convene representative focus groups that consider the exhibition concept and its subsequent phases of schematic and more detailed design as they emerge. They might include a selection of likely users of the exhibition—teachers, students, museum members, or visitors selected at random. They might simply be asked to respond to a survey, or as plans progress they might be "walked through" the plans, the text, and the storyboards to identify areas of miscomprehension or confusion. If the project is a major new permanent collection exhibition, the museum may be well advised to employ an outside evaluator.

Interpretative Plan (Design Brief)

Once the standing exhibition committee and the director have approved the exhibition concept and it has been added to the exhibition schedule and budget, an exhibition task force is established, and the project team starts work.

The first step is to write an *interpretive plan*, sometimes called a *design brief*. This is an important document that will guide the exhibition development process right through to opening day.

The interpretative plan or exhibition brief articulates the

- objectives of the exhibition;

- intended visitor experience;

- levels of explanation (for children, adults, and specialists, for instance);

- component-by-component description of the exhibition, including

  - communication objectives of each component—major artifacts, specimens or works of art, display cases, interactive exhibits, demonstrations, and theatrical presentations;

  - means of expression to communicate these objectives (multiple means for each objective), utilizing all appropriate display modes;

  - diagrams of visitor flow patterns on gallery layouts; and

  - initial concept sketches or renderings to give the feel of the exhibition.

If there is to be a parallel virtual exhibition on the museum's website, the interpretative plan should also provide an outline of that feature.

Curators or educators are often expected to draft the interpretative plan, although some larger museums will have *interpretative planners* on staff. Often the museum may choose to contract an experienced outside consultant specialized in interpretative planning, with the exhibition concept plan serving as the *terms of reference* for a *request for qualifications* or a *request for proposals* to select this person, who may be part of a museum planning firm or an exhibition design studio.

Whoever produces it, the interpretative plan will be reviewed by each member of the exhibition task force until the entire team and the director reach a consensus of agreement about it. This is the point at which all members of the project team should be consulted: it is as important to have the comments of the chief of security as the chief conservator, and as important to get the input of the visitor services director and the marketing and retail managers as it is to obtain a sign-off from the curatorial department.

Once the interpretative plan has been recommended by the project team and approved by the director, each member of the task force can begin to develop plans for his or her own area of specialization: the selection of artifacts, works of art, or specimens by the curators; a schedule for condition reports on them by the conservators; a schedule for the requisite loan forms by the registrar; a marketing plan by the communications department; any special security arrangements by the chief of security; and so on. If the museum has in-house exhibition designers, the interpretative plan becomes the basis of their design; if not, it becomes the *design brief* for a competition to select the exhibition designers (unless the interpretative planner was part of a design team already selected). This competition may be for design only, or it could be for a *design-build* or *turnkey* contract for both design and fabrication.

Schematic Design

Schematic design refers to the period during which designers are drawing up the layout and design of the exhibition to fulfill the interpretative plan. This is usually a combination of floor plans, sections, elevations, and three-dimensional views (often called "presentation drawings") of each exhibition component. There are usually several reviews until the designers (whether in-house or outside contractors) develop a solution that the exhibition task force chairperson can sign off on. Once this level of approval is reached, these drawings are not only useful for the exhibition design process but may also be invaluable to the marketing and development departments, especially if a sponsor is being sought for the exhibition. A preliminary "fly-through" graphic illustration of the experience of the exhibition may now be possible, which is even more helpful to all concerned—marketing, development, education, and others.

If the exhibition is to include a theatrical presentation, the schematic design stage is where a *script* and *treatments* should be developed, advancing beyond the interpretative plan's means of expression to draft a storyline and propose treatments of specific themes. This document, usually developed by a specialist in the cinematic or theatrical techniques being proposed, is attached to the schematic design and should be considered and eventually approved along with it. If there is to be a parallel virtual exhibition on the museum's website, text and images for it should also be prepared in draft at this time.

Here the value of the initial interpretative plan becomes apparent. The more accurate the interpretative plan, the less time it will take for the design team to develop an appropriate solution and for the exhibition task force to recognize and approve it. This is an important factor in staying within the exhibition schedule and the budget, as the schematic design should also be the basis for a more advanced costing by a museum planner or cost consultant with museum exhibition experience.

This is equally the "sketch stage" for all the specialists on the team. The educator, for example, can now draft a learning program based on the exhibition, making sure that there is sufficient provision for the space required by the groups of schoolchildren or adults expected to tour the show and providing for any adjacent hands-on labs or classrooms, as well as learning stations in the exhibition itself, such as performance areas for demonstrators. The security chief is able to look for surveillance issues *before* design is finalized. The retail manager can begin to plan the special exhibition shop and start to order the stock for it. Visitor services can consider whether there is sufficient space for queues and any special ticketing arrangements that are needed. Depending on the size of the project, schematic design can take from three months to a year, with the final product being approved by the task force and the director before detailed design or design development can start.

Design Development

As soon as schematic design is approved, *design development* should begin.

Design development elaborates the schematic drawings into complete designs for buildable exhibits, vitrines (display cases) for specific objects, and locations for paintings or graphic panels. Some design practices distinguish design development from a subsequent stage of *detailed design* for larger projects, whereas others see the two as closely intertwined, especially for smaller projects. At this stage the script and treatments of the theatrical presentation should be elaborated into *storyboards*, illustrating scene by scene what the viewer will see on the screen or on stage.

This is also the stage in which the text of all graphics and labels and any audiovisual scripts should be drafted for repeated editing to fit the space, as well as being subjected to the formative evaluation focus groups to test for clarity. Questions are often more effective communicators than assertions, and there is a paramount need to avoid the academic or technical jargon that creeps into the museum's language but may mystify the visitor, in addition to limiting the text of a graphic panel to sixty words or fewer so that a majority of visitors will pause long enough to read it. Curators usually initiate text, but the interpretative planner and/or the educators should massage it for length and clarity, with the final version submitted to the curator to check back for accuracy.

If the museum has a chief of communications or a publications director, it is also valuable to have them edit the text from the viewpoint of the museum's house style. Graphic designers (either in-house or contracted) will meanwhile be developing a graphic style for the entire exhibition that provides a comprehensive format and size guide for all levels of printed communication, from the exhibition title and gallery names through graphic panels to labels, monitor screen text, and publications, all planned in relation to the levels of communication identified in the interpretative plan. They should also be preparing the final version of the text and images for the parallel virtual exhibition on the museum's website, if one is planned.

With all of these activities in development at the same time as the educators and the marketing staff are developing their plans, it is not surprising that, depending on the size of the project, the design development stage takes three months to a year after schematic design has been approved.

Construction and Installation

The official approval of detailed design is the final point at which the exhibition task force or the museum director can make changes. Now *construction drawings* are prepared on the basis of the detailed design. For the audiovisual and theatrical components, a final recording schedule or shooting script is developed on the basis of the approved storyboards.

The construction drawings are then assembled with all other instructions to contractors, creating a bid, or tender, package that is issued with a request for proposals from exhibition fabricators. These may be issued as one large contract, with the understanding that the fabricator will employ various subcontractors, or the museum may prefer to manage separate contracts for such elements as display case construction, computer hardware and software programs, model and mannequin making, audiovisual production, and so on. Mount making—building the supports for artifacts or specimens that might range from a gold ring to a reconstructed drinking vessel, or from a trilobite fossil to a whale's skeleton—is a specialized field in itself, which may be assigned either to in-house technicians or to an outside contract with a good track record for that very specialized work. Audiovisual production for the museum's theater or within the exhibition gallery is usually a separate contract with its own timeline, hopefully coordinated with the rest of exhibition fabrication and installation so that it will be "alright on the night" of the exhibition opening.

The contractor selection process should be managed according to the museum's procurement policies by the museum's purchasing department or responsible financial officer, in close consultation with the exhibitions department and the task force. The museum should not be tied in advance to accepting the lowest bid—frequently a low bid may indicate simply a lack of understanding of the complexity of the project, a lack of experience commensurate with the quality the museum expects, or an attempt to win the job at a low price, counting on change orders to increase the actual expenditure to what is really needed. This applies equally to the audiovisual producer and to any other separate components if they are not grouped as subconsultants under the main fabricator.

Once the construction and installation process has commenced, the exhibition task force can intervene for quality control only at previously agreed points, when a prototype is being presented for approval or an inspection of a particular phase is prearranged. Keeping within the budget and the schedule is important at this stage, with hard decisions having to be made if, for instance, certain materials are not available in sufficient quantity, so that substitutions are proposed, or if expensive change orders are proposed by the museum or the contractors. Because of the special security concerns of museums, access by contractors' personnel needs to be closely supervised by the museum's security staff.

A major focus of the study team during this period should be the coordination of the education activities, special events, publicity, fund-raising, and plans for the opening. The parallel virtual exhibition on the museum's website may be launched in advance of the exhibition because it will stimulate advance excitement about the show, in addition to being valuable in itself.

The construction and installation stage is likely to take anywhere from nine to eighteen months for most exhibition projects.

One Last Look: Commissioning

The completion of installation is a relatively short but critical stage in exhibition development. Prior to final approval of construction and installation, the task force, led by its chair and the project manager, should tour the exhibition and draw up a *snag list* of deficiencies that the contractor is required to correct. Some negotiation may ensue regarding which deficiencies legitimately fall under the original contract and which are client changes, but in any case all problems identified on the snag list must be resolved before handover (commissioning) is complete. A similar screening of audiovisual components is needed before they are installed in their appropriate places.

The paint should be dry, the dust should be removed, and the contractors should be vacated from the site prior to the installation of the artifacts, works of art, or specimens, which is the responsibility of the curators and conservators. There should also be time reserved for a "soft opening" in which exhibit components can be pretested on school groups or other samples of visitors, with an allocation in the schedule for adjustments if needed. Then the visitor services and operations staff take over to arrange for the opening.

Evaluating the Exhibition

The exhausted project team still has one more job to do: evaluate the exhibition process. It is crucial, both for the museum and for the profession as a whole, to look back on a major exhibition project to identify aspects of the process that worked well and why and to recommend changes to the process that will improve chances for success in the future. The task force itself should do this much.

In addition, a *summative evaluation* of the visitor experience of the exhibition should be conducted by the museum's evaluation specialist or by an outside contractor. This type of visitor evaluation is most effective if it goes back to the original interpretative plan to determine whether or not the exhibition actually communicates what it was planned to communicate. The evaluation should be submitted to the director and the exhibition department, which could use it to improve the museum's *exhibition procedures manual* based on the cumulative experience of many exhibition project teams over the years. This type of manual can be a vital document to facilitate the creativity of future exhibition project teams.

APPENDIX F
Museum Marketing

This appendix outlines five steps for activating museum marketing, from analyzing visitor research to implementation and evaluation.

- The first step in museum marketing is to understand the museum's current visitors—the market segments they represent, the frequency of the visits, and their motivation. This may be accomplished by studying daily attendance records through observation and visitor surveys. For a new museum project, it is usually valuable to undertake such studies of comparable museums, either within the same city or area or of museums with similar collections or subject matter.

- The next step is to compare this reality with the demographics of the resident market (obtained from census data) and the tourists who visit the area (available from the local tourist board or chamber of commerce) and with visitor survey results from other museums or visitor attractions in the area that are willing to share that information. This should enable analysts to determine which market segments are underrepresented in the museum's visitor base.

- The third step is particularly challenging: to analyze what it all means, to set marketing priorities around *target market segments*, and to identify marketing strategies that will boost attendance from those market segments, consistent with the museum's mission, goals, and objectives. This stage constitutes a marketing plan for tasks ranging from advertising, promotion, and public relations to the creation of special events and programs. These tasks may be carried out by museum staff—say, in the education department for the creation of learning programs, or in the graphic design department to create advertisements—or they may be carried out by outside consultants, including public relations firms and advertising agencies. Whoever creates them, it is important to note that marketing strategies based on the same data may aim at developing underrepresented markets or, on the contrary, may choose instead to serve current market segments better—and the choice must be made by the museum's senior management consistent with the museum's goals and objectives, not by marketing personnel alone.

- The fourth step is implementation of the marketing plan. The role of the marketing manager is effectively to monitor the implementation of the plan or brief, coordinating completion of all the tasks on time, on budget, and to an agreed level of quality.

- The final step is evaluation of the results, recording what should be changed and the production of a manual for ongoing marketing efforts.

Visitor Research

Visitor research collects up-to-date and reliable data about the museum's visitors to enable the museum to

- improve its performance in its public role;

- focus on meeting public needs and expectations and achieving outcomes related to visitor and general public interests; and

- demonstrate to current and potential funders and sponsors, whether in the public or private sectors, the degree to which the public is served and which sectors of the public are using the museum.

In order to meet these objectives, there needs to be a balance between *quantitative* analysis of demographics and behaviors and *qualitative* methods that focus on feelings, attitudes, and motivations of visitors. This is particularly important because of these factors:

- Museums that thrive as civil society institutions will be those that are of real value to the community.

- Visitor data shows that "word of mouth" is often the most frequently cited motivation for a museum visit; this means that visitor satisfaction is likely to be the most significant generator of attendance.

- Museums have become more dependent on visitor-generated revenue and visitor spending in their gift shops and restaurants.

- The potential for converting visitors to become museum members and supporters is closely related to their level of satisfaction with the museum experience.

Visitor surveys and attendance counts are used to create a database of attendance, demographic, and lifestyle information, while methods such as in-gallery interviews, observation, workshops, and focus groups are used to understand visitor motivations and expectations and the quality of the visitor experience.

This type of research is particularly important in addressing the needs of audiences such as visible minorities and low-income earners because these groups are underrepresented in traditional museum surveys and therefore relatively little is known about their attitudes, expectations, and experiences in the museum. Thus, a focus group drawn from an underrepresented socioeconomic class may be of great interest, even if its members have visited the museum only once or not at all.

In surveying visitors, care must be taken to restrict questions to data that will really be of value. For instance, presenting a range of twenty occupation groups and asking visitors to indicate which one fits them most closely is of little value if the gradations between the occupation groups make no difference to the marketing strategy; broader classifications would be of greater value if they are the classifications on which decisions can be based.

The most effective and efficient approach to visitor research is to develop a comprehensive three- to five-year rolling program that focuses on quantitative research in some years and qualitative in others. The key is to involve representatives of all departments who work with the public in the audience research project team to ensure that all the museum's many evaluation activities (whether of education programs or from visitor comment cards) contribute to the visitor research database.

The museum may have an evaluator on staff (a full-time or part-time position depending on the size of the museum) to design and implement research or may contract outside consultants to do so; to analyze and disseminate the results through the project team and to formulate recommendations for the director to take to the trustees if necessary. Again, the decision on whether to pursue underrepresented markets or to emphasize improved service to current markets is one for the museum's senior management and must be consistent with the museum's long-range mission and goals, as well as current objectives.

Target Markets

There are many potential market segments that a museum may seek to attract. Selecting *target markets* means choosing from among these segments to focus the museum's energy.

The decision as to which markets to target will be based on many considerations, ranging from *affordability* (unless the market is saturated, it's less costly and risky to target more of the same kinds of people you are already attracting) to *responsibility* to engage a broader demographic to *creativity*, recognizing that new audiences will contribute new perspectives and new vitality to the museum. Five main factors need to be considered in selecting and prioritizing target markets:

- The size of the market and its growth potential.

- The importance of the market to the museum's mission and mandate. This applies particularly to the museum's role as a public educational institution in a culturally and economically diverse society.

- The capability of the market to contribute to visitor-generated revenues.

- The contribution of a particular segment to the tourism or economic development objectives of the city or region. There is a growing recognition of the central role of museums in attracting high-income cultural tourists and in helping to increase the length of stay and visitor spending of all tourists. Communities also value museums because they are symbolic of the quality-of-life factors in attracting new industry and service companies to the area. And there is the vital contribution that museums and other cultural institutions make to attracting and retaining knowledge industry workers, the group that economist Richard Florida has identified as *the creative class*, which he observes is crucial to a thriving urban economy today.

- The negative factor of the costs associated with attracting each segment.

These policy decisions should involve senior management. The director should then present them to the board on the basis of recommendations from the marketing manager, resulting in quantitative goals to be set for each market segment in the context of three- to five-year attendance projections.

Marketing Strategies

Marketing strategies are the many ways in which the museum can improve its communications and service to target audiences with the objective of boosting attendance and visitor spending. The marketing strategy also aims to build a closer relationship with the museum's audiences, leading to repeat visits, membership, and donations. Ideally, think of the relationship between marketing and audiences as a continual conversation rather than a speech from a podium to a listener. This is a continual process in which the manager of the museum's marketing activities must work closely with evaluation, curatorial, and public programming staff and development and visitor services departments, ideally through a task force project team.

Once the overall marketing strategy has been established, there may be as many as fifty specific marketing strategies to be implemented, such as new admission prices and categories (such as subscriptions, which seem to appeal to young adults rather than memberships that appeal to older age groups), an advertising campaign packaging with hotels to lure vacationers, evening openings targeted at the singles market, or seminars on contemporary art to appeal to collectors. Developing the right strategies requires expertise in museum marketing and knowledge of what has been successful elsewhere.

Museums can benefit greatly from learning about the successes and failures of museums of comparable size and scope. This is called *comparables analysis* and consists of interviews with staff in the comparable institutions.

Study of *best practice* examples is also helpful; this involves identifying examples of outstanding successes in institutions that may be much larger or smaller and carefully analyzing how their methods could be applied to this museum. In order to avoid taking the wrong lessons from comparables or imitating failures that look like successes, both types of research should be facilitated by staff or external consultants who have considerable experience in museum marketing and managing organizational change.

Marketing strategies should be implemented in a deliberate way, with opportunities for evaluation planned as part of the strategy. Regular reports to the interdepartmental task force on progress in their implementation, evaluating each step in the process, ensure results and control costs.

APPENDIX G
Preparing the Functional Program

This appendix outlines the main components of developing a functional program, through architectural concept to evaluation.

1. Pertinent principles, goals, and assumptions specific to the project that work to align stake-holders and serve as tools for measurement as the project proceeds (principles are not expected to change for the life of the project while assumptions may be changed).

2. Site characteristics and requirements for access, signage, security, and the like.

3. A list of all spaces in the building, organized by zone and function, as outlined subsequently in this section.

4. Functional area descriptions, describing how each major room or space will function with focus on intended use, adjacencies, and daily operation.

5. Access, adjacency, and circulation diagrams are graphic (diagrammatic) representations illustrating the relationship between rooms and spaces and indicate the best arrangement to ensure that visitors/collections/services flow in the best possible manner.

6. Building systems and standards required throughout the building, or by zone, with specific standards for the collection or parts of it, as well as human comfort standards.

7. Room data sheets are detailed, museum-focused information sheets for each room in the space program. The data is presented in a matrix format and correlates with the space program, adding depth of architectural and technical information such as museum zone, net area, primary adjacencies, anticipated/required occupancy, and critical environment.

A *facility strategy* usually includes some or all of the foregoing list but not necessarily the detailed functional requirements. Often a facility strategy will be produced for fund-raising as well as planning purposes, and the museum will proceed to a full functional program only after sufficient funds have been raised to justify this more detailed level of planning, or a facility strategy can be the basis for an architectural competition, with the functional program being produced for the selected architect. The facility strategy can also set the tone for further project development by exploring a number of framing questions that can be used for considering future options, for instance:

*   VISIONARY

    Does the project raise aspirations for what the museum can be in the future?

*   PROVOKING

    Will the project be a catalyst for the museum's community roles and profile?

*   RESPONSIBLE

    Does the project optimize capital and infrastructure resources?

*   FLEXIBLE

    Can the project accommodate future scenarios in a phased approach?

- BRAND BUILDING

   Will the project elevate the museum's identity locally, nationally, and internationally?

The drafting of this functional program or brief should not be assigned to architects or engineers. Their expertise does not lie in the statement of museum *requirements*.

The architects and engineers provide the *answers*, with their drawings and specifications, but the purpose of the functional program or brief is to get the *questions* right, to state the museum's *requirements* that the architect and engineers must meet in their work. The development of the museum planner as a specialized role within the museum profession has been very much in response to this demand for experienced museum professionals who have learned the language of the facility strategy and functional program or brief.

Museum Zoning

Within the functional program, museum spaces within the space program can be organized according to a system of zones, which identify the net (useable) area in terms of public and nonpublic functions and collections and noncollections functions. The zone model allows for the testing of specific areas against industry-proven norms and ensures "right-sizing" of building components and facilitates efficient capital costing estimates.

The five zones are as follows, with the last relating to exterior spaces, which are not included as useable building area.

Zone A, Public Amenities: In this zone, visitors are present, but normally, collections items are not. Lobby, gift shop, restrooms, event space, food service spaces, and public program areas are typical spaces for this zone. This space is among the most expensive to build due to the high level of finish but is less expensive to operate because it does not have tight temperature and humidity requirements.

Zone B, Galleries and Exhibits: This is where visitors encounter exhibitions or collections, as well as any art works borrowed from other institutions. It is the costliest part of the building (capital and operating) because it requires high levels of finish to meet public expectations, environmental controls, and security.

Zone C, Collection and Content Support: Collections and loaned objects are present in this zone, and access is typically restricted to authorized curatorial staff. All the collections handling, management, and support areas for the temporary exhibition program—from the shipping/receiving area inward—are part of this zone. It is less expensive to build as it only requires a basic level of finish, but it is more expensive to operate because the space requires tight temperature and humidity controls.

Zone D, Building Support: This zone includes areas that do not normally host the public or require specific environmental or security controls. Offices and work areas to support staff activities and programs and noncollections building support, storage, and work areas are in this zone. It is frequently the lowest cost of the building to construct because it requires neither a high level of environmental control and security nor the level of finish necessary to meet public expectations.

Zone E, Exterior Spaces: This zone tracks critical program elements not located inside the building. It identifies those spaces that the museum will rely upon to execute its outdoor events, programs, and visitor experiences. These include functional items like a bus drop-off as well as programmatic and revenue generating spaces, such as plazas, courtyards, gardens, and rooftops. No net useable area is assigned to exterior spaces.

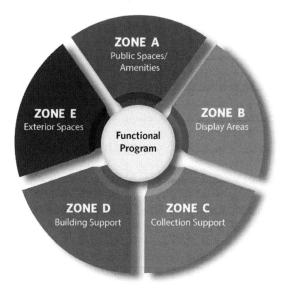

Figure 9.1. Museum Zones. *Lord Cultural Resources.*

Space allocations for each of the four interior museum zones for a collecting institution with collections stored mainly on site will typically fall within the range shown in figure 9.2.

Zone	Description	Typical Distribution
A	Public Ammenities	20%
B	Exhibits and Galleries	40%
C	Collection Support	20%
D	Building Support	20%
	Total	100%

Figure 9.2. Space Allocations. *Lord Cultural Resources.*

It is important to note that these percentages are not a fixed measure of distribution but rather rules of thumb that can be used as benchmarks against industry tested norms. They are presented as a reference for right-sizing proposed areas. Nevertheless, the analysis of the museum's space into these four categories is of immeasurable help to the architect and engineer in planning efficient adjacencies, as well as to the cost consultant (or quantity surveyor) and the construction manager in determining where and how to cut costs if that should become necessary in what is called a *value engineering process*. This four-zone analysis also allows us to see most clearly how efficient the building is or could be made.

Zoning of the building is also instrumental in planning for operating efficiencies or for planning to enhance "green" sustainability. These are usually challenging in a museum because its requirements for environmental controls and security may necessitate equipment or facilities that could be more efficient if standards were lower. Proper zoning of spaces allows engineers to work with museum planners to mitigate these effects wherever possible, and it at least permits the identification of those factors where cost savings and compromises can or must be made.

From Architectural Concept to Evaluation

Whereas the functional program or brief asks questions (and sets the requirements), the work of the architects and engineers is to provide answers.

Their drawings and specifications are called *architectural documentation*; in Britain it is sometimes called a *technical brief*. The museum project team and the building team should meet to resolve issues that arise as the functional program or brief is translated first into an *architectural concept* or *design concept* and then into progressive stages of *schematic design* and *detailed design* or *design development*, along with technical *specifications* by the engineers as well as the architects, in response to the requirements of the functional program. If museum planning professionals have been engaged in developing the program, they should also continue to be engaged in a design assist capacity working in partnership to review the designs and specifications as they are produced in order to advise on the degree of compliance with the requirements or to suggest compromises as needed.

For many museum projects there is both a *design architect*, who may do only the concept or may proceed only as far as schematic design, and an *architect of record*, usually a local architect licensed to practice in that jurisdiction, who may be responsible for continuing the process through detailed design and for issuing *construction drawings* as the basis for the documentation to be issued to contractors to bid on building or renovating the structure. An exhibition designer may also be part of the design team, especially for natural history, science and technology, or history museums involving complex, large-scale exhibits.

Throughout this process compromise is inevitable and welcome—but should always be made with an eye to ensuring the optimal achievement of the museum's functional requirements within the limitations of budget, time, and technology.

Consideration must be given to the usually inverse relationship of capital and operating costs—a savings in the former often leading to an increase in the latter, and vice versa. The design stage concludes with *bid* (or *tender*) *documents* on the basis of which contractors prepare their proposals, and the consequent contract negotiations after bids are opened. The cost consultant (or quantity surveyor) should have provided estimates at each stage, possibly beginning with very rough order-of-magnitude projections after the master plan, refining the estimates through the programming process, and costing each set of designs. The opening of bids or tenders proves how accurate the process has been. It is important to include a review of the competing bids in terms of their compliance with the functional program or brief as a prominent part of their evaluation. The selection should certainly not be made on the basis of lowest price alone.

The construction of new or renovated museum space proceeds toward *commissioning* (handing over the building to the client), as do most building projects, but it is important that the project manager, the museum project team, and/or the museum planners should be able to review the project at various stages of its completion to ensure that the museum's needs are being met. And the final stage of the process should not be forgotten, the *evaluation* of the building's performance, again measured against the requirements of the functional brief or functional program.

APPENDIX H
Security Policy Checklists

This appendix offers a series of security policy checklists and begins with a focus on risk analysis. A *risk analysis* involves answers to these four basic questions:

1. *What is to be protected?* The collection should be analyzed in terms of monetary value—classified by value categories of over or under certain monetary levels—and in terms of interest to thieves or vandals. Famous works of art or artifacts may be particularly vulnerable, and objects made of precious metals are always of interest to thieves because they can be melted down. Some artifacts are politically controversial or involve religious values that may attract attacks. Others may be of lower monetary value but may be of great value to the museum and the community for other reasons. Although the same high level of security should be maintained throughout the collection zones, it may be useful to classify the collections into categories A through C, strictly from the viewpoint of their value to be secured so that special attention may be given to category A objects.

2. *What are the threats?* An explicit identification of the risks will help to focus the security plan on reducing or eliminating them.

3. *What level of risk is acceptable?* Many threats cannot be eliminated entirely but may be reduced to the level that the museum's security policy can accept. Purely from a security viewpoint, the museum could remain closed to the public to maximize the safety of its collections, but because the museum is a public institution, its management must determine the degree of risk that is acceptable. There might, for example, be a policy against open displays of objects in category A (those with the highest monetary value).

4. *What countermeasures are appropriate?* Again, museum policy must determine acceptable standards among security options. One very busy museum in Manhattan, for instance, encourages its warders to be strict and even officious with the public because it prefers to err on the side of security rather than putting its emphasis on a visitor-friendly atmosphere. Another museum might make exactly the opposite priorities.

The threats to be evaluated in a risk analysis include:

- *natural disasters*, such as earthquakes, hurricanes, tornadoes, floods, forest fires, or simple power outages, which are becoming more common because of extreme weather due to climate change;

- *building faults*, such as electrical or heating system deficiencies or structural weaknesses;

- *theft*: art theft in particular is said to be second only to the drug trade as a source of revenue to criminals, and a distressingly high proportion of museum thefts are said to be "inside jobs" connected with or committed by a person who has joined the staff for that very purpose;

- fire;

- vandalism;

- *accidents* of staff or visitors; and

- *social or political hazards*, such as bomb threats, strikes, or demonstrations.

Risks may be evaluated in terms of their

- *probability*, from least to most likely to occur;

- likely *frequency* of occurrence; and

- seriousness of *consequences* for the museum.

Risks may be

- *eliminated*, for example, by changing staff procedures to stop causing or allowing a hazard;

- *reduced* by installing detection or response equipment;

- *transferred* to an insurer; or

- *accepted* as necessary to the fulfillment of the museum's public mission.

All four of these responses may be utilized in regard to a particular collection or exhibition, or indeed in protecting a single valuable object. Certain risks may be eliminated and others reduced with protective equipment for an insured object in the collection, but because the museum is dedicated to providing public access to it, some degree of risk will be accepted.

The museum's security policy should accordingly identify the following range of countermeasures (the famous "four Ds"):

- *Detection*: Methods of determining whether a threat is occurring, include surveillance by guards or warders, intrusion alarms, smoke detectors, display case alarms, and closed-circuit television.

- *Deterrence*: Methods of reducing the likelihood of threats may range from perimeter fences to case locks. The perception of deterrence may be just as important as the reality: most museums now recognize the value of making security obvious—so that visitors can see closed-circuit television screens near the entrance, for example.

- *Delay*: If a threat arises, the intention of security is to retard its progress. Two-hour firewalls around collection areas (with one-hour walls elsewhere) are a typical example, as is the practice of restricting egress from the building to one guarded exit rather than permitting multiple means of getaway.

- *Defense*: An *emergency procedures manual* should detail appropriate staff response in the event of a threat. All staff and volunteers should be provided with this manual—not just security staff—and there should be regular drills and rehearsals. In addition to fire drills, vandalism, theft, visitor illness, and accident scenarios should be enacted, with staff being tested on their ability to respond in accordance with the museum's security policy as detailed in the emergency procedures manual. All staff should know when and how to call for an ambulance or fire or police protection, and all should understand the legal implications of liability for actions taken or not taken, for the museum or for themselves (with legal advice consulted in preparing the manual). After-hours response should also be covered, especially for those who are to receive telephone calls if the intrusion alarm or the fire alarm should be activated. An *emergency measures team* of those employees empowered to coordinate responses to emergencies should be identified in the manual, and the team should meet regularly (at least semiannually) to review the museum's readiness.

It is possible to develop a risk analysis for individual objects, groups of objects, or an entire collection. An arbitrary scale of 1 to 10 for degrees of *criticality* and *vulnerability* may be devised, with "criticality" defined as how important the object is to the museum and "vulnerability" measuring the extent to which it is at risk: Risk = Criticality × Vulnerability.

Thus if a category A object of prime importance to the museum (high criticality) is moved from inside a case to an open exhibit, its risk factor would be greatly increased—so that the chief of security might suggest to the curators or the director that the relocation might be reconsidered.

The museum's security policy should define three levels of security for exhibition galleries:

- *high security*, for exhibitions of highly valuable items, with special provisions, possibly including constant surveillance during open hours;

- *moderate security*, for exhibitions of original works of art, artifacts, specimens, or original archival material, for which the museum's routine security patrols and surveillance should be maintained; and

- *limited security*, for exhibitions that do not contain original works of art, artifacts, specimens, or original archival material—these might be supervised by a person with duties other than those of a guard (such as an educator or even a volunteer) and might be mounted in a corridor or foyer.

Seven levels of security may be distinguished for collection storage rooms, all of which should have two-hour fire protection on all walls and doors:

- Alarmed vaults: with all interior masonry-reinforced walls, ceilings, and floors and heavy metal doors on a combination lock. All visits must be accompanied by authorized staff and recorded. Vaults may be required for gems, stamps, coins, precious metals, jewelry, and other relatively small items of high value.

- High-security collection storage: also with all interior masonry walls, ceilings, and floors, but with steel doors and frames with a minimum six-pin tumbler lock and key control. This would be required for works of art, weapons, furs, and other objects of high value.

- Permanent collection storage: the museum's main storage rooms, of solid construction with solid doors under key control, required for the main body of the museum's permanent collection. Storage should be organized by medium to facilitate specific environmental control set points; that is, separate storage rooms for metals, textiles, costumes, and works on paper, and separate rooms for painting racks, ceramics, glass, bronze, and so on.

- Temporary exhibition storage: solid walls and doors under key control in a nonpublic area adjacent to the crating/uncrating area, required for temporary loans to the museum or other works of art, artifacts, specimens, or archival materials in transit. This area must have conditions approximating those of the permanent collection storage because it is likely to be visited by couriers accompanying loans from other museums.

- Storage cabinets: these may be located in nonpublic areas or under or above exhibit cases in the galleries. Key control is critical, and objects stored should not be of high value.

- Offsite storage: key control, alarm response, and patrols of these areas present particular challenges and should be appropriate for the nature of the collections in such storage. Often required for larger items, such as vehicles or military equipment. An environmentally controlled van may be needed if there is to be frequent movement of objects in the collection to and from offsite storage.

- Hazardous materials storage: nonflammable and fire-retardant materials (at least a lockable metal cabinet with key control) should be used to store hazardous materials used in the museum (such as some conservation laboratory supplies). Occasionally some collection materials are themselves hazardous, such as certain types of photographic negatives in archival collections, and so require the same conditions.

In considering security planning for the museum site and building as a whole, it is useful to think of it as a series of concentric circles of protection, with the collection at the center and the following layers of protection, from the outside inward:

- *Museum grounds*: Landscaping can enhance security by eliminating trees overhanging or shrubbery near buildings. Parking areas should be separated from the building by an access area subject to surveillance. Exterior lighting is an important consideration. Closed-circuit television (CCTV) systems should be in operation here, as well as inside the building.

- *Building fabric*: Walls and roofing materials should resist intrusion; fire ratings should in general meet building code requirements; walls surrounding collection zones should be at least two hours. Doors and door frames are a particular concern, with fire rating required to be equal to the walls and with a solid core; doors in historic structures may require discreet reinforcement. Hinges should be interior, secured by nonremovable pins. Exterior openings should be protected with magnetic switches and glass breakage detectors, with doors secured by six-pin tumbler deadbolt locks with a minimum throw of 1 inch (25 mm). Windows, especially ground floor windows, present a major challenge: interior blocks (not visible on the exterior), bars, or shutters that descend over the openings when the museum is closed may all be considered. Roofs should be examined carefully because entry is very often gained through skylights or service doors there. Basement or half-basement windows or doors must also be reinforced.

- *Perimeter alarms*: Intrusion alarms should be installed at all entrances and on all windows, including any skylights or other roof access points, with direct telephone connection via dedicated lines to either a police station or the security company, whose response to an alarm should be detailed in the emergency procedures manual. A verified passive infrared detector system should extend to all interior spaces, with the same telephone connections. The CCTV system should utilize *close coupled discharge* color cameras, which should be positioned to record the faces of persons both entering and exiting the building at all points; computer software programs are available that combine CCTV cameras with computerized plans of the building so that security personnel observing them can actively select or record images of interest and store them in computer memory. Pressure alarms on the roof should also be provided, especially in buildings where the architect has made the roof publicly accessible at some points.

- *Security stations*: Many museums have two security stations, where guards operate and observe CCTV systems and monitor alarms. One is usually visible to entering visitors, providing access for guards (or warders in the United Kingdom) to intercept anyone attempting to enter or leave. The other is usually adjacent to the loading bay and the shipping and receiving door, with control over the personnel door through which all delivery personnel must approach the museum; CCTV and a sound system should be provided at this door so that guards may interrogate delivery personnel before allowing them access even to the controlled area within the personnel door. The personnel door should lead only to a foyer, from which further ingress into the museum is also controlled by the guard within the protected security station. This personnel door for delivery personnel may also function as the staff entrance; if not, a similar arrangement must be provided at the staff entrance. Some staff must enter before opening hours, while others leave after public hours, in both cases presenting some risk, unless their entry and exit is via such a security station.

- *Guards*: This force makes up the largest single group of employees in many museums. They are also the people with whom the public has the most frequent and sustained contact. It is therefore crucial that they be well trained and well motivated, especially because they are seldom well paid. They are traditionally uniformed, although this need not be paramilitary but can be simply an official but not unfriendly jacket and pants or skirt.

Attempts to mix education or interpretation functions with security have generally not been successful: guards must focus their attention on security. But they should be trained in the nature and value of the collection and in museum visitor service policy.

Security guards' operations manuals should include:

- their postings schedule;

- routines for opening and closing the museum to the public;

- after-hours patrol practices (possibly with punch clocks at various points within the museum);

- instructions for handling deliveries and other property control procedures;

- key control measures, today usually referring to control of access cards;

- locking and lock-checking routines;

- exhibition gallery surveillance requirements;

- crowd control measures;

- instructions on maintaining security during construction or exhibition replacement;

- instructions for monitoring building systems during nonpublic hours; and

- emergency measures procedures for all risks.

Procedures for removing objects from exhibitions and the use of a card notifying the public that an object has been temporarily removed should be controlled and recorded. Curatorial and conservation personnel must maintain close communication with security officers each time an object is removed from or added into a display. Especially when new permanent collection exhibitions are being planned, security officers should be notified, consulted, and given an opportunity to comment on designs from a security standpoint. Some years ago in the Australian Museum in Sydney a security guard participating in a planning meeting for a new permanent collection exhibition pointed out that the design of one gallery would require two surveillance personnel; with a few deft changes in the layout, the exhibition designer cheerfully reorganized the vitrines so that only one surveillance guard would be needed—thereby saving the museum thousands of dollars over the years that the exhibition has subsequently been on view.

An important management principle is a determination to consider security guards as members of the museum staff who can in some cases develop into other positions, rather than isolating them from other functions. This approach leads to security personnel who are likely to be far more involved in and aware of customer care as well as security issues. Requiring higher educational qualifications (and compensating accordingly), providing training, and offering personal development opportunities are all well-advised policies for encouraging a security guard staff to be engaged with the museum, its visitors, and its collections. The opposite but lamentably common approach of subcontracting these functions to an outside professional security company with little or no interest in the content of the museum is not recommended.

- *Interior alarms*: The system should include alarms to alert security personnel if visitors approach exhibits too closely, as well as intrusion alarms that activate to any movement after hours, connected to the police station or security company in the same way as the perimeter alarms.

- *Display cases*: Case design is an issue not only for the exhibition designer, the conservator, and the curators but also for the chief of security, who should be consulted when display cases are being planned. Their location should be examined to ensure that they do not block emergency escape routes and that they do not offer too easy an exit for a smash-and-grab thief. Proximity to fire exit doors is a serious concern. Polycarbonate glass or plastic should be used and can be laminated to include clear ultraviolet light filters. Small, freestanding cases should be avoided; by preference display cases should be substantial and well anchored to the floor or wall, and their locks should be tamper proof. Sliding glass panels are ill advised because they are difficult to protect from intrusion; lockable access panels should be hinged, preferably horizontally, with nonremovable pins. Corners and joints should be tight. Display materials, in cases or without, should be fire resistant; the security department (as well as conservators) should routinely test any new materials proposed. Works of art, artifacts, or specimens should be discreetly but securely fastened within the case; the Asian Art Museum of San Francisco has gone much further in developing support systems to protect its collections from earthquake, both in display cases and in storage.

- *Security screws*: Pictures are sometimes suspended by chains or rods from hanging rails, with the security concern being to anchor both the chain or rod and the point of attachment of the picture to the chain or rod. Far preferable—and often required by lenders—are security screws, which pin a "fishplate" to the wall behind the picture and to its stretcher (rather than the frame). Security screws can be turned only by specially fitted screwdrivers, more complex than the usual slots or squares. Unfortunately, the best equipped of thieves stock a wide selection of security screwdrivers, so the security screw is not foolproof, but it is a substantial deterrent because circumventing a security screw takes a considerable period of time unobserved.

Three "concentric circles" form three levels of security for the building as a whole, which incorporate the security levels described previously for exhibition galleries and collection storage:

- Outer Level 1: comprising the perimeter, exterior lighting, locks, the intrusion alarm system, and interior space surveillance of public zones A and B, most of which is inactive during public hours and in use only when the museum is closed;

- Median Level 2: comprising the nonpublic, noncollection zone D and some nonpublic collection work areas (zone C), which should always be alarmed when the museum is closed and may be alarmed during public but nonworking hours;

- Inner Level 3: comprising nonpublic collection zone C areas, such as collection storage rooms, which are always protected by alarms that can be deactivated only by authorized personnel or on their instruction. Security personnel ordinarily should control access to these spaces and maintain a log of all entrances and exits to these rooms.

Fire safety presents another range of concerns that must be addressed by the museum's security policy. The world over, fire presents the most serious threat to museums, not only in those housed in historic wooden structures but in many more recent structures as well. Although theft or vandalism may remove or damage specific items, fire can ravage whole collections and may destroy them completely.

Smoke detectors are the preferred means of detection of fire, except in kitchens where heat detectors should be used. Ionization, photoelectric, or projected beam photoelectric smoke detectors may be used.

Sprinklers used to be resisted by museum managers due to the risk of water damage, but widespread experience with fire response times, along with technical advances in sprinkler design, have rendered such fears outmoded, especially when compared with the very real destruction that even a few seconds' fire can cause. Individual-action on-off sprinkler heads (that turn off when the heat level drops), with copper, thermoplastic, or internally galvanized iron pipes and water cleaned to potable or boiler water standards, should be specified. There are differing opinions on the potential deployment of two stage "preaction"-type sprinkler systems—some museum operators find them acceptable when properly installed and maintained, while still other operators may find them problematic due to the delayed reaction time and the possible risk of corrosion products being spewed out with the water when activated; however, some lenders may not allow their objects to be displayed under water in pipes, so that if wet pipe sprinklers are used (with conservator-approved specifications), a supervised valve may be needed on the pipe serving the temporary exhibition gallery so that the pipes may be drained during the period of the loan if that is allowed by local fire officials. Mist sprinklers are now being authorized for heritage buildings (such as those of the State of New York) and offer a positive alternative because their fine mist suppresses flames yet does not have the negative effects of a deluge.

Halon systems and halon fire extinguishers are no longer legal in many jurisdictions for environmental and life safety reasons. The best remaining options for fire extinguishers appear to be a combination of pressurized water (for nonelectrical fires) and CO_2. All staff should be regularly (at least annually) tested in their ability to utilize the museum's fire extinguishers, and the tags signifying that extinguishers have been successfully tested should be examined regularly (at least quarterly) for the dated initials of authorized inspectors.

Museum facility planning should include provision for *firewalls* (two hours for collection zones, to code elsewhere), doors to match these *fire ratings*, and *fire compartmentalization*, especially in collection storage. This means that large storage rooms should be compartmentalized by firewalls at regular intervals rather than designed as one continuous area—a practice that may facilitate provision of separate storage rooms for each medium, with environmental control set points adjusted accordingly. Atriums and stairwells are danger areas, especially where they must be retained as an authentic feature of a historic building; they usually require enclosure on the landings, with fire doors for access. Renovation projects should be utilized by the chief of security as opportunities for provision of additional fire walls or doors, and museum facilities planners should include security consultation as part of the planning process.

There is an inherent conflict between two aspects of security—the desire to control egress from an area and the need to provide fire or other emergency exits. The latter requirement usually dictates panic hardware ("break bars") on fire doors that must allow the user to access the outdoors directly. Yet these fire exits may provide a thief a convenient exit from a gallery, sometimes directly to a parking lot. All fire exits should be audibly alarmed, and in some jurisdictions delays of some seconds are permitted on lower-level access doors allowing egress from fire escape stairwells. The chief of security needs to meet with fire and police officials and to balance fire safety requirements against the museum's concern to prevent theft.

Finally, it should be noted that good security depends on good housekeeping. Good cleaning and maintenance procedures, good signage (including "No Smoking" and a discreet but firm "Do Not Touch" for open exhibits), sound preventive conservation practices, and an alert and informed staff of guards will contribute to both the appearance and the reality of improved security for the collection and enhanced safety for visitors.

GLOSSARY OF FREQUENTLY USED TERMS IN MUSEUM MANAGEMENT

Accessibility: site, facility, work environments, services, or programs that are easy to approach, enter, operate, participate in, and use safely and with dignity by all.

Acquisition fund: the amount allocated for purchasing objects for the collection, and in some cases for the expenses associated with acquisition as well.

Acquisition methods: procedures that a museum follows to acquire artifacts by, for example, gifts, bequests, purchases, fieldwork, deposits from other museums, and acceptance of acquisitions from government programs or agencies responsible for cultural property protection.

Acquisitions committee: a group of trustees delegated by a museum's board to consider issues of collection policy and collection development strategy, as well as recommendations for additions to the collections (and deaccessioning), which should come only from the relevant curators.

Advisory board: a nongoverning entity usually appointed to represent the public interest and specialist expertise to make recommendations on policy matters to the museum's governing authority.

Aesthetic display: a mode of exhibition of works of art, specimens, or artifacts to inspire affective contemplation of museum objects for their beauty or style.

AI: abbreviation for artificial intelligence, it is the intelligence of machines or software, as distinct from the intelligence of human beings or animals.

Antiracism: the policy or practice of opposing racism and promoting racial equality.

Appraisals: the process of financial evaluation of objects, works of art, and specimens, conducted by qualified and certified appraisers, not by museum staff.

Architectural documentation or technical brief: an architects and engineers document that provides answers to drawings and specifications.

Arm's length: the metaphorical distance between a museum and the political authority allocating or granting funds to it.

Attendance, revenue, and expense projections: a forecast of all sources of income and all categories of expenditures.

Automation of collection records: the process of transferring manual records (for example, collection records) to computerized form.

AVR: a device used in generators with the purpose of automatically regulating voltage.

Best practice study: comparative analysis of outstanding successes in specific programs or activities in other institutions.

Bid or tender documents: formal issue of detailed technical scope of work for a competitive contract award for construction or fabrication.

BIPOC: acronym for Black, Indigenous, and People of Color.

Board, board of directors: the governing body with ultimate authority to ensure the continuity of the museum in fulfilling its mission including approval and monitoring of policies, long-range planning, and hiring/disciplining the director.

Brief: instructions for the architect or designer from the client or user pertaining to the requirements for space, facilities, or exhibitions.

Budget by objectives: a useful review process in which fluctuations in the current year's proposed allocations are evaluated in relation to the objectives identified in the museum's corporate plan and the outcomes they are intended to achieve.

Budget by program: projection of revenue and expenditures in terms of activities or services to be provided in accordance with the priority given to that activity in the current year's plans.

Budget or annual budget: a plan with money attached; monetary values allocated as the resources needed to attain the objectives that are the quantified short-term applications to the budget year of the museum's longer-range qualitative goals.

Building code: local authority requirements for buildings, including, for example, fire protection, health, safety, and the needs of the physically challenged.

Building management systems (BMS): a control system used to monitor and manage the mechanical, electrical, and electromechanical services in a facility.

Building team: composed of architects, engineers, landscape architects, and other technical specialists needed, along with the contractor and the construction manager, who report to the museum building project in a capital project with the duties of meeting the requirements of the functional program with technical drawings and specifications and with the actual construction of the building.

Business planning: the process of setting a museum's objectives and strategies in the context of the financial requirements to achieve them.

Capital budget (or funds): financial resources retained for planned development of the museum's site or buildings, such as renovation, relocation, new construction, or exhibition renewal.

Capital cost projections: the amount of money needed to upgrade or build the requisite space, to provide furnishings and equipment, or to build the planned exhibits.

Capital costs: the costs of acquiring a site and building or renovating a facility or exhibit.

Case statement: a document that articulates the rationale for donating funds for a particular project or for the continuation of the programs to be funded.

Cataloging: curatorial recording of works of art, artifacts, or specimens (more extensive than registration), aiming to record a full sense of each object's significance in relation to other objects in the collection, in other collections, and in the world at large.

Change order: a contract document issued by the client to the contractor authorizing an alteration in the original design or specifications of a building or exhibition under construction or installation.

Citizen science: the practice of public participation and collaboration in scientific research to increase scientific knowledge.

Civil society organizations: nonstate, not-for-profit, voluntary entities that are separate from government and corporations; many museums are civil society institutions or managed by a civil society organization.

Code of ethics: a set of principles affecting museum trustees and staff intended to avoid conflicts of interest and to respect relevant international and national professional standards that inform museum work and practice so as to maintain integrity and warrant public trust.

Collection: tangible natural or cultural (human-made) object(s) and/or intellectual property and intangible property directly owned by the museum and preserved as a public trust.

Collection analysis: quantitative and qualitative study of the contents of a museum collection in meaningful groups or classifications, and of the spatial and facilities requirements of the collection, including projection and provision for its future growth over a stated time period and for its security, documentation, and preservation.

Collection development strategy: the projection of both qualitative and quantitative growth of the collection.

Collection inventory: a list of objects that museums have brought into their collections, either permanently or temporarily.

Collection policy or collection management policy: the museum's fundamental document governing the scope and limitations of its intended collection, together with standards for its acquisition, documentation, preservation, security, and management.

Collective bargaining agreements: a set of principles, policies, and practices affecting the working conditions of personnel in unionized museums where the staff are unionized, approved by both the union and the museum.

Colonialism: the policy or practice of acquiring full or partial political control over another country or region or people, occupying, dominating, and exploiting them.

Communication audit: the process whereby the communications of an organization are analyzed by an internal or external consultant with a view to increasing efficiency and effectiveness.

Communication policy: the qualitative goals for such museum functions as the interpretation of the collection, exhibitions, wayfinding, graphics, Internet and Web communications, marketing, and media.

Competitive bidding: comparison of tenders submitted by contractors for work specified, the tender selected usually being the lowest in other sectors, but not always in the museum field due to the need for museum standards of quality.

Condition report: a document prepared by a conservator to record the state of a work of art, artifact, or specimen at the time of the report.

Connoisseurship: intimate knowledge rooted in aesthetic judgment and an acquired ability to perceive, to make distinctions, and above all to make judgments about the authenticity and relevance of works of art, artifacts, or specimens.

Conservation: the long-term preservation of artistic, historic, and cultural materials guided by a code of ethics intended to protect the integrity and authenticity of works of art and delay deterioration.

Conservation policy: the long-range qualitative standards for this endeavor, particularly with regard to preventive conservation measures.

Conservation research: a particularly important aspect of museum operations, whether it is directed at the testing of new materials proposed for display, at contemporary conservation and restoration techniques, or at investigation of the materials and methods of manufacture of the artifacts or works of art in the collection.

Conservation treatment plan: a detailed proposal for intervention in the condition of a work of art, artifact, or specimen aimed at enhancing its preservation through reversible procedures.

Contemplative mode: a type of presentation most commonly used in art galleries (but also found in other museums) in which works of art, artifacts, or specimens are presented in an aesthetic mode enhancing the visitors' affective experience or aesthetic appreciation of them.

Contextual, thematic, or didactic display: a mode of presentation in which artifacts, specimens, or works of art are placed in context so that their significance may be better understood; a "teaching" approach based on facts.

Contractor: individual or company who undertakes to fulfill defined functions in a defined period of time.

Contributed revenue: income from financial gifts, sponsorship, foundation or private sector grants, bequests, and donations. Some museums also include public sector or government funding in this category.

Control: a function of management, monitoring budgets, and scheduling to ensure that resources of time and money are utilized in accordance with allocations.

Corporate plan (or business plan): a document focusing all museum functions toward fulfillment of the museum's mission and goals within a specific planning period and financial framework.

Cost consultant: a professional specializing in the estimation of quantitative requirements to achieve qualitative goals, who therefore projects capital and occupancy cost estimates for buildings, systems, facilities, and functions.

Cost-effectiveness: a measure of the qualitative and quantitative extent to which the museum's expenditures achieve the intended result.

COVID-19 (pandemic): a global outbreak of coronavirus, an infectious disease caused by the severe acute respiratory syndrome coronavirus 2 (SARS-CoV-2) virus, as first detected in the year 2019.

Creative economy: the economic ecosystem of for-profit and not-for-profit industries that are based in knowledge work; for example, artists, educators, entrepreneurs, designers, and knowledge-based professions such as health care, finance, law, engineering, research, technology, and communications.

Criticality: correlation of the probability of a security risk and the degree of its impact (vulnerability), used to determine priorities among security requirements.

Cultural competency: a process of lifelong learning that results in knowledge, skills, behaviors, and attitudes that allow individuals to work effectively with others from different cultural backgrounds.

Cultural heritage: includes artifacts, monuments, a group of buildings and sites, museums that have a diversity of values including symbolic, historic, artistic, aesthetic, ethnological or anthropological, scientific, and social significance. It includes tangible heritage (movable, immobile, and underwater), intangible cultural heritage (ICH) embedded into cultural, and natural heritage artifacts, sites, or monuments.

Cultural preservation: keeping the artifacts and traditions of a community intact against factors trying to change them or wear them away.

Cultural tourism: pleasure travel motivated by cultural explorations such as visual performing arts, design, engineering, heritage, festivals, experiencing ways of life, sites, and monuments.

Curator: oversees collection care and development in a museum or manages a museum's exhibits.

Deaccessioning: a highly regulated process, guided by policy, by which an accessioned tangible or intangible object is removed from a museum collection.

DEAI: the acronym for diversity, equity, access, and inclusion, a key element in museum policies through all their functions with reference to staff, governance, audiences, and content.

Decolonization: in museums, decolonization refers to the process of deconstructing the ideologies of the superiority and privilege of the colonial thought and approaches in all aspects of a museum's functions, policies, and procedures.

Defense: a countermeasure identified in the museum's security policy that should be detailed in the emergency procedures manual for the appropriate response by staff in the event of a threat.

Delay: a countermeasure identified in the museum's security policy to retard progress of a threat.

Design concept: the initial drawings of a building or exhibition, which are generally based on a "brief."

Design day: a day of good (but not peak) attendance for which space and facilities are to be provided.

Design development: the stage in exhibition or building design in which the design concept is elaborated into detailed drawings, sometimes called information drawings (see also schematic design).

Design team: the group of practicing professionals who plan the disposition of spaces, materials, and facilities of a museum building or exhibition based on the approved brief or program.

Design year: the year for which a long-range plan, such as a master plan or a collection development strategy, is to provide—usually about ten to twenty years in the future.

Detection: countermeasures identified in the museum's security policy to determine whether and when threats occur, including surveillance by warders or guards, intrusion alarms, smoke detectors, display case alarms, and closed-circuit television.

Deterrence: a countermeasure identified in the museum's security policy to reduce the likelihood of a threat.

Digital asset management: activities associated with the creation, cataloging, storage, and retrieval of digital records and digitized assets.

Digital strategy: the vision, goals, and objectives that guide a museum's deployment of digital technologies and human organization.

Digitization of information: the process of converting data, records, documentation, content, and physical assets into digital formats.

Direct digital control (DDC): computer-operated electronic control system.

Display collections: assets that the museum owns for the purpose of display in exhibitions.

Display densities: the number of museum objects being displayed in specified surface units such as items per square meter or items per square foot.

Docents: individuals, frequently volunteers, who conduct approved guided tours in the museum.

Documentation procedures: an evolving series of clear instructions that standardize the research, recording, safekeeping, and use of information about museum collections.

Donation: a gift or bequest of artifacts, specimens, or works of art and/or of funds in support of the museum's mission.

Donation in kind: provision of goods (other than collections) and/or services in support of the museum's mission.

Earned revenue: museum's capacity to generate revenue from its operations such as admissions, retail, food services, and activities.

Education program: all those activities conducted by museum staff and volunteers with the goal of formal or informal learning.

Effectiveness: the qualitative measure of the museum's efforts of all kinds to achieve the intended result.

Efficiency: the quantitative measure of the museum's efforts to achieve intended results relative to the effort required to achieve it in time, money, space, or equipment.

Emergency procedure manual: a step-by-step guide to prepare for and respond to emergencies such as fire, flood, accident, extreme weather, and violence.

Employee development programs: training and other activities provided by the museum to assist staff in expanding their capacities based on their interests and goals.

Endowment fund: an investment fund of which a portion of the interest may be used to support operations (unrestricted fund) or must be used for designated purposes such as acquisitions, exhibitions, and lectures (restricted funds).

Ethnographic museums: those museums that conserve, display, and contextualize items relevant to the field of ethnography, the systematic study of people and cultures.

Eurocentrism: focusing on European culture or history to the exclusion of a wider view of the world; implicitly regarding European culture as preeminent.

Evaluation: qualitative and quantitative measurement of museum programs relative to their objectives.

Exhibition policy: the principal management tool for establishing the goals of the permanent and changing exhibition program including the philosophy of presentation and the number, frequency, size, and scope of changing exhibitions.

Extension: programs that museums offer outside the museum building or site.

External assessment: as part of a strategic planning process, an effort to see the museum as others see it and to learn from this external perspective by such means as visitor surveys; community surveys; workshops; focus groups; and interviews with knowledgeable persons in the field, community leaders, donors, sponsors, and funders as well as frequent museum users and—notably—nonusers.

Facilities programming: a broad planning activity usually undertaken by a specialist consultant to determine the space and facilities required by a museum undergoing new construction, expansion, or alteration, including the design and performance criteria of those facilities.

Facility planning strategy: a document deducing the space and facilities required for the museum to fulfill its functions at the level of quality expressed in its mission and foundation documents.

Feasibility study: a determination of the viability of establishing a new or expanded institution. In the context of a museum, feasibility does not refer to profitability but rather to identifying a manageable level of financial support from government and private sources to supplement earned income. The objective of a feasibility study should be not only accurate projections of operating revenues and expenses but also the development of ways and means to increase revenues and control operating costs.

Fire compartmentalization: the practice of dividing large spaces (such as a museum storage area) into smaller areas by means of fire walls, in order to contain the spread of fire.

Fire rating: a standardized projection of the time period that a building material or construction can withstand fire without collapsing or allowing the fire to pass through.

Formative evaluation: measures the effectiveness of an exhibition while the exhibition is taking shape (or form) so that the exhibition will communicate accurately and effectively with its visitors.

Foundational statements: basic policy statements that may be part of the museum's enabling legislation and bylaws that communicate the museum's mission, vision, values, and mandate and guide management and board leadership in their decision making.

Functions: the essential activities of a museum—collecting, documentation, conservation, research, display, interpretation, and the administration of these six core activities.

Fund-raising: programs or activities designed to stimulate contributed revenue.

Funding strategy: the plan of action to meet the museum's capital and operating requirements from public, private, and self-generated sources.

Goals: the long-range qualitative standards of program fulfillment or achievement toward which the museum is striving, usually articulated in a strategic plan.

Governance: the effective ownership of the museum or that organization to which the duties of governance are delegated. The governing body delegates management of the museum to the director and professional staff.

Grants: operating or project grants are nonrepayable funds or goods that provide financial assistance to museums.

Green economy: an economic system or sector based on or guided by environmentalist principles.

Green strategies: plans for construction and operation of museums to promote sustainable environments and achieve energy savings.

Grievance procedure: method of handling staff complaints about working conditions or treatment of personnel, usually defined in a collective bargaining agreement.

Guards: museum workers with the responsibility for security of the collection and safety of all persons in the museum.

Halon system: a method of control of fire by means of expulsion of halon gas from overhead, now illegal in many jurisdictions and being phased out everywhere due to environmental considerations.

Hands-on mode: museum exhibitions that encourage visitors to learn by doing, especially popular in children's museums and science centers.

Hazardous materials storage: a nonflammable, fire-retardant, lockable cabinet with key control to maintain safe conditions for dangerous materials used in museums (such as some conservation and laboratory supplies).

High-security store: a special level of security for museum storage usually required for works of art, weapons, furs, and other objects of high value; generally provided with all interior masonry walls, ceilings, and floors, and with steel doors and frames with a minimum six-pin tumbler lock and key control.

Human resources policy: the strategy that sets out the mission of the museum with respect to those who work in the museum, the benefits that the museum provides staff and staff responsibilities, addressing issues such as statutory regulations, salary, benefits, expense provisions, probationary period, hours of work and overtime, statutory holidays, vacation, sick leave, maternity or paternity leave and leave of absence, training and professional development, intellectual property provisions, grievance and harassment procedures, performance review, and termination conditions.

Hygrothermograph: a device for monitoring and recording fluctuations in relative humidity.

Implicit bias: a form of distortion that occurs unintentionally that nevertheless affects judgments, decisions, and behaviors.

Inclusion: the practice or policy of providing equal access to opportunities and resources for everyone working in or visiting the museum.

Indemnity: a process in lieu of insurance of objects on loan for museum exhibitions, under which the government secures the museum or the lender against any loss.

Information management: activities and programs facilitating the effective production, coordination, storage, retrieval, and dissemination of spoken and written text and images in all formats and from internal or external sources, leading to the more efficient functioning of the museum.

Information policy: a commitment by museum management to standards of documentation of and public access to records about and interpretation of the collection, addressing issues of intellectual property and the museum's participation in databases or other means of dissemination of museum records, including images.

Information system plan: an analysis of all data-related functions, both text and imagery, with recommendations for their efficient integration, compatibility, and future growth.

Institutional context: issues and opportunities related to the museum's relationship with other institutions and agencies, such as all levels of government, educational institutions, other museums, specialist groups, the tourist industry, and potential donors or sponsors in the private sector.

Institutional culture: a social system of meaning and customs and behaviors developed within an institution to assure its adaptation and survival under specific conditions.

Institutional plan: determines or reconsiders the museum's mission, its mandate, and its purpose, as well as its mode of governance and the structures through which it is administered and financed.

Intellectual property: a work that results from creativity of proprietary knowledge, such as a text, design, invention, or artwork, to which the originator(s) has legal ownership, and which requires a license for others to use.

Internal assessment: a step in the strategic planning process consisting of a review of the institution's programs and operations using available documentation and discussions with museum management, staff, volunteers, members, and trustees to develop an analysis of a museum's strengths, weaknesses, opportunities, and challenges.

Interns: recent graduates or students completing education programs who work in museums on a temporary basis at low levels of remuneration to gain training and museum experience.

Interpretation: the many ways that museums communicate with the public about its collections and research activities and their meanings.

Interpretive plan (or exhibition brief): a strategy that articulates the objectives of the museum in interpretation, the quality of the visitor experience intended, and a component-by-component description of the exhibition that lists the communication objectives of each component and the potential means of expression to achieve these objectives, along with diagrams of visitor flow patterns and concept sketches to give the "feel" of the exhibition.

Knowledge management: the system of distributing information to those who need it when they need it and facilitating information sharing and implementation to improve museum performance.

Leadership: the capacity to inspire people with a sense of the museum's mission in order to achieve goals.

Lifecycle costing: estimating how much money is required to pay for an asset over the course of its useful condition.

Line department museum: a museum administered as an integral division or agency of a government ministry, university, or corporation and funded primarily through allocations from the budget of the governing organization.

Lux: the metric unit for measuring the intensity of light (10.76 lux = 1 footcandle).

Lux level: the amount of visible light to which a museum object is being exposed; most accurately calculated as lux hours per annum, being the lux level at any given time multiplied by the number of hours the lights with that lux level are turned on the object.

Management: facilitates decision making throughout the museum and leads staff in fulfilling the museum's mission, goals, and objectives.

Mandate: the range of culture and content for which a museum assumes responsibility, which may be stated in terms of an academic discipline, geographical range, historical period, or specialization.

Market: the actual and potential public for a museum.

Market segmentation: analysis of the potential visitors to a museum into groups sufficiently homogeneous that programs can be effectively planned to meet the interests of each segment and prioritized accordingly.

Microenvironment: a climate-controlled and secure space for the display or storage of artifacts or specimens within a sealed case or frame, used in buildings where such control is not feasible in entire rooms.

Mission statement: an objective, brief, and hopefully inspiring assertion of a museum's long-range reason for existence, which serves as the foundation of all policy development.

Multimedia: the use of multiple methods of communication in one coordinated exhibit apparatus to appeal to multiple senses, usually employing computer and/or electronic technology.

Museology: the theory and practice of organizing, arranging, and managing museums.

Museum: a not-for-profit, permanent institution in the service of society that researches, collects, conserves, interprets, and exhibits tangible and intangible heritage. Open to the public, accessible, and inclusive, museums foster diversity and sustainability. They operate and communicate ethically, professionally, and with the participation of communities, offering varied experiences for education, enjoyment, reflection, and knowledge sharing.

Museum planner: a museum professional specializing in the planning of museum space, facilities, functions, services, operations, and/or administration.

Museum planning: the study and practice of facilitating the preservation and interpretation of material culture by ordering all those components that comprise a museum into a constructed or renovated whole that can achieve its functions with optimal efficiency.

Museum project team: the working group of museum personnel in a museum renovation or construction project whose task is to ensure that the museum's requirements are clearly stated in a functional brief or program and that those requirements are met by the architects, engineers, and contractors.

Museums service: an organization of museums and/or a government agency to serve a group of museums.

Nomenclature: a structured and controlled list of terms organized in a classification system to provide the basis for indexing and cataloging collections.

Objectives: short-range, quantified levels of achievement specified in plans and budgets as measures of fulfillment of longer-range qualitative goals.

Object theater: a mode of presentation to visitors in which artifacts, specimens, replicas, or other apparatus may be featured, usually by means of spotlights or other illumination, with a voiceover script and projected imagery interpreting them by relating a thematic storyline in which they appear.

Operating budget: a projection of allocations for the museum's running costs, usually prepared annually.

Operating grant: a grant-aid program that provides contributions to the operating costs of museums.

Operational business plan: a data-driven analysis that estimates the financial implications by considering key metrics such as staffing, operating hours, attendance, revenue, and overhead expenses in fulfilling the mandated museum functions.

Organizational chart: a diagram of an institution's management structure.

Orientation: information provided to welcome visitors to the museum, and the museum's mission and purpose as well as wayfinding—where they are, what services are available and where, in what languages service is provided, how to get help, what there is to see and do, and how to find it.

Perimeter alarm: an intrusion alarm that should be installed at all entrances and on all windows, including any skylights or other roof access points, preferably with direct telephone connection via dedicated lines to a police station or security company.

Permanent collection storage: the museum's main onsite or offsite storage, of solid construction with doors under key control, high security required for the main body of the museum's permanent collection.

Picture (or art) rental: a service to visitors of providing works of art for monthly hire to homes or offices, sometimes restricted to museum members only.

Planned giving: donations and bequests scheduled to meet the needs of the donor's estate as well as those of the museum.

Plural sector: composed of associations of people that are owned neither by the state nor by private investors.

Policy: a statement of the museum's commitment to its mission, mandate, and statement of purposes in relation to a particular museum function (such as a collection policy, conservation policy, security policy, exhibition policy, research policy, interpretation policy, and the like), and to the achievement of specific levels of quality in fulfilling this commitment.

Preparator: the trained staff who makes ready museum objects for display or loan and installs, dismounts, and returns them to stores as needed.

Preventative conservation: the applied science of providing an environment that minimizes the deterioration of works of art, artifacts, or specimens.

Private ownership museums: those owned and operated by individuals, foundations, or companies either for a profit or as private charities.

Procedures: the systematic means of accomplishing museum functions and activities in such a way as to achieve the objectives, usually codified and continuously updated in manuals.

Project manager: an individual or company, independent of or on the museum staff, whose function is to bring under a single coordinating authority all those involved in a project's implementation, in order to ensure that the project objectives are achieved and that it is completed on time, within budget, to an agreed level of quality, and with minimal disruption to other functions.

Public access policy: addresses how people can see, use, and reference museum collections, research, and content, gain access to museum buildings and sites, and how many people can engage with the museum.

Public private partnership (PPP): an agreement between a public service institution such as a museum or government organization and a private sector entity, which could be a for-profit corporation or a private nonprofit institution, to undertake a project or development together for mutual benefit.

Public program plan: provides dynamic activities and experiences that deepen the understanding of museum exhibitions and research.

Public trust: responsibility (in some jurisdictions a legal responsibility) for the collective material heritage of others, which is assumed by the governing body of the museum, to care for that heritage not only for the present generation but for their descendants in perpetuity with the same prudence that one would be expected to exercise if the property were one's own.

Racism: discrimination and prejudice toward people based on their race or ethnicity, which in museums may be reflected in exclusionary practices with respect to staffing, public services, collections, and their interpretation.

Recyclability: the process of converting waste materials into new materials and objects.

Redundancy: the capability for building systems to sustain operation despite malfunction or power outage to the regularly operating equipment.

Registration: the process led by registrars of numbering artifacts, specimens, or works of art in a museum collection and recording a range of data about each of them—such as name and function of the object, its artist or maker, source and provenance, place and date of origin, materials, and so on.

Relative humidity (RH): the ratio, expressed as a percentage, of the absolute humidity of sampled air to that of air saturated with water at the same temperature.

Repatriation: the process by which cultural items and human remains are returned to the community of origin, lineal descendants, or the descendant community.

Request for proposals: a formal document inviting companies or individuals to present their understanding of, approach to, and methodology and fees for a defined scope of work.

Request for qualifications: a formal document inviting companies or individuals to present their qualifications and experience relative to a defined scope of work.

Research: academic or applied investigations in disciplines relevant to a museum's collection or public programs.

Restoration: returning a building or artifact as far as possible or as far as desired to an earlier condition or appearance, sometimes (but not always) its original state, through repair, renovation, reconditioning, or other intervention.

Restoration policy: a statement of the museum's philosophical intent in restoring works of art, artifacts, or specimens, specifying standards of quality and levels of responsibility, including requirements for reversible processes and clear directives in regard to manifesting lacunae or wear in the original objects.

Restoration procedures manual: a step-by-step document for the execution of the museum's restoration policy, including a statement of the responsibility of curators or conservators, the role of paid or volunteer workers, and requirement for both written and photographic documentation of all processes.

Risk: the possibility of the occurrence of an event that may adversely affect the normal functions of an institution, which may be measured for a museum by assigning values to the criticality of a loss and the museum's vulnerability to it and multiplying the criticality index by the vulnerability index.

Risk analysis: the calculation of the priority of security needs in terms of the possibility of all threats, the criticality of those threats, and the vulnerability of the institution to them.

Risk management strategy: a plan that identifies threats to the museum and its collection and the measures that the museum takes to meet them.

Room settings: a mode of presentation in which artifacts, works of art, or specimens are grouped as they would have been found in their original setting.

Security: the entire range of activities concerned with the protection of the public, staff, and others in the museum, and especially the protection of the museum and its collections, from all threats to them.

Security policy: includes an ongoing process of recurrent planning and policy formulation and review of procedures manuals to update them to accord with present realities of certain risk analysis and measures to prevent any hazard toward the people and objects involved in its environment.

Self-generated revenue: funds earned by the museum's operations, including admissions, retail sales, catering, memberships, rentals, films, performances, special events, educational programs, publications, media, and contracted services.

Set point: the condition to be attained and maintained by environmental control equipment, such as humidifiers or dehumidifiers.

Snag list: a record of outstanding errors or shortcomings at the conclusion of a project to be remedied by a contractor or fabricator prior to completion.

Social cohesion: refers to the extent of connectedness and solidarity among groups in society.

Soft power: exercising influence through persuasion, attraction, and agenda setting, not by economic or political force. Soft power is often associated with cultural understanding.

Specifications: a detailed statement of work to be done by each contractor, materials to be used, standards to be met, procedures to be followed, matters of jurisdiction between contractors, procedures to resolve jurisdictional disputes, procedures for change orders, and so on, relating to an exhibition or a building project.

Sponsorship: the act of supporting an event, activity, person, or organization financially or through the provision of products or services.

Sprinklers: devices installed in the ceiling that respond to fire with a deluge of water.

Stakeholders: people who identify with or have an interest of any kind in the museum and in its history, location, collections, and stories.

Statement of purpose: a concise identification of the functions of a museum in relation to the objects defined in its mandate.

Strategic directions: in the strategic planning process, meaningful and memorable guidelines indicating the institution's approach or philosophy in resolving the key issues affecting that museum.

Strategic plan: determination of the optimal future for an organization and the changes required to achieve it.

Study collection: a collection acquired for purposes of comparative or analytical research, usually intended for indefinite preservation.

Sustainability: reducing consumption as much as possible; implementing recycling and reusing measures of materials; implementing environmental management systems.

Systematic collection: art, artifacts, or specimens selected to exemplify an entire range of significant types or variants within a collection category.

Task force: a group of individuals, usually from several departments, who cooperate to achieve a common, time-limited aim, such as an exhibition.

Technical program: the plans, drawings, and specifications of the architect and engineers that should meet the requirements of the functional brief or program.

Tender (bid): a proposal to undertake work on contract.

Tender documents: the detailed designs and specifications that are issued to competing contractors and that form the basis of the consequent contract with those who are awarded the contracts to undertake the construction, renovation, fabrication, installation, or other work necessary to complete a museum building or exhibition (see bid documents).

Temporary exhibition policy: guides sources, number, duration, frequency, size, and scope of changing exhibitions.

Temporary exhibition storage: (often called transit store in Britain) solid walls and doors under key control in a nonpublic area adjacent to the crating/uncrating area, required for temporary loans to the museum or other works of art, artifacts, specimens, or archival materials transit.

Terms of reference: a statement of mandate and requirements for a committee, a planning process, a program, or a project.

Thematic (or contextual) display: a mode of exhibition of works of art, specimens, or artifacts arranged to illustrate a theme, subject, or storyline in order to facilitate comprehension of their significance in relation to that theme, often employing graphic or other interpretative devices to place the objects in context for the visitor.

Training and development strategy: a plan agreed between the museum and the individual employee related both to the individual's needs for learning how to do their job to the requisite level of quality and their program of upgrading skills and capabilities for future advancement.

Transit store (or temporary exhibition storage): an area in which works of art, artifacts, or specimens loaned to the museum for temporary exhibitions are to be held, with levels of security approximating those of the permanent collection store, because it is likely to be visited by couriers accompanying loans from other museums and must meet insurance and indemnity requirements.

Trustees: members of the board responsible for the governance of the museum "in trust" for the public.

Trustees' manual: publication providing members of the museum's governing or advisory board with all relevant mission, mandate, and policy statements and the board constitution, as well as a history of the institution, current plans, staff organization charts, budgets and financial reports, board roles and responsibilities, and an outline of the committee structure.

Ultraviolet (UV) light: rays beyond the visible spectrum of light that are the chief cause of color fading and chemical changes due to exposure to light.

Value engineering: reconsidering plans or design for a construction or renovation project in order to reduce capital costs.

Vapor barrier: an impermeable barrier to prevent movement of water vapor into a building.

Visible storage, study storage, or accessible storage: collection objects are grouped by type as they would be in storage, except that they are intended for visual inspection and comparison, allowing the highest level of density and often the highest density of information as well, especially if the objects are keyed to an adjacent computer offering public access to the catalog information about them.

Vision statement: expresses the impact the museum aspires to make on people and the world.

Volunteer: an unpaid museum employee whose rewards are in the form of personal development and social recognition for work done.

Volunteer agreement: a contract between an individual and the museum that sets the terms and conditions of volunteering.

Volunteer manual: a document that links the museum's mission and mandate to the museum's volunteer policy and to practical details pertaining to the daily work of volunteers, including all museum policies and procedures relevant to the volunteers' area of work.

Vulnerability: the extent to which a work of art, artifact, specimen, or an entire museum collection is at risk.

Work plan: a statement of objectives and resources together with a budget and a schedule for achieving particular tasks.

Zeitgeist: the defining spirit or mood of a particular time and place, often reflected and interpreted through tangible and intangible museum collections.

Zero-based budgeting: justification of each allocation in relation to the programs it makes possible, as if it had no history.

NOTES

Chapter 1

1. International Council of Museums, *ICOM Prague 2022 Final Report*, 18.
2. "Museum Definition," ICOM, modified August 24, 2022.
3. Julia Halperin and Charlotte Burns, "The Burns Halperin Report: Introducing the 2022 Burns Halperin Report," Art Net News, December 13, 2022, https://news.artnet.com/art-world/letter-from-the-editors-introducing-the-2022-burns-halperin-report-2227445.
4. Henry Mintzberg, *Rebalancing Society: Radical Renewal beyond Left, Right, and Center* (Oakland, CA: Berrett-Koehler Publishers, 2015).
5. Dawn DiPrince, "The Messy and Vulnerable Truth about Trust and Museums," American Alliance of Museums, April 21, 2023, https://www.aam-us.org/2023/04/21/the-messy-and-vulnerable-truth-about-trust-and-museums/.
6. Gail Dexter Lord and Ngaire Blankenberg, *Cities Museums and Soft Power* (Washington DC: American Alliance of Museums Press, 2016).
7. David Graeber and David Wengrow, *The Dawn Of Everything: A New History of Humanity* (New York: Farrar, Straus and Giroux, 2021).
8. Eber Hampton, "Memory Comes before Knowledge: Research May Improve If Researchers Remember Their Motives," *Canadian Journal of Native Education* 21 (1995).
9. Ibid.
10. Tim O'Reilly, "What Is Web 2.0," O'Reilly Network, September 20, 2005, accessed August 6, 2006, http://www.oreillynet.com/pub/a/oreilly/tim/news/2005/09/30/what-is-web-20.html.
11. Jennifer L. Novak-Leonard and Alan S. Brown, *Beyond Attendance: A Multi-Modal Understanding of Arts Participation*, based on the 2008 Survey of Public Participation in the Arts, National Endowment for the Arts.

Chapter 2

1. Stephen E. Weil, *Making Museums Matter* (Washington, DC: Smithsonian Books, 2002).
2. David Gelles, "Smithsonian's Leader Says 'Museums Have a Social Justice Role to Play,'" *New York Times*, July 2, 2020, https://www.nytimes.com/2020/07/02/business/smithsonian-lonnie-bunch-corner-office.html.
3. "The History of the San in Southern Africa Told through Embroidery," Google Arts & Culture, accessed June 7, 2023, https://artsandculture.google.com/story/the-history-of-the-san-in-southern-africa-told-through-embroidery-origins-centre/FAWRd4Yd6lygrQ?hl=en.
4. The team includes Anatomy Museum curator Malcom MacCallum supported by John Harries, Nicole Anderson, and Henrietta Lidchi (all affiliated in various ways with the University of Edinburgh) and Cara Krmpotich, Marcel Robitaille, and Megan Boler (all affiliated in various ways with the University of Toronto).
5. Cara Krmpotich, email communication to the author, February 27, 2023.
6. John Carver, *Boards That Make a Difference: A New Design for Leadership in Nonprofit and Public Organizations*, third edition (San Francisco: Jossey-Bass, 2006).
7. See the museum definition in chapter 1.
8. "Canadian Museum for Human Rights," CMHR, accessed June 6, 2023, https://humanrights.ca/.
9. Canadian Museum of Immigration at Pier 21, accessed June 6, 2023, https://pier21.ca/.
10. "The Lowry," *AJ Architect's Journal*, accessed June 6, 2023, https://www.ajbuildingslibrary.co.uk/projects/display/id/2287.

11. "Cultural Funding," DCLA, NYC.gov, accessed March 31, 2023, https://www.nyc.gov/site/dcla/cultural-funding/cultural-funding.page.

12. "AAM Code of Ethics for Museums," American Alliance of Museums, last modified 2000, https://www.aam-us.org/programs/ethics-standards-and-professional-practices/code-of-ethics-for-museums/.

Chapter 3

1. Gail Dexter Lord and Ngaire Blankenberg, *Cities, Museums and Soft Power* (Washington, DC: AAM Press, 2015).

2. The Austen family were the wealthy Victorian and Edwardian era owners of Spadina house, a grand villa that overlooks the entire city.

3. Frederick Douglass was the great African American abolitionist and orator who was featured at the founding of the Canadian Antislavery Society in Toronto in 1851.

4. The portrait reproduced here in black and white has been accessioned into the collection of the Toronto museums.

5. "About Myseum," Myseum of Toronto, accessed June 20, 2023, https://www.myseumoftoronto.com/about/.

6. Richard Florida, *The Rise of the Creative Class* (Basic Books, 2012), 27.

7. Dexter Lord and Blankenberg, *Cities, Museums and Soft Power*, 14.

8. "National UF Butterfly Science Curriculum Engages Kids as Scientists," University of Florida, October 1, 2009, https://news.ufl.edu/archive/2009/10/national-uf-butterfly-science-curriculum-engages-kids-as-scientists.html.

9. "Community Engagement Programs," Perot Museum, accessed June 26, 2023, https://www.perotmuseum.org/events/children-and-families/tech-truck/.

10. "Meet the Whynauts," Perot Museum, accessed June 26, 2023, https://www.perotmuseum.org/events/children-and-families/whynauts/.

11. "Get in the Scrap!" The National WWII Museum New Orleans, accessed June 26, 2023, https://getinthescrap.org/.

12. https://www.instituteforlearninginnovation.org/project/science-museum-futures/.

13. "Museum International," ICOM, Taylor & Francis Online, accessed August 2023, https://www.tandfonline.com/journals/rmil20.

14. "History," Association of African American Museums, accessed July 13, 2023, https://blackmuseums.org/history-2/#:~:text=The%20Association%20has%20a%20longstanding,rallying%20around%20this%20worthy%20cause.

15. "About Us," International Coalition of Sites of Conscience, accessed June 26, 2023, https://www.sitesofconscience.org/about-us/.

16. Simon, "How Many Museums Are There in the World?" Arna Bontemps Museum, March 6, 2023, https://www.arnabontempsmuseum.com/how-many-museums-are-there-in-the-world/.

17. José Mariano Gago was Minister of Science and Technology in the XIII Constitutional Government (1995-1999) and the XIV Constitutional Government (1999-2002) and Minister of Science, Technology, and Higher Education in the XVII Constitutional Government (2005-2009) and in the XVIII Constitutional Government (2009-2011).

18. https://www.cienciaviva.pt/en/ciencia-viva-centres-network/rules.

19. C. Aaron Price and Lauren Applebaum, "Measuring a Sense of Belonging at Museums and Cultural Centers," *Curator The Museum Journal* 65, no. 1 (December 2021), https://doi.org/10.1111/cura.12454.

Chapter 4

1. "The Story of Owariya," Hoke-Owariya, last modified 2023, https://honke-owariya.co.jp/en/the-story-of-owariya/.

2. "Masterpieces@Home—An Augmented Reality App," The National Gallery UK, accessed June 16, 2023, https://www.nationalgallery.org.uk/national-gallery-x/masterpieces-home.

3. Stephen Fortune, "The Arts Organization as System: An Interview with Paul Bennum," *Digital R&D Fund for the Arts*, last modified June 26, 2013, accessed October 7, 2016.

4. Shimon Attie, Rome, projected image on a brick wall. Photo courtesy of the artist and Jack Shainman Gallery, New York.

Chapter 5

1. Maria Piacente, *Manual of Museum Exhibitions*, third edition (Lanham, MD: Rowman & Littlefield Publishers, 2022).
2. Barry Lord, *Manual of Museum Exhibitions* (Lanham, MD: Rowman & Littlefield, 2014).
3. AAM, "Museums Losing Millions, Job Losses Mount as COVID-19 Cases Surge," *American Alliance of Museums*, November 17, 2020, https://www.aam-us.org/2020/11/17/museums-losing-millions-job-losses -mount-as-covid-19-cases-surge/.
4. UNESCO, *UNESCO Report: Museums around the World in the Face of COVID-19* (UNESCO, 2021), https://unesdoc.unesco.org/ark:/48223/pf0000376729_eng.
5. National Centre for Truth and Reconciliation, "Truth and Reconciliation Commission Reports," December 2015, https://nctr.ca/records/reports/#trc-reports.
6. Charlie Wall-Andrews and Owais Lightwala, "Canada's Largest Arts Organizations Fail at Leadership Diversity," *Globe and Mail*, November 17, 2022.
7. Zachary Small, "U.S. Museums See Rise in Unions Even as Labor Movement Slumps," *New York Times*, February 21, 2022, https://www.nytimes.com/2022/02/21/arts/design/museums-unions-labor.html.
8. Small, "U.S. Museums See Rise in Unions Even as Labor Movement Slumps."

Chapter 6

1. Gail Lord and Kate Markert, *The Manual of Strategic Planning for Cultural Organizations: A Guide for Museums, Performing Arts, Science Centers, Public Gardens, Heritage Sites, Libraries, Archives and Zoos* (Lanham, MD: Rowman & Littlefield, 2017).
2. Barry Lord et al., *Manual of Museum Planning: Sustainable Space, Facilities, and Operations* (AltaMira Press, 2012).
3. "Indigenous Ways and Decolonization: Indigenous Art at the National Gallery of Canada Includes Works from Indigenous Peoples across Canada and Around the Globe," National Gallery of Canada, accessed July 13, 2023, https://www.gallery.ca/collection/collecting-areas/indigenous-ways-and-decolonization.
4. "Sakahàn: International Indigenous Art," The National Gallery of Canada (Ottawa, Ontario), last modified May 15, 2013, https://www.gallery.ca/for-professionals/media/press-releases/sakahan-international -indigenous-art-0.
5. Josee Drouin-Brisebois, Greg A. Hill, and Andrea Kunard, *It Is What It Is: Recent Acquisitions of New Canadian Art* (Ottawa: National Gallery of Canada, 2010).
6. Adrienne Huard, "An Indigenous Woman's View of the National Gallery of Canada," *Canadian Art*, September 27, 2017, https://canadianart.ca/reviews/canadian-and-indigenous-galleries/.
7. Barry Lord, Gail Dexter Lord, and John Nicks, *The Cost of Collecting: Collection Management in UK Museums (A Report Commissioned by the Office of Arts & Libraries)* (London: H.M.S.O., 1989).
8. Catherine Eagleton et al., "Turning a Pivot into a 'New Normal'? Online Teaching and Learning with Digitised Collections in Higher Education Contexts," *ICOM Voices* (June 2021).
9. Maria Piacente, *Manual of Museum Exhibitions* (Lanham, MD: Rowman & Littlefield, 2022).
10. American Alliance of Museums, *Museums and Trust* (AAM, 2021), https://www.aam-us.org/wp -content/uploads/2021/09/Museums-and-Trust-2021.pdf.
11. Brad King and Barry Lord, *The Manual of Museum Learning* (Lanham, MD: Rowman & Littlefield, 2015).
12. https://cosi.org/qed-dr-b.
13. https://cosi.org/cosi-connects/drbin3.
14. https://cosi.org/connects/kits/.
15. https://vimeo.com/517208326.
16. https://cosi.org/connects/color-of-science.php.
17. Lee Cheshire, "Louvre Retains Its Place as the Most-Visited Art Museum in the World," *The Art Newspaper*, March 27, 2023.

Chapter 7

1. The Green Museum, *A Primer on Environmental Practice* (Lanham, MD: Rowman & Littlefield, 2013).

2. Environment and Culture Partners (ECP) gathers data and reports study results in the cultural climate space. ECP is a US nonprofit accelerating climate action in the cultural sector by cocreating collaborative work to research and implement climate action for all sizes and types of cultural institutions. www.ecprs.org.

3. At the time of writing, there is no aggregation of sustainability policies in the cultural sector, but one can find museums committed to sustainability at America Is All In and through professional associations serving the field who have signed on to the US Culture Climate Collaboration Initiative. Reach out to neighbor institutions and professional colleagues to begin to build your sustainability network as you build your foundational documents.

4. The museum's website offers clear and accessible guides to green action: https://madisonchildrensmuseum.org/about/green-initiatives/.

5. Barry Lord, Gail Dexter Lord, and John Nicks, *The Cost of Collecting: Collection Management in UK Museums (A Report Commissioned by the Office of Arts & Libraries)* (London: H.M.S.O., 1989).

6. Randy Kennedy, "74 Are Laid Off at Met Museum; More May Follow," *New York Times*, March 12, 2009, https://www.nytimes.com/2009/03/13/arts/design/13metr.html.

7. "Colchester Museums Crowdfunding Success!," Colchester City Council, June 16, 2022, https://www.colchester.gov.uk/info/cbc-article/?catid=latest-news-june-2022&id=KA-04149.

8. Sooyoung Cho and Andreas H. Krasser, "What Makes Us Care? The Impact of Cultural Values, Individual Factors, and Attention to Media Content on Motivation for Ethical Consumerism," *International Social Science Review* 86, no. 1/2 (2011): 3–23, https://www.jstor.org/stable/41887471.

FURTHER READING

American Alliance of Museums. "AAM Code of Ethics for Museums." AAM. Last modified 2000. https://www.aam-us.org/programs/ethics-standards-and-professional-practices/code-of-ethics-for-museums/.

American Alliance of Museums. "TrendsWatch Building the Post-Pandemic World." AAM. Last modified 2023. https://www.aam-us.org/wp-content/uploads/2023/04/TrendsWatch-Building-the-Post-pandemic-World.pdf.

American Alliance of Museums and Wilkening Consulting. *Museums and Trust.* AAM, 2021. https://www.aam-us.org/wp-content/uploads/2021/09/Museums-and-Trust-2021.pdf.

Basu, Paul, and Wayne Modest. *Museums, Heritage and International Development.* London: Routledge, 2015.

Bechtler, Cristina, Dora Imhof, Chris Dercon, Soichiro Fututake, Eli Broad, Bernardo Paz, Dakis Joannou, Phillippe Meaille, Eugenio Lopez, Patrizia Sandretto Re Rebaudengo, Nadia Samdani, and Jochen Zeitz. *The Private Museum of the Future.* Zürich: JRP Ringier Kunstverlag, 2018.

Benjamin, Walter. *The Work of Art in the Age of Mechanical Reproduction.* London: Penguin Books, 1935.

Berg, Maxine, and Pat Hudson. *Slavery, Capitalism and the Industrial Revolution.* Cambridge: Polity Press, 2023.

Betsch Cole, Johnnetta, and Laura L. Lott. *Diversity, Equity, Accessibility, and Inclusion in Museums (American Alliance of Museums).* Lanham, MD: Rowman & Littlefield Publishing, 2019.

Brophy, Sarah S., and Elizabeth Wylie. *The Green Museum: A Primer on Environmental Practice.* Second edition. Lanham, MD: AltaMira Press, 2013.

Bruchac, Margaret. "NAGPRA, Scattered Relics, and Restorative Methodologies." *Museum Anthropology* 33, no. 2 (September 2010): 137–56. https://doi.org/10.1111/j.1548-1379.2010.01092.x.

Canadian Art Museum Directors Organization. *Roles and Responsibilities of Museum Boards of Trustees.* Ottawa: Canadian Museums Association, 2005.

"Canadian Museums Association Deaccessioning Guidelines." Canadian Museums Association. Last modified October 2020. https://www.museums.ca/site/deaccessioning_guidelines.

Carver, John. *Boards That Make a Difference: A New Design for Leadership in Nonprofit and Public Organizations.* Third edition. San Francisco: Jossey-Bass (Wiley & Sons), 2006.

Catlin-Legutko, Cinnamon. *The Inclusive Museum Leader (American Alliance of Museums).* Lanham, MD: Rowman & Littlefield Publishers, 2021.

Cerasoli, Eleonora. "What Does Sustainability Mean for the Art World?" *KeiSei Magazine,* June 27, 2021. https://keiseimagazine.com/what-does-sustainability-mean-for-the-art-world/.

Chambers, Iain, Alessandra De Angelis, Celeste Ianniciello, and Mariangela Orabona. *The Postcolonial Museum: The Arts of Memory and the Pressures of History.* London; New York: Routledge, 2017.

Cheshire, Lee. "Louvre Retains Its Place as the Most-Visited Art Museum in the World." *The Art Newspaper,* March 27, 2023. https://www.theartnewspaper.com/2023/03/27/louvre-retains-its-place-as-the-most-visited-art-museum-in-the-world.

Cheshire, Lee, and José da Silva. "The 100 Most Popular Art Museums in the World—Who Has Recovered and Who Is Still Struggling?" *The Arts Newspaper*, March 27, 2023. https://www.theartnewspaper.com/2023/03/27/the-100-most-popular-art-museums-in-the-worldwho-has-recovered-and-who-is-still-struggling.

Chmelik, Samantha. *Sustainable Revenue for Museums*. Lanham, MD: Rowman & Littlefield, 2019.

Cho, Sooyoung, and Andreas H. Krasser. "What Makes Us Care? The Impact of Cultural Values, Individual Factors, and Attention to Media Content on Motivation for Ethical Consumerism." *International Social Science Review* 86, no. 1/2 (2011): 3–23. http://www.jstor.org/stable/41887471.

"Code of Ethics for Museums." Museums Association. Accessed August 8, 2023. https://www.museumsassociation.org/campaigns/ethics/code-of-ethics/#.

Collison, Jisgang Nika, and Cara Krmpotich. "Saahlinda Naay—Saving Things House: The Haida Gwaii Museum Past, Present and Future." *The Routledge Companion to Indigenous Repatriation*, edited by Cressida Fforde, Tim McKeown, and Honor Keeler, 44–62. London; New York: Routledge, 2020.

Conaty, Gerald. *We Are Coming Home: Repatriation and the Restoration of Blackfoot Cultural Confidence*. Edmonton, AB: Athabasca University Press, 2015.

Coombes, Annie E., and Ruth B. Phillips. *Museum Transformations: Decolonization and Democratization*. Chichester: Wiley-Blackwell, 2020.

Curtis, Neil G. W. "Universal Museums, Museum Objects and Repatriation: The Tangled Stories of Things." *Museum Management and Curatorship* 21, no. 2 (June 2007): 117–27.

Dafoe, Taylor. "Museum Staffs Are Starting to Diversify, Particularly among Leadership Roles, According to a New Survey." *Artnet News*, November 16, 2022. https://news.artnet.com/art-world/museum-staff-diversity-survey-2022-2211671.

Davis, Natalie Zemon. *Trickster Travels*. London: Hill and Wang, 2007.

Davis, Natalie Zemon. *Women on the Margins: Three Seventeenth-Century Lives*. Cambridge, MA; London, England: The Belknap Press of Harvard University Press, 1997.

Davis, Peter. *Ecomuseums: A Sense of Place.* Second edition. London; New York: Continuum International Publishing Group, 2011.

Decter, Avi Y., Marsha L. Semmel, and Ken Yellis. *Change Is Required: Preparing for the Post-Pandemic Museum (American Association for State and Local History)*. Lanham, MD: Rowman & Littlefield Publishers, 2022.

Demos, T. J., Emily Eliza Scott, and Subhankar Banerjee. *The Routledge Companion to Contemporary Art, Visual Culture, and Climate Change*. Milton: Taylor & Francis Group, 2021.

Digital Benin. "Explore Digital Benin." Accessed February 25, 2023. https://digitalbenin.org.

Drouin-Brisebois, Josee, Greg A. Hill, and Andrea Kunard. *It Is What It Is: Recent Acquisitions of New Canadian Art*. Ottawa: National Gallery of Canada, 2010.

Dungca, Nicole, and Claire Healy. "Revealing the Smithsonian's 'Racial Brain Collection.'" *Washington Post*, August 14, 2023. https://www.washingtonpost.com/history/interactive/2023/smithsonian-brains-collection-racial-history-repatriation/.

Eagleton, Catherine, Kamila Oles, Maria Economou, Neil Curtis, Lisa Collinson, and Susannah Waters. "Turning a Pivot into a 'New Normal'? Online Teaching and Learning with Digitized Collections in Higher Education Contexts." *ICOM*, June 29, 2021.

Falconer, Shelley, and Shawna White. *Stones, Bones and Stitches: Storytelling through Inuit Art.* Toronto: Tundra Books, Lord Museum Books, 2007.

Falk, John H., and Lynn D. Dierking. *Learning from Museums*. Second edition. Lanham, MD: Rowman & Littlefield, 2018.

Farago, Jason, Kerry Hannon, James Barron, and Ted Loos. "MUSEUMS: 'Reinventing the Future: As Museums Emerge from a Devastating Pandemic, They Are Seeing Their Art and Their Purpose in a New Light.'" *New York Times*, May 23, 2021.

Fforde, Cressida, C. Timothy McKeown, and Honor Keeler. *The Routledge Companion to Indigenous Repatriation: Return, Reconcile, Renew.* Milton: Routledge, 2020.

Fischer, Daryl, and Laura B. Roberts. *Building Museum Boards.* Third edition. Lanham, MD: Rowman & Littlefield Publishers, 2018.

Florida, Richard. *The Rise of the Creative Class.* New York: Basic Books, 2002.

Fortune, Stephen. "The Arts Organization as System: An Interview with Paul Bennum." Digital *R&D Fund for the Arts*, June 26, 2013.

"The Future of Museum Labor: Exploring the Latest COVID Impact Data." *American Alliance of Museums*, February 17, 2022. https://www.aam-us.org/2022/02/17/the-future-of-museum -labor-exploring-the-latest-covid-impact-data/.

"The Future of Museums Post Covid-19." UNESCO, 2022. https://www.unesco.org/en/articles/ future-museums-post-covid-19.

Garthe, Christopher J. *The Sustainable Museum.* New York: Routledge, 2022.

Gelles, David. "Smithsonian's Leader Says 'Museums Have a Social Justice Role to Play.'" *New York Times*, July 2, 2020. https://www.nytimes.com/2020/07/02/business/smithsonian -lonnie-bunch-corner-office.html.

Genoways, Hugh H., Lynne M. Ireland, and Cinnamon Catlin-Legutko. *Museum Administration 2.0 (American Association for State and Local History).* Lanham, MD: Rowman & Littlefield Publishers, 2016.

Girault, Yves. *Contemporary Museums: Tension between Universalist and Communitarian Approaches.* New York: Wiley-ISTE, 2023.

Glass, Aaron. "Return to Sender: On the Politics of Cultural Property and the Proper Address of Art." *Journal of Material Culture* 9, no. 2 (July 2004): 115–39. https://doi.org/10.1177/ 1359183504044368.

Graeber, David, and David Wengrow. *The Dawn Of Everything: A New History of Humanity.* New York: Farrar, Straus and Giroux, 2021.

Greenblatt, Stephen Jay. *Tyrant: Shakespeare on Politics.* New York: W. W. Norton & Company, 2019.

Grimes, John R. "Why? People, Not Objects, Are the Future." *Muse Magazine* (Canadian Museums Association), March/April 2017. https://www.museums.ca/site/people_not_objects.

Halperin, Julia, and Charlotte Burns. *The Burns Halperin Report: Introducing the 2022 Burns Halperin Report.* Art Net News, 2022. https://news.artnet.com/art-world/letter-from-the-editors -introducing-the-2022-burns-halperin-report-2227445.

Hampton, Eber. "Memory Comes before Knowledge: Research May Improve If Researchers Remember Their Motives." *Canadian Journal of Native Education* 21 (1995): 46–54. https://doi .org/10.14288/cjne.v21i.195782.

Harris, Rodney. *Heritage: Critical Approaches.* London: Routledge, 2013.

Heritopolis: Heritage and the Metropolis—A Global University Consortium (Around-the-World Globinar on Shaping Future Heritage Policies for UNESCO). Mexico: UNESCO, September 2022.

Hicks, Dan. *The Brutish Museums: The Benin Bronzes, Colonial Violence and Cultural Restitution.* London: Pluto Press, 2020.

Hitchens, Christopher. *The Parthenon Marbles: The Case for Reunification.* London: Verso, 2008.

Hossaini, Ali, and Ngaire Blankenberg. *Manual of Digital Museum Planning.* Lanham, MD: Rowman & Littlefield, 2017.

Huard, Adrienne. "An Indigenous Woman's View of the National Gallery of Canada." *Canadian Art*, September 27, 2017. https://canadianart.ca/reviews/canadian-and-indigenous-galleries/.

ICOM. "Museum International." Accessed August 2023. https://www.tandfonline.com/journals/rmil20.

International Council of Museums. *Dictionary of Museology*. Edited by François Mairesse, Yves Bergeron, Bruno Brulon Soares, Peter Davis, John H. Falk, J. Pedro Lorente, Sharon Macdonald, Eiji Mizushima, and Markus Walz. Abingdon, Oxon: Routledge, 2023.

International Council of Museums. "ICOM Code of Ethics for Museums." Code of Ethics. Last modified 2021. https://icom.museum/en/resources/standards-guidelines/code-of-ethics/.

International Council of Museums. *ICOM Prague 2022 Final Report 26th ICOM General Conference 20–28 Aug*. ICOM, 2023. https://icom.museum/wp-content/uploads/2023/06/ICOM2022_FINAL-REPORT_EN.pdf.

International National Trusts Organisation. "Putting the Local into Global Heritage: A User Guide." May 27, 2021. https://www.into.org/putting-the-local-into-global-heritage-a-user-guide/.

Janes, Robert J., and Richard Sandell. *Museum Activism: Museum Meanings*. London: Routledge, 2019.

Jocelyn, Marthe. *A Home for Foundlings*. Toronto: Tundra Books, Lord Museum Books, 2005.

King, Brad, and Barry Lord. *The Manual of Museum Learning*. Second edition. Lanham, MD: Rowman & Littlefield, 2015.

King, Thomas. *The Inconvenient Indian: A Curious Account of Native People in North America*. Toronto: Anchor Canada, 2012.

Lord, Barry. *Art & Energy: How Culture Changes*. Washington, DC: American Alliance of Museums, 2014.

Lord, Barry, and Gail Dexter Lord. *Artists, Patrons, and the Public*. Lanham, MD: AltaMira Press, 2010.

Lord, Barry, and Gail Dexter Lord. *The Manual of Museum Management*. First edition. London: The Stationery Office, 1997.

Lord, Barry, and Gail Dexter Lord. *The Manual of Museum Management*. Second edition. Lanham, MD: AltaMira Press, 2009.

Lord, Barry, Gail Dexter Lord, and Lindsay Martin. *Manual of Museum Planning: Sustainable Space, Facilities, and Operations*. Lanham, MD: AltaMira Press, 2012.

Lord, Barry, Gail Dexter Lord, and John Nicks. *The Cost of Collecting: Collection Management in UK Museums (A Report Commissioned by the Office of Arts & Libraries)*. London: Her Majesty's Stationery Office, 1989. https://collections.britishart.yale.edu/catalog/orbis:889400.

Lord, Gail Dexter. "The Importance of Space and Place." *Curator* 48, no. 1 (2005): 23–26.

Lord, Gail Dexter, and Ngaire Blankenberg. *Cities, Museums and Soft Power*. Washington, DC: American Alliance of Museums Press, 2015.

Lord, Gail Dexter, Guan Qiang, An Laishun, and Javier Jimenez. *Museum Development in China: Understanding the Building Boom*. Lanham, MD: Rowman & Littlefield, 2019.

Lynch, Bernadette. "Reflective Debate, Radical Transparency and Trust in the Museum." *Museum Management and Curatorship* 28, no. 1 (March 2013): 1–13. https://doi.org/10.1080/09647775.2012.754631.

Manjarrez, C., C. Rosenstein, C. Colgan, and E. Pastore. *Exhibiting Public Value: Museum Public Finance in the United States*. Washington, DC: Institute of Museum and Library Services, 2008. https://www.imls.gov/sites/default/files/publications/documents/museumpublicfinance_0.pdf.

Matthews, Maureen. *Naamiwan's Drum: The Story of a Contested Repatriation of Anishinaabe Artefacts*. Toronto: University of Toronto Press, 2016.

Matthews, Maureen, Roger Roulette, and James Brook Wilson. "Meshkwajisewin: Paradigm Shift." *Religions* 12, no. 10 (October 18, 2021): 894. https://doi.org/10.3390/rel12100894.

Merritt, Elizabeth. "The Future of Museum Labor: Exploring the Latest COVID Impact Data." *American Alliance of Museums*, February 17, 2022. https://www.aam-us.org/2022/02/17/the -future-of-museum-labor-exploring-the-latest-covid-impact-data/.

Mintzberg, Henry. *Rebalancing Society: Radical Renewal beyond Left, Right, and Center*. Oakland: Berrett-Koehler Publishers, 2015.

Mishra, Arunima. "Museums in the Middle East Are Thriving. So What's the Big Picture?" *Fast Company Middle East*, November 15, 2022. https://fastcompanyme.com/impact/museums-in -the-middle-east-are-thriving-so-whats-the-big-picture/.

Monkman, Kent. *Shame and Prejudice: A Story of Resilience*. Toronto: Black Dog Press, 2020.

Mousavi, Seyed Sina, Naciye Doratli, Seyed Nima Mousavi, and Fereshte Moradiahari. "Defining Cultural Tourism." *4th International Conference on Advances in Agricultural, Biological & Ecological Sciences*, no. 16 (December 2016): 70–75. https://doi.org/10.15242/iicbe.dir1216411.

Murawski, Mike. *Museums as Agents of Change: A Guide to Becoming a Changemaker (American Alliance of Museums)*. Lanham, MD: Rowman & Littlefield Publishers, 2021.

Museums Association. *Museums Change Lives*. London: Museums Association, 2017. https://www .museumsassociation.org/app/uploads/2020/06/28032017-museums-change-lives-9.pdf.

National Centre for Truth and Reconciliation. *Truth and Reconciliation Commission Reports*. Canada: NCTR, December 2015. https://nctr.ca/records/reports/#trc-reports.

Native American Graves Protection and Repatriation Act Report. Washington, DC: Congress USA, 1990. https://www.congress.gov/bill/101st-congress/house-bill/5237.

NEA Research Report. *A Decade of Arts Engagement: Findings from the Survey of Public Participation in the Arts, 2002–2012*. Washington, DC: NEA, 2015. Accessed 2023. https://www.arts.gov/ sites/default/files/2012-sppa-feb2015.pdf.

Novak-Leonard, Jennifer L., and Alan S. Brown. *Beyond Attendance: A Multi-Modal Understanding of Arts Participation*, based on the 2008 Survey of Public Participation in the Arts, National Endowment for the Arts.

Peers, Laura. "Repatriation: A Gain for Science?" *Anthropology Today* 20, no. 6 (2004): 3–4. http://www.jstor.org/stable/3695256.

Pennings, Mark. "Art Museums and the Global Tourist: Experience Centers in Experience Scapes." *Athens Journal of Tourism* 2, no. 4 (2015): 209–21. https://doi.org/10.30958/ajt.2-4-1.

Piacente, Maria. *Manual of Museum Exhibitions*. Third edition. Lanham, MD: Rowman & Littlefield Publishers, 2022.

Piketty, Thomas. *A Brief History of Equality*. Cambridge, MA: The Belknap Press of Harvard University Press, 2022.

Piketty, Thomas. *Capital in the Twenty-First Century*. Cambridge, MA: The Belknap Press of Harvard University Press, 2017.

Prianti, Desi Dwi, and I Wayan Suyadnya. "Decolonising Museum Practice in a Postcolonial Nation: Museum's Visual Order as the Work of Representation in Constructing Colonial Memory." *Open Cultural Studies* 6, no. 1 (2022): 228–42. https://doi.org/10.1515/culture-2022-0157.

Price, C. Aaron, and Lauren Applebaum. "Measuring a Sense of Belonging at Museums and Cultural Centers." *Curator The Museum Journal* 65, no. 1 (December 2021). https://doi.org/10.1111/ cura.12454.

Prince, Bryan. *I Came as a Stranger: The Underground Railroad*. Toronto: Tundra Books, 2004.

Putnam, Robert D. *Bowling Alone: Revised and Updated: The Collapse and Revival of American Community*. New York: Simon & Schuster, 2000.

Reséndez, Andrés. *The Other Slavery: The Uncovered Story of Indian Enslavement in America*. Boston: Mariner Books, 2016.

Rijksmuseum. *Rijksmuseum: Accessibility without Limits*. Rijksmuseum.

Roppola, Tiina. *Designing for the Museum Visitor Experience*. New York: Routledge, 2014.

Sarr, Felwine, and Bénédicte Savoy. *The Restitution of African Cultural Heritage: Toward a New Relational Ethics*. Translated by Drew S. Burk. Paris: Ministére De La Culture/Université Paris Nanterre, 2018.

Saunders, Doug. *Arrival City: How the Largest Migration in History Is Reshaping Our World*. New York: Vintage Books, 2012.

Scheland, Nora. "Celebrating the Firsts: First Painting by a Native American Artist Acquired by the National Gallery of Art: Copyright." *The Library of Congress*, November 23, 2022. https://blogs.loc.gov/copyright/2022/11/celebrating-the-firsts-first-painting-by-a-native-american-artist-acquired-by-the-national-gallery-of-art/.

Schep, Mark, and Pauline Kintz. *Guiding Is a Profession (The Museum Guide in Art and History Museums)*. Rijksmuseum, Amsterdam: Pictoright, 2017. https://www.lkca.nl/wp-content/uploads/2020/02/guiding-is-a-profession.pdf.

Shannon, Jennifer. "Collections Care Informed by Native American Perspectives: Teaching the Next Generation." *Sage Journals* 13, no. 3–4 (2017): 205–24. https://doi.org/10.1177/155019061701303-4.

Shellman, Cecile. *Effective Diversity, Equity, Accessibility, Inclusion, and Anti-Racism Practices for Museums: From the Inside Out (American Alliance of Museums)*. Lanham, MD: Rowman & Littlefield Publishers, 2022.

Silberberg, Ted. "Cultural Tourism and Business Opportunities for Museums and Heritage Sites." *ELSEVIER* 16, no. 5 (1994): 361–65. https://doi.org/10.1016/0261-5177(95)00039-Q.

Simon, David, Claus-Peter Echter, and Can Emre Memis. *Heritage and the Metropolis: Current Status, Emerging Trends and Contributions to Sustainability*. Heritopolos, 2022.

Simon, Nina. *The Participatory Museum*. Santa Cruz, CA: Museum 2.0, 2010.

Small, Zachary. "Even as NFTs Plummet, Digital Artists Find Museums Are Calling." *New York Times*, October 31, 2022. https://www.nytimes.com/2022/10/31/arts/design/nfts-moma-refik-anadol-digital.html.

Small, Zachary. "There Are Almost Two Dozen Director Roles Vacant in U.S. Museums Right Now. Why Does Nobody Want Them?" *ArtNet News*, November 22, 2021. https://news.artnet.com/art-world/u-s-museums-director-vacancies-2038335.

Small, Zachary. "U.S. Museums See Rise in Unions Even as Labor Movement Slumps." *New York Times*, February 21, 2022. https://www.nytimes.com/2022/02/21/arts/design/museums-unions-labor.html.

Smith, Sarah E. K., and Sascha Priewe. *Museum Diplomacy: How Cultural Institutions Shape Global Engagement*. Lanham, MD: Rowman & Littlefield, 2023.

Smith, Saumarez Charles. *The Art Museum in Modern Times*. New York: Thames & Hudson, 2021.

Solomon, Tessa. "The People and Places That Made a Stage for Indigenous Art in 2022." *ARTnews*, December 30, 2022. https://www.artnews.com/list/art-news/news/indigenous-art-visibility-1234652388/a-landmark-indigenous-lending-collection/.

Strasser, Christian, Irene Preissler, Erwin Uhrmann, Louisa Hutton, Matthias Sauerbruch, Gail Dexter Lord, Adrian Ellis, and Vitus Weh. *World Culture Districts: Spaces of the 21st Century*. Verlag für moderne Kunst, 2022.

Suchan, Laura. *When Disaster Strikes: Lessons Learned (and Survived)*. Oshawa: Muse Magazine (Canadian Museums Association), November/December 2018. https://museums.in1touch.org/site/Muse_Online_novdec_disaster.

Perera, Kamani. "The Role of Museums in Cultural and Heritage Tourism for Sustainable Economy in Developing Countries." Conference: International Conference on Asian Art, Culture and Heritage, ResearchGate, 2013. https://www.researchgate.net/publication/237099471_The_Role_of_Museums_in_Cultural_and_Heritage_Tourism_for_Sustainable_Economy_in_Developing_Countries.

UN. *United Nations Declaration on the Rights of Indigenous Peoples ((UNDRIP): A Manual for National Human Rights Institutions*. United Nations Office of the High Commissioner for Human Rights, 2007. https://www.un.org/development/desa/indigenouspeoples/wp-content/uploads/sites/19/2018/11/UNDRIP_E_web.pdf.

UN. "United Nations Declaration on the Rights of Indigenous Peoples." Accessed February 28, 2023. https://social.desa.un.org/issues/indigenous-peoples/united-nations-declaration-on-the-rights-of-indigenous-peoples.

UNESCO, Ernst & Young, and I. G. Bokova. *Cultural Times: The First Global Map of Cultural and Creative Industries*. International Confederation of Societies of Authors and Composers, 2015. https://unesdoc.unesco.org/ark:/48223/pf0000235710.

Wall-Andrews, Charlie, and Owais Lightwala. "Canada's Largest Arts Organizations Fail at Leadership Diversity." *Globe and Mail*, November 17, 2022. https://www.theglobeandmail.com/arts/art-and-architecture/article-canadas-largest-arts-organizations-fail-at-leadership-diversity/.

Warick, Jason. "Sask. Art Gallery Reviewing 2,000 Pieces Following Return of Stolen Indian Statue." *CBC News*, December 2, 2021. https://www.cbc.ca/news/canada/saskatchewan/art-gallery-reviewing-pieces-after-return-stolen-statue-1.6269603.

Weil, Stephen E. *A Cabinet of Curiosities: Inquiries into Museums and Their Prospects*. Washington, DC: Smithsonian Institution Press, 1995.

Weil, Stephen E. "From Being about Something to Being for Somebody: The Ongoing Transformation of the American Museum." *Daedalus* 128, no. 3 (1999): 229–58. http://www.jstor.org/stable/20027573.

Weil, Stephen E. *Making Museums Matter*. Washington, DC: Smithsonian Books, 2002.

INDEX

employee development programs, 128, 315
endowment fund, 244–45, 254, 256, 315
energy-saving, in buildings, 216, 218–20
engagement, 15–16, 224, 260, 263; audience, 169, 198; public, 14, 102, 198, 258; visitor, 198–201, 256–57
entry documentation, 282
environmental control, 170, 206, 213, 219–20, 284–86; BMS and, 217–18; loans and, 216
environmental display, 165, 175
environmental sustainability, 218; data and, 223, 226, 330n2; policies and, 223–26, 330n3
Environment and Culture Partners (ECP), 69, 330n2
equipment budgets, 170–71
equity, 5, 117, 127, 160–63, 196–97
equity, diversity, and inclusion (EDI). *See* diversity, equity, access, and inclusion
Equity Task Force, of MacKenzie Art Gallery, 10–12
ethics, 10–11, 54, 69–70; code of, 57–58, 311; trustees and, 57, 277
ethnocentrism, 31, 61, 116, 264
ethnographic museums, 66, 315
Etihad Museum, Dubai, *89*
eurocentrism, 200, 315
Europe, 132–33, 194–95, 213, 242; NEMO, 167, 183, *183*
evaluation, 207, 292–93, 295, 300–301, 315; formative, 287, 316; of functions, 31–32; governance and, 76; of grants, 244; visitor, 46–47
exclusion, of people, 61–62, 101
executive role, 55–56, 148, *149*; meetings and, 149–51; planning and, 142–45; policies and, 145–47
exhibition brief, 318. *See also* interpretive plan
exhibition catalogues, 47, 153, 161, 175, 198
exhibition procedures manual, 292
exhibitions, 46, 69, 160, 221–22, 297; blockbuster, 176–77, 251; collection management and, 172, 184; concept plan of, 287–88; curators and, 115, 123, 185; development of, 178, 186–87, *187*, 287, 290; for families, 181–82; labels and, 188–89, 290; policy for, 174, 177, 316; public programs and, 122, 184; research and, 181–83; schedule of, *177*, 289–91; schematic design and, 289; security and, 302; sponsorship and, 55–56, 287; task force for, 122–23, 184–85, 288–92; virtual, 97, 167, 169, 287–92; visitor experience and, 174–78, 186
exit documentation, 282
expansion, of museums, 7–9, 72, 145, 204, 213
expenses, 249–53, *252*; projections of, 145, 310. *See also* costs
experiences, 258–60; negative, 61, 228. *See also* visitor experience

expertise, 77, 87, 96, 123–24, 185
extension, 103, 144, 194–98, 316
external affairs department, 115, 120
external assessment, 143, 316

facilities, 206; of art museums, 215, 232–33; auditorium in, 188, 235–38; programming of, 316; requirements of, 145, 158, 164–66, 204, 210, 212; special events and, 236–37; strategy for, 205–6, 296–97
facility planning, 204, 213, 218; architect and, 210–12; contractors and, 208–9, 214, 217, 220–21; museum planner and, 208–10, *209*, 212, 214, 319; museum shops and, 231; site selection and, 207–8; strategy for, 316
families, *47*, 181–82
feasibility studies, 145, 212, 316
fenestration, 215–16, 285
fiduciary boards, 48–49, 54
financial management, 55–56; expenses and, 249–57, *252*; revenue and, 227–49; risk and, 135
fire, 301; safety and, 306–7
fire compartmentalization, 316; fire walls and, 280, 302, 307
fire rating, 316
fire walls, 280, 302, 307
Florida Museum of Natural History, 67
Floyd, George, 5, 117, 127, 129, 134
focus, 22–25
focus groups, 16, 287
food services, 231–33
formal communication, 150–51
formative evaluation, 287, 316
foundation, of museums, 23, *25*, 66
foundations, 73, 243–44
foundation statements, 20–25, 245, 267–76, 316; branding and, 200; digital change and, 95–96, 107; executive role and, 142; functions and, *26*, 26–32, *28–30*, *32*; policies and, 145–46
France, Louvre, 11, 43, 69, 200, 227, 239–40
free admissions, 43, 72, 78, 101, 228–29, 234–35
free-choice learning, 67–68
functional brief. *See* functional program
functional program, 204–5, 295–300, *298*; for facility planning, 212–13
functional requirements, 210, 280–81, 296
functions, of museums, 5, *114*, 114–16, 254, 316; foundation statements and, *26*, 26–32, *28–30*, *32*; repatriation and, 33–34
funding, 7, 30–31, 44, 73, 83, 223; arm's length museums and, 40; creativity and, 135; endowments and, 244; government, 71–72, 241–43, 255–56; for restoration, 79, 81; site selection and, 207–8; strategy of, 145, 316; taxes and, 242–43

ABOUT THE CONTRIBUTORS

Joy Bailey-Bryant
Photo by author.

Frederic Bertley
Photo by Anna Trankina. Image courtesy of Frederic Bertley.

Dr. Lisa R. Biagas
Image courtesy of the Pennsylvania Academy of the Fine Arts.

Cheryl Blackman
Image courtesy of the City of Toronto.

Annemies Broekgaarden
Photo by Maarten Kools. Image courtesy of Annemies Broekgaarden.

Kathleen Brown
Photo by author.

Karen Carter
Photo by Natalie Asumeng. Image courtesy of Karen Carter.

Muna Faisal Al Gurg
Photo by & courtesy of Dubai Culture & Arts Authority.

Dov Goldstein
Photo by author.

Daniel Hammer
Photo by Keely Merritt. Image courtesy of The Historic New Orleans Collection.

John G. Hampton
Photo by Andrew Parry. Image courtesy of the MacKenzie Art Gallery.

Ali Hossaini
Photo by Leslie Cummins. Image courtesy of Ali Hossaini.

Umbereen Inayet
Photo by Hyghly Alleyne & Eric Black. Image courtesy of Umbereen Inayet.

Sandra Jackson-Dumont
Photo by author.

Javier Jimenez Fernandez-Figares
Photo by Cañadilla Fotógrafos. Image courtesy of Javier Jimenez Fernandez-Figares.

Tim Johnson
Photo by author.

Mary Kershaw
Photo by author.

Judith Koke
Photo by Wendy Woon. Image courtesy of Wendy Woon.

Cara Krmpotich
Photo by Alysse Rich. Image courtesy of Cara Krmpotich.

Sri Anjani Kumar Singh
Photo by author.

Robert LaMarre
Photo by author.

Natalie MacLean
Photo by author.

Marc Mayer
Photo by MIV Photography, 2022. Image courtesy of author.

Gwendolyn Perry Davis
Photo by Maria Ponce. Image courtesy of Gwendolyn Perry Davis.

Terry Simioti Nyambe
Photo by Bernad Gani. Image courtesy of Terry Nyambe.

Sean Stanwick
Photo by author.

Sarah Sutton
Photo by author.

Yvonne Tang
Photo by author.

Rosalia Vargas
Photo by author.

Elizabeth Wylie
Photo by author.

Joy Bailey-Bryant is managing partner and president, Lord Cultural Resources. She is a specialist in civic engagement around arts and culture. A certified interpretive planner and outreach facilitator, Bailey-Bryant works with government, institutional leaders, and developers, in global municipalities like Chicago; New York; Dhaka, Bangladesh; and Dharan, Saudi Arabia to creatively plan cities and bring people to public institutions. Bailey-Bryant has been an integral part of the development of identity museums where people of color are engaged in telling and interpreting their own story. Bailey-Bryant led the teams for planning on remarkable projects like the National Museum of African American History and Culture in Washington, DC, reaching thousands of stakeholders across the country to learn their expectations for the new museum, and the National September 11 Memorial and Museum at the World Trade Center, and directing citywide engagement in locations as large as Dallas and Chicago and small as Decatur, Georgia.

Frederic Bertley, PhD, is the president and CEO of the Center of Science and Industry (COSI). Dr. Bertley, affectionately known as "Dr. B," is a scientist, scholar, immunologist, and educator. His innovation has led to experiences including the COSI Science Festival, the Color of Science™, EiPIC, and COSI STEM kits. Under his leadership, COSI received the prestigious 2023 IMLS National Medal. He graduated from McGill University where he studied physiology, mathematics, and the history of science, and earned a PhD in immunology. Bertley has worked internationally in South America, Africa, Europe, and throughout the Caribbean and is the creative behind the Emmy Award–winning television show *QED with Dr. B* and the animated online series *Dr. B in 3.*

Dr. Lisa R. Biagas is chief human resources officer at the Pennsylvania Academy of the Fine Arts. She holds a doctoral degree in higher education management, an MBA, an MS in organizational dynamics from the University of Pennsylvania, and a BA in psychology from Temple University. As an undergraduate, Dr. Biagas joined the Army ROTC and, as a cadet, successfully completed Army Airborne School basic (military parachutist) training. She spent several years on active duty as an army officer, serving during Desert Storm. Dr. Biagas's doctoral research applied positive psychology principles to presidential leadership. She holds specialty certifications in human resources, leadership, executive coaching, diversity, Title IX, and project management. Her specialty is organizational culture, change, and leadership. In her university appointments she has explored the influence of culture on transformational change. She has led a variety of workshops and retreats and consults with higher education institutions on topics ranging from executive coaching and strategic planning to organization redesign.

Cheryl Blackman is the director of museum and heritage services with the City of Toronto. With ten city-owned and operated historical museums, the city's collection of historical objects, archaeological specimens, and moveable fine art includes forty heritage buildings. Blackman also served as the interim general manager of economic development and culture, where she led efforts to create arts and culture plans and roadmaps for cultural vitality. She is the vice president of the Ontario Museum Association (OMA). She holds a bachelor's of social work (BSW) and a master's of business administration (MBA), is the past president of the Robert McLaughlin Gallery Board, and is a board member of the Gardiner Museum.

Annemies Broekgaarden is the head of education at the Rijksmuseum, Amsterdam, the Netherlands. After a career in marketing and communications, Broekgaarden set up the Dick Bruna House Foundation, creating a home for the collection of renowned Dutch artist Dick Bruna. She served as the head of the Tropenmuseum Junior, and her skills in communications, management, cultural anthropology, and education eventually led her to the Rijksmuseum, where in 2008 she began formulating the museum's education policy and programming for its reopening in 2013.

Since 2016, her responsibilities have included academic program, digital learning, accessibility, and diversity and inclusion. Other responsibilities include codirector of the Children in Museums Award; steering committee member and jury member of the EMA Art Museum Award; Member Thinktank of the Global Art Museum Summit Shanghai; international member of the Public Education Experts Committee of NAMOC, Beijing; and supervisor of CJP (Youth Cultural Passport).

Kathleen Brown, senior practice leader at Lord Cultural Resources, has over four decades with public and private institutions and organizations across the United States and Canada, including staff and consulting positions with cultural attractions, community organizations, government, and academia. Her thirty-plus years of experience as a consultant keep her in demand as an advisor on key projects in which Lord is engaged. A skilled and effective communicator, she excels in pinpointing and articulating key project goals and finding solutions to achieve them while meeting the needs of diverse stakeholders. Her excellent reputation for producing positive results stems from the ability to engage key constituents, think strategically, and solve complex problems with solid, working solutions. Among her most recent projects are the Kwanlin Dün Cultural Centre, the Chinese Canadian Museum, the Museum of Northern Arizona, the Natural History Museum of Utah, and the Long Beach Cambodian American Cultural Center.

Karen Carter (she/her) has over twenty-five years of experience working and volunteering in a range of arts, culture, and heritage settings. She is the former executive director of Heritage Toronto, the founding executive director of Myseum of Toronto, and cofounder of Black Artists' Network and Dialogue (BAND). She is also the founder and president of Karen Carter and Associates Cultural Consulting, a firm that focuses on building new community-centered cultural organizations, projects, and initiatives, as well as the founder of CArt, a Caribbean Art Fair launched in 2020. Carter's most recent project is as the cofounder of the BIPOC Fellowship to help support the development of a more diverse cultural landscape in Canada.

Muna Faisal Al Gurg has been the chief executive officer of the Museums and Heritage Sector at Dubai Culture and Arts Authority since 2022. She joined the Authority in 2012 as a collections specialist and has since played a crucial role in the development of the museum sector in Dubai. Throughout her career, she has been privileged to work on the establishment of iconic cultural institutions in the city, including the Etihad Museum and Al Shindagha Museum.

She graduated with a BA in visual arts from Zayed University, Dubai, and holds a master's degree in museum studies and history of art from Paris-Sorbonne University in Abu Dhabi.

Muna currently leads the Museums and Heritage Sector, overseeing the development and operations of several museums and heritage sites within the emirate of Dubai.

Dov Goldstein is managing partner, Lord Cultural Resources. With over twenty years of experience in urban and cultural planning, he has led large projects such as the Canadian Museum for Human Rights, the King Abdulaziz Center for World Culture in Saudi Arabia, and Mexico's Museum of Energy and Technology. His area of focus includes strategic, cultural, and master planning; project management; and client representation services for museums, libraries, multiuse cultural developments, and cultural institutions, as well as for municipalities and private sector companies.

Daniel Hammer, president and CEO of the Historic New Orleans Collection, is dedicated to preserving the history and culture of New Orleans through his work at the Historic New Orleans

Collection, where he has worked for eighteen years, serving in various capacities, including as head of reader services and deputy director, before being named president and CEO in 2019. He earned a bachelor's degree in German literature from Reed College and a master's degree in historic preservation from Tulane University School of Architecture.

John G. Hampton is the executive director and CEO of the MacKenzie Art Gallery in Regina (Oskana kâ-asatêki). They entered the arts through studio practice and then started their career in the Artist Run Centre community as curator at Neutral Ground then artistic director at Trinity Square Video. They have also previously served as curator-in-residence (then adjunct curator) at the Art Museum at the University of Toronto and executive director of the Art Gallery of South-Western Manitoba. Hampton is a citizen of the Chickasaw Nation and examines intersections of Western and Indigenous culture through practice, policy, and theory. They hold a master's of visual studies–curatorial studies from the University of Toronto and a bachelor's in visual arts from the University of Regina.

Ali Hossaini is an associate of Lord Cultural Resources who has worked with museums, cultural districts, and cities globally. When developing plans, he brings a wealth of experience from his work as an artist and researcher. He is a senior research fellow in the Department of Engineering at King's College London, where he focuses on cultural applications of information and communications technology. As codirector of National Gallery X, he showed how the artistic canon can maintain relevance by inspiring new perspectives in robotics, AI, and other research programs. His work embraces diversity, equity, and sustainability, and it ranges from the development of standards for safe, equitable AI to developing strategies for correcting unequal health and social outcomes. Through his consulting, he converts theory into practice by working with museums and other clients to align their values with technological and organizational change.

Umbereen Inayet is a multi-award-winning TEDx speaker, curator, artistic director, and producer. With a master's degree in social work from the University of Toronto and an undergraduate degree in cultural anthropology and women's studies, Inayet's personal style is to bridge pop culture with contemporary art, using her roots in anthropology, culture, psychology, and social work to inform her artistic practice. Inayet has led the visioning for major City of Toronto events, recently creating the Lieutenant Governor of Ontario Heritage Award–winning program "Awakenings" for Toronto History Museums. Having worked on Nuit Blanche Toronto for over a decade, Inayet has worked with artists and studios such as Ai Weiwei, Bill Viola, John Akomfrah, Director X, Drake, Floria Sigismondi, Philip Beesley, Daniel Arsham, Hank Willis Thomas, Creative Time, and more.

Sandra Jackson-Dumont is a curator, author, educator, administrator, and public advocate for reimagining the role of art museums in society. She is currently the director and chief executive officer of the new Lucas Museum of Narrative Art in Los Angeles where she oversees all curatorial, educational, public, and operational affairs for the fast-developing institution. Throughout her roles with some of the country's most renowned museums, she has collaborated extensively with living artists, communities, creatives, and historical materials. Her work catalyzes the presence of increasingly dynamic and diverse audiences in cultural spaces while exploring issues of relevance.

Javier Jimenez Fernandez-Figares is managing partner, Lord Cultural Resources. He is an established cultural planner who has worked with prominent cultural institutions in more than twenty countries, including the Guggenheim Museum, V&A, Nanjing Museum, and Grand Egyptian

Museum, to name a few, and city cultural departments of Bilbao, Dubai, Chicago, and Belfast. In all his assignments, Javier pays detailed attention to both local sustainability and global outreach and brings advanced skills in strategic thinking, operations, and financial feasibility. He collaborates regularly with the academic sector. He is an invited lecturer at the master in cultural diplomacy, Università Cattolica del Sacro Cuore, Rome, Italy, and jury member for the Leading Culture Destinations Award. In 2019, he coedited *Museum Development in China—Understanding the Building Boom*, published in collaboration with the Chinese Museum Association. Jimenez Fernandez-Figares holds a master's degree in cultural management and is currently based in Madrid.

Tim Johnson is the senior advisor of heritage and legacy at the Niagara Parks Commission, senior advisor of the National Indigenous organization Plenty Canada, Indigenous advisor at Lord Cultural Resources, artistic director at the Great Niagara Escarpment Indigenous Cultural Map, and conceptual author and executive producer of the multiple award-winning documentary *RUMBLE: The Indians Who Rocked the World*. He also holds board memberships with several organizations, including the Niagara Escarpment Biosphere Network, Niagara Peninsula Aspiring Geopark, Bruce Trail Conservancy, Niagara-on-the-Lake Museum, McMichael Canadian Art Collection, and the Shaw Festival. Jonson's previous role as associate director for museum programs at the Smithsonian Institution's National Museum of the American Indian allowed him to oversee critically acclaimed exhibits and programs. He played a key role in promoting Indigenous art and history through books and the establishment of the museum's Indigenous Community Services Department.

Mary Kershaw is the executive director and CEO of Museum of Northern Arizona since June 2019. In 2010, she became director of New Mexico Museum of Art, modernizing it and raising $12.5 million for a new art venue. During her twenty-five-year museum career in England, she was head of museums and arts for Harrogate Borough and senior management at York Museums Trust. She served on the Museum Association Board, UK, national panels, was a curatorial advisor, and collaborated internationally. She was awarded an FMA, Fellow of the Museums Association (UK), in recognition of an advanced level of achievement in museum work.

Judith Koke is a senior researcher and the director of professional learning at the Institute for Learning Innovation. She works at the intersection of research, practice, and policy to support museums to deliver on their mission and purpose. Her experience in both research and museum leadership allows her to focus strongly on capacity building, culture change, and integrating research into practice.

Cara Krmpotich is director and associate professor of museum studies at the Faculty of Information, University of Toronto. She codirects GRASAC, a research alliance focused on Indigenous cultural belongings and histories of the Great Lakes. She researches, teaches, and writes in the areas of repatriation, critical collections management, digital heritage, and decolonial museology. She is happiest when connecting communities with their belongings and supporting active collections in museums.

Anjani Kumar Singh is the director general of Bihar Museum. He has served as project director of the Bihar Education Project and principal secretary of the Education Department and has earned several awards for his literacy campaign, including the Satya Mitra National Literacy Award. Singh played a leading role in the planning, construction, and completion of the Bihar Museum and has been awarded the India Today Art Award and Seema Art Award for his efforts and vision to create more cultural spaces. He helped pioneer the first "Museum Biennale" in India, has been instrumental in promoting contemporary folk artists of Bihar, and has helped conceive many other art institutions in Bihar to promote art at a grassroots level.

Robert LaMarre, vice-president, Lord Cultural Resources, is based in Hanover, Germany, and has been actively engaged in the cultural tourism sector in Canada, Europe, Southeast Asia, and across the MENA Region. Educated in tourism management-planning and development at Georgian College in Canada, LaMarre has specialized in applying success factors on projects around the globe since the 1980s. In addition to planning work on more than one hundred museums, cultural centers, and heritage sites, LaMarre has worked on-site at five world expositions, two international government summits, and on several of the world's most ambitious cultural destination projects, including the Singapore Heritage Precinct, the Saadiyat Island Cultural District in Abu Dhabi, and the Grand Egyptian Museum in Giza.

Natalie MacLean is a senior consultant on the organization and strategy team at Lord Cultural Resources. She uses her research and analytical skills to provide clients with important data and analysis, leading to practical and actionable solutions. Her expertise in digital strategy helps organizations connect with and inspire audiences across multiple platforms. MacLean holds a BFA from the Massachusetts College of Art and Design, an MA in art history from York University, and an MBA specializing in arts, media, and entertainment management from the Schulich School of Business. Her graduate research focused on the impact of social media use on visitor experience in museums and galleries. Previously, Natalie worked as a curator at Wreck City, an independent arts organization in Calgary, Alberta, that organizes art events in underutilized urban spaces. She has also worked as a codirector of Pith Gallery and Studios, an arts hub focused on providing resources to emerging artists.

Marc Mayer, a former director and CEO of the National Gallery of Canada from 2009 to 2019, is a writer and independent curator based in New York. Among other positions that he has held are director of the Musée d'art contemporain de Montréal; deputy director for art of the Brooklyn Museum; director of the Power Plant Contemporary Art Gallery at Harbourfront Center, Toronto; and curator of the Albright-Knox Art Gallery, Buffalo, New York. He has published widely on contemporary art and has organized numerous exhibitions, notably the 2005 Jean-Michel Basquiat retrospective for the Brooklyn Museum and the 2014 Jack Bush retrospective with Sarah Stanners for the National Gallery of Canada.

Gwendolyn Perry Davis is the chief operating officer at the Museum of Contemporary Art Chicago, one of the country's largest museums dedicated to contemporary art. She provides direction and oversight for the MCA's daily operations, including the care of the MCA's three-thousand-object permanent collection; employee resources and planning; maintenance of over 300,000 square feet of physical plant; and the museum's diversity, equity, and inclusion program. She is a trustee of the Poetry Foundation and Sarah Lawrence College. She was named one of Crain's Chicago Business 2021 Notable Black Leaders and Executives and a 2022 Chicago Defender Women of Excellence.

Terry Nyambe, vice president of the International Council of Museums (ICOM), has been an executive board member of ICOM since July 2016. He was a member of several committees in ICOM before joining the executive board. He was a member of the Ethics Committee (ETHICOM) from 2011 to 2016. He was a member of the ICOM Strategic Planning committee from 2014 to 2019. He was also a board member of the International Committee on Documentation (CIDOC) from 2013 to 2016. Currently, he serves as vice president of ICOM. He has over twenty years' experience as a curator in Zambian museums.

Sean Stanwick, BArch, MEDes (Architecture), director of facilities planning at Lord Cultural Resources, is an experienced architectural designer, facilities master planner, and programmer with over twenty years of experience in the field. He has dedicated his career to creating inspiring places and experiences that advance clients' cultural, interpretive, and operational goals. As a director of facilities planning, Stanwick leads and manages planning and programming projects for cultural institutions worldwide, bringing a unique understanding of the needs of all users from collections to staff and visitors. He has led the development of multiple space programs and strategic site and facility master plans for complex institutional projects including museums, galleries, and educational facilities, involving new buildings, renovations, and campus reorganization plans. Stanwick is also a published author, having written three books and multiple articles on contemporary architecture and experience. His first book, *Wine by Design*, has been translated into multiple languages and is in its second printing.

Sarah Sutton and **Elizabeth Wylie** have been advocating and agitating for environmentally sustainable practices in the cultural sector for almost two decades. Their seminal and widely referenced book *The Green Museum, A Primer on Environmental Practice* made the case for museums, zoos, gardens, aquariums, and cultural heritage sites, who are in the business of saving things for the future, to see environmentally sustainable practices as mission work. Since 2006, Sutton and Wylie have written dozens of articles and presented at scores of conferences to educate the field and funders about the importance of this work, emphasizing that communities and institutions benefit when the cultural sector is connected to the web of efforts on environmental and human health, climate mitigation and adaptation, and community resilience.

Yvonne Tang is director of visitor experience at Lord Cultural Resources and has worked on a global scale for over twenty years, ensuring a safe and welcoming space for all. She envisions and achieves unique solutions that assist institutions to respond to their visitors, from the hyperlocal to international. Tang believes in holistic engagement, including developing all aspects of human connection, looking out as well as reflecting in, from staff and audience needs, to community and partnership building. She has also contributed her exhibit design expertise to the second and third editions of *The Manual of Museum Exhibitions*. Tang is cofounder of SafePet Ontario, a charity dedicated to arranging pet safekeeping for families escaping domestic violence and human trafficking across the province.

Rosalia Vargas is the president of Ciência Viva, the National Agency for Scientific and Technological Culture in Portugal, a role she has held since 1996. She has also served as the director of Pavilhão do Conhecimento (Pavilion of Knowledge), the Lisbon Science Centre, since 1999. A former Ecsite president, she was also previously elected city councilor for education, youth, and culture at Lisbon City Hall (2007–2009). Vargas is a board member of the Association of Science Technology Centers (ASTC).

ABOUT THE AUTHORS

Gail Lord is co-founder and chair of Lord Cultural Resources, one of the world's leading cultural planning firms focused on museums, cultural districts, and the creative economy. Based in Toronto and New York, Lord has offices in Los Angeles, Madrid, and Mumbai. It has now completed over 2,700 projects in 57 countries and 450 cities.

Gail is an art critic, commentator, public speaker, and coauthor of six museum-planning manuals and several books.

Gail cofounded Lord Cultural Resources with her husband Barry Lord in 1981 to provide specialized planning services to museums, the arts, cultural districts, and the creative economy with the goal of making the world a better place through culture. With Barry, she is coeditor of *The Manual of Museum Planning* (1991, 1999, 2012), coauthor of *The Manual of Museum Management* (1997 and 2009), and with Kate Markert the first edition of *The Manual of Strategic Planning for Museums* (2007). In 2015, Gail coauthored with Ngaire Blankenberg *Cities, Museums and Soft Power*. In 2019, Gail coedited *Museums in China: Understanding the Building Boom* with Guan Qiang, An Laishun, and Javier Jimenez.

Gail's clients include the Canadian Museum for Human Rights; Smithsonian Institutions, Washington, DC; Constitution Hill in Johannesburg, South Africa; the National African American Museum of History and Culture in Washington; the Museum of the African Diaspora in San Francisco; the Canadian Museum of History in Ottawa; the National Holocaust Monument in Ottawa; the National World War II Museum in New Orleans; the Poetry Foundation, Chicago; the Pennsylvania Academy of the Fine Arts, Philadelphia; the Museo Guggenheim Bilbao; and the Tate Modern.

Gail is a member of the Order of Canada (2016) and Officier de l'Ordre des Arts et des Lettres de France (2014). In 2016 she was awarded an Honorary Doctor of Letters by McMaster University.

Barry Lord (1939–2017) was internationally known as one of the world's leading museum planners. Dedicated, thorough, and knowledgeable, Barry brought over fifty years of experience in the management and planning of museums, galleries, and historic sites to the hundreds of projects he has directed.

Educated at McMaster and Harvard Universities in philosophy and the history and philosophy of religion, Barry planned and managed cultural and heritage projects that ranged in topic from marine archaeology to industrial technology, from heritage villages to the complex stories of a nation. His profound knowledge of planning for art museums stemmed from his early work as an art curator, critic, and educator. He held positions as curator, education officer, and director at several art galleries and museums in Canada as well as curated freelance exhibitions for Canadian and American galleries.

As an author and editor, Barry was originally known for *artscanada magazine* (1967) and for *The History of Painting in Canada: Toward a People's Art* (1974), as well as numerous exhibition catalogs, art magazine articles, and newspaper art criticism. Together with Gail Dexter Lord, Barry edited and wrote the world's first book on the subject, *Planning Our Museums* (1983), and what is now considered the guide book in the profession, *The Manual of Museum Planning* (third edition, 2012, coedited with Gail Dexter Lord and Lindsay Martin; second revised edition, 2003, coedited with Gail Dexter Lord; second edition, 1999; first edition, 1991, coedited with Gail Dexter Lord), followed by *The Manual of Museum Management* (1997; second edition, 2009), which Gail and Barry coauthored, and *The Manual of Museum Exhibitions* (2002), which they edited. Barry also coauthored *The Cost of Collecting* (1989), a landmark study in collection management costs. Barry both authored and edited *The Manual of Museum Learning* (2007). Gail and Barry coauthored *Artists, Patrons, and the Public: Why Culture Changes* (2010). Many of these books are being successfully used in university museum studies programs. Barry authored *Art & Energy: How Culture Changes*, showing that major cultural shifts accompanied each energy transition since mastering fire (2014).

Barry's international reputation as president of Lord Cultural Resources, which he and Gail founded in 1981, is reflected by his many invitations to speak at conferences and seminars and teach frequently in museum management, planning, and training programs at universities and museum organizations around the world.

Barry often directed functional briefs or programs and facility strategies for museums, having developed a unique approach to zoning museum spaces and a comprehensive, systematic approach to space planning and functional requirements for museums. He also directed hundreds of master plans, feasibility studies, collection analyses, and exhibition planning, design, and installation projects for museums around the world.